Do You Have What It Takes to Be a Model?

So, you want to be a model, but you're not sure whether you have the right stuff? Answering the questions in this quiz (truthfully!) will help you find out!

1. You need a step stool to reach:
   A. The bathroom sink
   B. The top shelf of your locker
   C. The place where your mom hides the cookies on top of the refrigerator
   D. The moon

2. You're old enough to:
   A. Cross the street
   B. Baby-sit
   C. Drive
   D. Get your ears pierced

3. The foods you eat most often include:
   A. Candy, chips, and soda
   B. Hamburgers and French fries
   C. Cereal, sandwiches, and juice
   D. Fruits, vegetables, and fish

4. You were supposed to start working on an important book report a month ago. It's now the night before it's due. You:
   A. Call your friend to see if she has the book
   B. Are almost finished reading the book
   C. Are halfway finished writing the report
   D. Put the finishing touches on the finished product

5. You're sitting in your favorite class next to your best friend. How long can you go without talking to her?
   A. 10 seconds
   B. 10 minutes
   C. You don't say anything to her but, 10 minutes before the bell, you pass her a note about your after-school plans
   D. The whole class

6. The clothes you wore yesterday are:
   A. On the floor where they fell off your body
   B. On the floor under the bed where you kicked them
   C. In the family hamper
   D. Washed, dried, folded, and put away—you do your own laundry

7. The cutest guy in the school wants you to go for a swim at a romantic but dangerous cove where a bunch of kids have been hurt. You:
   A. Buy a new swimsuit and shave your legs
   B. Practice your crawl in the school pool in case something happens
   C. Agree to go, but invite along some friends who took lifesaving classes
   D. Politely decline—a guy who doesn't care about your safety and well-being isn't worth dating

alpha
books

Do You Have What It Takes to Be a Model?...continued

8. How did you pay for your most recent clothing purchase?
   A. You whined until your mother gave you the money
   B. You hit your dad up for money when your mother was out of the room
   C. You paid for half with your baby-sitting money, and your mom paid for the other half, because you also needed money for a new CD
   D. You saved up your money from your part-time job

9. You have an 11:00 curfew. As the clock strikes 11, you're:
   A. Just starting another game of pool
   B. Looking for your car keys
   C. Careening home in your car, breaking every speed limit
   D. Walking in the door

10. Your relationship with your parents most resembles which movie:
    A. *Saving Private Ryan*
    B. *Clueless*
    C. *Hope Floats*
    D. *Sense and Sensibility*

11. You joined the school drama club because you really love to act. But instead of playing the lead, you're stuck painting backdrops and hauling furniture backstage. You:
    A. Quit as soon as you learn about how you were cheated out of a part
    B. Miss a lot of rehearsals to show them how unhappy you are
    C. Do everything you're asked, but really slowly and sullenly
    D. Act as cooperative as possible, because a good attitude may help you land a part next time.

12. How long would it take you to find your school ID card in your room:
    A. 2 years
    B. 3 days
    C. 10 minutes
    D. 7 seconds

For every A answer, give yourself one point. For every B answer, give yourself two points. For every C answer, give yourself three points. For every D answer, give yourself four points.

If you scored 36 points or more, congratulations! You're definitely on the right track to a successful modeling career.

If you scored 24 to 35 points, you may have what it takes to be a model, but there may be some things you need to work on. Look at the questions where you scored only one or two points, and work on improving those things.

If you scored 23 points or under, you're probably a lot of fun and the life of the party, but you have a way to go before you're ready for the responsibilities of a professional modeling career.

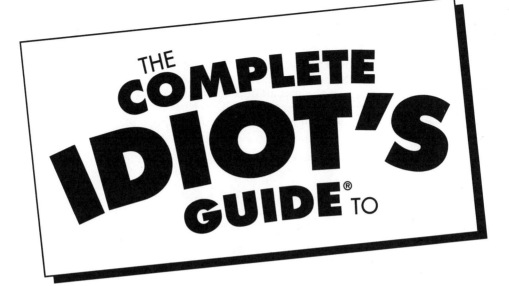

THE COMPLETE IDIOT'S GUIDE® TO

Being a Model

by Roshumba Williams
with Anne Marie O'Connor

alpha books

A Division of Macmillan General Reference
A Pearson Education Macmillan Company
1633 Broadway, New York, NY 10019-6785

Contents at a Glance

Contents

5   Which Look Are You: The Seven Basic Model Types   63

Appendices

Foreword

There's no denying that modeling is an incredible career. It offers people without any special skills a fantastic opportunity to make money, travel, and improve their style of life. That's because modeling is somehow magic—it opens doors, it impresses people, it is an incredible status symbol. You go to beautiful places (often shoots take place in gorgeous resort areas). You meet all sorts of interesting people. The money you make, even for a model doing relatively poorly by *industry* standards, is amazing. I've also found that models do well after they've left the business because they've had so much experience of the world, they have learned other languages, and they've made great connections.

But because there is so much interest in modeling, a lot of people try to take advantage of aspiring models who don't know the real facts about getting into the business. Very often, people think getting into modeling is a very involved process, in which you have to spend a lot of money on portfolios, classes, photos, etc. While it's true that for many people, a certain degree of formation is necessary, it's also true that for a lucky few, all they need to do is send a couple of snapshots to an agency, or drop by when the agency is seeing potential new models.

That's why this book is so important. It gives aspiring models the guidelines and tips they need to get started in the industry, without spending a lot of money needlessly. This is extremely useful, especially to people who have no other access to the necessary information about getting into modeling.

Roshumba is the ideal person to write this book. She is a very down-to-earth person and the advice she gives in this book is straightforward, no-nonsense, and professional, which is great for people who don't know much about our business. She's got many natural qualities that have allowed her to survive and grow and improve, and people reading this book will benefit from that.

She's also a very well-known, well-respected name in the industry, and she's had a very successful career. She's been involved with every aspect of modeling—she's worked in runway, she's done all kinds of magazine work, she's done advertising and catalogs. And of course, she was a *Sports Illustrated* model for four years. In addition to all that, she's someone who has a lot of character as a person, as well as a model.

I also know from watching her host the Elite Model Look, an international model search sponsored by Elite Model Management, which scouts models from all over the world, that Roshumba is a great teacher. She's great with the Elite Model Look contestants, and that's why I think she's the perfect person to share her knowledge with her readers.

Everything she knows about the modeling industry she had to learn on her own, and I've seen how much she enjoys imparting all her experience to aspiring models. I also know she will really inspire them as they start their own careers.

John Casablancas

John Casablancas is the chairman of Elite Model Agency Group, which represents some of the most glamorous women in the modeling industry today. Born in the United States of Spanish parents, Casablancas spent his childhood in the United States, Mexico, and Europe. In 1969, he opened his first modeling agency in Paris; in 1971, he founded Elite Model Management. Casablancas now has agencies all over the world, including New York, Los Angeles, Chicago, Atlanta, Miami, Paris, and Milan, among others. In 1979, he founded the John Casablancas Modeling Centers; today, there are over 60 of these well-respected modeling schools located throughout the world.

Introduction

It seems that everyone at one time or another dreams of becoming a model. Maybe you're a magazine junkie who loves looking at your favorite models in the pages of *Vogue, Mademoiselle,* or *Seventeen.* Or maybe you've watched fashion shows on TV or at a local store, and you've thought strutting up and down the runway looks like your kind of fun. Or maybe you love perusing catalogs and wondered how those models get hired. Although it can be a tough business to break into and aspiring models face many pitfalls, I'm living proof it can be done.

I was once sitting in my bedroom at home in Peoria, Illinois, looking at magazines and dreaming of a career on the runway and in front of a camera. And with a lot of luck, hard work, and determination—and despite a lot of rejection and numerous setbacks— I managed to go from my small hometown to appear on magazine covers and in fashion shows. In *The Complete Idiot's Guide to Being a Model,* I'd like to share my hard-won knowledge and experiences with you. I will explain how the modeling business works and take you step by step through the process of getting an agent and getting started in the business, while warning you about all the hazards I've seen in my 10 years in the business.

Every model has a reason for wanting to be in front of the camera or on the runway. Some love clothes and are attracted to the fashion industry; some just want to make a lot of money and then get on with their life. Others want to be as famous as their favorite supermodels. No matter what your reason, to get started in the modeling industry, you'll need to convince a lot of people that you have what it takes to shine in their magazine, ad, or catalog, because becoming a model isn't all about the way you look. It's also about a great personality and a good attitude. To give you an edge up, I'll explain my secrets for making a (good) impression that lasts.

Not only can the modeling industry be difficult to break into, but it can be very harsh and crazy once you're a part of it. On the other hand, it can be every bit as glamorous and exciting as you've heard. In this book, I'll give you my advice on giving the modeling world your best shot, and I'll also share with you my tips for establishing the kind of career that's long-lived, lucrative, and enhances your life. Finally, I'll also give you guidance on avoiding the many pitfalls and scams that every model faces.

How to Use This Book

The modeling industry is easy to understand once you break it down into its six major components. Each part of this book explains a different aspect of the industry. By the time you've read them all, you will have a firm grasp on everything you need to know to give a modeling career a try.

Part 1, "Modeling: The Ultimate Dream," examines the many reasons people want to get into modeling. It will give you a realistic assessment of what it takes to make it and whether you have what it takes. It will also talk about how world fashion trends can affect your career, and how you can stay on top of industry developments.

Part 2, "Breaking into the Business," is where you find out all you need to know to conquer the first major hurdle to becoming a model: finding an agent. Here, I'll explain the materials you'll need (don't worry, they're minimal and inexpensive) and everything you need to do to stand out when you start looking for an agent. Next, I'll explain the pros and cons of open calls, model searches, model conventions, and modeling schools. Finally, there's a special chapter just for parents of aspiring models.

Part 3, "Now That Your Foot's in the Door, What's Next?" discusses the challenges you face once you've found an agent. I'll explain how an agency works, the model musts you need to be familiar with (test shoots, portfolios, composites, vouchers), as well as give you a behind-the-scenes look at a test shoot. I'll also talk about go and sees, those all-important job interviews for models, and tell you my secrets for shining at them.

Part 4, "Oh My God, I've Booked a Job, Now What?!" will tell you everything you need to know to get through your first few photo shoots with grace and style. I'll tell you everything you need to know to prepare for that all-important first job. I'll also explain who everyone at the shoot is, give you my tips for working with them, and discuss the differences between working in the studio and working on location.

Part 5, "There's Something for Everyone," discusses the many aspects of modeling, including magazines, fashion shows, advertisements, and catalogs. I'll talk about the pros and cons of each, and I'll also discuss opportunities for models who don't meet the stringent criteria for fashion modeling, including plus-size models, elegant (older) models, and real-people models. I'll also talk about how men and children can get started in the business.

Part 6, "Career and Personal Management," tells you everything you need to know about making the most of your career once it's up and running. I'll talk about establishing clientele, finding a niche, and managing your finances. In addition, I'll share my thoughts on staying sane in a crazy business. Finally, I'll give you my tried-and-true tips on keeping your outer self picture-perfect.

And to make sure you don't get confused by modeling lingo, there's a glossary that contains all the terms you'll need to sound like an insider in conversations with agents, editors, fashion designers, and casting directors. I've also included a list of must-read books and Web sites for aspiring models, a directory of modeling agencies around the country and abroad, and a list of key tourist offices in major modeling centers.

Extras

In every chapter, I'll give you the insider scoop on the modeling industry. These boxes contain four different types of information:

Mod Squad

Here I tell you fun stories and wacky tales about various models and their exploits, both exemplary and cautionary.

Catwalk Talk

Modeling terms are defined for you here, so you'll always be fashion-forward when the talk turns technical.

Roshumba's Rules

These are my best tips on making the most out of your modeling career. You can't go wrong following the rules!

Reality Check

These are warnings about the worst aspects of the modeling industry. Read these carefully, and avoid these pitfalls at any cost!

Acknowledgements

From Roshumba:

I would like to thank God for giving me the inspiration and dedication needed for this book. I would also like to thank the following: Gail Parenteau, Sheree Bykofsky, Anne Marie O'Connor, Gary Krebs, Kathy Nebenhaus, Georgette Blau, John Casablancas, Debra Hall, Cathy Gould, Erin Lundgren, Ellen Harth, Calvin Wilson, Karen Lee, Laura McClafferty, Ryan Kopko, Kwame Brathwaite, Joya Delaney, Alvaro, LaVonne Joslin, Natalie Laughlin, Christiana Cordel, Christopher Cordel, Patti Abbott-Claffy, M.L. McCarthy, Corynne Corbett, Christiana Anbri, Stephen Schmidt, Lynn Northrup, Christy Wagner, Susan Aufheimer, Nikki Suero-O'Brien, and Andrea Fairweather.

From Anne Marie:

I would like to thank my very funny friend Janet Rosen, the warm and wonderful agent Sheree Bykofsky, the beautiful Roshumba Williams; as well as my model friends and family.

Special Thanks to the Technical Reviewer

The Complete Idiot's Guide to Being a Model was reviewed by an expert who double-checked the accuracy of what you'll learn here, to help us ensure that this book gives you everything you need to know about a career in modeling. Special thanks are extended to Debra Hall.

Debra Hall is a published author with national recognition and over 16 years of experience in the modeling and television industries. She currently writes a monthly column for *16 Magazine* and produces the award-winning PBS teen television series *Hall Pass,* covering all areas of the modeling industry and other teen-related topics. Formerly, Debra was vice president of Barbizon International, where she produced model search competitions, and worked in all professional areas of the modeling industry.

Trademarks

All terms mentioned in this book that are known to be or are suspected of being trademarks or service marks have been appropriately capitalized. Alpha Books and Macmillan General Reference cannot attest to the accuracy of this information. Use of a term in this book should not be regarded as affecting the validity of any trademark or service mark.

Part 1
Modeling:
The Ultimate Dream

So you think you want to be a model! You've probably heard about the glamour, excitement, and big money of an international modeling career, and you want to give it a shot. Maybe your friends and family tell you you should be a model, or perhaps strangers stop you and ask if you're a model.

But the modeling industry can be full of pitfalls, scams, and other trouble for the naive and uninformed. So I'll start out by talking about everything you need to know about modeling before you launch a successful career. First, I'll look at the modeling business itself, how it all works, and what you need to be aware of. I'll also talk about the physical—and mental—prerequisites for becoming a professional model. Because the best models are the ones who know and understand the fashion industry, I'll also talk about the preparations that are needed for a successful career. Finally, you'll find out about the different types of models, and learn how your type will affect your career. To find out if you have what it takes, and for more information on getting started, keep reading!

Chapter 1

Why Become a Model?

The million-dollar paychecks. The closets full of designer clothes. Jet-setting from Paris to New York to Jamaica. Flocks of men pursuing you. Your face on the cover of magazines. Fans from all over the world asking for your autograph. Dressing up and getting your hair and makeup done—and getting paid for it. Who wouldn't want to be a model?

But the truth is, this is the side of modeling you see only in the movies, on TV, and in magazines. Sure, for a very fortunate few supermodels—perhaps 10 to 20 women in the world at any one time—this is a true picture of a modeling career. But behind all the glitz and glamour is a completely different reality and a lot of blood, sweat, and tears. Although female models garner more attention than male models, they face many of the same obstacles. For more information on male models, see Chapter 22, "Specialty Models."

The Dream vs. the Reality

The reality is, the vast majority of models will never reach the supermodel stratosphere of limos, champagne, and million-dollar paydays. To give you just one example, of the thousands of girls who every year enter the Elite Model Look—a nationwide model search contest to find the next generation of models—only a few of them end up with modeling contracts with the Elite modeling agency, and maybe just one of them—if she's lucky—may go on to *supermodel* status.

Although the rewards can be incredible for those fortunate few, a professional modeling career at any level involves a lot of hard work and sacrifice—many models have to leave their friends, boyfriends, and family behind to move to a big city where they can pursue a career. They also usually need to leave or defer going to school in order to model or make special arrangements to complete their basic education. Because most models travel so much, they may need to live out of a suitcase, wearing the same few outfits for weeks at a time, spending more time sitting on planes than at home. Many models, feeling lonely and homesick, also get caught up in drug or alcohol abuse, or are taken advantage of by abusive boyfriends; many end up losing everything they worked so hard to earn. Before you decide whether you want to pursue modeling, it's important that you get a realistic picture of what a career entails.

Catwalk Talk

A **supermodel** is a model who is so successful she becomes a household name, well-known to an audience outside the fashion industry. Super-models include Cindy Crawford, Christy Turlington, Christie Brinkley, Kathy Ireland, and Roshumba Williams.

Missing Out on Fun

Many professional models who rise to the top of the industry start their careers when they're as young as 13. (Age 15 or 16, however, is the average.) Usually, they continue to attend high school and may model just on Christmas break, spring vacation, and during the summer. Other times, they may choose to miss a few days of school for a very important assignment.

Catwalk Talk

A **go and see** is a job interview for a modeling job. It's called a go and see because a model goes to the client's office so they can see what she looks like in person.

As exciting as it may sound to spend your vacations modeling in a big city, the reality is that while your friends are having fun going to the beach, attending parties, shopping together, playing tennis, or learning to drive, you may be exhausted from walking around a large city all day, map in hand, going from one job interview, known as a *go and see,* to another (we'll tell you more about these in Chapter 15, "Go and Sees"). Believe me, being lost on the streets of Chicago after your twentieth go and see in 95-degree heat is neither fun, exciting, nor glamorous. And yet it's an aspect of modeling you don't see on television shows.

Modeling sounds more glamorous than it really is. In reality, it involves a lot of exhausting schlepping around big cities and going from one appointment to another, often getting lost.

Rejected and Dejected

We've all had some disappointment or rejection in our lives—we didn't make the school play, didn't get that cushy lifeguard job, didn't ace the test we studied for all semester. Models have to deal with that rejection every day, all day. I've gone on as many as 15 go and sees in one day—killing myself rushing around town to make sure I was on time to every single one. Even though I was exhausted and had aching feet by the end of the day, sometimes not one of the clients I met ended up hiring me.

There probably isn't one other business in the world in which one human being can receive as much rejection as in the modeling industry. So if you decide you want to become a model, get ready! Plan to have doors slammed in your face and hear very blunt criticisms of your body and features: Her hips are too wide; his shoulders are too small; we don't want any black girls (yes, I really did hear that once!); no Asian girls; her jaw's too square; and so on.

So if you decide you want to have a modeling career, you'll need to be prepared for a whole lot of rejection. Even though you eventually learn that these comments aren't meant to hurt you personally, it's hard to deal with them every single day. But it's a fact of life in the modeling business. (We'll discuss how to deal with rejection in Chapter 25, "Personal Management.")

Poor and Alone: Not as Glamorous as It Sounds

Even after a week or month of meetings and go and sees, you may still not have gotten even one modeling job; some models have a harder time than others getting a career off the ground (and others find theirs never takes off). One client after another may decide you're not exactly right for them. You may be completely broke living in a teeny two-bedroom apartment with six other models and surviving on peanut butter and jelly sandwiches. Besides not having any money, you can become extremely depressed expending all that time and energy trying to find a modeling job, only to be rejected again and again.

Roshumba's Rules

If you're just starting out on a modeling career and things are slow getting started, consider getting a supplemental job. Not only will you earn money to live, but staying busy will keep you from becoming dejected.

Meanwhile, your friends at home may still live in their own rooms in their parents' house, have full access to a well-stocked refrigerator, a TV, stereo, video games, a phone, and a car with gas already in it. Except for the occasional problem at school or work, they live pretty cushy and stress-free lives. But if you want to be a model, you may have to forego these comforts of home.

Skipping School

At the same time that you're going on go and sees and trying to launch a modeling career, your friends back home may be finishing high school, attending college, or learning marketable skills on the job. Even if you're one of the lucky few who makes it as a model, in five or 10 years your career may be coming to an end. (The average career span of a model is eight years.) Your friends from home, meanwhile, may have graduated from college or acquired skills that will allow them to support themselves throughout their lives. In those same years, you may have been working full-time and making good money, but you've had to forego the education and job experience necessary for a career beyond modeling.

Even though it may sound tempting to drop out of school to pursue modeling, you need to consider just how much you're giving up. The truth is, people with college degrees usually earn far more than those with just high-school diplomas, and that gap is growing all the time. If your career takes off, that's great, and you could make enough to be set for life. But if it doesn't, and you skipped college to give it a shot, you could end up with dim prospects for the future. (For tips on planning your future after modeling, see Chapter 24, "Managing Your Career.")

The Downside of the Glamorous Life

Many of the things that make modeling sound so exciting—the travel, the cute guys who flock around successful models, the parties—can actually be negatives. Your fifth plane flight in a week isn't as much fun as that first time, those cute guys can turn out to be con artists and predators, and too many parties can take their toll on your looks and career. So before you say yes to modeling, you need to take a closer look at the darker side of some of its (so-called) fringe benefits.

On the Road

Most successful models travel constantly, all around the world. This *sounds* great, but the downside is that you may also not get to see your family and friends as much as you'd like. Even though I've seen some incredible sights—the Louvre Museum in Paris, the pyramids in Egypt, the beaches of Jamaica—I've also missed a lot of fun at home, including my best friend's birthday, my brother's graduation, and many Christmases with my family.

Traveling so much also means spending a lot of time alone; although I enjoy this, some models find that they often feel very lonely and isolated. On top of that, it's exhausting and stressful to always be running to catch a plane, train, or automobile to get to the next job.

Roshumba's Rules

A good way to stay close to your loved ones is to set aside quality time to spend with them. When I first moved away from home, my mom and I would set up specific times when we were both free to have heart-to-heart chats. This helped me stay close to my family.

The reality of modeling is traveling all the time is rushing through airports dragging heavy suitcases.

A Scam a Minute

Models at all stages of their careers, from beginners to supermodels, are targeted by con artists hoping to profit from their hopes, dreams, and naiveté. Although you may be complimented by their attention, don't fall for their scams.

Aspiring models are generally very young, and their desire to model may occasionally cloud their judgment. There are many horror stories about disreputable people who offer drugs to young models, who coerce them into modeling nude, who demand sex in exchange for a modeling job, or who want the model to pay them to get a job.

Another big source of frauds and swindles is photographers who try to get young models who are just starting out to pay hundreds (or thousands) of dollars for photos, *portfolios* (an album of specially selected pictures models take with them on job interviews), and *composites* (a card with several photos on it that's sent out to potential clients). They will insist these materials are necessary in order to find a modeling agency that will represent a beginning model, or that they're needed to get started in the modeling business. These con artists will insist that agents won't accept them if they don't have a portfolio full of pictures. Don't fall for this common scam; professional photos are definitely not necessary to get started as a model; in fact, they can actually hurt your chances of making it. (For more on scams, see Chapters 8, "Modeling for Experience (Hobby Modeling)," and 10, "Modeling in the Fashion Capitals.")

Many established models have also been victims of scams. Successful models often find themselves in the middle of a swarm of men who are dying to meet them. As exciting as that may seem, it also exposes models to shady people who want to take advantage of them emotionally and financially. Many of these con artists date models, hoping to convince the models to give them money to set up investment companies, where they buy risky stocks. Other con artists want to open their own businesses, such as health clubs, nightclubs, restaurants, and resorts. Many models, inexperienced in business or head over heels in love, fall for the hype and give them money. More models than I can count have lost their peace of mind, their careers, and all their savings to unscrupulous guys.

Catwalk Talk

Your **portfolio** is an album of specially selected pictures you bring with you on job interviews; your **composite** is a $8^{1}/_{2} \times 11$-inch or 5×7-inch card with several photos on it.

Reality Check

If a photographer tries to convince you to spend a lot of money (more than $100) on a photo session and/or pictures, he is either not knowledgeable about the modeling industry or scamming you. In either case, refuse to give him any money. The truth is, once you have an agency, they will arrange for any necessary professional photos. Any professional photos taken without an agency's guidance are useless.

Just Say "No!"

Many models are also frequently invited to parties, nightclubs, new restaurants, gallery openings, charity galas, and other events. Although this is very enticing, it's also true that too many nights on the town can contribute to drug and alcohol abuse and leave you looking less than camera-ready.

The number of models who've used drugs and lost everything—careers, friends, possessions—is depressingly large. Besides the well-known cases, such as Margaux Hemingway and Gia—who were top models in the late 1970s and early 1980s—there are many less-famous models whose careers were derailed by drugs. Although it's probably true that these people might have become addicted even if they hadn't become models, it's also true that the pressures, rejection, and superficial values of the modeling industry can exacerbate drug problems. The fashion industry is also quite tolerant of models' drug problems: Kate Moss admitted that she smoked marijuana (and drank alcohol) pretty much continuously throughout her career, until a stay in a rehab clinic. Although not every model becomes an addict, drugs are a common problem throughout the industry.

Alcohol is also widely available in the fashion world. Backstage at runway shows, the champagne is always flowing, even at nine in the morning. While one glass of champagne isn't a problem, the easy accessibility of alcohol makes it more likely that some models develop problems. And the frantic pace and stress of some models' careers—they appear in a dozen fashion shows in three days, they have to fly somewhere new every night, or they're just running around town meeting 15 potential clients—makes it easy to understand why some models start to drink too much.

If you're still gung-ho about a modeling career, even after hearing all the pitfalls of the fashion industry, your next step is to figure out what level of model you'd like to pursue.

The Three Basic Levels of Modeling

Although the big-time models on the cover of *Vogue* get most of the attention, there are actually three different levels of modeling: *hobby modeling, secondary-market modeling,* and *big-time modeling.* Each has its own requirements, which means there are opportunities for many different types of models.

Maybe you're not ready to leave your friends, family, and education for a modeling career in a big city such as New York or Paris. Maybe you just want to have some fun, express yourself creatively,

Catwalk Talk

The three levels of modeling are **big-time modeling,** which refers to professional modeling in the fashion capitals (New York, Paris, and Milan); **secondary-market modeling,** professional modeling in other cities; and **hobby modeling,** amateur modeling that can be done anywhere.

and get involved with the fashion industry. In this case, you may want to consider hobby modeling. Hobby models model at local malls, in local TV commercials and ads, and for their hometown newspapers. Hobby models generally earn little or no money. (For more information on hobby models, see Chapter 8.)

Maybe you'd like to make some money, get a chance to be the center of attention, and develop a stronger sense of self-esteem, but don't want the stress and loneliness of traveling all the time and never seeing your friends and family. In this case, you may want to pursue secondary-market modeling, modeling in cities such as Miami, Chicago, and Los Angeles. Secondary-market models appear in catalogs, advertisements, local runway shows, and regional publications. Many manage to carve out lucrative careers, without the continual travel, competition, and stress of big-time modeling.

Or maybe you're prepared to make the necessary sacrifices to give big-time modeling a shot. Maybe you've been dreaming of seeing your face on a magazine cover or on a billboard in Times Square, and you're ready to leave your friends and family to work harder than you ever have before to give big-time fashion modeling a try. Although the rewards are great, so is the competition. Even though you realize you may not make it, your dream is so strong you're willing to risk everything to give it a shot.

Why Do You Want to Model?

Your reasons for getting into modeling will help determine the level of modeling you want to pursue. Most models get into the business for more than one reason. They may love fashion, they may be attracted to the glamour of dressing up and posing for the camera, they may want to get out of their small hometowns, or they may want to express themselves creatively. Some may harbor a secret desire to become rich and famous—or at least to make some extra money and be the center of attention for a short time. Your reasons for wanting to get into modeling, and how much you're willing to give up to pursue your dream, can help you determine what kind of modeling career to pursue.

Catwalk Talk

The **runway** (also known as the **catwalk**) is a long narrow stage that juts out into the audience. At a fashion show, the models walk down the runway, which allows the audience to see the clothes up close.

Your physical characteristics—height, weight, body type, facial structure (see Chapter 3, "Do You Have What It Takes?" for more details)—will play a part in determining the path of your modeling career. Also important are your reasons for wanting to pursue a modeling career. (Yet despite your desire to model and make all the sacrifices, keep in mind there's still no assurance that you'll even be able to get your foot in the door!)

But before you take your first step down the *runway*, you need to figure out why you want to model.

There are as many reasons to model as there are models. Are any of the following reasons yours?

➤ I love clothes and makeup and want to be more involved with the fashion and beauty industries.

➤ I love to perform and be the center of attention.

➤ I'd like to be famous.

➤ I'd like to make a lot of money.

➤ I want to express myself creatively.

➤ I want to build my self-esteem.

➤ I want to be independent.

➤ I want to experience new things and be introduced to a more sophisticated world.

➤ All of the above!

Let's take a closer look at each of these reasons.

I Love Clothes and Makeup

Do you have a unique sense of personal style, a flair for hair, a passion for makeup? Do you love to shop and put together outfits in different ways? If so, you may be attracted to modeling for the opportunities it offers to get more involved with the fashion and beauty industries. You may love the idea of wearing beautiful, interesting clothes and getting your hair and makeup done in new and different ways every single day.

Reality Check

Although getting your hair and makeup done before every photo shoot and fashion show sounds like fun, it's actually not all that glamorous. It usually takes the hairstylist an hour to do your hair, and the makeup artist 45 minutes to apply your makeup. Having to sit still that long while someone pulls on your hair and dabs makeup on your face is not all it's cracked up to be.

I Love Being the Center of Attention

Do you love dance, theater, or music? Do you love to perform? Do you love to get your picture taken? Are you confident and self-assured? Are you comfortable with a roomful of people looking at you? If so, modeling may be right for you because it offers you an opportunity to play a part, create a character, or set a mood, whether you're playing a waitress in a photo shoot or a bride on the fashion runway.

I Want to Make a Lot of Money

If making money is your sole motivation, you should know that it's a long shot that you'll make millions. Unlike other lucrative professions, such as doctor, professional athlete, or investment banker, modeling requires no particular training or expensive schooling; but knowledge of the profession makes it more likely that you'll have a successful career.

For a lucky few, modeling can be a means to earn a significant amount of money. It's true that top models such as Claudia Schiffer and Cindy Crawford make several million dollars a year. Even the many models you've never heard of—the people in the Spiegel catalog or in a newspaper ad—may make $100,000 a year or more. (It's estimated that $100,000 a year is the standard earnings of the average working model.) But many others make very little modeling, or nothing at all. Despite giving it their best shot, they can't get their foot in the door. Because modeling is so lucrative and so competitive, trying to get hired for a modeling job is very difficult.

I'd Like to Be Famous

Some people pursue a modeling career hoping that it will make them famous, whether appearing on the cover of *Vogue*, or being featured in a local newspaper that all their friends will see. It's true that some models—Christie Brinkley, Kathy Ireland, Linda Evangelista, Tyson Beckford, Vendela, and Stephanie Seymour—have become household names. This sort of prominence is rare, however, and is usually a result of exceptional physical attributes and incredible luck.

Modeling can also be an excellent stepping stone to other careers, which has been proven by the many models who have gone on to distinguish themselves in other careers. Modeling can open the doors to many opportunities. I know that for me, my modeling career helped me get my foot in the door when I decided to pursue acting (in movies such as Woody Allen's *Celebrity*) and broadcasting (as a veejay on VH1).

Mod Squad

The list of ex-models who have accomplished impressive things in other fields is impressive: Former cover girls Andie MacDowell and Rene Russo are busy, accomplished actresses; Kim Basinger even won an Oscar. Cybill Shepherd and Brooke Shields star in their own network sitcoms. Martha Stewart is renowned as the doyenne of domesticity and runs a multimillion-dollar conglomerate. Iman developed her own line of cosmetics. B. Smith owns a successful Manhattan restaurant and has her own TV show. Believe it or not, even Whitney Houston started out as a model; it gave her the exposure she needed to get her career off the ground, and her beautiful voice did the rest. Even male models have taken advantage of opportunities that have come from modeling. Michael Bergen is a successful actor on *Baywatch*.

Even if you don't ever produce your own calendar or appear on the cover of a fashion magazine, you may still be able to enjoy your 15 minutes of fame, starring in a school fashion show or modeling at a local department store. The poise and self-assurance you learn modeling can also help you throughout your life, interviewing for jobs, making presentations, and giving speeches.

I Want to Express Myself Creatively

If you're an artistic person and want to get involved in an artistic field, modeling could be a great way to get an up-close and personal experience with the creative world of fashion.

When you're hired for a modeling job, you get to be an actress for the day. For instance, when you go into a photo studio, the photographer will give you an idea of the kind of image he's after and the story he wants to tell in the picture. Whatever the photo is going to be about, you need to be able to play the part, whether it's a working woman in a catalog selling business attire, or the belle of the ball in a stunning gown for a magazine story. The set is there, the clothes are there, the hair and makeup people can help you create the look, but the magic has to come from you. Models are essential because they're the ones who interpret the idea and make it come alive.

For one *Sports Illustrated* shoot, I was dressed in an antique bolero jacket and carried a fan, so I knew the photographer wanted to capture the image of a matador in the ring with a bull. I remember asking myself who I was supposed to be and how I could project that image. I began to pose, interpreting the energy of a bullfighter facing off with a fierce bull. In the photo, you really get an idea of a matador in the ring.

A model has to be able to creatively express personality and emotion with her body and face, sort of like an actress in a silent movie. But if you like performing and other creative endeavors, such as drama, dance, and music, modeling could be a great outlet for your artistic aspirations.

I Want to Build My Self-Esteem

Growing up I was insecure and self-conscious about my weight and height. I was always too tall for my age—I was 5'10" when I was 13, and as skinny and flat-chested as a string bean; everyone else was average height and had started filling out. I stuck out, which made me feel very insecure. But as soon as I became a model, I was celebrated for exactly those things I thought were so weird about me. Realizing my height and string-bean body were my best assets helped me get over not liking those parts of myself.

Models are constantly complimented on their beauty. Industry professionals are always stroking model's egos, which makes young girls feel like they're on the top of the world. People go out of their way to flatter you and listen to what you have to say. You're always the center the attention on the job. At work, the whole day is built around you, your needs, and your wants, and making you look good and feel comfortable.

Although models do face a lot of rejection, there is also a lot of praise (especially once you start working regularly). This can be a great ego booster, particularly for young models who lack self-confidence.

I Want to Be Independent

Because models start their careers at such a young age, and because they often have to move to a big city, they're often forced to become independent, self-sufficient adults earlier than their friends back home. One of the great things about modeling is that it allows you to live independently at a very young age. This means, for one, that you get to set your own schedule. If you don't want to work, you tell your agent you're not available and then you're free to take off for the beach for the week. You have no curfew. If you want to come in at 3 A.M., no one will say a word.

At the same time that models have a lot more freedom than their friends at home, they're also forced to be a lot more responsible. They're responsible for their schedules and for making sure that they get to jobs on time. (See Chapter 25 for more information on personal management.)

Reality Check

It may seem like a minor thing, but if a model shows up late to a shoot, it could cost thousands of dollars, because the whole day is thrown off schedule. The photographer, hair, and makeup people all have to be paid extra, and the photography studio has to be rented for a longer period. That's why it's so important that models be on time.

Once you've finished work for the day, your life is in your own hands. But along with freedom comes responsibility. You can live anywhere you want, but you have to go out and find your own apartment. You can eat whatever you want, but you have to go buy and prepare your food. You can choose your own sheets and towels, but you have to go to the store, pick them out, pay for them, then put them on your bed. You have to take care of the not-so-fun things as well, such as going to the gym, the dentist, and the doctor. Still, it can be a great feeling to know that you can handle that kind of responsibility, especially if you've never lived on your own before.

I Want to Experience New Things

I spent my high-school years in Peoria, Illinois, the quintessential American small town. But being a model has exposed me to all sorts of new things I never would have experienced if I'd stayed in Peoria. In the cosmopolitan environment of modeling, you start to notice the different ways people do things and to learn from them. Once you've seen the clever way the photographer from New York ties her scarf, or the beautiful natural manicure of a French makeup artist, you may be inspired to improve yourself, to try wearing scarves or to toss the purple nail polish you thought was so cool back home and buy a chic, understated, natural color.

You're exposed to people who come from places where manners and etiquette are different from yours, and you may find that some of the things other people do appeal to you. For instance, maybe you'll be motivated to learn another language, start taking European-style steam baths or saunas, or wear bell bottoms—things that you may not have considered if you'd remained at home.

For one thing, once I became a model, I began to learn a lot more about nutrition. I soon realized that we Americans have just about the worst diets on the planet. We eat so much junk food, and we eat such huge portions of everything. I discovered a healthier diet, which is to eat better-quality, nutrient-rich food (fruits, vegetables, grains, fish), and to consume smaller portions. (For more information on a model eating plan and developing your own exercise regimen, see Chapter 27, "The Outer You.")

Learning from My Experience

In this book, I'll give you the benefit of my many years of experience in the modeling business. I've been where you probably are now—sitting in your bedroom, reading *Elle* magazine, dreaming of becoming a model.

Since then, I've experienced modeling on every level: I started out modeling for local stores in Peoria; I spent a year in a secondary market (Chicago) struggling to break into the business with little to show for all my efforts. Then I went to Paris with just $150 and a return ticket, and with an incredible bit of luck, I ended up getting hired my first week by fashion designer Yves Saint Laurent. I've hit some bumps in the road, but I've always managed to move ahead. So I think I can confidently say I know the modeling business inside out.

Unfortunately, as it is with everything else, wishing to be a model doesn't make it so. Modeling is a business like any other, and you'll increase your chances of success and avoid common pitfalls and scams if you're knowledgeable about the modeling industry. In the chapters ahead, I'll give you the inside scoop on what modeling is really like, and I'll give you advice that will give you your best shot at success!

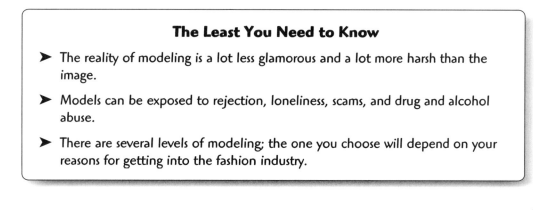

The Least You Need to Know

➤ The reality of modeling is a lot less glamorous and a lot more harsh than the image.

➤ Models can be exposed to rejection, loneliness, scams, and drug and alcohol abuse.

➤ There are several levels of modeling; the one you choose will depend on your reasons for getting into the fashion industry.

The World of Modeling

Now that you know a little about the pros and cons of modeling as a career, you probably want to know more about the work itself. Modeling encompasses everything from appearing on the cover of a top fashion magazine, to posing for pictures in a catalog, to walking around a store in the local mall dressed in the latest styles. In this chapter, I'll discuss the major types of modeling: print (magazine and newspaper), catalog, runway, fittings, advertisement, and endorsements.

It's also important that aspiring models understand how the modeling business affects the fashion industry, the advertising business, and the corporate world in general. So in the second half of this chapter, I'll talk about why the modeling business really is a business.

Cover Girl: The ABCs of Editorial Modeling

Editorial work refers to modeling for magazines. It's one of the most important sources of work for models. Large national publications such as *Glamour, Mademoiselle,* and *Seventeen,* as well as local magazines such as *Chicago* or *Boston* magazines, hire models to appear on their covers and in their stories.

Editorial work includes fashion stories, which showcase the latest style trends (the newest look in coats, the must-have shoes for spring, or the new suits for fall). A second major type of editorial story is beauty related, which means anything having to do with skin care, hair care, makeup, or cosmetic procedures, such as facials or massages. Models are also used to illustrate lifestyle pieces, stories about relationships, jobs, money, food, health, and fitness.

Editorial is generally considered the most prestigious type of modeling. This is because magazines set the standard for the fashion industry as a whole; they decide what styles are in, what designers are important, and which models embody the look of the moment. (We'll discuss how magazines help create trends later in this chapter.) Once you start appearing in magazines, everyone else (fashion designers, advertisers, catalogs) will follow the magazines' lead and probably soon be clamoring to hire you.

Catwalk Talk

Modeling for a magazine is referred to as **editorial work**, because the models appear in the editorial stories (the pages created and written by the publication's staff) as opposed to the advertisements.

The downside of editorial work is that it doesn't pay well, but models who appear in a lot of magazines actually end up making the most money. Doing editorial work establishes a woman as a top model, and it creates a demand for that model from the rest of the industry. (We'll talk more about the pros and cons of editorial work in Chapter 19, "Print Work.")

The Lucrative World of Catalog Modeling

Catalog work—posing for photos that will appear in the catalogs that are mailed out to people across the country—generally doesn't get as much attention as magazine and runway work, but in reality, catalogs employ more models than any other sector of the industry. In addition, catalogs pay very well. Many models make a good living doing catalog work alone.

Roshumba's Rules

Studying the models in catalogs is a great way to learn how to model clothes in ways that show off their best attributes. Notice how the models stand, where they place their arms, and which direction they're facing.

Catalog modeling includes modeling for catalogs published by specialty houses such as J. Crew, Spiegel, and Tweeds, and catalogs produced by department stores such as Neiman Marcus, Saks Fifth Avenue, Filene's, Macy's, and Dillard's. Department stores often produce a dozen or so different types of catalogs: One might feature designer clothing, another might show bridge lines (designers' secondary, less-expensive lines, such as DKNY and Anne Klein II), and a third might include moderate merchandise. They may also publish catalogs with seasonal themes, such as Christmas and Mother's Day. For each different catalog, a team of models will be hired.

Catalog work is not fancy or creative—I like to call it bread-and-butter work. The purpose of a catalog is to sell merchandise, and the purpose of a catalog shoot is to show the merchandise at its best so people will buy it. The buyers for the catalog have already spent millions of dollars purchasing the clothing being featured in the catalog. They want to make sure those clothes sell, so the focus of the catalog is to make those garments look appealing to customers. The model, photographer, hairstylist, and makeup artist are all chosen because of their ability to make the clothes appealing and desirable. On the other hand, editorial or runway modeling is about creating an image or selling an attitude.

Modeling for catalogs is one of the most lucrative types of modeling; it pays a very high *day rate,* and because there are so many catalogs, there is a lot of work available in cities around the country.

Catwalk Talk

A model's **day rate** is the amount of money she earns for a full day of work. A model's experience, popularity, and the caliber of the client all determine her day rate.

On the Runway

You've no doubt seen footage of fashion shows on TV or in magazines, where models strut up and down a long narrow stage (called the runway or catwalk) dressed in the newest fashions. Runway shows allow fashion designers to present their latest creations to the press, executives of clothing stores from around the world, and wealthy customers. For these fashion shows, the designers hire a squadron of models to wear the clothes and walk up and down the runway in them.

Although it's generally only the top fashion designers' shows that are showcased on television and in the press, there are many other types of fashion shows that hire models, including local events at malls and stores around the country. These shows are known as *consumer fashion shows.* (While a few wealthy individuals may attend designer fashion shows of famous designers, they're mostly attended by fashion industry professionals, such as store buyers and the fashion press.)

Consumer fashion shows take place at malls and stores around the country. Their purpose is to give local shoppers an idea of the newest design trends and styles; hopefully, the audience will then buy the fashions they saw on the runway.

Top designers today prefer using the top editorial models—models featured frequently in the pages of fashion magazines—for their shows, although many designers, especially in Paris and Milan, are always on the lookout for fresh new faces. There are also some models who specialize in doing runway, and who travel continually doing fashion shows in cities around the world. For fashion shows outside of Milan, Paris, and New York, local models are generally hired.

How much a model earns doing runway depends mainly on the caliber of the client. Some of the models in the Victoria's Secret runway show, for instance, can earn up to $30,000 for a show that lasts less than 30 minutes! Models for a lesser-known designer may make a few hundred dollars. Fashion shows in a mall may pay little or nothing. (For more information on runway modeling, see Chapter 20, "The Exciting World of Runway Modeling.")

Modeling on the Small Screen

Models also appear in many of the national and local commercials you see on television. TV commercials generate a lot of potential work for all types of models, from the classic beauty to the "real-person" model (a model who doesn't meet the prerequisites for fashion modeling, but who embodies a specific character type, such as the mom, the student, the businesswoman, for example) in cities large and small. The variety of models used in TV commercials can range from the quirky young woman selling Diet Coke to the "family man" type shopping at a local car dealership. (See Chapter 3, "Do You Have What It Takes?" for more information on the prerequisites of fashion modeling.)

The bad news about TV commercials is that models are competing not only with other models but also with actors and "real-people" types to land those spots (for more information about real-people models, see Chapter 23, "Real-People Models"). Often, it doesn't necessarily matter how beautiful someone is; it's more important that the model embodies what the client is looking for. Even the most beautiful girl in the world could be turned down if her personality doesn't capture what the client is trying to sell.

Most models start going on auditions for TV commercials from the beginning of their careers. Although the competition is stiff to land a job, many commercials pay well, especially at the national level, and offer a model an opportunity to try her hand at a new medium, working in front of a *live-action camera*. But because working in front of a live-action camera is much more complicated and requires a much larger behind-the-scenes crew than modeling in front of a *still camera*, filming TV commercials can be very demanding, repetitive work. (For more information on television commercials, see Chapter 21, "Advertisements, Endorsements, and TV Commercials.")

Roshumba's Rules

The best way to increase your chances of landing a TV commercial is to take acting and/or commercial technique classes. These will teach you the skills necessary to perform your best in front of a live-action camera.

Catwalk Talk

A **live-action camera** is a camera that captures more dimensions: walking, talking, and movement. **Still cameras** capture only the dimension of a still photo; movement is captured frame by frame.

Salespeople: Advertisement and Endorsement Modeling

Appearing in an advertisement in a magazine, newspaper, or on a billboard can be a very lucrative job for a model. Of course, because they generally pay well, jobs doing ads are harder to land.

Models who land advertisement bookings often have physical attributes that relate to the product. If it's an ad for a body lotion, the model will have beautiful, flawless skin. If it's a hair ad, she'll have healthy, beautiful hair. If it's for exercise clothes, she'll have an extremely fit, athletic body.

Other times, the model will need to embody the image of the product. (We discuss more about image later in this chapter.) A model appearing in an ad for platform sneakers will need a trendy, cool, young look. A model posing as a doctor in a medical ad, however, will need to look older, more professional, and responsible. So although it can be difficult to find the right match for your exact look, the good news is that there is modeling work for many different types of looks (and hopefully yours, too!).

Even more lucrative and prestigious than advertising work is endorsement work. Landing an endorsement deal is as fabulous (and as rare) as winning the lottery. With an endorsement deal, a company signs you on to represent their products and their company for a certain period of time, usually at least a year. As part of the deal, you may appear in all of that company's advertisements and represent it at various events for consumers at malls and stores; you may even be asked to meet the company's employees and investors at major corporate meetings.

Endorsement deals are coveted by all models because they (usually) pay so much. (Many models live off endorsement deals alone.) For example, L'Oréal might hire a model to endorse its hair-care, makeup, and skin-care products for three years at a rate of $1 million a year. But the model may be required to work only a relatively few number of days—20, perhaps—to earn that money. Granted, only a very few models—less than 1 percent—ever land endorsement deals, but if you become one of them, you've hit the modeling jackpot!

Reality Check

Don't think that you can't model in advertisements because you don't live in New York or another very large city. Even smaller and mid-size cities have local ad agencies that create advertisements for area clients, such as clothing stores, hair and beauty salons, health clubs, restaurants, banks, appliance stores, and car dealerships. Often times, local models will be hired to appear in these ads. Economics can play a big part in the hiring process. Local clients often don't have budgets to fly in big-name models or celebrities.

Mod Squad

Certain models have such widespread appeal that numerous companies clamor to use them in their ad campaigns. Christy Turlington is one of those fortunate few models who has appeared in numerous advertisements. Her classic looks have earned her very lucrative contracts with Maybelline cosmetics, Calvin Klein fragrances and underwear, and Ellen Tracy sportswear. Model Niki Taylor, who embodies the healthy, girl-next-door look, is one of the busiest models around; besides appearing on dozens of magazine covers, she has endorsement deals with Cover Girl, Liz Claiborne, and Nokia cell phones. Another model who has parlayed her beauty and name recognition into some profitable advertising contracts is Claudia Schiffer, who has represented Chanel, Versace, Revlon, Valentino, and Victoria's Secret.

The Business of Modeling

When people think about modeling, they mostly think about the glitz and glamour of photo shoots and fashion shows. But behind all the fabulousness is a business, a very big business, which is an intrinsic part of the fashion industry and a myriad of other corporations that sell consumer products, such as soft drinks, potato chips, cars, stereos, videos, sports equipment, and so on.

Models are responsible for the bottom lines of many companies, because it's their pictures that sell the mascara, the soft drink, the shoes, the candy bars—you name it. This is why major corporations pay top models so much to help market a wide range of products. If a desirable image is connected to a product, that product can be transformed from an obscure and unprofitable item to a multimillion-dollar success.

Creating an Image

Say someone has an idea for a new perfume. She knows her perfume has a lovely scent, but it needs a desirable presentation to launch it in the marketplace. What does her company do? It hires an advertising agency to create an *image* for the product and to design an advertising campaign that will create desirability, and thus, demand, for the product. This is where models come in, to lend their image, personal style, physical looks, and personality to the product.

How does image sell a product? Let's look at three examples:

➤ You're in a grocery store and have the choice of buying either a can of Diet Coke or a can of generic diet cola. What's your first choice? Probably the Diet Coke.

Obviously, you may just like its taste. But part of your decision may be influenced by the fact that over the years you've seen dozens of advertisements for it showing good-looking people having a good time. Eventually, it's only natural that you associate fun times with Diet Coke.

➤ When the TV commercial says, "L'Oréal ... because I'm worth it," it makes you think something positive about yourself—yes, you're worth it, too. So when it comes time to buy hair color, you may find yourself leaning toward buying L'Oréal, because it's the choice of beautiful women who deserve the best in life—you.

➤ A commercial shows a beautiful, healthy couple running along a white sandy beach with the wind blowing through their hair. On some level you want a piece of that beautiful, carefree image, even if it means buying something completely unrelated, such as a bar of deodorant soap. Everyone wants to be young, beautiful, and sexy, which is what that deodorant soap wants to associate itself with—images of youth, beauty, and sex.

The Face of a Product

One way to build an image for a product is by hiring one particular model whose looks and personality lend a specific aura to a product. A good example of this is the care fashion designers take in selecting a model to be featured in their advertisements. A lot of money is spent designing beautiful garments, developing advertising campaigns, manufacturing, and distributing the merchandise. That's why designers pay so much attention to models who will embody what they feel is aesthetically perfect, to make their products look as appealing as possible.

A designer's idea of the perfect beauty may come from a vision that came to her in a dream, from a beautiful relative remembered from childhood, or from her favorite movie star. Whatever the case, perfection doesn't come cheap. So important is the model to the success of the whole collection that much care (and often money) is taken to hire the right model. But the designer knows that this is a good investment, because the image will often pay off through increased sales.

A model may also be hired to give a product a whole new image and a whole new appeal. Hiring African American male model Tyson Beckford to represent designer Ralph Lauren's preppy, conservative clothes may have seemed like a strange choice for Lauren. But Beckford's rugged good looks and cool homeboy style gave the company a younger, hipper image and made Lauren's clothes appealing to a whole new block of buyers—trend-setting urban youth.

Models give life to fashion trends, like the halter top, Capri pants, and feathered handbag shown here.

Mod Squad

Cosmetic companies often use a single model to embody their name and company image. One example is Estée Lauder, which has established itself as an upscale, classic line of beauty products, primarily through an advertising campaign featuring a single model who is signed to an exclusive contract. Elizabeth Hurley is the model who currently embodies the Estée Lauder image. (Her predecessors were Paulina Porizkova and Willow Bay.) Her classic features, beautiful skin, and lovely smile are associated in consumers' minds with Estée Lauder products; on some subliminal level, buyers think they can become just as beautiful if they use those products.

Sex Sells

Besides the image of an individual model, another thing that advertisers use over and over again to sell everything, even socks, is sex. If the image created to advertise a product is sexy, most people want to have a piece of it because it makes them feel sexy and desirable themselves. Have you seen the commercial with the sexy blonde who pulls over to the side of the road, jumps out of her car, strips down to her birthday suit, and begins to bathe in a rain shower? That commercial gave Clairol Herbal Essence body wash a sexy image and told consumers this was more than just boring old soap.

Using sex in advertisements can be very controversial, which gets people talking—and shopping. The ads for cK one fragrance were so inflammatory they were yanked from magazines and billboards. Despite all the (supposedly) negative publicity, thousands of people bought cK one, making it one of the most successful fragrance launches ever.

Reinventing an Old Product with a New Image

Just as new products need to define their images and find ways to project them, older products whose sales might be declining need to bring new life to their images, too.

Sometimes, all it takes is a remake of a beloved commercial, such as the Oscar Mayer B-O-L-O-G-N-A commercial. Bologna is something we are all familiar with. There are many different brands on the market, so why does one particular bologna, Oscar Mayer, stand out from all the rest? Well, it's because we've all heard that famous song, "My bologna has a first name…" Now what company comes to mind when you hear this song? Oscar Mayer.

But everyone had heard this song so often that it had lost its fresh appeal, so it was retired. A few years passed, and a new advertising campaign was needed. The advertising company chose not to come up with a whole new campaign, but to give it a fresh new slant, capitalizing on the affection consumers have for that first commercial. A worldwide search was set up to find a new child to represent the product.

Roshumba's Rules

Whenever you see an ad, try to figure out how it's trying to make you feel and how that relates to the product being sold. This is the first step toward being a knowledgeable consumer.

Now, when we see that fresh new face and hear that adorable voice singing the Oscar Mayer jingle on the new television commercial, the advertiser is hoping that we find ourselves falling in love with the Oscar Mayer B-O-L-O-G-N-A commercial—and buying Oscar Mayer bologna—all over again.

Fifteen Minutes of Fame: How Fashion Trends Originate

Besides helping creating an image for a product and helping to sell that product to consumers, models are also key players in helping to initiate fashion trends. Every time a new style comes in and is embraced by even a segment of the population, millions of dollars change hands. Models play an essential role in making that happen.

Whenever you've been shopping, reading a magazine, or watching a TV show about fashion, you've probably wondered who decides what's in and what's out. It often happens that you see a story in a magazine with a model wearing the new short skirts, the new flat shoe, or the new brown nail polish. Then, the next time you go to the mall, there are the new short skirts, the new flat shoes, and the new brown nail polish in all the stores.

That doesn't happen by accident. It's a large, well-coordinated effort on the part of the fashion industry to inform you about the newest fashion trends—and more important, to encourage you to buy them.

The fashion industry, which includes clothing designers and manufacturers, magazine editors, advertisers, photographers, hairstylists, and makeup artists, is constantly redefining what's considered beautiful and what's "in." These people can take a new idea (or recycle an old one), refine it, package it, and make us want to buy it:

➤ Italian designer Miuccia Prada may send a new knee-length skirt down the runway at her fashion show in Milan, and, instantly, women all over the world will be clamoring to buy it.

➤ The Gap can declare that khakis are the new look for spring and feature them in a big ad campaign, and, before long, just about everyone in the country is wearing them.

➤ *Allure* magazine can print pictures of a new red lipstick, and suddenly we all need it to feel hip and modern.

➤ *Vogue* can put actress Cameron Diaz on the cover of the magazine, dressed in a silk skirt and top, and dub her the new "It" girl. Since we all want to feel like a sexy, popular "It" girl on some level, we may be inspired to copy her hairstyle and buy her makeup and clothes.

Roshumba's Rules

If you're on a budget, fashion experts suggest splurging on classics that don't go out of style—jackets, turtlenecks, tailored shirts and pants—and buying cheaper versions of trendy items (platform shoes and halter tops).

Catwalk Talk

A **fashionista** is a woman or man, often someone who works in fashion or retail, who follows every trend. She or he is always wearing the latest styles, carrying the most fashionable purse, and sporting the hottest sunglasses.

Even colors are subject to fashion trends. One season many designers may feature gray garments in their fashion shows. The color to have that season is gray, and all the *fashionistas* will run out to buy something gray—a shirt or pants or a sweater. The next season, gray might be out and brown will be the color to have. Fashionistas then will be replacing their gray shirts and pants and sweaters with brown shirts and pants and sweaters. Models help create the demand for each trend as it comes along.

Why do fashion trends change so much? Partly to keep the fashion designers and magazine editors busy working. Partly to keep people's attention. But mostly to keep people buying and buying and buying—the latest clothing, makeup, shoes, hats, belts, coats, and nail polish.

What Is "The Look"?

All the fashion trends, taken together, are what's called "The Look." The Look of the Moment, however, is just that—it lasts only a moment; it changes constantly. Let's consider the many different things that can affect The Look.

Fashion History in the Making

Historical events leave their mark on The Look. Events such as Prohibition, the Great Depression, World War II, the Vietnam War, Women's Lib, a bull run of the stock market, and grunge rock have all been reflected in the styles of the times. Certain material items are totems of each of those decades: 1920s flapper dresses, Depression-era Bakelite jewelry, the bobby socks of the World War II era, the full skirts of the prosperous 1950s, the love beads of the rebellious 1960s, the braless look of the Women's Lib era in the early 1970s, the power suits of the corporate 1980s, and the thrift-shop chic of the early recessionary 1990s. In each of these eras, it was models—in magazines, in advertisements, at designers' fashion shows, and at consumer fashion shows—who embodied these trends and created demand for them.

Style Makers

As times change, so do the influential people who dictate the trends, and that can affect fashion as well. Diana Vreeland was the editor in chief of *Vogue* in the go-go 1960s. Her fashion flair was perfectly suited to the crazy experimentation that was going on at the time. When she was replaced by Grace Mirabella, a new aesthetic was ushered in, one that valued practicality over frivolity, and was more suited to women's new roles in the workplace. These style makers also help choose the models who best embody The Look of the Moment.

Roshumba's Rules

Don't try to copy all the fashions, makeup, and hairstyles you see in magazines. Often times, certain looks are done for dramatic effect in a photo; they are not meant to be worn on the streets!

Hollywood's Influence

Another big influence on The Look is Hollywood and the personal look of popular entertainers, such as Marilyn Monroe's hourglass figure, Julie Andrew's pixie haircut, Ali McGraw's hippie style, Grace Jones's hard-edged, postmodern look, Madonna's shocking hair and wardrobe changes, or Ally McBeal's super-short skirts. Today, with the increase in the coverage of celebrity style by media such as *In Style* magazine and E! Entertainment Television, Hollywood is a bigger influence than ever on the fashion industry. And conversely, Hollywood is more fashion-conscious than ever before.

Street Style

Often, The Look doesn't originate on the fashion runways or in the photo studio. Instead, the powers-that-be in the fashion industry—designers, photographers, magazine editors, and advertisers—take to the streets to find out what's hot and what's not.

Inspiration can come from the funky, individual style of club kids: The fashion of wearing slips and bras (which are normally considered to be underwear) as outerwear was inspired by a club trend. Even over-the-top drag queens have originated fashion trends: Wearing very dark, obvious lip liner with light lipstick was a look started by drag queens, and then recycled by the fashion industry.

Designers Ralph Lauren and Tommy Hilfiger have based entire collections on the cool style of the hip-hop homeboys and funky diva attitude of the homegirls, as well as the preppy style of rich East Coast kids. The thrift-shop chic of college girls has inspired Todd Oldham and Miuccia Prada. Even the uniforms of garbagemen have been used as a springboard for designers. But it takes a beautiful model wearing that thrift-store-inspired dress or those huge, baggy jeans to make them desirable, cool, and in fashion.

Reality Check

Don't think you have to buy every new thing that comes into fashion in order to make it as a model. In reality, classic styles are preferable when you're trying to break into modeling. Being aware of why fashion changes so much—to force you to buy new things all the time in order to keep up—can make you a smarter shopper.

Designers borrow ideas from street trends, like the baggy clothes and baseball cap shown here, a look that was adapted from rappers.

Signs of the Times

In every era, there are models, clothes, accessories, hairstyles, and makeup that are so prevalent that they become associated with that time period. Looking back at four decades of evolving fashion trends will help show how each decade has its own Look, how that Look is shaped by the dominant fashion and beauty trends, how models embody those trends, and how they end up being the faces of their generation.

The 1960s

The 1960s was the Age of Aquarius—of youth, idealism, hippies, and flower power. Young people were protesting the Vietnam War and rebelling against the system, which they saw as the outdated, racist, classist, sexist, and prudish ways of the establishment. Young people were experimenting with life, pushing the boundaries, and challenging stereotypes, sexual boundaries, women's roles, and strict fashion and etiquette rules (for example, the 1960s saw the end of gloves and hats for women). The fashions reflected the radical, fast-changing era: microminis, go-go boots, "groovy" sunglasses, long, beautiful hair, and lots of eye makeup. Twiggy was the most popular model of the decade, and with her offbeat, innocent look—rail-thin, girlish, with super-long limbs, big eyes, a pixie haircut, and a sweet smile—she was the perfect representative of her time.

The 1970s

The 1970s were all about the Sexual Revolution. Halston, an American designer whose clothes were extremely body-conscious, was all the rage. The legendary nightspot Studio 54 in New York City was a fashionable international playground where excess was the order of the day. Everywhere, everybody was shaking their booty and having a really good time. For women, it was a time of exploring their newfound personal, professional, and sexual freedom, and this was reflected in the models. For me, the ultimate 1970s women were Charlie's Angels—Farrah Fawcett, Kate Jackson, and Jaclyn Smith. They were self-confident, independent, healthy, natural, and comfortable with their bodies and their sexuality, as were the decade's top models, Cheryl Tiegs, Lauren Hutton, and Beverly Johnson. (These three were also the first supermodels.) When Tiegs appeared on the cover of *Time,* it was a sign that models had become household names (and faces), and that she was a bona fide representative of the modern-day woman.

The 1980s

The 1980s were all about money—making it and spending it. Fashion houses such as Chanel, Yves Saint Laurent, and Calvin Klein established themselves as the ruling powers. They licensed out their names and their merchandise appeared everywhere, including umbrellas, jewelry, luggage—you name it. The economy was booming and the world was shopping. Everyone wanted a designer label on their jeans, underwear, handbags, and scarves. You *had* to have a Louis Vuitton bag or a Perry Ellis coat. TV shows like *Dynasty* and *Dallas* added fuel to the fire. As Joan Collins and Linda Evans strutted around their mansions in those designer clothes, they fired the demand of thousands of people. It was no longer about what you were wearing, but *who* you were wearing. It was the era of the shoulder pads, the power suit, pounds of jewelry, high heels, lots of makeup, and big hair—anything that added to an image of luxury and opulence. The top models embodied that glamour and sophistication: Kim Alexis, Paulina Porizkova, Christie Brinkley, and Carol Alt.

Mod Squad

The early 1990s was the era of the waifs. Kate Moss and the other waif models were the answer to the overdone, voluptuous supermodels who had dominated the runways in the late 1980s and early 1990s. The waifs were super skinny and undernourished-looking, had lank, lifeless hair, and expressionless faces. Soon their pictures were everywhere, in magazines, on television, on billboards. For once, the general public rebelled against a look promoted by the fashion industry. The debate was fanned by the fact that for most women, Moss's adolescent thinness was completely unattainable except through extreme, unhealthy means of dieting. This controversy—and fashion's continual search for new standards of beauty—meant that the heyday of the waifs was short-lived. This time period was also the moment of "heroin chic." Models appeared in magazine editorial layouts and clothing advertisements looking drugged out and lifeless.

The 1990s

If I were to sum up fashion and pop culture in the 1990s, I would have to say it's been a decade of exploration. One trend is to reinvent the good old days through the revival of 1970s styles such as bell bottoms, blue eye shadow, and even platform shoes. As exercise has become more prevalent, clothes have gotten more body-conscious. Fashion is also more about line and silhouette than it is about decoration; jewelry, for instance, is either small and discreet, or nonexistent.

Today (fortunately) no one type of model is dominant; there's room for a variety of beauties. Cindy Crawford, Christy Turlington, Linda Evangelista, Claudia Schiffer, Stephanie Seymour, and Kathy Ireland have been the top models throughout the decade. Exotic types such as the baby-faced African model Alek Wek and the Siberian beauty Irina are also everywhere. Oddball models with quirky looks like Kristin McMenamy are popular. Waif Kate Moss, meanwhile, is also still busy, but has publicly admitted that her bad-girl ways have come to an end and is cleaning up her act. She is now the poster girl for rehab, as are many of her other heroin-chic buddies.

The Least You Need to Know

➤ Modeling work encompasses photo shoots for magazines, catalogs, and advertisements as well as TV commercials and runway shows.

➤ Modeling is an intrinsic part of advertising and marketing.

➤ Fashion changes continually in an effort to keep consumers buying.

➤ The predominant fashion styles of an era help define that time.

Do You Have What It Takes?

Have you been told that you look like a model, or that you should give modeling a try? Many pretty girls have been told at one time or another that they should become models. But to be a successful fashion model—the type of model who appears in magazines, catalogs, and fashion shows—a person needs to be more than just pretty. Because fashion models need to be able to fit into special sample-size garments and to look a certain way when photographed, it's also necessary that they meet other requirements: They need to be tall, slim, well-proportioned, within a certain age range, and have photogenic features, including beautiful skin, hair, teeth, and nails.

As you read this chapter, keep in mind that these physical requirements apply to fashion models only. So even if you don't meet all these requirements (for instance, many people who are interested in modeling aren't tall enough), don't despair! There are still other modeling opportunities for you, including parts modeling (where only one part of your body, such as your hands, legs, or feet, is photographed) and "real-people" modeling (which relies as much on personality type as physical qualifications). We'll discuss the special requirements for male models, plus-size models, petite models, and elegant (older) models in Chapter 22, "Specialty Models."

But there's a lot more to being a model than meets the eye—literally. A lucrative modeling career, like anything else, requires hard work, dedication, a good attitude, and good physical and mental health. Many otherwise beautiful models have seen their careers fizzle out because they were immature, irresponsible, disorganized, or didn't manage their careers in a business-like manner. Others couldn't handle the stress and rejection of the modeling industry, while others got involved with abusive boyfriends, developed mental problems, depression, or eating disorders, or started abusing drugs or alcohol. In the second part of this chapter, I'll talk about the mental and emotional requirements for a modeling career.

Catwalk Talk

Real-people models appear mainly in ads and TV commercials (not fashion magazine covers and fashion shows). They generally represent a type, such as a mom, a cute kid, a kindly granddad, a balding "regular Joe," or a businesswoman. **Parts models** specialize in modeling specific body parts—legs, hands, or feet. These body parts must be free of scars and bruises and kept well maintained.

Finally, at the end of this chapter is a fun quiz that will help you figure out if modeling is for you.

Basic Physical Requirements

There's no getting around the fact that fashion models are hired for the way they look; therefore, height, weight, body structure, skin, hair, and other physical attributes are extremely important. Fortunately, there's a demand for many different types of fashion models—whether it's a magazine looking for a classically beautiful cover girl, a designer looking for an exotic-type model to walk in her runway show, or an advertiser looking for an athletic model to represent its new line of sneakers. (We'll talk more about the different types of models, and the kind of modeling they specialize in, in Chapter 5, "Which Look Are You: The Seven Basic Model Types.") There are also opportunities for *real-people models* and *parts models,* and we'll talk about special requirements for them, too, in Chapter 23, "Real-People Models."

Height

The minimum required height for a fashion model is usually about 5'8". Although there are exceptions to this rule (Kate Moss, for instance, is only about 5'7"), they are extremely rare, especially in the fashion capitals such as New York, Paris, and Milan, where the majority of models work. In certain secondary markets, such as Chicago and Los Angeles, where models are needed for the many teen and junior catalogs that are shot there, a fashion model may be able to get away with being as short as 5'6".

For parts models or real-people models specializing in TV commercials, height is not an issue. Real-people models can range from short, dweeby guys in computer commercials to 5'5" mom types to towering giants.

People often ask me, "I'm 5'2". Why can't I be a model?" The answer is, when designers make garments to be shown on the runway, in a photo shoot, or in an advertisement, they make a sample size to fit one body type; a full range of sizes has not yet been manufactured. Models need to fit into that one sample available, which is generally a woman's size 4 or 6. Samples are also cut longer to fit a taller model. Long, lean bodies move and look better on the runway. That is why models' body proportions, especially height, are so important.

The maximum height for a model is generally six feet, although again, there are rare exceptions. Gabrielle Reese, a model who's also a professional volleyball player, is around 6'3".

Weight

This is tough to answer because people have different body structures, muscle tones, and heights. In general, fashion models need to be tall and slim in order to fit into the single sample-sized garment that's available for a shoot or fashion show. Generally, models weigh 10 to 15 pounds less than the generic height/weight table.

Instead of judging aspiring models on weight, many agencies look at their bust, waist, and hip measurements. "Hips should probably be no bigger than 35 inches," reports Cathy Gould, a model scout who was the director of the Elite Model Look model search, who has met thousands of aspiring models. "Usually hips are the biggest problem we have with girls. Bust size is not as important," she says. "Some models are busty, some models are really flat-chested; it's not a major issue."

The ideal waist measurement is your hip measurement minus 10 inches. So if your hips are 34 inches, your waist should be around 24 inches.

Roshumba's Rules

Don't think you need breast implants to make it as a model. It's actually preferable that models be smaller rather than larger in the chest, because clothes tend to hang better unless a model specializes in bathing-suit and lingerie modeling.

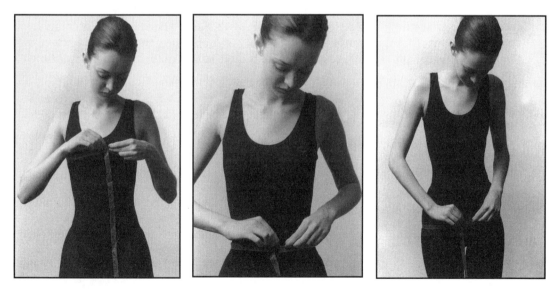

Body measurements, not weight, are used to evaluate models' figures. Here, a model takes her bust, waist, and hip measurements with a tape measure.
Photographer: Kwame Brathwaite. Model: Laura McLafferty.

Again, for real-people models, weight is not an issue. The same goes for parts models, as long as the part they're modeling (hands, legs, feet) still looks attractive.

Preferred Body Types

Many people don't realize that being tall doesn't automatically make you fashion-model material. Body proportion is also important: You want to project an impression of length, and that usually means long, long legs (as opposed to a long torso and short legs). You should have a toned, lean body so you can fit into sample-size clothing. Of course, there are exceptions to the rule, such as lingerie and swimsuit models, who are fuller in the bust and hip area.

Real-people models come in all shapes and sizes. Parts models need to have attractive, well-proportioned parts, but the rest of their body proportions are not important.

Acceptable Clothing Size

Generally, fashion models should be no smaller than a women's size 2 and no larger than a women's size 6.

Real-people and parts models don't need to meet any specific requirements when it comes to clothing size.

Age Range

Beginning fashion models can range in age from 12 up to 22, although again, there are exceptions. In general, *modeling agents* start to scout models around the age of 14 (occasionally, they will work with even younger girls). This doesn't mean a girl will drop out of junior high school to move by herself to New York or Paris to become a model. It means that the agency starts grooming and prepping the girl for her career. In fact, agents usually encourage girls to finish high school before starting a full-time modeling career.

Catwalk Talk

A **modeling agent** finds girls who have the potential to be successful models, signs a contract to represent them, markets them to clients (including magazines, advertisers, and fashion designers), and guides their careers.

As Cathy Gould explains, "It takes a while to get a girl marketed, to get her developed, to get her book [portfolio] out there. It could take a year before something really starts to happen. So we start scouting [them] around 14.

"That doesn't mean they're a full-time model at 14. It means a girl may come to New York for a week to put a portfolio together. Then maybe she'll come back over the spring holiday to start to go see the magazines, then maybe she'll come for a week in the summer. She may do that for a year or two, until she's 16 or 17. It's a good gauge to see how clients are responding to the model, how the model is responding to the industry, and whether or not she has a career once she graduates high school.

"Once a girl hits a certain age, I'd say after 22, it's a little difficult [to get a career started in a major market like New York or Paris], because it takes a while to get a girl developed, to get her book out there. In New York, we like to have the models up and running between 18 and 22, as opposed to just starting out at 22. In other cities, like Miami, Chicago, or Los Angeles, it's probably skewed a little older." So if you're over 22 and want to become a fashion model, you're best bet is to try to break into a secondary market, such as Miami, Chicago, or Los Angeles.

Real-people models can be of all ages, from quirky kids featured in cereal commercials to feisty old ladies in fast-food commercials. Parts models can also be of any age, as long as their "part" looks young and beautiful, or fits the image of the product being advertised, for example: rugged, outdoorsy hands in a lawn fertilizer ad.

Model Skin

Healthy, clear, beautiful skin is a must for models because bad skin doesn't photograph well. People with skin that is sun damaged, marked from acne and blemishes, or people who look tired and have dark circles under their eyes from lack of sleep may have problems launching a modeling career because of their skin.

But even if you think the condition of your skin could be an impediment, don't worry—all hope is not lost. Fortunately, your skin is something you can actually work on to improve. First of all, even at a young age, it's important to learn how to take care of your particular type of skin properly. (Check out Chapter 27, "The Outer You," for my skin-care advice.) You can also ask your doctor or pharmacist for advice on the best ways to cleanse, moisturize (if necessary), and medicate (if you have mild acne) your skin. If you have more serious problems with acne (as many teenage girls do), see a dermatologist (get your parents' permission first) to get the necessary treatment.

It's also important to stay out of the sun and to wear sunscreen every day. Sun damage can start to show up on the skin as young as 16. Your face is your fortune, and you need to take care of yourself. Get enough sleep, eat healthy, balanced meals, and drink plenty of water (see Chapter 27 for more tips)! These healthy habits will all benefit your skin.

Reality Check

Although young children can often get away with eating anything, a bad diet (eating lots of chips, candy, cookies, and soda) is unhealthy, tends to make you gain weight, and starts to show up in your skin when you become a teenager. So instead of eating junk food or fast-food, eat more fresh fruits and vegetables, whole grains, fish, and chicken.

A Cover-Girl Smile

Healthy, pretty, well-maintained teeth are also crucial to modeling success. During my time on the road as the official host for the Elite Model Look model search, I've seen many otherwise beautiful girls turned away by the scouts and judges because their teeth were discolored, crooked, or just not in good condition.

The ideal teeth are straight and white. Even if yours are not, there are many things you can do to make them look better. Consult your dentist about what you can do to get your teeth in tiptop shape. But don't sign up for expensive cosmetic dental procedures such as bonding or laminates except on the advice of an agent, and only with your parents' permission, if you're under 18.

Healthy teeth and a pretty smile are key elements for success for both male and female models.
Photographer: Kwame Brathwaite. Models: Ryan Kopko and Laura McLafferty.

Having braces doesn't mean you can't be a model; it means only that you'll have to delay your career just a bit. In fact, one of the national finalists in this year's Elite Model Look model search had braces. Agents would much rather see girls with braces than girls with bad teeth! "We'd rather have you in braces at 14, 15, and 16, as opposed to finding out at 18, when you can model full-time, that now you need braces," explains Cathy Gould. "It's important at a younger age, if you really want to get into modeling, to take care of that."

Hair, Beautiful Hair

Aspiring models often ask me, "What is good hair?" Good hair is healthy hair that's clean, well cut, not overcolored, overpermed, overprocessed, or overstyled. "Hair is an individual thing," says Cathy Gould. "We're not looking for any specific hair type; anything goes today. That's the exciting thing—you see all different styles of hair, all different colors."

Fortunately, girls aren't usually disqualified from modeling because of the condition of their hair, but it's a good idea to keep yours looking its best. Work with a hairstylist you trust to make sure your cut suits your face, and that it's a modern, youthful style. Also ask the stylist for tips on keeping your hair its healthiest.

Real-people models can have almost any kind of hair, from balding guys to curly maned girls to white-haired older women. For parts models, hair is generally not an issue.

Nailing It

For all types of models, nails should be short, clean, manicured, and polished with a clear or natural-colored polish. No bitten nails! Another turnoff is nails that are long, scraggly, or unmanicured. And skip the outrageous black or green nail polish when you're meeting with an agent.

Of course, well-manicured hands are even more vital for hand models, since all the focus will be on your hands. You'll want to get regular manicures, with clear- or natural-colored polish. (For more information on taking care of your nails, see Chapter 27.)

Reality Check

When agents look at your hair, they're checking to see what can be done to it, not admiring what you did to it, so in general, the simpler the style, the better. When you're going to meet an agent, whether it's at a model search, modeling convention, or the agency itself, shampoo and condition your hair, style it simply, and skip all the gels, sprays, and hair goos.

Mental and Emotional Requirements for Modeling

Modeling is a business, and like any business, it wouldn't be very profitable if the employees (the models) didn't show up for work, were late for jobs, stole half the merchandise, treated the other employees rudely, or threw tantrums every time something didn't go their way. Believe me, there have been models who have done all those things, and many of them are not modeling anymore. That's why it's important to know the kind of behavior that's acceptable for a model, to figure out if your current actions reflect what's generally expected, and if not, to find ways to improve them.

There's no denying the fact that models face rejection constantly. My first day looking for an agency in Paris I was rejected six times, by six different agencies. Even today, 10 years later, I still face rejection every day. These constant rebuffs are hard to deal with even if you're happy, self-confident, and well-adjusted; for a model who's very young, insecure, and has low self-esteem, this endless rejection can be devastating, even to the point of causing serious mental and physical illness. That's why it's so key that an aspiring model have the mental stamina necessary to survive in the business.

Finally, models face many temptations: partying, drugs, adorable boyfriends who turn out to be abusive monsters. Knowing what's right and wrong, and being able to say no to things that will cause you and others harm, is equally important.

In the next sections we'll talk about the most important emotional and mental require-ments for a model, and why they are vital to a successful career—and a happy life.

A Strong Sense of Responsibility

Being responsible is key for a model. Modeling is a job, and your behavior affects a lot of people. If you're late to a *booking,* or decide you just don't feel like working that day because you're tired or not in the mood, your irresponsibility will cause a lot of time and money to be lost and have a negative impact on many people.

Catwalk Talk

When a model is hired for a job, whether it be to pose for a magazine or advertisement or to appear in a runway show, she is said to be "booked" for the job; a **booking** is any job a model is hired to do.

The model who is booked for a job is the center of attention. The photographer is paid a lot of money to shoot her; hairstylists, makeup artists, and fashion stylists are hired to prepare her. A location is rented for the shoot. If a model doesn't show up, or shows up late, this could cost the client (be it a magazine, a fashion designer, a cosmetic company, or a catalog) a lot of time, money, and energy. So it's important to be on time, pleasant to work with, and willing to give your best effort.

If you're considering a modeling career, it's very important that you know the whats, hows, whys, and wherefores of responsibility. Responsibility is not one of those virtues that will just suddenly appear the day you get your first modeling job; it's something that has to be developed and worked on, starting (hopefully) before you take on a modeling career.

Roshumba's Rules

If you're often late, start practicing getting places on time. Figure out in advance how you're going to get where you're going, how long it will take you to get there, and then allow yourself plenty of time.

Arrive on Time

There are many components of responsibility—the first one is being on time. Do you get up on time in the morning? Are you on time for school and other activities? Do you complete your homework and turn it in on time? Do you arrive home before your curfew? Do you get to work on time, and don't ask to leave early?

Finish What You Start

Responsibility also entails knowing exactly what an assignment entails, and then following it through to completion. A model who decides to fly home halfway through a five-day shoot on location in the jungle because she doesn't like the food is just as bad as one who doesn't show up at all.

If you want to make it to the top, you need to be the type of person who finishes what she starts, even when the going gets tough. A good time to start learning how to complete what you start is when you're still at home contemplating a modeling career. For instance, when asked to do chores around the house, don't do them halfway—if

40

you have to do the dishes, don't just pile them in the sink. Wash them, dry them, and put them away. Don't quit a team halfway through the season because you're bored or got a new boyfriend. If you do tend to get distracted halfway through a task, start making a point of completing what you begin.

Motivate Yourself

Responsibility means being self-motivating—taking the initiative to do things on your own without being asked or having to be reminded 25 times. The staff at a modeling agency will tire quickly of a model who has to be told over and over that she has an assignment or an appointment, and they may soon decide that it's not worth the trouble to book that model for jobs. That's why being self-motivating is so key.

While still at home and in school, test your self-motivating skills by knowing what your assigned chores and homework assignments are, and doing them without being asked. When you need extra spending money, don't depend on your parents for handouts, find your own part-time job. Taking small steps to be more self-reliant will make a big difference when your career gets going.

Get Organized!

Responsibility also requires being organized. The model who forgets to put her portfolio in her backpack for an audition, or leaves her datebook at the photo studio where she was shooting, or is always losing things may find her career cut short. That's why it's so important to be organized, to plan ahead, and to know what you'll be doing, and what you'll need, for the next day. Buy a datebook and write all your appointments in it. The night before, lay out your clothes and pack up everything you'll need for the next day—all of this is great practice for your future modeling career.

Roshumba's Rules

Buy a datebook and start using it. No model worth her Prada bag goes anywhere without hers. It contains her whole life: where she's going, when she has to be there, what time the car is coming to pick her up.

Acting Your Age

Maturity is also necessary for a successful modeling career. Numerous beautiful young models have done immature things such as succumbing to peer pressure, partying all night, drinking, or doing drugs. Not surprisingly, these girls aren't around anymore. Also, models who whine, complain, and pout when things don't go their way quickly find themselves to be highly unpopular and find their behavior costs them jobs, and eventually their careers.

How mature are you? Do you constantly tease and fight with your siblings? When something happens that's not to your liking, do you throw a tantrum and make the situation worse? Do you do things that are guaranteed to get you in trouble, just because your friends are doing them? If so, you may need to work on acting more mature.

41

Instead of fighting with your brothers and sisters, especially the younger ones, help and encourage them when they need it. Instead of getting upset about difficult situations, find a peaceful, mutually agreeable way to deal with them. And instead of getting into trouble with your friends, politely say goodbye and head home—no excuses or explanations required. It may be hard, but believe me, learning the mature way to act will pay off numerous dividends once your career takes off!

Knowing Right from Wrong

It sounds old-fashioned, but knowing right from wrong is key to being a model. The reason? Because the temptations and pitfalls are even greater in the modeling world than in your hometown. I won't lie—drugs are common in the fashion industry, and if you give in to them, you could find yourself addicted, unemployed, or even dead in just a matter of months.

Even minor indulgences such as going to parties, shopping, eating too much, and falling in love be hazardous to your health, your well-being, and your career, if you don't know when to say when. I like to have a good time as much as the next person. I like going to clubs and dancing with my friends to the wee hours of the morning, I love to shop, I love to eat, and I love men. But I do these things selectively and in moderation because overdoing any of these things will have a negative impact on my life and my career.

Roshumba's Rules

The guidelines I follow are, first and foremost, respect yourself; and second, do unto others as you would have them do unto you. These rules have served me well, both in modeling and in life.

Being out in the clubs all night wears you down. You look tired the next day, you get black circles under your eyes, and your skin loses its fresh, healthy glow—not the look employers are after. Shopping is fun, but yes, there is such a thing as shopping too much, like when you max out your credit cards every month and have to borrow money (and worse) to pay them off. Overeating is unhealthy and makes it impossible to maintain a model-slim figure, so you need to plan and manage what you eat. And finally, men are great, but I've seen relationships with controlling, drug-addicted, or abusive boyfriends cost more than one model her career. There are many pitfalls out there, which is why it's so important for a young model to have a sense of what's right and what's wrong, so that she knows what actions will threaten her career and well-being.

The same problems that can derail your modeling career may already be present in your life before you even get started: You give into pressure to have sex even though you're not in love with the person, or don't feel mature enough to have sex, or don't want to get pregnant or catch a disease. Your friends talk you into getting drunk, taking drugs, or staying out past curfew. You cut class to go to the mall, even though you know you'll be expelled if you miss another day of school. You tease people who are less fortunate than you, or who have mental or physical handicaps. (This shows a mean spiritedness, a pathetic lack of judgment, and an insecurity about yourself.) You treat your parents badly or even curse them out. (If you can't deal with parents, who represent your first experience with authority figures, in a respectful manner, your future will be plagued with difficulties.)

If you have bad habits such as these, you need to stop them now, because you could find yourself in far worse trouble later. In fact, the modeling industry will only aggravate your bad habits. That's why recognizing—and then avoiding—self-destructive behavior is key if you want to be a model.

Mod Squad

There was one model who was incredibly popular from the moment she was discovered. She was on many magazine covers and all the designers wanted her for their shows. But she had some very bad habits that ended up costing her her career. First of all, she had a reputation as being a compulsive liar—you couldn't trust anything she said. Then she stole another model's credit card and used it to buy expensive clothes and airplane tickets. The model she stole from found out who had taken her credit card by calling one of the stores where her card had been used; then she called the police. The model/thief's agency had to pay thousands of dollars just to keep her out of jail. Even though she was absolutely gorgeous, she's hardly ever worked since then.

You can tell that you're headed in the wrong direction if your actions hurt yourself or others, or if you find yourself lying about almost everything in order to cover your tracks when things have gone wrong. If you do find yourself in these sorts of situations too frequently, your ability to determine right from wrong may be clouded. Get back on track by reading books by positive spiritual teachers, or maybe taking a class dealing with religion or spirituality, whether it be a mainstream or an Eastern religion. (But by no means am I suggesting that you join a cult of any sort!) Meditating on spiritual teachings can help you get a firmer grasp on a more positive, moral way of life. Also, there are many 12-step programs available to help people overcome bad habits and abusive behaviors.

Making Friends with Yourself

Self-esteem is really important in modeling because it's a very competitive industry, one in which you're constantly judged on your external beauty and youth. The competition is stiff; in fact, you'll be up against some of the most incredible-looking people in the world. Being constantly told you're too short or too heavy or just "not right" can take its toll on you, no matter how strong you are. That's why you need to develop a sense of self-confidence and accomplishment before you even enter the industry, so when you're faced with all that rejection, you'll have something to fall back on. All of this is good training for life, too, and makes you a better person—whether or not you model.

Develop Other Talents

When I entered the modeling business, I was fortunate in that I already had a strong sense of self-confidence. I got good grades in school, so I knew if modeling didn't work out, I could go on to another profession. I could speak and move well, so if I didn't succeed in modeling, I could get into dancing or acting. In other words, my sense of self was not totally based on what I looked like; I knew I wouldn't be devastated if I didn't make it an industry where looks are key. Although my ego was often put to the test, I knew I would be okay because I had other talents.

Some ways to develop self-esteem include getting involved in extracurricular activities that will allow you to find and nurture your own unique talents, such as excelling at academics, getting involved in athletics or drama, volunteering, or developing a skill such as cooking.

Mod Squad

One great way I found to validate myself and build self-esteem was to help others less fortunate than I. When I was in high school, I volunteered for the Special Olympics. We organized a fundraiser, Rocking for Dollars, in the mall. We worked to get sponsors and to plan the event. We also helped out at the Special Olympics themselves. This experience validated me early on and has kept me grounded throughout my career: After witnessing the handicaps, mental and physical disabilities, and misfortunes of others, I realized how blessed I am. I realized that I am extremely lucky in that I have no handicaps, and that everything on top of that is just gravy.

Independence Day: Can You Survive?

Living independently means there is no mommy or daddy to buy and cook your meals, do your laundry, clean your room, get you out of those little jams, and put up with your bad moods. The staff at the modeling agency may help you a great deal when it comes to things related to your career, such as scheduling, personal maintenance, traveling, getting paid, and job selection. But at the end of the day when you've finished working, then what? You'll need a place to live and food to eat. You'll need to buy your own food, do your own laundry, and clean your own apartment. You'll have to pay your bills and maintain your health. You may even need to find a job outside of modeling until your career takes off. In other words, you will be entering the adult world of responsibility.

Models often have to start living independently long before their peers, who may still be living with their parents or in the more nurturing atmosphere of a college dorm. That's why it's important for aspiring models to start learning to take care of themselves while they're still at home.

Wake yourself up in the morning in time to get ready for school or work. Keep track of all your own appointments in a datebook. Get where you're going on time and be alert and attentive once you're there. Become involved in activities that require discipline and scheduling, such as student council, the school newspaper or yearbook, or sports. Take responsibility for scheduling your own doctor, dentist, and orthodontist checkups. Pay your own bills. Learn how to take care of your laundry properly and to cook simple, healthy meals. The experience you gain by doing these things while you're still at home (and able to ask for advice from your parents and other family members) will prove to be valuable once you start your modeling career and find yourself out there on your own.

Reality Check

If you're determined to start your career and move away from home before you're 18, you'll need a parent or guardian to accompany you. You need someone to be legally responsible for you, who can cosign all the various legal forms involved with modeling. That's why most agencies recommend that you wait until you're 18 to begin modeling full-time.

The Skeletons in Your Closet

One big mistake many people make is believing that the money and fame that come with a successful modeling career will cure all their problems. If you want to become a rich, famous, and successful model because you think you'll be leaving all your troubles and issues behind and your whole life will be magically okay, you are mistaken. Whatever problems you have now, whether they're physical, mental, emotional, or sexual, will not be erased just because you make it big as a model. The truth is that nothing can solve deep mental and emotional problems, except psychological help that addresses your personal issues.

If you have an eating disorder, abuse drugs or alcohol, suffer from depression, have been raped or experienced sexual abuse, or have a history of getting involved with abusive or controlling boyfriends, modeling is not the answer. Not only will it not solve your problems, but it will make them far worse because of all the stress and competition involved in modeling.

At some point, hopefully sooner rather than later, you'll work out those issues with a minister, priest, or other spiritual guide, therapist, or school guidance counselor, or in a 12-step program. (The good thing about modeling is that some of the money you earn can be used to pay for the professional help you need.) So if you have any of these skeletons in your closet, address them now; they'll get only worse later on.

Quiz: Do You Have What It Takes to Be a Model?

Answering the questions in this quiz (truthfully!) will help you figure out if you have what it takes to be a model.

1. You need a step stool to reach:
    A. The bathroom sink
    B. The top shelf of your locker
    C. The place where your mom hides the cookies on top of the refrigerator
    D. The moon

2. You're old enough to:
    A. Cross the street
    B. Baby-sit
    C. Drive
    D. Get your ears pierced

3. The four words that best describe your diet are:
    A. Candy, chips, and soda
    B. Hamburgers and French fries
    C. Cereal, sandwiches, and juice
    D. Fruits, vegetables, and fish

4. You were supposed to start working on an important book report a month ago. It's now the night before it's due. You:
    A. Call your friend to see if she has the book
    B. Are almost finished reading the book
    C. Are halfway finished writing the report
    D. Put the finishing touches on the finished product

5. You're sitting in your favorite class next to your best friend. How long can you go without talking to her?
    A. 10 seconds
    B. 10 minutes
    C. You don't say anything to her but, 10 minutes before the bell, you pass her a note about your after-school plans
    D. The whole class

6. The clothes you wore yesterday are:
    A. On the floor where they fell off your body
    B. On the floor under the bed where you kicked them
    C. In the family hamper
    D. Washed, dried, folded, and put away—you do your own laundry

7. The cutest guy in the school wants you to go for a swim at a romantic but dangerous cove where a bunch of kids have been hurt. You:
    A. Buy a new swimsuit and shave your legs
    B. Practice your crawl in the school pool in case something happens
    C. Agree to go, but invite along some friends who took lifesaving courses
    D. Politely decline—a guy who doesn't care about your safety and well-being isn't worth dating

8. How did you pay for your most recent clothing purchase?
    A. You whined until your mother gave you the money
    B. You hit your dad up for money when your mother was out of the room
    C. You paid for half with your baby-sitting money, and your mom paid for the other half, because you also needed money for a new CD
    D. You saved up your money from your part-time job

9. You have an 11:00 curfew. As the clock strikes 11, you're:
    A. Just starting another game of pool
    B. Looking for your car keys
    C. Careening home in your car, breaking every speed limit
    D. Walking in the door

10. Your relationship with your parents most resembles which movie:
    A. *Saving Private Ryan*
    B. *Clueless*
    C. *Hope Floats*
    D. *Sense and Sensibility*

11. You joined the school drama club because you really love to act. But instead of playing the lead, you're stuck painting backdrops and hauling furniture backstage. You:
    A. Quit as soon as you learn about how you were cheated out of a part
    B. Miss a lot of rehearsals to show them how unhappy you are
    C. Do everything you're asked, but really slowly and sullenly
    D. Act as cooperative as possible, because a good attitude may help you land a part next time

12. How long would it take you to find your school ID card in your room?

    A. Two years

    B. Three days

    C. Ten minutes

    D. Seven seconds

How did you do?

For every "A" answer, give yourself one point. For every "B" answer, give yourself two points. For every "C" answer, give yourself three points. For every "D" answer, give yourself four points.

If you scored 36 points or more, congratulations! You're definitely on the right track to a successful modeling career.

If you scored 24 to 35 points, you may have what it takes to be a model, but there may be some things you need to work on. Look at the questions where you scored only one or two points, and work on improving those things.

If you scored 23 points or under, you're probably a lot of fun and the life of the party, but you have a way to go before you're ready for the responsibilities of a professional modeling career.

The Least You Need to Know

➤ Fashion models need to be a certain height, weight, and age and have good body proportions; the requirements for real-people and parts models are less stringent.

➤ Models have to have healthy, beautiful skin, teeth, hair, and nails.

➤ Models need to be responsible and mature to have a successful career.

➤ A successful modeling career won't cure all your problems.

SILENCE!
STUDY
AREA

VAGUE

Chapter 4

Doing Your Homework

In This Chapter

➤ Catching up on all the latest trends

➤ Checking out fashion magazines and books

➤ Must-see TV shows for aspiring models

➤ Fashion and modeling resources on the Internet

This may sound funny, but in order to properly manage and get the most out of your modeling career, it's important to first do some homework. Believe it or not, it will be to your advantage to study for a successful modeling career. These studies may not be formal (and they actually can be a lot of fun), but they are really important. The more you know about this new profession, the better prepared you will be, so that you can avoid common pitfalls and make the most out of what already tends to be a short-lived career.

This is as true of modeling as any other profession. Can you imagine an aspiring actress who doesn't know Meryl Streep, Jodie Foster, or Susan Sarandon? Or a newcomer to the pro basketball leagues who has never heard of Michael Jordan?

A Great Place to Start: Fashion Magazines

Fashion magazines are inexpensive, easily accessible, and fun to read. Monthly magazines such as *Vogue, Harper's Bazaar, Elle, Glamour, Mademoiselle, Seventeen, YM, Allure,* and *Cosmopolitan* are must-reads for any aspiring model. Although they all may seem alike, these magazines actually have different editorial missions, readerships, and advertisers. They provide necessary information on fashion, makeup, and hair trends. They can teach you how to dress and present yourself so that your best assets stand out. When you know the latest trends, you can make sure that your look is current. Here are some of the best ones to read:

Vogue

Vogue is the fashion bible. It's extremely sophisticated and elegant in both look and tone. It features fashions by all the most important high-end designers. It's read by everyone in the fashion industry and by some of the wealthiest, most style-conscious women in the country. Appearing in the pages of *Vogue* is one of the most prestigious assignments a model can land; once she graces the cover of *Vogue*, a model's career is pretty much made.

Harper's Bazaar

Harper's Bazaar is another high-fashion magazine that's bold, edgy, and arty in its photography, fashion, and style. It's read by urbane, sophisticated women. It features the highest-end and most avant-garde designers and takes a lot of risks in the photographers and models that it uses—*Bazaar*'s models tend to be very dramatic, expressive, and exotic.

Elle

Elle is a fashion magazine that incorporates cultural and design influences from all over the world, including Africa, India, and Asia. In addition to high-end fashion, it features the work of more cutting-edge and avant-garde designers. *Elle*'s readers are young and adventurous. The models, who are often athletic or exotic types, are often pictured in motion—running, jumping, or skipping.

Glamour

Glamour takes beauty and fashion trends from the runway and translates them for working women. The fashions it features are more practical and less expensive than the fashions in high-end magazines. *Glamour* is also great for learning how to take care of your skin, hair, and body, and how to apply makeup. The models are fresh, healthy, girl-next-door types.

Roshumba's Rules

It's not necessary to buy every fashion magazine. You can browse through issues at your school library or the public library. You can also check them out at hair salons and coffeehouses. Keep in mind that buying a subscription is cheaper than buying single issues.

Mademoiselle

Mademoiselle is young, fun loving, and hip. It features less-expensive versions of clothes seen on the runway, and it contains a lot of how-to information on beauty and fashion that's important to know. The models reflect the readers: young women who are finishing college or getting started on a career.

Seventeen and YM

Seventeen and *YM* are the first fashion magazines most women ever read. They're geared toward young teenage girls; they interpret beauty and fashion and make them accessible and appropriate for their readers. Both feature lots of helpful how-to hints on styling your hair, taking care of your skin, dealing with acne, applying makeup, dressing stylishly, working out, and eating right. These two magazines use mainly models who are just starting out; in fact, *Seventeen* and *YM* have launched many models' careers.

Allure

Allure is THE beauty magazine. It focuses almost exclusively on beauty trends, products, breakthroughs, and news. It keeps readers abreast of beauty trends and offers how-to advice on applying makeup, choosing makeup colors, taking care of your skin and hair, and related topics. *Allure* uses a wide variety of models, because they want to show all women how to be beautiful.

Cosmopolitan

Cosmopolitan is more of a lifestyle magazine, which means that it focuses more on relationships, sex, jobs, self-image, and personal experiences. But it's the only magazine that gives extensive information on its cover girls, such as their age, zodiac sign, biological data (where they were born, where they live), and what they're up to in their career.

Other Magazines

Other publications you may want to pick up include two men's magazines: *GQ,* an upscale men's magazine that features the top menswear designers and male models with classic good looks; and *Details,* a magazine for younger men that features cutting-edge designer clothes and uses young, funky, artistic-looking models. You should also check out the music magazines *Rolling Stone* and *Vibe,* which profile top performers in the music industry and spotlight cool downtown fashions. Finally, for everything you ever wanted to know about celebrity fashion and beauty, there's *In Style.*

Spotting Fashion Trends

While you're reading these magazines, be on the lookout for fashion trends: Are bellbottoms and blue eye shadow in again? Did the Audrey Hepburn gamine look come back into style? What's the hot new color for the season? Being aware of fashion trends can also influence your personal style and help you to embody and project a modern, contemporary image. Can you make subtle changes in your look that will incorporate the newest trend? Maybe the look of the season is soft sweaters and tapered knee-length skirts complemented by a low-key beauty. Small

Reality Check

Now that you're reading so many fashion magazines, you may feel the urge to follow every trend you read about. Don't do it! Models should be beautiful blank slates on which clients can create their visions. Although it's good to project a modern image, there's a big difference between buying a cool new eye shadow and dyeing your hair the newest shade of purple!

changes, like a new lipstick, haircut, or highlights in your hair, could freshen up your look and give you the necessary edge to enhance your career.

The more an aspiring model knows about fashion and beauty trends, the better. Study magazines to learn about the ins and outs and dos and don'ts of style.

Beauty Products to Know and Love

Magazines also keep you up to date on the newest beauty products, including skin-, hair-, and body-care items. Science is always coming up with new improvements, so you need to keep on top of things to stay "in the know." It's important to know which products are which and who makes them. Models, hairstylists, and makeup artists will constantly refer to these products, and you'll want to know what they're talking about. Knowing the latest products will also help you present a more professional image; people will see that you're informed about the latest developments in the industry. Also, these items will probably be used on you by a makeup artist or hairstylist at some point in your career. You may also want to experiment with some of them, so you'll know in advance how your skin/body/hair will react.

It's a good idea to try out some of the new looks you see in magazines, to see how well they suit you.

Models of the Moment

Fashion magazines can also help you to learn about the top models of the moment. The hottest models will be featured in *fashion spreads*, or stories about the latest beauty trends. Some magazines even print interviews with top models. Also, seeing which models work for which magazine can give you the inside scoop on whether or not a particular magazine is into your look—at least at that moment.

In addition to knowing their names and the magazines they work for, you'll want to learn what type of work the top models do (do they appear in fantasy high-fashion spreads, down-to-earth beauty stories, or bathing suit pieces); which photographers they work with most; which advertisements they appear in; and which one you think you most resemble.

Other things to pay attention to are the poses and expressions of the important models. Learn from their poses, the way they tilt their heads, the lines and energy of their bodies, the intensity in their eyes, and their smiles. Also, study the image they project: Are they ice-cold and aloof, sultry and sexy, bold and aggressive, or animated and smiling? Try out the different poses you see, and learn what works for you. You can also pick up some tips on how to dress and present yourself for your own success.

Catwalk Talk

A **fashion spread** is a story spotlighting a particular fashion trend. It appears toward the back of the magazine, where there are no advertisements. Because there are no ads, the pictures can "spread" across the page.

Other Names to Know in the Fashion Industry

Fashion magazines also help you familiarize yourself with the important people in the industry (and you may even meet them if your career takes off). Fashion insiders bandy about many of their names a lot ("Anna" is Anna Wintour, editor in chief of *Vogue*), and it's good to know who they're talking about. The best way to find out is by reading the *masthead*.

Also check out the cover credits. This list includes the names of the model appearing on the magazine's cover, as well as the photographer who took the shot and the hairstylist and makeup artist who helped create the cover girl's image. The clothing, accessories, and makeup the model is wearing is also identified. Sometimes, the name of the fashion stylist (the person who selects what the model wears) is also listed.

Looking at the names listed under the cover credits, as well as the names of those responsible

Catwalk Talk

The **masthead** usually appears between the table-of-contents page and the first article in a magazine. The masthead lists everyone responsible for putting together the magazine, including the editor in chief, fashion editors, and model editor.

for the fashion and beauty pictures inside the magazine, will give you a feel for which photographers, hair and makeup artists, and fashion stylists are hot at the moment. It's a good idea to familiarize yourself with these people, because they usually work with the magazine's editors to create the look and the appeal of the magazine. They are the ones who will be responsible for transforming you from a 16-year-old small-town girl to a full-blown glamour gal. They also often recommend models they think have what it takes to fulfill the image they're trying to create.

Check These Out: Books on Modeling and Fashion

There are many books available on the subject of models, modeling, fashion, designers, and photographers. First of all, lots of models, including Kate Moss, Claudia Schiffer, and Marcus Schenkenberg have all done semiautobiographical "picture books," which are photography-oriented books with minimal text. These books feature lots of photos and take you on an interesting journey of their modeling evolution.

More biographical books on or by models are great research material. They show and tell you what life has been like for some of the most successful models, from the very beginning of their careers. Examples include *Thing of Beauty: The Tragedy of Supermodel Gia,* by Stephen M. Fried; *True Beauty: Positive Attitudes and Practical Tips from the World's Leading Plus-Size Model,* by Emme; and *Veronica Webb Sight: Adventures in the Big City,* by Veronica Webb. (Check out Appendix B, "Model Knowledge: Essential Books and Web Sites," for details on all the books I mention in this chapter and more.)

Modeling: The Big Picture

Books about the modeling industry in general tell the stories of the models who came before us and explain useful tidbits about the business in general. Two good ones are *Skin Deep,* by Barbara Summers, which is the history of African American women in the modeling industry; and *Model: The Ugly Business of Beautiful Women,* by Michael Gross. *Model* is good because it gives biographical background on dozens of models, from the early part of the century through the present. It also provides a thorough history of the modeling business, which is both interesting and important to know.

The information you glean from books about models can also help you to understand the cycle of fashion trends. By knowing which models were big in the 1960s, 1970s, and 1980s, you can tell whose shoes you're filling in the 1990s and onward. You'll know what a photographer means when she says she wants a Penelope Tree sad smile. You'll be equipped to compliment photographers on their award-winning ad campaign from 10 years ago or give fashion designers the needed inspiration when they're experiencing a creative block. And

Reality Check

Many of the books I discuss in this chapter are expensive art books, some of which cost as much as $80. So unless you have a lot of disposable income, I suggest looking for them at your local public library. If you can't find them, ask the librarian about interlibrary loans, which allow you to borrow books from other collections.

most important, you'll learn about the history of the industry and its many evolutions, giving you wisdom, depth—and an edge over the competition.

How-To Books

How-to books, such as the one you're reading right now, provide valuable information on getting started in modeling, pitfalls to watch out for, and career management tips. They give you the tools necessary to be confident, professional, and business minded about your career.

Books About Fashion Photographers

Major fashion photographers such as Herb Ritts and Richard Avedon have published books featuring their work, allowing you to familiarize yourself with their style of photography. (Photography books tend to be very expensive, so you may want to check them out of the library or look at them in the bookstore.) Other important fashion photographers whose works are available in books include Irving Penn, Peter Lindberg, Arthur Elgort, Bruce Weber, and David La Chapelle.

Books About Fashion Designers

Books on or by photographers and fashion designers are really great to read, too. They're full of historical information, which can help you understand why and how fashion, photography, and modeling have developed and changed over the years. They'll fill you in on the key players of the past and how their work has affected the industry.

In fact, my favorite books to read are books about fashion designers. They tell the story of the great designers and the design houses they founded, such as Coco Chanel, Christian Dior, and Yves Saint Laurent. They inspire me so much. In addition to charting the evolution of fashion, these books capture the allure, decadence, and true art of designing clothes. Not only do they tell the stories of the designers and the visions they were trying to achieve, but they teach you about costume structure, fabrics, color, and how garments complement a woman's body. They provide information on the heart of the industry, seeing how the designers' dreams are realized. A few good ones to check out include *Chanel: Her Style and Her Life,* by Janet Wallach; *Versace,* by Richard Martin and Grace Mirabella; and *Obsession: The Life and Times of Calvin Klein,* by Steven Gaines.

Beauty Books

Makeup and hair books can teach you the basics, such as how to care for your type of skin properly, pluck your eyebrows, apply foundation, change the look of your eyes with eye makeup, trim your bangs, or blow-dry your hair. They can also guide you if you want to experiment with makeup and different hairstyles. This practical, how-to information is really important to know because at some point during your modeling career you'll be asked to do your own hair and makeup.

Good books on makeup include *Bobbi Brown Beauty: The Ultimate Beauty Resource,* by Bobbi Brown and Annemarie Iverson; and *The Art of Makeup,* by Kevyn Aucoin.

Good books on hair include *Andre Talks Hair,* by Andre Walker and Teresa Wiltz; and *1001 Beauty Solutions,* by Beth Barrick-Hickey.

Books on Fashion History

These books describe fashion looks from the past, how trends are reinterpreted and recycled, what artists inspired various designers, what events in history have triggered new fashion trends, and the stories of various fashion houses.

They're also loaded with information on the top models of the past, such as Dovima, the quintessential haute-couture model of the 1950s; Twiggy, the waifish sensation of the 1960s; and Pat Cleveland, an ultraglamorous model of the 1970s. These women are our mentors: They blazed the trail before us and made it possible for the models of today to be considered an integral part of the creative process, to make the money they do, and to demand the respect they get. Long before Roshumba, Cindy Crawford, or Linda Evangelista, there were incredible beauties such as Amalia, Paulina Porizkova, and Joan Severance. These women laid the foundation and set the standards for us to live up to.

Mod Squad

Dovima was the top model of the 1950s, and some consider her the greatest model of all time. Diagnosed with rheumatic fever at age 10, she spent the next seven years in bed. But then she arose, like Sleeping Beauty, to almost instant success and acclaim. Almost immediately she began charging the top rate of the time—$30 an hour. She was soon so busy she was forced to change clothes in taxis and in telephone booths. Dovima appears in one of the most famous fashion photographs of all time, *Dovima and the Elephants,* by Richard Avedon. The gazelle-like Dovima is pictured in an elegant evening gown flanked by two enormous circus elephants.

Books to read on fashion history include *The Art of Haute Couture,* by Victor Skrebneski; *D.V.,* by Diana Vreeland; and *New York Fashion: The Evolution of American Style,* by Caroline Rennolds Milbank.

Must-See Chic TV

Over the past decade, television has been good to models and the modeling industry. Coverage of modeling and fashion has increased exponentially. Only a few years ago, models were only seen—on a magazine cover or in its pages—but now, because of all the television shows featuring models, these women are now seen *and* heard by millions of people who might otherwise not read or buy *Elle* magazine. On television, you get to know their voices, movements, and personalities on a more intimate level. Here are the style shows you should be watching.

MTV's House of Style

MTV's *House of Style* has been a great vehicle for the models who have hosted it, such as Cindy Crawford, Amber Valletta, Shalom Harlow, Rebecca Romijn-Stamos, and Niki Taylor. It has not only given them on-camera broadcast skills, but it's been great exposure for them personally and for modeling in general. Also, the show has fun and informative features on other models, as well as important designers and new trends in the fashion industry. *House of Style* is not only fun to watch, but it teaches you a lot about the fashion business.

VH1 Fashion Awards

The VH1 *Fashion Awards* allow you to see the heavy hitters of the fashion industry, put names to the faces you've seen in every magazine, and put faces to designer names like Donatella Versace, Tom Ford of Gucci, Calvin Klein, and Ralph Lauren. The awards ceremony features fashion shows of top designers, giving you insight into the latest fashion trends and which designers are using which models.

Also, be sure to check out the presenters and the awardees: They usually include the hottest people in the industry at that moment. Recent presenters have included models Tyra Banks and Stephanie Seymour, and Anna Wintour, editor in chief of *Vogue*. Recent winners have included Tyson Beckford (for Best Male Model), Kate Moss (for Best Female Model), Tom Ford (for Best Menswear Designer), and Cameron Diaz (for Best Personal Style). And at least one person in the audience will be sporting THE must-have cashmere coat or sunglasses of the season!

Here I am backstage at the VH1 Fashion Awards, *one of the biggest events for the fashion industry.*

"E!" Entertainment Television Fashion File

E!'s *Fashion File* features profiles on up-and-coming models. It covers how they got their start, who they have worked for, and what makes them special. This show also spotlights the latest fashion trends—a new futuristic fabric in a designer's latest collection; the natural, matte, or shimmery makeup look; hair styles that are straight and sleek or fluffy and curly; and blondes, brunettes, or redheads, whichever are in.

E!'s The Making of a Supermodel

E! Entertainment Television also airs a yearly special called *The Making of a Supermodel*. This show usually premieres in early fall and continues to air throughout the year. It contains a lot of important, interesting information on the Elite Model Look model search and its young contestants. *The Making of a Supermodel* is an up-close and personal look at the young aspiring models as they go through the model-search process, from regional contests to the big international finals. The show also explores life behind the scenes, revealing all the work it takes to put on a production of such magnitude. It introduces the team that puts on the show—the model scouts, runway coordinator, hair and makeup people, judges, and host. It spotlights the counseling and guidance given to each aspiring model by the team.

This is definitely must-see TV for all who aspire to enter the modeling business!

CNN's Style with Elsa Klensch

Style with Elsa Klensch has been around for a long time, and it's great for learning not only about fashion, but also about art and culture. Host Elsa Klensch takes viewers backstage to the season's hottest fashion shows in Milan, Paris, London, New York, and Tokyo, giving them an insider look at the backstage madness of a fashion show. You see designers putting the final touches on a dress, models getting their hair and makeup done, stylists dressing the models … the whole creative flurry. Klensch gives us a front-row look at the decadence, mystery, and allure of the ultimate fashion event, the couture runway show, with the models strutting those fabulous designs on the runway.

Style also does excellent model profiles. It not only covers the basic questions—how did the model get started, what's it like being a model, and what are her plans for the future—but it takes it a step further, delving into the model's personal life: How does she keep her sanity in the crazy fashion world; what motivates her; what's a day off like for her. Klensch gives us an accurate picture of the day-to-day activities of a real working model, as well as the mental activity modeling requires.

Klensch not only covers models and modeling, but she also goes behind the scenes, delving into the private lives of fashion designers, photographers, magazine editors, and hair and makeup artists. I find these shows especially revealing because they take some of the mystique out of these great designers and photographers whom we tend to revere. It shows them as real human beings, and we can learn a lot from them both as people and as artists.

Mod Squad

One of the most wonderful experiences in my life was the interview I did with Elsa Klensch for *Style*. Not only did she cover the basic questions (plus a few extras), she and her crew followed me all day long, from a photo shoot, to a meeting with my agent, and finally to my African dance class—which at the time was a great source of inspiration for me and influenced me a great deal. These classes also helped me to open up and project a lot of my real self through my work. After the interview aired, many people came up to me and complimented me on it. It gave me a whole new visibility.

You are guaranteed to walk away from *Style with Elsa Klensch* better informed about fashion, art, and design than you were when you first tuned in.

VH1, MTV, and E! Entertainment Television

It's also important to watch VH1, MTV, and E! Entertainment Television, because the worlds of fashion, movies, and music are totally intertwined. Watching these channels will help you keep informed about the newest fashion trends, as well as the coolest music and the hottest movies. They not only cover the world of music, fashion, and movies, but they also influence them. If VH1 features a new hot musical artist, his music and personal style could be the inspiration for the next Versace fashion show. And conversely, a really amazing fashion show could influence the style of a major recording artist such as Seal.

What's more, artists like Madonna and Michael Jackson have influenced the style and dress of millions of youth worldwide. Millions of people wanted Michael Jackson's leather jacket from his *Beat It* video after they saw it on MTV. The Spice Girls' sexy, sassy costumes and girl-power anthem made everyone stand up and take notice. Big, baggy, oversized clothes worn by homeboys and homegirls, skateboarders, and inline skaters ushered in a look that had all the cool kids running to the mall to keep up with this latest fashion trend and gave designers like Tommy Hilfiger a new generation to design for. These TV channels have their fingers on the pulse of the entertainment and fashion worlds, so if you have plans for a career as a model, stay tuned.

Roshumba's Rules

If you can't watch MTV because you don't get cable, you can still check out what the hottest musicians are wearing in magazines like *Rolling Stone*, *Vibe*, and *In Style*.

Fashion Documentaries on TV and Video

Television documentaries and rental videos on fashion can be great sources of information as well. The *Sports Illustrated* swimsuit issue documentary and other special-interest programs such as *Supermodels in the Rain Forest* are not only entertaining, they offer a practical look at the industry. You'll get the inside scoop on what really goes into modeling—waking up at 5 A.M. for a photo shoot, lying in chilly water for a long time until the photographer gets the shot, and working with a group who are traveling great distances for the shoot. You can also pick up tips about how to pose in a bathing suit and how to show your body off to its best advantage.

At the video store, you could also rent *Unzipped,* a documentary about designer Isaac Mizrahi as he prepares for a fashion show; and *Ready to Wear,* a fictional movie about the Paris collections and all the behind-the-scenes shenanigans. These shows give you an in-depth look at the good, the bad, and the ugly that go into creating something of beauty. And for a less-realistic but utterly charming look at the fashion industry of the 1950s, check out Audrey Hepburn in *Funny Face.*

Modeling.com: Beauty and the Internet

Modern-day science has brought us the Internet, which happens to be loaded with information on modeling and the modeling industry. Log on and check out an interview with your favorite supermodels, hear what they have to say about their careers and extracurricular activities, download their photos, and purchase merchandise such as calendars, posters, and videos they may be selling.

Reality Check

Beware of entering contests or sending money to any Web sites, unless you're ordering specific merchandise, such as a poster. Even then, make sure the company's phone number and address are listed. Some experts advise ordering by phone, not over the Web. If the site is demanding a lot of money or if the promises they are making sound too good to be true, they're probably not legitimate.

Many modeling agencies have Web sites; the Ford Model Agency, for example (www.fordmodels.com). These sites may have information on the agencies' history, their top models, events they may be hosting, and merchandise they may be selling.

Supermodel.com is one of the premier model sites. Also check out individual supermodels' own sites. (For more on these and other Web sites, check out Appendix B.)

Many magazines have their own Web sites, too. These sites are supercool because they're interactive, meaning you get to click on and participate in quizzes and chat sessions with other readers. You can also download information on your favorite models. They're filled with fun beauty tips, advice on relationships, and how to lose a couple of extra pounds.

If you have any doubts about the legitimacy of a company, don't give them your charge card number (or don't order from them at all). If you're under 18, don't order from a site without your parents' permission.

Not only could you lose money if you order, say, a poster from a disreputable Web site, it's possible an aspiring model could hook up with someone over the Internet who says he's a fashion photographer or agent, but who's really a perv.

The world of cyberspace can be a con artists' paradise because it's so difficult to monitor. You'll find all types of modeling Web sites, but it's a good idea to stick to gathering information from more reputable sites, such as the top modeling agencies, Elite and Ford; well-known magazines, *Vogue, Elle,* and *Seventeen;* or sites on top models whose names you're familiar with: Roshumba, Niki Taylor, Cindy Crawford, and others.

The Least You Need to Know

➤ Fashion magazines keep you up to date on the hottest fashions and the most popular models and provide lots of how-to advice for looking fabulous.

➤ Books are a great source of knowledge and inspiration for aspiring models.

➤ Watching TV can be educational—when you want to learn more about fashion and modeling.

➤ The Internet can be a great resource, but be careful to avoid scams, con artists, and worse.

Which Look Are You: The Seven Basic Model Types

Even though there are some basic qualifications for modeling, as I explained in Chapter 3, "Do You Have What It Takes?" the truth is that there are really a number of different types of models representing a range of looks. Every niche of the fashion business prefers a certain type. The clean-scrubbed, all-American, J. Crew-catalog model might have a tough time getting a job walking the runway for an avant-garde fashion designer. Meanwhile, the sexy, big-haired Barbie type who's a knockout in the Victoria's Secret catalog is way too overdone for *Seventeen,* a magazine geared to high-school girls. Not only does each facet of the fashion industry use different types of models, but fashion is also always changing and looking for the next new thing. So someone who couldn't get arrested two months ago may suddenly be the next million-dollar face!

Figuring out which type of model you are is very important so you don't waste your time pursuing the wrong kind of work. If you're a strapping six footer, you may have a difficult time getting hired for the European runway shows; they're usually looking for thinner, more delicate models. On the other hand, if you are slender and fragile looking, you're probably not going to be modeling too many bathing suits.

Basically, there are seven distinct types of fashion models, each of which I describe in depth in this chapter. As you read each description, try to figure out where you fit in. The list at the end of each category will help you pinpoint your type.

The Amazon

The Amazon is a special breed of superwoman. This type is often six feet tall (or just looks like she is) with a strong, imposing, big-boned body. Like Xena, Warrior Princess, or Wonder Woman, the Amazon has a strong, defined jawbone, an intense look in her eyes, and a full head of hair.

Catwalk Talk

Editorial refers to modeling done for the covers and inside pages of major fashion magazines. **Runway** means modeling in the fashion shows, when designers present their latest creations.

Her universal appeal adds up to a lot of modeling opportunities. Amazons often do editorial work, primarily because their image is very distinctive and compelling. They project a strong sense of personality that's hard to miss, even on a crowded newsstand shelf. Conversely, Amazons rarely do high-fashion runway shows because their intense personalities and well-built bodies overpower the exquisite, refined clothing. In smaller cities, Amazons appear in advertisements and catalogs.

The Amazon is tall, strong, and imposing-looking: Think Roshumba Williams or Xena, Warrior Princess.

Cindy Crawford

Perhaps the most successful Amazon type is Cindy Crawford. Even though she's not six feet tall, she definitely looks it. She projects a strong, bold, majestic image, almost like a living Statue of Liberty. Still, she definitely embodies the essence of a real woman. She's intelligent, she has breasts, hips, and curves, and she's very sexy, but in a wholesome way.

As proof of her tremendous appeal, Cindy has appeared on countless magazine covers and in hundreds of magazine stories. She has had an extremely lucrative long-term cosmetic contract with Revlon. She's done many ready-to-wear runway shows, which is unusual for an Amazon. Cindy also has the personal popularity and presence necessary to branch out beyond modeling. She's done her own television show (MTV's *House of Style*), as well as a movie, exercise videos, and a beauty book.

Roshumba Williams

I remember when I first hit the scene and started modeling professionally in 1987. For whatever reason, at that moment, I had an Amazon look the fashion industry couldn't seem to get enough of. I was six feet tall, had a strong, curvy body, and thick, kinky hair, yet my features were chiseled and refined. I was determined to succeed, but at the same time I was kind and respectful to others, especially those who were trying to help me get my career going. Before I knew it my look was all the rage. (And yes, imitation is the highest form of flattery: I knew I had made it when a lot of new models were imitating my look and getting work, and many established models were changing their looks to resemble mine.)

I'm proud to say the image I ushered in over a decade ago still reigns supreme. I have been fortunate enough to have worked with most of the top designers, such as Yves Saint Laurent, Versace, Valentino, and Anne Klein. I have also graced the covers of many magazines, including *Elle* and *Marie Claire,* appeared in ads for Navy Cover Girl, Maybelline, and Clairol. My most fulfilling accomplishment was becoming the first African American to be featured four years in a row as a *Sports Illustrated* swimsuit model. While still maintaining my modeling career, I've also branched out into film (Woody Allen's *Celebrity*) and television, hosting lifestyle shows for Lifetime Television, veejaying on VH1, writing my own book, and hosting the Elite Model Look model search.

Other famous Amazons include Grace Jones, Elle Macpherson, Nadja Auermann, and Brooke Shields.

Roshumba's Rules

When people ask me for the secret to success, I tell them to select a favorite model and adopt her as a role model. Copy her good habits and career moves and learn from her mistakes.

You know you're an Amazon if:

- ➤ You're close to six feet tall or more.
- ➤ You have a powerful and striking physique, with wide shoulders, full breasts, hips and thighs, and long, shapely legs.
- ➤ You have large, pronounced features: expressive eyes, prominent cheekbones, and full lips.
- ➤ Your hair is lustrous and full-bodied.
- ➤ Personality-wise, you're outgoing, vivacious, determined, and optimistic.

If you're an Amazon, some of the modeling jobs you may be best suited for (but are by no means limited to) include bathing suit, lingerie, and sportswear modeling; product endorsements; and beauty stories in magazines.

The Classic Beauty

Classic Beauties are born, not made. These are the lady-like Grace Kellys of the modeling world, with perfect faces—almond-shaped eyes, beautiful, slim noses, high cheekbones, medium-full lips, and sleek jaw lines.

Reality Check

Being nice, polite, and cooperative are all good qualities in a model that can help advance your career. But there is such a thing as being too nice. Don't let people take advantage of your niceness and youth to try to coerce you into doing things you don't want to do. Remember, you always have the right to say no, at any stage of your career.

Classic Beauties are the envy of other models because they can do almost any kind of work. Magazines editors adore them and are constantly putting them on the covers and in the pages of their publications. Their beauty can make any product look good, so they're also coveted for advertising campaigns. They get many of the lucrative beauty contracts, representing huge advertisers such as Estée Lauder, Revlon, Cover Girl, L'Oréal, Lancôme, Clairol, and Chanel. Even when they get older, and other models their age have long since taken their last walk down the runway, Classic Beauties continue to work. Dayle Haddon, who is in her 40s, still models; as does the silver-maned beauty Carmen, who started modeling over 50 years ago, and is still modeling today at 60-something.

In smaller cities, Classic Beauties are in demand for all kinds of work: catalog, advertisements, TV commercials, and runway.

Classic Beauties have perfectly symmetrical features: oval faces, almond-shaped eyes, slim noses, high cheekbones, and chiseled lips.

Christy Turlington

One of the great Classic Beauties of all time is Christy Turlington. She has the delicate, exquisite features of a doe: beautiful oval eyes, high cheekbones, a perfect nose, and dew-kissed lips. Her lean but curvy body is perfectly proportioned; her shoulders, hips, and thighs are medium-small.

Because Christy's classic look appeals to just about everyone, she is in constant demand for every type of modeling work imaginable. She has appeared, many times over, on the covers and in the pages of nearly every fashion magazine. She has a long-term contract with Calvin Klein, representing underwear, clothing, and fragrances. She's the face of Maybelline cosmetics and has appeared in ads for many major fashion designers, including Prada, Versace, Yves Saint Laurent, Valentino, and Chanel. Christy has also done almost every major runway show, from wild and wonderful Dolce & Gabbana to classy and elegant Bill Blass.

Beverly Johnson

Beverly Johnson is another model with a classic oval face, high cheekbones, warm, creamy skin, and a beautiful smile. In fact, her beauty was so extraordinary that she managed to transcend racial barriers to become the first black woman to appear on the cover of *Vogue,* in 1974. She went on to grace the covers of dozens of other magazines and was also the first ethnic model to appear in mainstream advertisements, most notably as one of Revlon's Most Unforgettable Women. She's written a beauty book and has appeared in a number of movies.

Other famous Classic Beauties include Amber Valletta, Vendela, Elizabeth Hurley, and Christie Brinkley.

You know you're a Classic Beauty if:

➤ You're around 5'8"—Classic Beauties are usually not too tall. You're thin but not too skinny.

➤ You have an oval face, almond-shaped eyes, a slim, delicate nose, sculpted cheekbones, and medium-full lips.

➤ Your skin is flawless, with no blemishes or blotches, your hair is healthy and lustrous, and your teeth are perfectly straight and pearly white.

➤ You're polite, ladylike, and calm.

If you're a Classic Beauty, you may be best suited for (but by no means limited to) beauty stories in magazines, beauty-oriented advertising campaigns, TV commercials, classic runway shows, and catalog work.

The Barbie Doll

The Barbie Doll is defined, first and foremost, by her hair, which is often blonde (but many brunette and redhead Barbies do exist). It's big—really big—so much so that it can dominate her whole face. She has a round, slightly irregular face, big blue eyes, a cute little nose, and a great big Farrah Fawcett smile. Her body may be thin or even slightly plump, but she's definitely bosomy. She has long legs, slim hips, and a cute tush.

The Barbie look goes in and out of fashion. But when it's hot, you'll see the Barbie on every magazine cover and in lots of beauty and fashion advertisements. This type also does a lot of lingerie and swimsuit modeling. Top Barbies will appear in the Victoria's Secret catalog and in the *Sports Illustrated* swimsuit edition and many also have their own pinup calendar.

The Barbie is the kind of model who's definitely too sexy for her shirt: She's beguiling, often blonde, and extremely curvaceous.

Claudia Schiffer

Although she occasionally tries to escape it, Claudia Schiffer is the epitome of the Barbie model. With her long, blonde hair, blue eyes, full breasts, narrow hips, and long legs, she fits the Barbie image to perfection. Claudia was a 17-year-old high-school student when she was spotted by a modeling scout in a disco in Dusseldorf, Germany. Her image as a Barbie was cemented when she emulated Brigitte Bardot in a Guess? Jeans advertising campaign. She was then hired to model in the Chanel runway show. Her slightly awkward walk charmed the fashion press and the public, and her career then went into overdrive.

Claudia went on to grace the covers of almost every major magazine. She's also appeared in advertisements for Chanel, Revlon, L'Oréal, Victoria's Secret, Valentino, and Versace. She's written a book and starred in her own exercise videos, and (of course) her own calendar.

Pamela Anderson Lee

Pamela Anderson Lee is an extreme version of the Barbie look, with huge, teased blond hair, blue eyes, long legs … even the plastic body parts (which she's since had removed). And she definitely knows how to work it! In contrast to her voluptuous body is her sweet, innocent personality. Modeling for *Playboy* magazine put Pamela on the map and helped launch her acting career. She's since appeared on *Home Improvement, Baywatch,* and her own TV series, and in movies. In addition, she's been featured in her calendars and in movies (as well as some infamous home videos!).

Other Barbie types include Stephanie Seymour, Anna Nicole Smith, and Carmen Electra.

You know you're a Barbie if:

➤ You have long, thick hair, preferably blonde.

➤ You have big blue eyes, a button nose, and juicy, pouty lips.

➤ You're 5'7" to 5'10".

➤ You're slender with large breasts, slim hips, and a cute butt.

➤ You're friendly, outgoing, perky, and not as naive as you seem.

If you're a Barbie type, you may be best suited (but by no means limited to) lingerie and swimsuit modeling, modeling for designers of sexy fashions such as Hervé Léger or Dolce & Gabbana, in ads that want that Barbie look, and nude modeling (if that's your thing).

The Chameleon

The Chameleon is constantly changing her look, dyeing her hair from brunette to blond to red to polka dot, depending on the trend. She's willing to gain 10 pounds, lose 15, get a tan, put on full body makeup—whatever she needs to do to keep her career alive and the spotlight on her. Usually rather average-looking, Chameleons depend on hairstylists, makeup artists, and designer clothes to help them create their look. In fact, if you saw a Chameleon on the street, you probably wouldn't guess that she was a model. What often sets her apart from other types are a creative personality and dramatic temperament that drive her to experiment constantly with various looks.

Chameleons do a lot of editorial work, which allows them the freedom they need for creative expression. They often team up with the most famous photographers (some Chameleons become muses to certain photographers because they work so often and so closely together). Chameleons are rarely featured in advertisements because their distinctive looks and personalities compete too much with the sales message. That's why you're much more likely to see the Chameleon in a fantasy fashion spread in *Harper's Bazaar* than in an ad for a mainstream client such as Liz Claiborne or in a mainstream catalog such as JCPenney.

Roshumba's Rules

Consult your agent before you make drastic changes in your appearance, such as dyeing or cutting your hair, getting a dark tan, or undergoing plastic surgery. These changes could have a negative impact on your career.

Because of their high level of creativity, Chameleons can have a tough time in smaller markets, where most of the work is doing catalog and advertisements. The best bet for a Chameleon in a smaller market is to find a look that appeals to the local clients and stick with it. Avoid the outrageous—bright orange hair, radical haircuts, and strange outfits.

The Chameleon is always changing her look, trying out new hair colors, new hairstyles, new makeup— whatever it takes to stay on the cutting edge of style.

Linda Evangelista

Linda Evangelista is the ultimate Chameleon model. She continues to reinvent herself, always making each new look seem effortless. Surprisingly, it took Linda several years to establish herself as a premier model. She kept experimenting with various looks before she finally found the one that made her a darling of the fashion world: At a time when all the other models had long hair, she cut hers short, instantly launching a worldwide trend.

Linda has worked with many of the hottest photographers in the business. She is willing to do whatever it takes to fulfill the photographer's vision. This strategy has paid off for her: She has been a reigning supermodel for nearly a decade and was once quoted as saying she didn't get out of bed for less than $10,000 a day (a remark she's been trying to live down ever since). True Chameleon that she is, she has done a phenomenal amount of editorial work and has graced the cover of just about every fashion magazine in the world, time and time again. She has even managed to cross over into advertising work (for Clairol, Kenar, Yves Saint Laurent, Versace, and Chanel), which is unusual for a Chameleon.

Naomi Campbell

Like Linda, Naomi Campbell is also a major trendsetter and trend interpreter. Naomi has dared to do things that no ethnic model—and few models of any type—have ever done before. She bleached her hair blond for Versace, spray-painted herself silver for an arty photo shoot, endlessly changed hair styles and colors, and even sported green contact lenses. Because she's not a Classic Beauty, she changes her look to attract attention and keep her career on track, a strategy that has worked in her favor.

Naomi's daring and willingness to do whatever needs to be done to create an image, coupled with one of the best bodies in the business, has enabled her to work in every aspect of fashion. She has appeared in hundreds of magazines internationally, on dozens of magazine covers, in countless runway shows in Europe and the United States, and in ads for Versace and other high-end designers. She has also crossed over into TV and film work.

Other famous Chameleons include Kristen McMenamy, Carolyn Murphy, Sarah O'Hara, and of course, the most famous Chameleon of all, Madonna (who did some modeling early in her career).

You know you're a Chameleon if:

➤ You meet the basic model qualifications: tall, thin body, good hair, skin, and teeth (see Chapter 3 for more details).

➤ Your hair, skin, and eyes are neutral-colored (brown or dark blond hair, medium skin, brown eyes).

Roshumba's Rules

For certain types of modeling jobs, such as catalog, TV commercials, and advertising, the focus is on the product, so your best bet is to figure out what the clients want and give it to them.

71

➤ You have an expressive face and dramatic or unpredictable body language.

➤ You're not afraid of artistic experimentation.

➤ You would prefer to be in a creative environment more than anyplace else in the world.

Reality Check

Enjoy your 15 minutes of fame when it comes, but don't start to believe the hype. Many a beautiful star has fallen from the sky when her ego got so out of hand that people found her impossible to work with. Very few models are so extraordinary they can't easily be replaced. Remember, there are hundreds of girls who are dying to take your place.

If you're a Chameleon, you may be best suited for (but by no means limited to) editorial and runway work, creative ad campaigns, and art photography. Personally, the Chameleons are my favorite models because they look like they have the most fun making all those drastic changes and letting their imaginations run free.

Also be aware that although the Chameleons do get to play the most with their looks, all that hair dye, weight gain and loss, and change of persona may not be good for your health and well-being. So when you're not in the public eye, try to stay grounded and focused on who you are, and leave the role-playing for work. Otherwise, you may lose your sense of self, which can lead to serious problems. (For more information on this, see Chapter 25, "Personal Management.")

The Exotic Beauty

Exotic Beauty models are unique, one-of-a-kind beauties who usually come from faraway places, have exotic names, and were discovered completely by chance. They possess chiseled bone structures, piercing eyes, high cheekbones, pouty lips, and beautiful, radiant skin. Their bodies are lean and shapely, with gorgeous long legs. As children, their good looks made them stand out from the crowd, and they eventually grew to be full-fledged beauties. They often have to travel great distances and over-come tremendous odds to enter the modeling business. Once their personal histories become known, the Exotics are admired for the courage and quick wits that allowed them to overcome amazing odds to land on the fashion runways.

Exotic models are often very much in demand when they first hit the fashion scene. They're promoted as the It Girl of the moment, and they get all the prized modeling jobs, including magazine work, runway jobs, and even advertising. Because they can easily become a passing trend, Exotics must be very clever, hard working, and lucky to maintain a lasting career. They may come in with a big bang, but they can disappear just as quickly once the initial fascination is over. Some, however, manage to be continually alluring and captivating.

Because most of the work available in smaller cities is commercial (catalogs, TV commercials, advertisements), it can be tough for an Exotic Beauty to find a lot of work in a smaller market, where clients tend to want to hire models who appeal (and look like) their customers. The exception is those cities where there is a large local population of people of the Exotic model's background, for instance, a Latin model in Miami.

Exotic models hail from the far corners of the globe. They often face great obstacles, even danger, to break into modeling.

Iman

Iman, perhaps the greatest Exotic Beauty of all time, is my mentor and one of the main reasons I became a model. When I was an aspiring model, reading magazines and watching the fashion shows in Peoria, Illinois, she was the person I focused on most. I studied the way she moved, the energy she projected, and the mystery she exuded. I knew that I had to meet her and eventually work with her.

Mod Squad

To embellish her image as an Exotic Model, Iman was first introduced at a press conference by photographer Peter Beard as a savage African woman whom he had found living with a nomadic tribe in the wilds of Somalia. The truth was actually quite different: Iman was a privileged student at the University of Nairobi in Kenya, and she was the daughter of a prominent diplomat. In fact, she was discovered on a trip to the Sudan by Beard, who brought her to the Wilhelmina agency. The truth eventually came out, but it didn't stop Iman's rise to the top: She soon became one of the hottest models of the late 1970s.

Iman has beautiful, exotic model features: long legs, a slender, shapely body, a neck that goes on for miles, deep-set almond-shaped eyes, a perfect chiseled bone structure, and gorgeous high cheekbones. When she looks at you, she seems to look through you, right into your soul, a quality that's present even in her photographs. Her movements are as nimble and graceful as a lioness stalking her prey, while her bearing is that of a regal princess.

Iman has walked the runways for many of the top designers, including Calvin Klein, Versace, and Yves Saint Laurent. She was also featured in Revlon's Most Unforgettable Women advertising campaign. In addition, she's appeared in movies and on television and produced her own cosmetic line.

Irina Pantaeva

Irina Pantaeva is similar to Iman in that her perilous journey from the steppes of Siberia to the runways of Paris is very inspiring. Although she possesses the basic physical characteristics of a model (tall and lanky), what defines her as truly exotic are her sexy, slanted eyes, her razor-sharp cheekbones, her dramatic coloring, and her Eskimo heritage. In photos and on the runway, her demur personality and childlike fascination with the world at large comes through.

From the minute that Irina first hit the runways of Paris, her career took off because her look was fresh and new. When the story of her treacherous journey from her small home in Siberia was revealed, it made her all the more desirable, because not only did she have a look, she had a story. Modeling opened the door to a future unimaginable in her impoverished Russian hometown.

Since then, Irina has appeared in most of the major fashion magazines and in dozens of runway shows. She has been featured in ads for fashion-forward designers such as Issey Miyake, Kenzo, and others. She's even written a novel, snagged a major role in a *Mortal Kombat* movie, and has made guest appearances on several TV shows.

Other exotic models include Kadija, Anna Bailey, and Warus.

You know you're an Exotic Beauty if:

➤ You possess the basic physical requirements of a professional model: tall, thin body with good skin, hair, and teeth (see Chapter 3 for more details).

➤ You have exotic facial features: distinctive eyes, a pronounced nose, healthy hair, and extra long neck.

➤ You have an exotic name or come from an obscure foreign country (or just seem like you do).

➤ You have an uncanny ability to survive and overcome the most impossible obstacles.

If you're an Exotic Beauty, you may be best suited for (but not limited to) very creative modeling work, including editorial and runway jobs. Chances are you have luck on your side or you would not have made it out of that remote corner of the world to a fashion capital. But it will take hard work and planning to maintain a modeling career once the fashion industry's fascination with you has waned.

Surround yourself with experienced agents and managers who can help you sustain and further what you've built. If you've got an incredible look and a great story, market yourself outside of modeling—tell your story to magazines, write your autobiography, or go on the lecture circuit, talk shows, and other television shows. Use your story as well as your looks to advance your career. Finally, learn to speak the language of your new country properly and with ease; also familiarize yourself with its customs and etiquette. At the same time, learn to share your customs in a unique and positive way.

Roshumba's Rules

It's a good idea, whether you're an Exotic model from a remote country or an American in Paris, to learn to speak the language of the country where you are living. This will give you a big advantage with clients.

The Oddball

What can I say about the Oddball? According to all conventional wisdom, she should never even consider the modeling business! Her features are nothing like a model's: Her eyes are too small or too big, and her nose and teeth are crooked. She may be too tall or too short, or maybe she moves in an odd manner. Chances are, no one would ever stop her on the street and ask if she's a model. But somehow all these peculiarities, taken together, make her stand out from the crowd.

When an Oddball first gets noticed, the industry often falls head over heels in love with her. Suddenly, a slew of lookalikes appears on the scene, and for a short time, a new trend shakes up the fashion business. During this time, you can find the Oddball on the covers and in the pages of all the major fashion magazines, on the runways for the most popular designers, and in major ad campaigns. But inevitably, a more conventional look returns, and unless she's smart and lucky, the Oddball's career may be over quickly.

Right now, Oddball models are especially in demand for editorial work in the big fashion capitals—New York, Paris, and Milan. But because most of the work available in smaller cities is commercial (catalogs, TV commercials, advertisements), it can be tough for an Oddball to find a lot of work in a smaller market, where clients tend to want to hire models who appeal (and look like) their customers. In a smaller market, the Oddball's best bet is to try to maximize her commercial appeal with a classic haircut and makeup that makes her best features stand out and her "oddball" features less noticeable.

With their unique, quirky beauty, Oddballs defy the conventional wisdom on what model beauty is. They may have unusually large or small features, very short or very long hair, but somehow they stand out from the crowd.

Kate Moss

When Kate first came along, no one understood her appeal, not even other models. She was short, her eyes were too close together, she had thin lips, and was too skinny. Well, Kate laughed all the way to the bank. (She has since grown about an inch and gained a little weight.) Sulky, helpless-looking Kate actually helped establish a whole new category of model: the *Waif*. What made the Waifs so successful was that they came along at a time when the industry was tired of looking at the same old high-maintenance, overdone supermodels.

Catwalk Talk

A **Waif** is a model type who's super-skinny and not classically pretty. The Waifs were the talk of the fashion world in the early 1990s. Their heyday put an end (at least temporarily) to the reign of the supermodels.

Now Kate is a household name in her own right, thanks in part to Calvin Klein, who has featured her in several ad campaigns. She has also appeared in all the major fashion magazines and in all the big designer runway shows.

Alek Wek

Alek Wek is another very unusual beauty. Against all odds, she was dubbed the It Girl of late 1990s. Her striking baby-faced look, teamed with her model-thin body and extraordinarily long legs, caught the eye of the fashion world, and suddenly she was everywhere. She has appeared on the cover of American *Elle* and in many of the other top fashion magazines, as well as in ads for

Clinique and Francois Nars. She's also walked the runway for top designers Yves Saint Laurent, Ralph Lauren, and Issey Miyake.

Other Oddballs include Twiggy, Rossy De Palma, Lauren Hutton, and Betty Lago.

You know you're an Oddball if:

➤ Your body structure is similar to a model's (you're 5'8" or taller, thin, and well-proportioned).

➤ You look unusual or distinctive in photographs or are attractive in a unique way.

➤ You exude a strong sense of personality and people love being around you.

➤ Your personal style is very fashion forward, which makes you stand out.

➤ You have an overwhelming desire to be a model, even though you know that you don't meet the standard requirements.

If you're an Oddball, you may be best suited for (but not limited to) creative, less-commercial modeling jobs, including editorial and runway work. Take advantage of every opportunity that comes your way because your career as a model may be very limited (for instance, working for only one client) or short-lived.

Keep a positive attitude. Sometimes when your looks are out of the ordinary (especially when you're surrounded by Classic Beauties all day), you may start to feel bad about yourself. But remember, other models may have great careers because their looks are more conventional, but your odd qualities are the secrets to your success. Work to improve yourself as a talent and a person. Surround yourself with agents and managers who can help you make the most of your 15 minutes of fame, and hopefully further your career.

Roshumba's Rules

If you're tempted to cosmetically alter your look (get a nose job, have your teeth bonded), remember that the very feature that you hate may be the secret to your success.

The Athletic Girl Next Door

The Athletic-Girl-Next-Door models are divided into two categories: beautiful athletes who model part-time or full-time models who look healthy and athletic. In either case, these women are usually six feet tall or taller (or just look like they are). They look like they spend hours at the gym, perfecting their strong, muscular bodies. They have broad shoulders and powerful legs, but what makes them stand out from ordinary athletes are their pretty faces. They have medium to big eyes with a fierce, competitive look in them. They have high cheekbones, perfectly proportioned, though not necessarily small, noses, medium-full lips, fresh-scrubbed skin, and healthy hair.

Magazines and advertisers use them for covers and inside pages when they want to project that healthy, natural appeal or just want a more sporty look, especially fitness editorials that demonstrate specific exercises such as seen in *Self* magazine. The Athletic Girl Next Door also appears in ads for bathing suits, sportswear, and athletic products. They're usually not found on the fashion runways because their bodies can be too muscular and overpowering for the clothes.

In smaller markets, the Athletic-Girl-Next-Door type is one of the most popular types of models. Her healthy and wholesome looks appeal to just about everyone, so clients such as catalogs and local advertisers love to hire her.

The Athletic Girl Next Door is pretty and healthy and has a wholesome look that appeals to many consumers.

Reality Check

Don't freak out if your body starts to change as you mature. It's rare that a 25-year-old model is the same body type she was when she was just starting out at 16. This could be a great opportunity to expand your career. As your body changes, your model type may change, too, and you may be able to do modeling jobs you never could before.

Gabrielle Reese

Gabrielle Reese (better known as Gabby) is the perfect example of a full-time athlete/part-time model. She is a professional volleyball player who is known worldwide for her killer skills on the court. She's 6'3", with broad shoulders and a muscular body. She has beautiful, long healthy hair. Gabby has appeared on the cover and in pages of *Elle* and *Shape* and other fitness magazines. She endorses Nike, and her volleyball matches are televised seasonally.

Niki Taylor

Niki Taylor is the embodiment of the other type of athletic model: Although she's not an athlete, she looks like she's played sports all her life, drinks the requisite eight glasses of water a day, and leads a very healthy life.

Her body is strong and womanly, with broad shoulders, full, defined hips, and muscular, athletic legs. Her features are similar to those of the Classic Beauty: almond-shaped eyes, perfect little button nose, medium, pouty lips, and high cheekbones. Combined with the most dazzling smile in modeling, Niki projects a healthy, down-to-earth appeal.

Niki made a splash in the early 1990s when she snagged a lucrative contract with Cover Girl. She's also been featured in the pages of every major magazine (she once appeared on seven covers in one month). She endorses Liz Claiborne clothing, has walked the runway for many designers, and has hosted shows for MTV's *House of Style* and *Fashionably Loud.*

Other famous athletes include Lisa Lesley, Kathy Ireland, and Kim Alexis.

You know you're an Athletic Girl Next Door if:

> ➤ You're six feet tall or taller (or just look like you are).

> ➤ You have a strong, muscular body, and a pretty, photogenic face.

> ➤ You're an athlete and want to continue your sports career while earning extra income.

> ➤ You're competitive and driven, yet fun to be around.

If you're an Athletic Girl Next Door, you may be best suited for (but not limited to) modeling bathing suits, athletic clothes, sportswear, and other athletic products, in both editorial and advertisements. Catalogs are another potential lucrative source of work. Athletes who are models are really lucky because they have two potentially lucrative careers going for them, which feed off each other. You should assemble a good team of professionals who can help you harmoniously manage both careers. For those models who are not professional athletes, it may be a good idea to tune in to the world of sports. You should also pay special attention to staying in shape and maintaining a healthy lifestyle so you can build on your image as an active, physically fit beauty.

The Least You Need to Know

> ➤ There are seven basic types of models, each with its own physical characteristics.

> ➤ Your type depends on your facial features, body structure, and to some degree, your personality.

> ➤ Even the most famous, successful models can be categorized as one type or another.

> ➤ It's essential that you know which type you are, because it will have a big impact on your career.

Part 2
Breaking into the Business

So now that you've learned everything you need to know about the modeling business, your next question is probably, "How do I get started?" In this chapter, I'll tell you everything you need to know about launching a modeling career.

Because the first step in becoming a professional model career is finding an agent to guide and manage your career, I'll start by detailing the basic materials you'll need to find an agent, and I'll talk about the many options for finding one. Because many successful models start their careers with unpaid modeling jobs (which are called hobby modeling jobs or modeling for experience), I'll discuss how aspiring models can find these types of jobs. The next step, of course, is modeling professionally, and I'll describe what it's like to model in the international fashion capitals (New York, Milan, and Paris) as well as in secondary markets (Miami, Chicago, and Los Angeles).

Finally, one whole chapter is devoted entirely to parents, telling them everything they need to know about the business so they can insure that their child's career is a safe, successful, and happy experience for everyone.

Chapter 6

Getting Started

In This Chapter

➤ Breaking into the modeling biz

➤ Keep it simple: clothing, hair, and makeup tips

➤ Tips for taking the snapshots you'll need

➤ Other materials you'll need: statistics card and letter of introduction

---

In Part 1 you learned a lot about the modeling industry. Although it can be a difficult field to break into, the very first steps you need to take are relatively easy, painless, and inexpensive.

You've probably seen models in magazines, so you may think you have a pretty good idea of how you need to look to get started. Believe it or not, looking like the models in the magazines when you first start out is the *opposite* of what you want to do. I'll tell you the real scoop on how to look to get your foot in the door. Once you know how to look the part, you'll want to start getting together some essential (but simple to assemble) materials—snapshots of yourself, an index card with your vital statistics on it, and a letter of introduction to send to agents.

Your ultimate goal in all of this is to find a modeling agency to represent you. Your agency will help develop your look, send you on auditions and job interviews with potential clients, and guide and develop your career. Agencies have special employees, called modeling scouts, who are always on the lookout for new talent. With the simple materials that I describe in this chapter, you'll have everything you need to contact agencies and impress their scouts, whether it's at open calls at their offices, at modeling searches, conventions, and schools, or by mail.

Looking the Part

When you're just starting your modeling career and are going to meet with an agent or a model scout for the first time, whether it be at an open call, a model search, convention, or modeling school, you'll probably want to look your most fashionable. Maybe you'll want to wear your cool new baggy Tommy Hilfiger jeans with a Polo sweatshirt. Or maybe you look your best in high heels and a sexy little black minidress. Or perhaps you're thinking about wearing that beautiful prom dress that is an exact copy of the dress Calista Flockhart wore to the Golden Globe awards.

But believe it or not, none of those outfits is what a model scout wants to see. They're there to look at beautiful young girls, not the latest fashions. They want to see natural-looking girls who would be lovely raw material that agents, fashion editors, advertising clients, hairstylists, makeup artists, fashion editors, and clothing stylists can use to turn into an exquisite image of beauty.

That's why you want to dress so they'll notice *you*—your tall, slim body, fantastic legs, thick, healthy hair, and pretty eyes—not your overstyled hair, funky fashions, and superlong acrylic nails.

Reality Check

In general, it's a good idea to avoid decorative body art. This includes everything from long, acrylic nails, to large, obvious tattoos, body piercings (other than the earlobes), and other types of decorative body art. Models make their living by using their bodies to sell products, and it's best if your body is as close to its simple, natural, healthy state as possible.

Dressing for Success

The way to create a positive first impression is to dress as simply as possible, so the real you shines through; don't cover yourself up with elaborate makeup, overstyled hair, and exaggerated fashions. Whether it's for an open call, convention, model search, or for your snapshots, dress in a comfortable, simple manner that's appropriate for your age and that shows your shape. Neat jeans or a fitted, above-the-knee skirt, worn with a T-shirt, denim jacket, or sweater are perfect. Flat comfortable shoes or sneakers are also good. Avoid high heels—agents and model scouts will want to see at a glance how tall you are. (Not to mention if you're tottering around in stilettos, you'll be focusing way too much attention on staying upright, which could make you come off as nervous, unsteady, and uncomfortable.) Clothes that are too tight often come off as vulgar or trashy—not the image you want to project. Oversized or baggy clothes hide your shape and look like you have something to hide. Also avoid anything trendy, messy, dressy, or overdone.

Reality Check

There's no need to spend a lot of money on designer outfits or the latest fashions. Model scouts aren't looking for the girl who can afford the most expensive, most fashionable outfit in the whole mall; they're looking for beautiful girls, who look great even in the simplest, most casual outfits. Trust me on this: Keep it simple!

Makeup Tips

Another mistake a lot of aspiring models make is wearing too much makeup. When you're going to meet a model scout, don't glop on every product in your bathroom—heavy foundation and powder, big stripes of blush, tons of eye shadow, a couple of layers of mascara, and a pound of lipstick.

Model scouts don't want to see girls with a lot of makeup on their faces; they're not interested in how skillful you are with concealer or eyeliner. They want to see how you look naturally. They're looking for empty canvases on which beautiful images can be created. In fact, sometimes scouts will even tell girls to go into the bathroom and wash the makeup off their faces if it's too heavy.

Ideally, you should wear little to no makeup, maybe just a little mascara to make your eyes stand out and some natural-colored lip gloss to make your lips look soft and supple and to enhance your smile.

Model Hair

Model hair is healthy, shiny, well cut, clean, and conditioned. Beautiful, healthy hair that can be used in ads for hair products—shampoos, conditioners, styling products, hair colors—is in high demand and can make models a lot of money. So keep your hair looking its best. When you're going to be meeting with a model scout, make sure that your hair is clean, free from split ends, and lightly styled. If you're attending a model search, convention, or open call, don't pull your hair back into a ponytail; the model scout will want to see how it looks hanging free.

Be very careful about coloring your hair, because certain colors can make you look older, clash with your skin tone, or may not match your eyebrows. Also, if color is not done properly, it could damage your hair and change its texture. If you do decide you have to color your hair, go to a competent professional, and choose a color within a couple of shades of your natural hair color. Anything else tends to look too unnatural and unattractive. Better yet, leave your color alone. Once an agency has signed you, they will decide if you need to have your hair colored and will send you to a colorist whom they trust.

Perming your hair should be avoided as well. Again, the model scout wants to see what your hair looks like naturally. Also, the chemicals in the solutions used in perms could severely damage your hair. Another reason that I would caution you about perming your hair is that perms tend to be problematic once they start to grow out, and redoing them increases the chances of damage exponentially. So it's probably best to leave your hair its natural texture and let the agent decide what should be done with it.

Roshumba's Rules

When you're meeting model scouts, don't load your hair up with excessive amounts of styling products, such as gels, mousses, and sprays. It can be blow-dried, as long as it looks natural, not elaborate or exaggerated.

African American women often chemically straighten their hair to make it easier to maintain. Although that's not a problem, just make sure it doesn't get damaged from overprocessing. Keeping it conditioned also helps.

Drastically cutting your hair is also generally not a good idea. Although short hair has its moments in the fashion spotlight, agencies generally prefer models with mid-length or long hair, which is more versatile than short hair. A drastic haircut could also throw off the balance of your face and body. And remember, it's a lot easier to cut your hair later than have to sit around and wait for it to grow back.

The Photos You'll Need

One big mistake that many aspiring models make is spending tons of money on photos, portfolios, and composites before they get an agent. This is a total waste of money and time, and people who tell you otherwise either don't know what they're talking about or are scamming you.

Once you have an agent, she will make arrangements for all the photos, test shoots, portfolios, and composites you'll need. Most reputable agencies will even pay for them up front, and the cost will be subtracted from the money you earn once you start working. All photos taken without an agent's guidance are essentially useless because the photos may not capture the image the agent plans to build for you and promote to the fashion industry. When agents are looking for new models, they want to develop the model's own natural beauty into a marketable style, so spending a lot of money on professional photos that probably won't project the image they're after is not necessary. (Be wary if an agent asks you for money up front to pay for any of these photos, portfolios, or composites because it's not the usual practice.)

Once you have an agency, they will provide you with a portfolio and composites. The portfolio will have the agency's name and logo on it. The agent will also want to put together a composite card of you. The composite usually consists of a beautiful head shot and a body shot, and maybe a couple of additional photos showing your personality or exceptional attributes, such as beautiful legs or a lovely smile. The photos used in the composite are generally selected from test photo shoots that the agent has set up. Or the agency may want to incorporate pictures from magazine tear sheets (pictures of you that are cut out of the publication in which they appeared). The composite will also usually have the agency's logo on it. (For more information on test shoots for your book, see Chapter 13, "Testing, Testing, 1, 2, 3: Test Shoots"; to learn more about composites, portfolios, and other model materials, see Chapter 14, "Tools of the Modeling Trade.")

Photographers often prey on young, unsuspecting models and their parents, suggesting that models need loads of professional pictures, composites, portfolios, and elaborate, expensive photo sessions before they've found an agent or started their careers. They'll tell the models that agents won't accept them if they don't have a portfolio full of pictures. In these cases, the photographer is probably trying to scare the unsuspecting model in order to make money off the photo session, the development and processing of the film, and the printing of contact sheets and photos. If anyone tells you that you need to spend a lot of money on pictures, hairstylists, makeup artists, photographers, or clothes to get started in this business, either he's not completely informed about the modeling process or he's scamming you. In either case, grab your wallet and run!!

Sometimes, however, young, inexperienced photographers will volunteer to do photo sessions with aspiring models to get experience and develop their own books. This is called a "test shoot for experience," and it can be a great learning experience for a model. But the difference here is that there is no charge, or that it's minimal (under $100), just enough to cover the processing and printing of the film. See Chapter 8, "Modeling for Experience (Hobby Modeling)," for more information on test shoots for experience.

Getting in the Door Is a Snap(shot)

The most that's needed to get your foot in the door are a few snapshots that by no means require a professional to take. As I've said, anything more is really a waste of time and money. (But if you already have test shots that you feel you would like to use, by all means, use them.)

These pictures can be handed out at model searches, conventions, and open calls. (See Chapter 7, "Finding an Agent," for more information about these.) Also, they can be mailed to agents whom you can't meet in person. Keep your photos simple; don't bother spending a lot of money on fancy effects or special clothes. Again, the model scouts aren't looking for fabulous photography; all they want to see is what you look like, and if they can tell that from the photo, then that photo is a masterpiece.

Ask a friend or family member who's handy with a camera to shoot you. You'll want to take both head shots, which are close-ups of your head and shoulders, and body shots, which are pictures that show your body from head to toe.

Roshumba's Rules

Use a whole roll of 24- or 36-exposure film so you'll be able to choose the best shots on the roll.

Getting Camera-Ready

In the photos, your face should be clean, and you should be wearing little or no makeup. At most, apply a little mascara, which will enhance your eyes, and some natural-colored lip gloss; if you're having a bad skin day, use a small amount of concealer to discreetly cover a zit or two. Remember, the agent is interested in seeing the real you, not the made-up you. Make sure your hair is pulled off your face, or simply styled.

For the head shots, it doesn't really matter what you wear, because your clothes won't show in the photo. For the body shots, you'll want to pose in a solid-colored, one- or two-piece bathing suit or leotard, which will give agents the best look at your body. Avoid anything too revealing; thongs, G-strings, and T-backs are too flashy. Leopard prints, bold graphics, or stripes on a bathing suit or leotard will make it harder to see your body's natural silhouette. Also, prints may make you look chunky or make your arms and legs look shorter, so it's best to keep it simple.

Bathing suits that are too revealing can be distracting and make you come off as overly sexy. If you are a naturally sexy girl, it will show through in your personality. Besides, when you meet with agents you will be in a public business environment, so it's best to have some decorum and be respectful.

Pose in front of a plain white or pale-colored background; a blank wall is perfect. Make sure the lighting on your face makes you look healthy and pretty (check yourself with a hand-held mirror first).

Shooting Star

You'll need several different shots, including:

➤ **Two head shots.** These close-up shots of your head and shoulders give agents a good look at your head, facial features, and smile. Take two full-frontal face shots. In one of the photos, you should be smiling; in the other, you should be relaxed and natural looking. A profile (side) shot is optional. If you think you have a great profile, by all means shoot it.

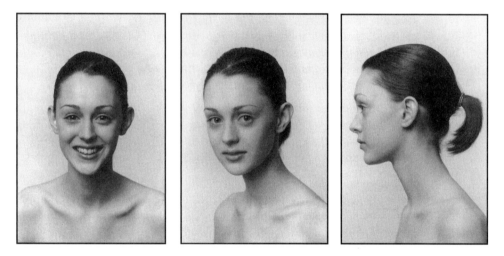

You'll want two snapshots of your head and neck, one smiling and one relaxed and natural looking. A profile (side shot) is optional, but a good idea if you have a nice one. Photographer: Kwame Brathwaite. Model: Laura McLafferty.

➤ **Three full-length snapshots of your body.** These shots give agents an idea of what your body measurements and proportions are. Agents want to see your body shape, the size of your bust, waist, and hips, as well as the length of your neck, arms, torso, and legs. These are important factors when it comes to determining what type of clients you'll be best suited to work for. You'll want one full-length (from head to toe) shot from the front, one from the side, and one from the back. Make sure that the shot shows your whole body.

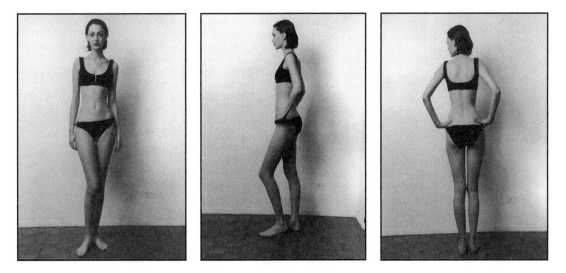

You'll want three full-length photos of your body: a frontal shot, a side shot, and a back shot. Photographer: Kwame Brathwaite. Model: Laura McLafferty.

➤ **A casual snapshot (optional).** This could be a shot of you having fun or hanging out. Casual snapshots should capture your personality in a fun environment. These pictures give agents a feel for the real you. Feel free to use your imagination here.

Mod Squad

I've seen girls send in all kinds of casual snapshots of themselves. One girl who was into horses sent in a picture of herself dressed in riding gear, posing on her horse. A couple of girls who were members of the school basketball team have sent in photos of themselves pictured in the school gym in their basketball uniforms. Another girl was photographed posing under a tree playing the guitar. My casual snapshot showed me dressed in a leotard, stretching in the backyard; I wanted to show agents that I was very health-conscious. The important thing is to capture yourself doing something you like, which allows your special talents to show through.

A casual snapshot, like this one, gives agents an idea of your personality. Photographer: Kwame Brathwaite. Model: Laura McLafferty.

Once you've shot the pictures you need, take the roll of film to be developed. (Getting them developed at the local drugstore is fine; there's no reason for expensive processing.) Choose the best shots, and have several prints made of each, so you'll be able to give them out. Be sure to write your name, phone number, and measurements in felt-tip pen on the back of each photo.

Your Statistics Card

Agents need to know your height, weight, and body *measurements* in order to determine what body type you are, and to decide what kinds of modeling (runway, bathing suit, petite) you're best suited for.

Catwalk Talk

Measurements are usually written as a series of three numbers: for example, 34-24-34. The first number is the bust size, the second is the waist measurement, and the third is the hip size.

Your statistics card, which lists all your vital measurements, gives them all that information at their fingertips. To create your own statistics card, write down the following measurements on several blank 3" × 5" index cards to give to agents. Your card should list the following information:

➤ Name (or modeling name)

➤ Address

➤ Phone number (include best time to call)

➤ Age

➤ Height

➤ Weight

90

➤ Bust, waist, and hip measurements

➤ Dress size

➤ Shoe size

➤ Eye color

➤ Hair color

➤ Special talents (for example, you study ballet or speak a second language)

This card, along with your snapshots, are all you need to get started. Good luck!

Just in case you're not familiar with how to take your measurements, here's a little guidance. All you'll need is a measuring tape with inches on one side and centimeters on the other. Take the end of the tape that begins with one inch and place it in the center of the front of your body or body part you'll be measuring. Wrap the tape around the back of your body, bringing it around until both ends meet. Pull it taut, but not tight. Write down the measurement.

➤ **Bust.** To take bust measurements, wrap the measuring tape around the fullest part of your chest. To figure out your cup size, wrap the tape around your chest, directly underneath your breasts. Subtract the second measurement (your chest under your bust) from the first (your full bust); that number will tell you your cup size. If the difference between the two numbers is one, you're an A cup. If the difference between the two numbers is two, you're a B cup. If the difference between the two numbers is three, you're a C cup, and so on. If this is too complicated, you can take the size from a bra that fits perfectly.

➤ **Waist.** Measure your waist at your natural waistline, where your belly button is.

➤ **Hips.** Measure your hips where your rear end is fullest.

A Letter of Introduction

The last thing you'll need to get started in the modeling business is a letter of introduction that you'll enclose with your photos and statistics card when you're writing agents to see if they're interested in representing you. Also include a self-addressed, stamped envelope when you're sending photos, if you want the agents to return them to you. (If you'll be meeting model scouts in person, at a search, convention, or open call, you can skip the letter.) Address the letter to the "New Faces Department."

Use this letter to introduce yourself to the agent. It should list several vital statistics—age, height, weight, dress size, and eye and hair color. If you can tell them something that's unique about you (such as hobbies or special talents), be sure to mention it. Finally, it should ask the agency if they're interested in representing you, or if they have any advice for things you can improve that will help get your modeling career off the ground.

Most important, be sure it has your name, address, and phone number on it! It's also a good idea to have someone proofread your letter. Here's one of the letters I sent to an agency when I was just starting out.

Roshumba Williams
10 Main Street
Anywhere, Illinois 12345
Phone: 309-555-5555

March 3, 1986

To: New Faces Department

Dear Sir or Madam:

My name is Roshumba Williams, and I am very interested in being a model. I am 16 years old and 5'10" tall. I weigh 115 pounds, and my measurements are 34-23-33. I wear a dress size 2 or 4. My eyes and hair are brown.

I live in Peoria, Illinois, where I am a high school junior. I am enrolled in my school's work-study program. I work as a receptionist at the Salvation Army.

Please contact me and let me know if you think I have what it takes to be a model, and if you would be interested in representing me. If not, I would appreciate your advice on how I can improve myself, or any suggestions of other agencies that might be interested in my look.

I am enclosing some photos, my statistics card, and a self-addressed, stamped envelope. I would really appreciate it if you could return my photos and any advice or comments.

Thank you so very much.

Sincerely yours,

Roshumba Williams

Enclosing the correct materials (photos, statistic card, self-addressed, stamped envelope) and including a professional but friendly letter will let the agency know that you are serious enough about modeling to have done your homework and know how to go about getting into the business. If you don't receive a response two weeks after sending the letter, contact the agency for feedback.

The Least You Need to Know

➤ Dressing simply, not like a model in a magazine, is the best way to impress an agent.

➤ When meeting with an agent, keep your hair and makeup simple.

➤ Don't spend a lot of money on photos; do-it-yourself ones are fine.

➤ List all your measurements on a statistics card to give to agents; if you aren't meeting with them in person, send a letter of introduction.

ents

Chapter 7

Finding an Agent

> **In This Chapter**
>
> ➤ Why a model needs an agent
>
> ➤ How you can shine at open calls, model searches, and model conventions
>
> ➤ What can a modeling school teach you?
>
> ➤ The easiest and least expensive way to find an agent
>
> ➤ Exploring other options in the fashion industry

Finding an agent can be one of the most difficult obstacles a fledgling model must face. Fortunately, there are many ways to find an agent, including open calls at modeling agencies, regional model searches, model conventions, modeling schools, or simply sending photos of yourself to an agency. In this chapter I'll tell you everything you need to know!

Why Have an Agent?

Finding an agent is the first major hurdle on the road to becoming a model, whether you're a fashion model or a specialty model such as a real-people model, a parts model, or a plus-size model. Agents help models get their careers off the ground. They help the model to make sure her look is as marketable as possible. They send them on job interviews and manage their careers. An agent will help with testing with the right photographers and will help a model develop her portfolio, making sure it captures her best attributes. Finally, the agent is the key link between the model and her clients.

Opening Doors at Open Calls

Open calls are a little like a modeling agency's version of an open house. Agencies are always looking for new models to represent, so they invite aspiring models to come into their offices to meet them to see if they have modeling potential. Anyone who is interested in getting into modeling is free to drop by the agency during open calls, which are held at certain set times, to meet with the agents and bookers. Some agencies hold open calls as frequently as twice a week, others have them less often, and some don't hold them at all.

Before you go, call the agency to confirm the time, date, and location of the open call. Also, ask what you should wear and what you need to bring. Usually, the agency will want you to bring in a couple of snapshots of your face, a few of your body in a simple swimsuit, and a shot capturing your personality, as well as your statistics card listing your age, height, weight, body measurements, hair, and eye color. (See Chapter 6, "Getting Started," for more information on these materials.)

Making a Good Impression

As the saying goes, you have only one chance to make a first impression, so you'll want to look your best at an open call. Follow the tips I gave you in Chapter 6: Go light on the makeup, and dress simply in clean, comfortable clothes that fit you well.

*The models in these photos are wearing the perfect type of outfits for finding an agent: casual but neat, body-conscious but not too tight or revealing.
Photographer: Kwame Brathwaite. Models: Laura McLafferty and Ryan Kopko.*

Another common mistake is wearing the wrong clothes. Yes, you want to look fashionable, but don't wear anything that is too tight, too baggy, or too trashy. Clothes that are too tight come off as cheap and tacky, which reflects badly on you. Agents can't see your body's silhouette in big, baggy clothes, and they may suspect you're trying to hide something. Also avoid overly dressy clothes—they set the wrong mood. What you should wear: clean, simple, youthful clothing that fits comfortably. Body-conscious jeans, khakis, T-shirts, and sweaters are perfect.

The two aspiring models on the left have it all wrong: One is wearing way-oversize hip-hop togs and too much jewelry, the other is overdressed in a formal prom dress. The neatly dressed model on the right will probably get the most positive response from agents.

Keeping Your Cool

When you arrive at the open call, you'll be asked to sign in and take a seat in a special room or in the reception area until the agent comes out. I advise getting there early so you can sit down and get comfortable with the environment before you meet with the agent. Modeling agencies are frantically busy, with models rushing in and out, messengers delivering packages, phones ringing off the hook, and people running around. You also may want to check yourself in the bathroom mirror to make sure you look fresh. And then just try to relax.

It's only natural to feel uncomfortable sitting in a room full of beautiful girls who are all trying to get the same thing you are. You'll probably want to

Roshumba's Rules

While you're waiting at the open call, do whatever you do to relax and make yourself comfortable. Take a series of deep breaths or read a book of positive affirmations, such as *The Seven Spiritual Laws of Success: A Practical Guide to the Fulfillment of Your Dreams* by Deepak Chopra.

start doubting yourself as you observe the other girls and see their books. It's an uncomfortable moment, but if you're prepared for it in advance, you'll be better able to deal with it. Try not to allow yourself to get distracted by the other girls. Don't look at the other models' pictures or portfolios, and don't let them look at yours. Be friendly and cordial, but if they ask to see your pictures, just say, politely but firmly, "I prefer not to." Don't make the mistake of starting to compete with all the other girls; don't start thinking everyone is more beautiful. You probably have something the other girls don't have, and it may be just what the agency is looking for! Try to project a calm, happy, friendly, positive attitude. Your focus should not be on anything else except how you can put your best self forward to let the agent know who you are and what a wonderful person you are to work with. Finally, try to enjoy the experience.

Show Time!

The agents or bookers will come out to meet with you or invite you into their office. They'll look at your face and figure and view your snapshots and statistics card. They're looking to see if you meet the basic physical requirements for modeling— that you're the right height, weight, age, and have the right body proportions (see Chapter 3, "Do You Have What It Takes?" for more specifics). They may ask you to walk for them, to get an idea of how you will move in front of the camera and on the runway. They'll also evaluate your facial expressions and try and see if they can visualize you in an advertisement or on the cover of a magazine. To try to get a feel for your personality, which is almost as important as looks for a successful model, they may ask you why you're interested in modeling, who your favorite model is, what your family is like, and where you go to school.

Often, a great personality can be the clincher at an open call, so cultivate whatever is special about you, whether you're an athlete, a painter, or speak another language. At one of the open calls I was involved with, the agent asked a girl why she wanted to model. She said that she wanted to get into modeling to help launch a singing career. The agent then asked her to sing something, and this girl sang this amazing blues song that truly expressed her personality. Everyone immediately fell in love with her, and she was signed on the spot. If you're given a chance to show off a particular talent or a charming personality, go for it!

Reality Check

Some girls at open calls are actually snippy to the agents, acting like they're doing the agent a favor by even coming to the open call. Some act like, "I know I'm going to be a star, if you don't take me, somebody else will." But even if these girls do find an agent willing to sign them, chances are their careers will be short-lived.

Why Attitude Matters

In addition to a certain look and a winning personality, the agency is looking for girls who would be a pleasure to work with (for more on the importance of a good attitude, see Chapter 3). Being nervous is no excuse. The truth is there are hundreds of beautiful women, but if an agent picks up that someone is uncooperative and has a bad attitude, that can quickly overshadow her beauty. An agency is not going to risk alienating a million-dollar client or a valuable booking by sending a model with a bratty attitude to a job, because it will ultimately reflect badly on them and could cost them a client.

Play the Field

If you are unable to land an agent in your first few meetings, go on as many open calls at reputable agencies as you can. They're a great experience and will help you get over the shock and scariness of walking into an agency cold turkey, so your confidence will increase. Furthermore, every agency (and every agent) has different tastes in models. Some agents might represent mostly Amazons, others have more success with Classic Beauties, others do best with the Athletic Girl Next Door. (See Chapter 5, "Which Look Are You: The Seven Basic Model Types," for more information on the different types of models.) Even if 10 agencies turn you down, the eleventh might think you have that special something.

Mod Squad

I must confess, I didn't follow my own advice. I arrived in Paris on June 27, 1987, with enough money to last only two weeks. I didn't have time to wait for the agencies' next open calls, so I just dropped by their offices. Some of them were polite and turned me down, others were incredibly rude and turned me down, a few said come back at the next open call. My last stop was at a small agency called Cosa Nostra, which booked models for fashion shows. They were welcoming and supportive, and they helped me get my first job, modeling for designer Yves Saint Laurent—the very next day!

If circumstances force you to drop by an agency when they're not having an open call—maybe you're only in town for a few days—you should know in advance there's a good chance the door will be slammed in your face and you'll be told to come back during an open call. But then again, you might want to take that chance. Someone may spot you and love your look. If you do decide to just drop by an agency, do a little research first to find out more about the agency by reading magazines, searching the Internet, and watching fashion shows on television (see Chapter 4, "Doing Your Homework," for how-tos). Be prepared for the possibility that the agency's staff may be extremely rude and dismissive. But if you think you can handle that, go for it!

Possible Results: Yes, No, Maybe

Models the agency is interested in will usually get a *callback,* requesting that they come in for a second meeting. Congratulations! This is a very good sign that you caught someone's eye. Callbacks allow the agency to see and meet with you another time to make sure you're right for them. You'll probably be introduced to the other people in the agency—bookers, department managers, even photographers—to see if they like your look, if they think that you fit their company's image, and if they have ideas about how to develop your talent.

Other times, an agency may think you have modeling potential, but that you maybe need to polish your presentation. (This is especially true of very young girls, say, 13- and 14-year-olds.) In this case, they may invite you to participate in a model search or model convention and ask you to keep in touch. If invited to participate in a search or convention, by all means attend. These competitions will allow you to make contacts with professional makeup artists, hairstylists, and runway coordinators (the person who teaches models how to walk on a runway and show their personality). This process gives the agent a chance to see how you behave and blossom in an intimate modeling situation.

Catwalk Talk

When an agency asks you to come back for a second interview because they're considering representing you, they are giving you a **callback.** You can get a callback by phone or by mail.

If the agents aren't interested in representing you, they may just politely glance at you and your pictures during the open call, then thank you for taking the time to come in. Some may be direct and tell you right then and there that they're not interested; often times, you'll be able to tell from their attitudes. Others will send you a letter a week or so later. In some cases, an agency may not contact you at all.

If you think you want to work with a particular agency, but haven't received any feedback since meeting with them, wait a week, then call back and ask to speak with the person in charge of the open call. Let him know who you are, tell him you're interested in working with the agency, and ask him if he's interested in you. If he's not, ask why and does he have any advice for you. It's a good idea to find out what he doesn't like, because it may be a simple thing you can easily work on to improve.

Reality Check

Never harass an agency! Never call them every day and bug them. Agencies get hundreds of calls a day, and they handle the careers of hundreds of girls—they don't have time to field dozens of calls from one person. Word gets around about harassers, and they can quickly find themselves shut out of every agency in town.

Listen to what the agents tell you. If you happen to notice that people are repeating the same thing—if they're all suggesting that you cut your hair, or lose weight, or wait until you're older and get your braces off—it makes sense to heed their advice. After all, they are the professionals, and following their suggestions will increase your chances of launching your career.

Finding Out About Open Calls

The best and safest way to find out about model searches is to call the agency you are interested in and ask when they hold open calls.

Looking for a Winner: Model Searches

Model searches are contests that are held all over the country, in cities large and small, at all times of year to try and spot the next Niki Taylor or Cindy Crawford. I've found model searches (which are also called model contests) to be fun and exciting. During my time as the host of the Elite Model Look model search, I've seen many young models getting their first taste of the business. Watching all the girls getting their hair and makeup done and walking on the runway was really emotional for me, because it took me back to when I first started and how special I felt.

Not only are the contests fun, but they can also be a crucial turning point in your career. Prizes vary depending on the sponsor (contests are usually sponsored by modeling agencies, magazines, clothing, and cosmetic companies), but they're often quite valuable. Some offer lucrative modeling contracts worth as much as $1 million. In other contests, winners may appear in the pages or even on the cover of a famous magazine or be featured in a product advertisement. Generally speaking, model searches are looking for models to work in the fashion capitals of New York, Paris, and Milan, not in smaller cities.

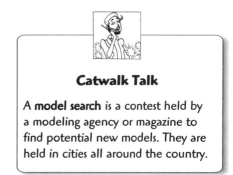

Catwalk Talk

A **model search** is a contest held by a modeling agency or magazine to find potential new models. They are held in cities all around the country.

Why You Should Enter a Model Search

"Model searches are the agencies' biggest scouting tools," explains Erin Lundgren, a model scout for the Elite Model Look model search, who travels around the country finding new models for the Elite Modeling Agency. "Searches are the best way to be seen by modeling scouts from New York and get free advice and direction from modeling professionals. Even if you don't have the chance to get to New York, you're being seen by a big New York agency. The scouts at a search can also steer you in the right direction. So even if you're not right for modeling in New York or maybe you're not right for editorial work, you [may be better suited to] catalog or runway modeling in your local market. It's a really good help session for girls, almost like a college fair for kids going to college, except [it's] for kids going into modeling."

To Pay, or Not to Pay

The biggest searches are sponsored by the Elite, Next, IMG, and Ford modeling agencies, *Seventeen* magazine, and Cover Girl Cosmetics. Most charge nothing (or a nominal fee, around $5) to enter. At other searches, a number of agencies will send scouts; in

101

these cases, a more sizable entrance fee will be charged. Sometimes it can be beneficial to pay to enter a modeling search because representatives from several agencies may be attending, which increases your chances of finding someone interested in your look.

Although some legitimate searches can cost up to $400 to enter, you should never pay more than $500 to enter one. "I honestly think it's not a necessity to pay to get into a model search, because it's so easy to get into the modeling industry," Lundgren says. "If you're struggling just to live, I wouldn't suggest paying anything because you can just mail photos in, or enter one of the model searches that don't have entrance fees."

Reality Check

Even if a search is legitimate, you still need to be on your guard. Searches attract unscrupulous photographers who come and take pictures of the participants and then try and sell the photos to them at exorbitant prices. Never pay a lot of money to have photos taken unless you already have an agent and she has directed you to have them taken. Even then costs should be kept down. At this point, the agency pays the cost for photos and photo sessions up front and the model reimburses them when she starts working.

Is It Legit?

To find out if a model search is legitimate, find out what agencies are sending representatives, advises Lundgren. "If top agencies such as Elite, Ford, Next, and IMG are attending, then it's got to be a good model search, because a major company like Elite wouldn't send a rep to a bad model search. If it's companies you've never heard of, then I don't know if I would be willing to pay any money to go to it."

One advantage model searches have over conventions is that searches are much smaller events, Lundgren says. "Both are really strong ways to get into the modeling industry. Conventions are really huge, so you may not get much of a chance to really talk in detail with the scouts. But at searches, you get more hands-on attention, you get to talk more directly to the scouts, and you can get more information out of them."

Model Searches, Step by Step

Most model searches happen in stages. The Elite Model Look, for instance, starts with a preliminary round, which is held in small cities around the country. This stage generally lasts one day and takes place at local malls or at hot spots such as Planet Hollywood. Anyone can enter, and contestants are responsible for their own hair, makeup, and clothes. First, participants fill out the application. Next the model scout from the agency will talk to them a little bit about the industry. Then it's time for each contestant to walk the runway, so the agents can see what they look like and how they move. At the end of the day, the winner is announced; she will go on to compete in the regionals.

The regional competitions of the Elite Model Look model search are held in big cities such as Chicago, Dallas, or Atlanta. The regional contests are more elaborate than the preliminary stage. "At Elite's regional search, contestants get instructions from a New

York runway coordinator, their hair and makeup is done over, and they get to model in a professional runway show," says Lundgren. Contestants often get to meet established models and find out about the industry from a working supermodel." The regional winners are awarded a two-year contract with Elite, plus they win an all-expenses-paid trip to New York City, where the national competition is held. The national winners compete at the international competition in France, where the grand prizes are guaranteed modeling contracts with Elite that are worth close to $1 million.

Search contestants range in age from 14 to 21; the average age is 15 or 16. If you're under 18, you'll need to bring your parent or guardian, because you need his or her signature on the entrance form. (And it's a good idea anyway to have a guardian's moral support and common sense along with you.) Often, girls bring their own cheering sections, including moms, dads, boyfriends, grandparents, and friends.

Roshumba's Rules

Be respectful and cooperative during the model search; do what is asked as long as it's reasonable; if you're difficult to work with at the preliminary stage, agents may not want to have anything more to do with you.

How to Succeed at a Search

Make sure you're freshly showered and are wearing deodorant. Avoid strong perfume, which can leave a smell on clothes that will be worn for the contest. To increase your chances of success at a search, know what events are taking place, when they start, and then make sure you're where you need to be on time. Keep your hair, makeup, and clothing simple and natural.

It's also a good idea to bring snapshots of yourself, preferably a couple of head shots and a couple of body shots, to show the agency representative how you look in photographs. (See Chapter 6 for more information on photos.)

Ruling the Runway

When it's your turn on the runway, take your time and walk naturally. Even if you're nervous and jittery because you're not used to being on stage in front of an audience, don't just run on and run off. It could be the scouts' one chance to see you. And remember, they're not judging you on how well you do a model's trademark catwalk sashay. "That's something they can learn," Lundgren says. Model scouts want to see you and your body move comfortably and naturally, and this may be their only chance.

While it's good to show some personality, the model-search runway is not the place for wild antics. Lundgren says, "I've had some people do some really weird things on the runway. I've had some girls do dances, wave to friends, blow kisses. I even had somebody do the Michael Jackson Moonwalk, and then proceed to get up on her tiptoes and shout at the audience." So while it's good to show personality, don't go overboard!

103

Pretty Is as Pretty Does

Be cooperative, polite, and respectful to the representatives from the modeling agency. Introducing yourself to the scout and being friendly and outgoing is a very good idea. "I like it when somebody comes up and asks me questions because I can see their personality," says Lundgren. "It helps me to get to know them a little bit, especially when we're there for just a short period of time." So go up to the scout, introduce yourself, and make a good impression by asking her some intelligent questions (you may want to think of them in advance). I can't stress enough the importance of showing good attitude and a pleasant personality.

Search Etiquette

Even if you don't win a contest, it doesn't mean you should give up on being a model. The best thing you can do, according to Lundgren, is go up and talk to the scout and ask why you didn't win and what you can do to improve your chances of breaking into the industry. Lundgren says, "I see thousands of beautiful girls, but [very few with supermodel potential]. They have to have height; they have to look the way that's in that year. To model in New York, height is a very big requirement—you have to be 5'9" and above, unless you're Kate Moss. And generally speaking, that doesn't happen."

Keep in mind that the national model searches are looking for girls to model in New York only. Even if you don't have the physical qualifications to make it in New York, it's still possible you can have a very successful modeling career in a *local market,* where the requirements are more flexible.

Models in these cities can earn a lot of money and have successful careers modeling for catalogs, in advertisements, and for local publications. If one of the scouts at a contest tells you you'd be better off modeling in a particular city, heed her advice. "We're all pretty much professionals, we know what we're doing; if we encourage you to go into your local or secondary market instead of New York, you should take it into consideration and really listen to that advice," says Lundgren. Ask the scout at the search for a listing of local agencies in your area.

Catwalk Talk

New York is where most models in the U.S. work, but many models also work in other cities, such as Miami, Chicago, Los Angeles, Dallas, Atlanta, and Los Angeles. These cities are referred to as **local** or **secondary markets.**

Whatever you do, be a gracious loser. "I've had some girls be really obnoxious wondering why we didn't pick them," says Lundgren. "If you have a question about why you weren't chosen, you can come and ask us. But don't accuse us. I had somebody who was only about 5'5" and just wasn't right for Elite, shouting at us and taking it way over the edge and calling us names. It was just crazy."

Finding Out About Model Searches

To find out about model searches in your area, look for advertisements in magazines, newspapers, or on the radio. Often, there is a 900 number to call to register. Before you enter, do some research to make sure the contest is reputable. Normally there is no cost to enter, but if there is, find out how much, and what it covers, before entering.

Modeling Conventions

Attending *modeling conventions* is another good way for aspiring models to find an agent to represent them and launch them in the modeling business. Conventions usually draw more partici- pants than searches (1,000 to 6,000 contestants is not uncommon at conventions, whereas usually no more than several hundred girls participate in a search). Conventions generally last from two to four days, are held in hotels in cities around the country, and have more sizable entrance fees (up to $500). Some of the better-known model con- ventions include IMTA, Model Search America, Manhattan Model Search, and New York Model.

Catwalk Talk

Modeling conventions are events attended by many different agents looking for new models to represent. Unlike searches, they charge sizeable entrance fees, and they usually last several days, unlike searches, which take place in one afternoon.

Why You Should Consider a Convention

Aspiring models should consider attending a convention because agents and scouts from many different agencies will be in attendance. Conventions offer a great opportu- nity to meet agents from the big New York agencies without having to travel to New York. One advantage conventions have over searches is that agents from many differ- ent agencies may be in attendance, increasing your chances of catching someone's eye. Also many agents from around the world—Paris, Milan, London, and even Tokyo— attend conventions looking for models.

Conventions also provide a great crash course in modeling. You'll gain experience working with hairstylists, makeup artists, and clothing stylists (at conventions where they're provided); at the very least, you'll learn how to do your own hair and makeup for a runway show. You'll find out what it's like to walk the runway, and get used to people looking at you. You'll also meet other models and learn from their experiences. Finally, you'll gain a lot of knowledge and information from talking to the agents present.

Conventional Wisdom

How can you tell if a convention is reputable? Find out who the sponsors are, or if it's linked to a major modeling agency. Some of the judges should be from major maga- zines, such as *YM* or *Seventeen,* or advertisers, such as Cover Girl or Keds. Also, ask the convention representative what well-known models have gone on to successful careers after participating in their convention. (Beverly Peele's career was launched after she was discovered at the IMTA Convention.) Reputable companies will have press kits or brochures. And don't be afraid to ask questions; a legitimate convention will be happy to answer all your questions because they're proud of the work they do.

The Parent Trap

Most girls at conventions are accompanied by a parent or guardian. Even though you may prefer to leave Mom at home, she can be a great asset for you at a convention. Sometimes a young, aspiring model's desire to launch her career may overshadow her logic, or she may find herself in a situation she isn't equipped to deal with. That's when it's key to have a parent or guardian along who can scrutinize the circumstances, ask questions, be objective, and read between the lines.

The Convention Itinerary

The first order of business at a convention is registration. Then there's usually a short interview, called a *meet-and-greet*. Also on the first day are rehearsals for a runway fashion show, then the show itself.

On the second day of the convention, a callback sheet is posted. The callback sheet lists all the agents' names, followed by the names of the girls in whom they are interested. The agents all have their own tables, and models line up to meet with the different agents.

Catwalk Talk

A **meet-and-greet** is a short interview that the judges and agents conduct with participants. You'll be asked basic questions, such as where you live, what grade you're in, and why you want to be a model.

At a convention, it's possible you could get a callback from five or six different agencies, in which case you would meet with each one at its designated table. Making it onto the callback list doesn't mean that the agency definitely wants to represent you, just that they're interested in seeing you and meeting you again. Sometimes girls are signed on the spot; other times, they are told the agency will be in touch.

Even if no one is interested in signing you, approach a couple of the agents and ask for their advice on how you can improve (but don't yell at them for not picking you!). Even if you don't find an agent, don't think it was a waste of time: For one thing, you learned more about modeling than you ever knew before, and for another, you had an experience that won't soon be forgotten. Move on and try other options.

Tips for Success

Interviewing and interpersonal skills are even more essential at a convention than at a search because the interviews with the agents at a convention are longer and more involved. "You need to treat this as a job interview," advises Lundgren. "We want to see your personality. If you're asking us questions or if you're answering our questions with more than just a yes or a no, then that's going to show us that you have some personality, and it's going to distinguish you from the next girl who answers every question with yes, no, yes, no."

Agents also look for a good personality because it's a key element in a successful modeling career. "If you're going out on a casting (which is basically an interview for a specific job), we want to make sure you can handle yourself, you can talk to the client, and show them a little bit of yourself," Lundgren says. "If they can't distinguish you from the next girl, they'll forget you the minute you walk out the door. Besides your looks, your personality is probably right up there with being the most important thing an agent looks at. It's always good to be outgoing, to be talkative … or else we're not going to remember you."

Nice Girls Finish First

As at open calls and searches, you should also try to be as cooperative as possible. "Yes, you have to be careful about certain things," says Lundgren. "I understand if you're going to a photo shoot and the photographer wants you to be naked, that's okay to say no to. Or if [you're asked to wear] something that's really revealing and provocative that you don't feel comfortable in. But otherwise, you should be pretty open. If someone wants you to wear your hair a different way than you normally wear it, don't say no and give [them] attitude, do it. Or if they want to dress you in a dress that might not be your favorite color and that you think is ugly, wear it." If you're already saying no before you're even established, you may find it difficult to get your career off the ground.

Finding Out About Modeling Conventions

Before the date of the event, conventions will run a lot of advertisements on the radio, in the local papers, and even on TV. Another option is to call a local modeling agency or modeling school in your area and ask them when the next convention is being held.

Modeling Schools

Some people feel that *modeling schools* are a big scam, but I don't agree. It is true that graduating from a modeling school won't guarantee you a modeling career. It's also true that they can be rather expensive. But girls who attend modeling schools learn a lot about modeling opportunities in their area, including the best agencies. They also learn to develop a sense of style, grace, poise, and self-confidence. They also learn about good grooming and beauty techniques, healthy eating,

Catwalk Talk

Modeling schools teach people interested in modeling about the modeling industry, as well as various modeling skills and techniques, including posing for a camera, walking on the runway, and grooming.

and exercise, as well as how to handle themselves in public situations. Basic modeling skills are taught, too: how to apply makeup, walk the runway, and move in front of a camera. Still, don't let anyone tell you that modeling schools are a necessity for a modeling career.

Like everything, modeling schools have good and bad aspects. I think the best thing they do is to give girls confidence and poise, help a shy, awkward girl grow out of her shell, and give you experience in your market. If you're very fresh, and not yet very knowledgeable about fashion, beauty, or modeling, it's a good way to find out about the industry.

Model Curriculum

At a good modeling school, you'll learn about the modeling industry as a whole and how it works; how to develop good posture and graceful movements; how to move in front of the camera; how to walk on the runway; and how to model in groups. You'll also learn about clothes, makeup, hair, and skin care; nutrition, diet, and exercise; interviewing and social skills; and how to develop poise and self-confidence. These classes can help prepare you for anything you do in life. You'll learn how to best present yourself at a job interview or public speech, including how to dress properly and ask the right questions. It's a good way to learn the right way to do things, and this knowledge will help boost your confidence, especially if you're shy or have low self-esteem.

Reality Check

If a modeling school insists on you having professional photos taken with a photographer of their choosing before you can enroll in their school, RUN FOR THE DOOR! A legitimate modeling school will charge models for a full curriculum, teaching her poise, grace, how to walk on the runway, makeup and hair tips, as well as test shoots, photos, and prints. These monies can be paid in advance or in install-ments. Only illegitimate schools who are running scams will charge crazy fees for photos just to get your foot in the door. Their focus is on making money, not developing talent.

Spotting Modeling School Scams

Even though most modeling schools are ethical, legiti-mate businesses, there are others that are not. They prey on the unsuspecting and the naive, so you need to be on your guard and do some research to protect yourself from their scams. Many modeling schools are attached to modeling agencies; in fact, some of the best modeling schools are affiliated with large, reputable agencies. These affiliated schools will be able to provide you the access you'll need to agents, agencies, conventions, and contests in your area. But other times, schools will be affiliated with agencies that are not reputable.

When a modeling school is associated with an agency, the school and the agency should operate separately. Legitimate modeling agencies make money on a com-mission basis, meaning they get a percentage of the fees you earn working as a model; they don't make money by insisting on being paid up front, whether it's for classes or special photos. You shouldn't be required to enroll in the modeling school before the agency will represent you. Good schools will also give you a realistic assessment of your chances to become a model, and they won't promise you will work if you enroll at their school.

The Cheapest Way to Find an Agent

Say you're unable to attend a model search or convention (maybe you just missed it, or the closest one is too far away). There aren't any modeling agencies near you, and you're not able to travel to a big city for an open call. Or maybe you're not the fashion model type, but you think you could break into the industry as a parts model, plus-size model, or older model. Don't despair! There's a quick and easy way to get in touch with an agent for just the price of postage!

All you need to do is to send several snapshots of yourself to a few of the agencies listed in Appendix C, "Directory of Modeling Agencies," in the back of this book. Just ask a friend or family member who's handy with a camera to take some photos of you (follow the tips in Chapter 6). Although some agencies require additional shots, generally all you need is around six pictures. Be sure to write your name, phone number, and measurements on the back of each photo.

Along with the photos, you'll want to include a letter of introduction and your statistics card (see Chapter 6). Include a self-addressed, stamped envelope, put it all in an envelope, and send it off! If you don't receive a response within two weeks, call to make sure your photos were received and request (politely) they return them, along with any comments.

Although this method of contacting an agency is easy and inexpensive, it has one big disadvantage—agents aren't getting to meet you, so they can't see what you look like in person and what a great personality you have. Still, with so little to lose (the cost of the photos and postage), it's worth taking the chance.

Not Model Material?

If you've tried everything to break into the modeling business but have gotten no positive feedback, you may need to face the fact that fashion modeling is not for you. But this definitely does not mean that you aren't pretty and attractive! Keep in mind that many famous beauties, including many Hollywood actresses, don't have the necessary requirements to be a model.

And sometimes, even girls with all the basic qualifications (age, height, weight) aren't able to break into the business, even after going to numerous open calls, model searches, and conventions. If you've been receiving a lot of rejections, ask for comments on your look and advice on how you can make yourself more suitable and marketable as a model. If you still can't seem to break in, it doesn't mean you aren't beautiful, it just means that modeling isn't the career for you.

Fortunately, modeling is just as glamorous behind the camera as in front of it. There are many other ways you can get involved in the fashion industry, such as:

➤ Photographer

➤ Clothing designer

➤ Model scout

➤ Model booker

➤ Hairstylist

➤ Makeup artist

➤ Clothing stylist

➤ Magazine writer or editor

To find out more about careers in these fields, contact your local university, community college, art center, or art school (for more information on photography); a journalism school at a local university (for careers in magazine writing or editing); local beauty school (if you're interested in becoming a hairstylist or makeup artist); or the Fashion Institute of Technology in New York City (for careers in fashion design and merchandising). Another good idea is to ask the model scouts at the next model search in your area—they'd be happy to direct you to the right people.

The Least You Need to Know

➤ Open calls at a modeling agency are one of the best ways to find an agent.

➤ Model searches are great ways to be seen by model professionals from New York.

➤ Modeling conventions expose you to agents from a number of agencies, increasing your chances of catching someone's eye.

➤ Modeling schools can help you develop poise, grace, and modeling skills.

➤ The cheapest way to find an agent is to mail in pictures of yourself to an agency.

110

Chapter 8

Modeling for Experience (Hobby Modeling)

In This Chapter

➤ What is hobby modeling?

➤ Where to find hobby–modeling jobs

➤ How hobby modeling can lead to bigger and better things

There are basically three different stages of a fashion model's career: hobby modeling in your hometown, which is like an unpaid internship for fun and experience; professional modeling in local and secondary markets (various big cities around the country); and big-time modeling in the fashion capitals of Milan, Paris, and New York.

While many big-time models started out as hobby models, not every hobby model moves onto professional modeling in a secondary market or in the fashion capitals. Some may discover they don't really like modeling all that much, or maybe they become interested in pursuing other careers but enjoy modeling as a hobby. In this chapter we'll discuss the first phase of modeling and how you can get involved.

Getting Started: Hobby Modeling

The first stage of modeling is *hobby modeling,* also called *modeling for experience.* The types of jobs a hobby model might do include modeling in fashion shows at the malls, at hair shows for a local salon, or for local newspaper advertisements. These jobs are generally done for the experience, so girls are usually not paid. At this stage, a girl might also be doing test shoots for experience, which we discuss in Chapter 13, "Testing, Testing, 1, 2, 3: Test Shoots." Hobby modeling can be done almost anywhere in the country. My very first hobby-modeling jobs were in Peoria, Illinois—not exactly a raging metropolis!

Mod Squad

I still vividly remember my first modeling job. I was hired to stand in the display window of a boutique at the mall and pretend I was a mannequin while dressed in some of the latest fashions. I found the job by going to the local mall and asking the managers of stores there if they used models. In one of the upscale boutiques in the mall, the store manager told me they didn't normally use models, but that sometimes they let girls come in and pose as dress mannequins in the display window. There was no pay, but I didn't care: I was just so happy to finally have my first real modeling job.

Modeling for experience is done both by very young girls (ages 13 to 15) who are interested in exploring the possibilities of a career on the catwalk and by people who have fun modeling but don't want to make a career of it.

Catwalk Talk

Hobby modeling and **modeling for experience** are two terms that mean the same thing: modeling that is done primarily for the experience and fun of it. Hobby modeling is usually unpaid.

Some girls, however, skip the hobby stage. Either they're natural-born models who are blessed with the ideal physical makeup and temperament, or an incredible opportunity arises (they're recruited by a big New York agency, for instance) before they've even gotten to the hobby-modeling stage.

Although you generally don't get paid for hobby modeling, the experience and knowledge you gain from it is extremely valuable: This is the time to figure out if you have the temperament for the modeling business. Can you stand to sit still for two hours while your hair and makeup are being done? Do you enjoy being the center of attention on a fashion runway? Do you love to have your picture taken? Do you like the way you look in pictures? When you do modeling for experience, these jobs will let you explore how well-suited you are to modeling and if you have the necessary physical requirements, the right temperament, as well as the desire to pursue it further.

Reality Check

Someone who does hobby modeling generally doesn't have an agent, because most of the work is unpaid. This means that a hobby model needs to find her own jobs, which can be frustrating.

Modeling for experience can be done almost everywhere in the country. In fact, it's actually a disadvantage to be in one of the fashion capitals (Paris, Milan, and New York) and other fashion centers in the United States (Chicago, Miami, and Los Angeles), where you'll be competing with professional models for the same jobs.

Models Wanted: Looking for Hobby-Modeling Jobs at Local Shops

It's good to use the resources available to you in your town—modeling in mall fashion shows, displays for store windows, fashion shows for local designers, or in school fashion and other productions—to familiarize yourself with the industry and to test yourself to see if this is something you really want to do. Remember that while some of these jobs will pay, most of the time you'll be doing them for free.

One of the best places to start looking for modeling jobs is your local mall. Most malls have fashion shows, sponsored by individual stores, by several stores, or by the mall itself. Newspapers and local news publications may have listings that specify that models are needed for hair shows, music videos, or exhibition conventions that come to town (car shows, etc.). But be careful with newspaper ads, they can be scam heaven. When answering these ads, ask as many questions possible to make sure the job is legit. Or take a male friend, parent, or guardian to ads that you answer in person.

To get involved with the fashion scene at your local mall, Erin Lundgren, tour coordinator for the Elite Model Look model search, suggests calling the mall and asking if they have a teen board or fashion board. These boards consist of a group of local people who sign up at their local mall to be part of mall fashion events.

"A lot of the malls have teen boards or fashion boards," Lundgren says. "I always suggest this to girls who aren't sure they want to model or don't have the money to go to a modeling school. It's a really good way [to get into modeling]." She explains that every six months to a year, the boards select a new group of models. These models will be involved in any fashion-related events at the malls, including fashion shows and other special promotional events. They also have links to local fashion events in the community. "A lot of the fashion boards and teen boards actually help us when we do our events [for the Elite Model Look], so they're getting some experience with that," says Lundgren.

Reality Check

When you're talking to adults in business situations, whether they be model scouts, agents, store managers, or store customers, don't talk to them in the same casual way, using the same slang, that you use when you're talking to your peers. Avoid slang, trendy words and expressions, and of course, cuss words. Treat people with respect and courtesy; it will pay off, because they will take you more seriously.

Becoming a Part of the Fashion Scene

According to Lundgren, joining and working with a teen or fashion board is "a way to kind of put you into the fashion scene, to learn how to dress and how to act in interviews. It's kind of a whole learning experience. You're actually getting to model, to see if you like it. I would say, without having to go to an agency, [joining a fashion board] is probably one of the best things you can do. All you have to do is call your local mall and ask if they have a fashion board or a teen board." Because fashion boards use people of all ages, from toddlers to senior citizens, you're never too old or too young to join.

Catwalk Talk

Fashion boards, also known as **teen boards,** are groups sponsored by malls that provide models for modeling events at the mall. They're a great way to try out modeling.

Roshumba's Rules

When you're looking for modeling jobs for experience, wear something simple and classy: a skirt or tailored pants and a blouse or sweater, and no hose or flesh-tone hose, depending on the season.

In addition to getting on fashion and teen boards, it's a good idea to visit individual businesses in the mall to see if they use models. First stop: the large department stores, such as JCPenney, Sears, Nordstrom, Bloomingdale's, Macy's, and Marshall Field's. Go to all the various women's clothing departments—juniors, misses, casual wear, designer—and talk to the sales clerks.

Introduce yourself politely, then ask if they ever use models for fashion events. If the salespeople aren't sure, ask them to call the manager and ask her. If they do use models, you're in luck! If they don't, ask them if they can refer you to someone who does. Retail professionals often network frequently with the managers and employees in other stores and malls and can be a great source of information.

You might also want to stop by the personnel department of the larger stores and ask if they ever use models for fashion shows or other events, and if they would consider using you. (The personnel department may not be responsible for hiring models, but often it can direct you to the person who is.)

Other Potential Employers

Visit the chain stores in the mall, which may include The Gap, Banana Republic, The Limited, Express, and Strawberry's; as well as upscale boutiques and bridal shops. Again, ask to speak to the store manager; introduce yourself politely, then ask if she ever hires models for fashion shows, in-store promotions, or displays. Also ask her if she's heard of anyone else who uses models.

Another good place to ask is hair salons. Not only do they occasionally sponsor hair shows, but often they are up on a lot of the fashion-related events going on around town.

If someone agrees to use you as a model, congratulations! You've taken the first step on what could be a long catwalk to fame and fortune! Before you leave the store, find out everything you can about the event: what it will entail, where and when it will take place, what will be required of you (hair, makeup, shoes, for instance). Also ask if you will be paid (if you won't be, don't worry; you're doing this for the experience, not the money). Be sure to get the name and phone number of the person giving you the information, as well as the name and number of the person organizing the event.

Roshumba's Rules

When looking for hobby-modeling jobs, try to find those where your hair and makeup will be done by a professional, so you can get a feel for what it's like.

Join (or Start) a Fashion Club

Another way to gain experience in modeling is by joining a fashion club at your school, church, or community center. If one doesn't exist, look into starting one. Here are some of the things you could do as part of a fashion club:

➤ Put on fashion shows featuring either clothes from local stores or the creations of sewing and fashion-design students.

➤ Take field trips to the mall to get makeovers to update your look (be sure to call ahead, however).

➤ Invite guest speakers to come and teach you how to do your hair and makeup.

➤ Set up evenings when the club members get together to watch the latest fashion shows on television, such as the VH1 *Fashion Awards,* MTV's *House of Style,* or E! Entertainment Television's *The Making of a Supermodel.*

Finally, let your family and friends know of your interest in doing some modeling. They might hear of someone who needs models for a fashion-related event at your church or a local convention center. As in so many areas of life, it's all about who you know. Word of mouth can be a great source of job referrals.

Safety First!

I believe that getting modeling experience at the mall, local stores, hair salons, and at school- and church-related functions is the safest way to start out. There are a lot of con artists out there who prey on unsuspecting young models. You will probably be most vulnerable to them during this stage in your career, when you're still quite young and inexperienced with the job market in general and the modeling business in particular. Department stores, smaller chain stores, boutiques, and hair salons are all businesses that must maintain good reputations in the community in order to stay in business. The chances of their doing something illegal or unscrupulous to harm or take advantage of a young person are therefore slim.

The Things You'll Learn

Hobby modeling allows you to acquire the modeling skills you'll need for the next phase of your career. You'll learn how to walk in high heels, carry yourself in an evening dress, show off a beautiful garment to its best advantage, and walk gracefully down the runway. You'll learn about fine clothes and grow more comfortable being around sophisticated adults. You'll become more conscientious about taking care of your body, skin, hair, and teeth, and you'll learn tips for applying makeup and styling your hair.

Besides allowing you to gain actual modeling skills, hobby modeling will give you a preview of the determination and spunk you'll need to pursue modeling in a secondary market or in the big-time fashion capitals. If you have the grit it takes to go to the mall and ask store managers to consider using you as a model, that will give your self-confidence an incredible boost, and give you a great advantage over other models, when the time comes for you to see the model editor of *Vogue,* who's considering you for a fashion spread. If you can make a success of modeling for experience—being on time, following directions, working harmoniously with fashion professionals, and being patient and respectful—you'll be one step ahead of the competition at the next stage of your modeling career.

Also, jobs that give you a chance to walk on the runway and show garments are really important. Being familiar with the runway helps you get a feel for how your body moves, feels, and looks on a runway. It also helps to prepare you for performing in front of a live audience, which can be very scary until you get used to it.

Test shoots for experience, inexpensive, amateur photo shoots done just for the experience, which I discuss at length in Chapter 13, will help you become more comfortable in front of the camera—something that's very important once you move into the realm of professional modeling.

I know that for me, all my hobby-modeling experience paid off when I arrived in Paris and went to work for Yves Saint Laurent on my second day in town. I'd already acquired a lot of the knowledge and skills needed. I wasn't intimidated, I wasn't fumbling, and I wasn't making dumb mistakes, like sitting in an expensive evening gown and wrinkling it after it was pressed, or folding my arms and wrinkling the sleeves of an elegant business suit.

Roshumba's Rules

When you're wearing a garment that wrinkles easily, be very careful of how you move in it. Don't sit down in it or don't bend your arms; don't do anything that will cause it to wrinkle.

When Saint Laurent spoke to his team, I knew how to stand quietly and patiently and wait for him to explain how to fix a garment that did not fit properly. I learned to quickly figure out what effect he was looking for—whether it's a masculine effect for a tailored suit or a soft, sensuous look for an evening gown. When he asked me to walk around during a fitting, I already knew how to be graceful, classy, and elegant because I had gained experience as a hobby model at the local mall.

Why You Don't Want to Make Your Modeling Debut Center Stage

To try to learn these sorts of things (confidence, poise, and grace) in the professional arena, however, can be awkward. The pace in the fashion world can be frenzied and people don't have time to stop and explain every little thing. Also, you don't want to embarrass yourself in front of other models, because the environment is often very competitive.

Mod Squad

Another one of my first modeling jobs was doing informal in-store modeling at a local boutique. The store would have local girls come in and model the latest collection of dresses in the store. The customers would be able to admire how the dresses looked on the models and judge whether or not they wanted to buy them. After doing my own hair and makeup, I would put on a dress, and then wander around the store for about half an hour. Not only did I learn a lot about how to best show fine clothes, but I grew more comfortable being around older, wealthier, more sophisticated adults, which made the transition to professional modeling much easier.

It takes time to learn how to carry your body and interpret a designer's vision; you don't just wake up with those skills. A good analogy is playing tennis. The first time you pick up a racquet you don't want to find yourself center court at Wimbledon. It's a lot better to learn the basics of the game on a public court in your hometown.

Erin Lundgren agrees that modeling for experience can really give a girl an edge when she starts her professional career. "It's so good for the girls' confidence," she says. "Because when you come to New York, you're in this big city going to casting calls with hundreds and hundreds of girls. You have to have something that's going to make you stand out over everybody else, and your personality is going to be that thing. Of course, at first it's going to be how you look, but after that it's going to be your personality that's going to [make you stand out] from those 300 other girls who are at that casting. If you don't have the confidence, you're not going to do as well, because you're going to come off as shy. You're not going to click in [the clients'] minds; they won't really remember you."

For me, every single "job"—whether it was posing as a mannequin in the store window or modeling in fashion shows at the mall and at my church—was invaluable for my growth as a model. Even though I didn't get paid, they were worth their weight in gold to me.

A Great Confidence Builder

Hobby modeling helped me find the confidence I needed to get on a plane and fly to Paris, even though I didn't know anyone there and didn't speak a word of French at the time. Although I was really gung-ho about modeling, it was only after being a hobby model that I felt confident, experienced, and prepared enough to go. It also gave me some sense of what professional work was like.

Finally, the best part about hobby modeling is that it's so much fun. It's a great feeling to have the whole audience admiring you as you walk the runway, no matter where that runway is. I remember my hobby-modeling jobs with special fondness because at that time I felt very awkward. I was 16, 5'10", and about 115 pounds. So I was taller than most of the kids my age, and had been since I was about 13. I was so skinny that most of the clothes I wore had to be altered or custom made because they were either too big or too short. Walking on the runway in my hometown in front of my family and friends made me feel so special because instead of feeling embarrassed about the way I looked, I felt proud and beautiful.

Modeling Experiences You *Don't* Want

While you are modeling for experience, you are in a particularly vulnerable state: Most hobby models are very young, and their desire to model may occasionally cloud their judgment. But you should definitely just say no to anyone who offers you drugs, tries to get you to pose nude, demands sex in exchange for a modeling job, or wants you to pay him to hire you to model.

These are not the kinds of experiences that will benefit your future modeling career, nor will they enhance your growth and development as a person. As a matter of fact, they may harm your chances of making it as a model, and they will certainly have a negative impact on your self-esteem, self-confidence, and peace of mind. So avoid them at all costs. (See Chapter 11, "Advice for Parents," for more advice about spotting scams.)

Roshumba's Rules

I strongly urge you to tell your parents, school guidance counselor or teacher, or another trusted adult about any negative experiences you have while modeling for experience. Let them decide whether the police should be called.

Fortunately, I had mostly positive experiences as a hobby model, which is why I strongly encourage all aspiring models to get involved. My first modeling jobs offered invaluable experience: They helped me learn how to walk on the runway and other modeling techniques. I also learned about clothes and fashion and how to do my own hair and makeup. They increased my confidence and sense of responsibility.

And if I can start a modeling career in Peoria, Illinois, the quintessential American small town, you can start yours anywhere!

The Least You Need to Know

➤ Hobby modeling is the first stage of modeling. It's a great way to explore modeling and whether it's right for you and to learn modeling techniques and gain self-confidence.

➤ Hobby-modeling jobs are available almost everywhere in the country; the best place to look is the local mall.

➤ Often hobby modeling can be a springboard to a professional modeling career.

Chapter 9

Modeling Professionally in Secondary and Local Markets

> **In This Chapter**
>
> ➤ Finding out about the major secondary and local markets
>
> ➤ Why these markets may be the best choice for you
>
> ➤ What kinds of modeling jobs will you be doing?
>
> ➤ Getting started in secondary and local markets

Modeling professionally in a secondary or local market is the intermediary step between hobby modeling (which I discussed in Chapter 8, "Modeling for Experience (Hobby Modeling)") and big-time modeling (which I'll tell you about in Chapter 10, "Modeling in the Fashion Capitals"). Unlike hobby modeling, this stage is considered professional modeling, since you're usually paid for your work. Also, professional models in secondary and local markets almost always have a modeling agent who represents them and helps them find jobs.

Some models spend their whole careers in secondary markets, for any number of reasons, which I'll also discuss. But spending time in a secondary or local market is also a great intermediary step for a model who wants to give big-time modeling a shot; it gives a model skills and experience that will be of great benefit when she moves on to the intensely competitive world of big-time modeling. In this chapter, I'll also discuss which types of models do best in local and secondary markets and which types may have a better shot as a big-time model.

What Are the Secondary and Local Markets?

When industry insiders talk about *secondary* and *local markets* in the United States, they're basically referring to any city outside of New York City, which is considered a fashion capital, where a majority of models live and work. New York City, along with the European fashion capitals of Milan and Paris, are considered the three fashion capitals of the world because so many fashion and cosmetic companies, fashion magazines, and advertising agencies are based there.

Models in the fashion capitals Milan, Paris, and New York are considered big-time models, because they are working for top national and international magazines, shooting lucrative advertising campaigns and TV commercials, and working for the highest-end catalogs and the most famous fashion designers.

The three major secondary markets in the United States—Chicago, Miami, and Los Angeles—don't have the intense concentration of fashion designers, cosmetic companies, and advertising clients who hire models. These three cities do, however, have a sizable number of clients who hire models, including catalogs, advertisers, TV commercial producers, and to a lesser extent, magazines and newspapers. This is where the majority of models who aren't located in New York live and work.

Other big cities, such as Atlanta, Boston, Toronto, Dallas, and Nashville, are considered local markets, because they have limited opportunities for models. Except for retail stores and beauty salons, there are few fashion-oriented businesses. Generally, models in these cities are hired for local advertisements and TV commercials.

Each secondary market is known for having specific types of clients. Following is a quick survey of each one.

Catwalk Talk

The **secondary markets** in the United States are Chicago, Miami, and Los Angeles. **Local markets** refers to any other city in the country (with the exception of New York, which is a fashion capital).

Mod Squad

Cindy Crawford is a textbook case of a model who started out as a hobby model then moved onto secondary-market modeling. Her first modeling job was appearing in a fashion show at a local store in her hometown of DeKalb, Illinois. Soon afterward, she volunteered to model in a hair styling show sponsored by Clairol in Chicago, the closest secondary market. Then an agency there agreed to represent her; they recommended that she have her famous mole removed, but she refused. She quickly snagged her first professional job—a bra ad for local retailer Marshall Field's. Soon after, she was so busy modeling she was forced to rearrange her school schedule so she could model every day in Chicago.

Chicago

Chicago is a major catalog and advertising market. Many, many catalogs are shot there, says Erin Lundgren, a model scout with Elite Model Look model search, so there's a constant stream of work for catalog-type models. That huge Spiegel catalog that takes up your whole mailbox is headquartered in Chicago, as are many smaller catalog houses. Many of the major retailers, including JCPenney, Sears, and Marshall Field's, do shoots in Chicago.

Chicago also has a sizable number of advertising agencies who hire models for everything from McDonald's commercials to advertisements for hotels.

There's a limited amount of editorial work in Chicago, mainly for the local newspapers (the *Chicago Tribune* and the *Chicago Sun-Times*) and for local magazines such as *Chicago* magazine. There is also some runway work for consumer fashion shows, as well as *in-store modeling*.

Catwalk Talk

With **in-store modeling** (which is also called informal modeling), the models are dressed in the clothes from the store; they walk around and let the customers see the clothes up close as they shop.

Miami

Over the past 10 years, Miami has developed into a major modeling center. The enormous popularity of South Beach (an ultra-cool section of Miami Beach that is jam-packed with restaurants, clubs, hotels, and modeling agencies), combined with the warm weather (which makes year-round outdoor shoots possible) and the celeb quotient (Madonna and Sylvester Stallone both have houses in the area) have all contributed to the growth of the fashion market there.

Although it has a reputation for being all-bathing-suit shoots, much of the modeling work in Miami is for the various catalogs that are shot there because of its scenic locations and warm weather; the majority of clients are from national and international marketplaces. Local advertising agencies also hire models to appear in TV commercials and print ads for area businesses.

In addition to catalogs and advertisements, Miami also attracts high-fashion, editorial clients, according to Lundgren. "South Beach has become such a big fashion center; they're doing a lot of fashion shoots there. I know *Women's Wear Daily* just did a huge, really nice photo shoot in Miami. So that's a really good market right now."

There is also a limited amount of runway work, including consumer fashion shows and in-store modeling.

Los Angeles

Because there are so many TV studios there, numerous TV commercials are shot in Los Angeles, says Lundgren. L.A. is also a good destination if you're interested in getting into acting as well as modeling. Because of the large number of teen publications based in the area, there's also a lot of work for junior-type models. With the beautiful weather, there's a lot of swimsuit modeling as well.

There is also a limited amount of runway work, including consumer fashion shows and in-store modeling.

The Major Local Markets

Other big cities, such as Atlanta, Boston, Toronto, Dallas, and Nashville, are considered local markets, because they have (at most) small numbers of fashion and beauty businesses, and because they offer more limited opportunities for models. Generally, models in these cities are hired for local advertisements and TV commercials; there is also the occasional consumer fashion show and in-store modeling event.

The major markets produce and hire models for the big national ads, but think about the advertising circulars you get in your mailbox and with your Sunday newspaper. Chances are they were created by a local ad agency, who hired the models from a local modeling agency.

Television work is available just about everywhere as well. Locally produced commercials, like those you see for car dealerships and other local retail and service establishments, all provide work for local models. Models may also be hired for consumer fashion shows sponsored by local retailers or malls.

In these smaller markets, there is virtually no high-fashion advertising or magazine work, says Lundgren. "Fashion has really targeted certain markets, and if you're outside of that market, the opportunities for other types of work are just not there." Following is Lundgren's up-close view of a few local markets around the country.

"Atlanta is primarily a catalog market," she reports. "It's starting to come up, but it's not a huge market yet." Toronto is another strong market, and it's one of the only markets where there is high-fashion editorial and advertising work. "They even work a lot of high fashion," she says. "We have an Elite there, and they do exceptionally well. They've even done stuff for Armani and Chanel."

Roshumba's Rules

You may want to consider taking acting or broadcasting classes, which will give you a leg up in landing TV commercials. Modeling in television commercials is available in just about every market and is a big source of work for local models.

Although it's still a small player, models in Dallas have been doing pretty well. Lundgren explains that it's a market where editorial models—models who have the quirky looks preferred by magazines these days—have trouble getting work. "Texas is very [into the] homecoming queen, beauty pageant girls. It's very commercial and catalog," she says. But if you're that type, you could find a steady stream of work. (I'll discuss editorial versus commercial models a little later in this chapter.)

"In Nashville, they do a lot of music videos, mostly country. I know some girls we have who lived in that area and done music videos," adds Lundgren.

Why Secondary Markets Can Be the Best Choice

There are two kinds of models in secondary and local markets: those who will work there for their whole careers and those who spend a couple of years working there gaining experience and waiting until they're old enough to move on to big-time modeling.

Many models can benefit by staying in secondary markets for their whole careers, instead of trying to break into modeling in a fashion capital, says Lundgren. "I see thousands of girls every year, but probably only 10 to 15 of them will actually make it as an *editorial model* [a big-time model in New York]. The majority of them will be more *commercial models* [also called catalog models], who won't benefit by coming to New York, because New York is more high-fashion. They could benefit [from staying in a] local market, doing local work, like catalogs or runway shows in department stores. Girls shouldn't overlook their local market; they shouldn't think they can only make it in New York. Your local market can be as fulfilling."

How can you tell if you have what it takes to make it in New York and the other fashion capitals? Not only do you need to meet every one of the physical requirements (height, weight, body proportions, dress size, and so on) we talked about in Chapter 3, "Do You Have What It Takes?" but you also need a high degree of perseverance, self-confidence, motivation, sense of self, and all the other mental requirements we talked about in the second part of Chapter 3. In addition, there are certain model types who fare better in the fashion capitals and certain types who thrive in local markets.

Catwalk Talk

Commercial models work primarily in local or secondary markets and appear mainly in catalogs and advertisements. **Editorial models,** also known as high-fashion models, work in the fashion capitals where they appear in magazine stories, designer fashion shows, and high-end advertisements.

High-Fashion Models vs. Commercial Models

As we've seen, much of the work in secondary markets is commercial (catalog and advertising) work, as opposed to high-fashion (magazine and high-end advertising) work. Commercial work requires a different type of model—a pretty, wholesome-looking type who will appeal to the average American consumer. Basically, the catalog-commercial girl has that "all-American girl" look—pretty, healthy looking, and appealing. She can be a Classic Beauty, an Amazon, an Athletic Girl Next Door, or sometimes a Barbie (see Chapter 5, "Which Look Are You: The Seven Basic Model Types," for more information on the different types of models).

An editorial model, on the other hand, has more of a quirky or exotic high-fashion look. These girls are often more striking or unusual than classically pretty. Oddballs, Exotic types, Chameleons, and sometimes Amazons can fall into the category of high-fashion models. Classic Beauties that fit into the high-fashion world of modeling usually radiate a special magic or have other qualities that make them stand out.

Oddball models such as Kristen McMenamy, for instance, are highly successful editorial models who probably wouldn't have had much success doing commercial work because their look is so radical and so extreme. Kristen provokes strong reactions from people—both negative and positive.

Mod Squad

Kristen McMenamy is not what you'd call a conventional beauty: She's tall, rail thin, and androgynous looking; her hair is cropped, her eyebrows are shaved, her nose is outsized, and her eyelids are droopy. Although she's far from commercial looking—you'll probably never see her in a Liz Claiborne ad or a Cover Girl commercial—Kristen is a very successful model. Her career took off at a time when the fashion world had (temporarily) grown weary of the Classic Beauties generally found on the catwalk and in front of the cameras. She's been called the queen of anti-fashion fashion, and to prove her coming of age, she has appeared in photo shoots for Versace and Karl Lagerfeld, in countless magazines, as well as on the cover of American *Vogue*.

Until the 1980s, pretty, wholesome-looking models (especially blue-eyed blondes) dominated both the commercial and high-fashion realms. But the emergence of dark-haired, olive-skinned beauties such as Cindy Crawford, Chameleons such as Linda Evangelista, and Oddballs such as Kate Moss, changed the editorial landscape. "Editorial has [undergone] such a change from the Christie Brinkleys," notes Lundgren. While this type of pretty, wholesome, smiling, all-American blonde was considered a perfect editorial model in the late 1970s and early 1980s, now she would might be considered more a catalog-commercial type.

Roshumba's Rules

Market yourself to the people who will be interested in buying you and your look. If you're a catalog-commercial type, that would be clients who want your look, i.e., clients in local markets.

Still, some models who have more of a commercial-catalog look manage to have successful editorial careers. "Niki Taylor, I would say, is really more commercial-catalog ... But she's still a very successful model," says Lundgren. "She does more catalog work ... and TV commercial work, than runway work or high-fashion work. But you also have your Tatiana Patitz, who's a beautiful girl, but she also does editorial. It really depends on how they photograph [as well as the type of model they are]."

But just because a model doesn't have the quirky or exotic looks that clients in New York, Paris, and Milan currently prefer doesn't mean that local clients in Miami or Los Angeles, who may have different requirements, may find her ideal for appealing to people in the immediate area. The bottom line is: You want to figure out which type of model you are, which will be one of the factors you can use in determining which direction your career should take.

Other Reasons for Staying in Your Local or Secondary Market

There are other reasons besides marketability why some models choose not to move on to big-time modeling, but instead spend their whole careers in secondary markets. One big reason is that they are comfortable with the quality of the work they are doing in a local market. Maybe they have lucrative catalog clients who book them regularly. Maybe they do numerous advertising shoots and TV commercial jobs and are making a good living. They're satisfied with the quality and amount of work they're getting, and they see no real reason to give up steady work to move on to New York or another fashion capital.

Another reason models may opt to stay in a local market is that they're not ready, willing, or able to deal with the full-blown crazy lifestyle of an international model— the intense competition, the high rates of failure, the grinding schedule, and the often back-stabbing atmosphere.

Other models may stay in their local markets because they are attending college, or they don't want to leave their families or boyfriends behind and move to New York, Paris, or Milan. They may be big stars in their local markets, and they're very happy with their current situations. Besides, models in secondary markets can have a lot more career longevity than models in the fashion capitals.

Another possibility is that they may have tried to get their foot in the door in New York or another fashion capital, but physically, they weren't the right type. Maybe they were a couple inches too short, their bodies weren't the right proportions for more upscale or national clients, or they didn't have the right look (the fashion capitals tend to prefer Oddballs, Chameleons, and Exotic types).

Modeling Mastery

Even if you know you want to give big-time modeling a try, it's still a good idea to spend a year or two modeling professionally in a secondary or local market, instead of jumping right into big-time modeling without any experience.

Even if you've done extensive hobby modeling (see Chapter 8), you'll gain many important additional skills and professional modeling experience working in a local

Reality Check

You may not want to be in a fashion capital when you're 15 or 16, because your body may be going through some awkward changes: You may still be growing, your skin may have a tendency to occasionally break out, and even your hair may undergo changes. By 17 or 18, you'll be ready to move on, *if* you decide you want to pursue big-time modeling.

or secondary market. Everything you do at this stage can help prepare you for big-time modeling: Modeling professionally in a local or secondary market will help you develop your ability to work with industry professionals and learn to develop yourself into a marketable product. It will help you conquer your fears and insecurities and develop increased confidence.

You'll learn how to start to develop and maintain a mutually beneficial relationship with a modeling agent and agency. You'll have the opportunity to learn what it's like to be directed by professional photographers, learn how to best work with different personalities, and how to play up your best attributes in front of the camera. You'll also have a chance to learn how to woo a client and sell yourself. This is the time for developing your interview skills, so you can shine on go and sees (job interviews). If you get nervous meeting new people, this is the time to work it out.

A Great Dress Rehearsal

Your time in the secondary market is where all your growing up and confidence building should be done. Although clients in secondary markets expect professional behavior and standards of work, the atmosphere tends to be a little more low-key and not as intense and fast-paced as in the fashion capitals. Clients in the fashion capitals pay models a lot more and consequently are a lot more demanding when it comes to professional standards. People in the fashion capitals are much less tolerant of panic attacks, temper tantrums, and inexperience from beginning models.

Mod Squad

After graduating from high school, I moved to the secondary market closest to me, Chicago, in order to purse modeling more seriously. My grandmother lived there, so I had a place to stay. I landed a job with a local Chicago fashion designer, Sterling Capricio, who needed a fit model on whom he could fit his designs to see how they hung. I would try on the dresses and stand, walk, or pose in the garments, whatever was required. Sterling taught me all that: how to stand, how to pose, how to walk, and how to present a garment to a designer. That knowledge was invaluable when I got my first job in a fashion capital as a fit model for Yves Saint Laurent.

In New York, Paris, and Milan, it's fast times and big bucks. It's not about nurturing and baby-sitting, because people's time and money are on the line. When you get to the fashion capitals, people are too busy and too impatient to be doing a lot of hand-holding for inexperienced, immature models. In these major markets, girls who always need cajoling and baby-sitting, or who are always throwing temper tantrums, quickly find themselves with a bad reputation throughout the industry, and unemployed soon thereafter.

These photos show me in two different modes. In the one on the left, I'm posing for a catalog, which is typical of the work done in local and secondary markets. In the one on the right, I'm doing a high-fashion editorial shoot, which is a good example of the type of work done in the fashion capitals. Both photos: Charles Tracy.

Working Out the Kinks

Secondary-market modeling is also a great dress rehearsal for that next step. When you do move on to New York, Paris, or Milan, you want to be completely developed already; you want to be a competent professional model. Once you've made the big move to New York, you'll suddenly be competing with Cindy Crawford for big modeling jobs.

You're going to be the underdog, and besides fighting the obvious disadvantages, you don't want to add inexperience and unprofessionalism. You want to be able to arrive in the fashion capitals ready to work: to be able to walk in a runway fashion show or appear in a photo shoot the day you get to New York and know what you're doing.

Reality Check

Even the most beautiful model in the world probably won't get hired if she's so nervous at a job interview that she can't talk to the client. If a model is that uncomfortable in an interview, the client will probably be afraid that she will be absolutely petrified in front of a camera.

When you're ready to venture out to a fashion capital, you want to be savvy, confident, and able to wow that client at an interview, work the camera at a photo shoot, and walk down a fashion runway with confidence.

If you've already had the experience of meeting the representative for the Sears catalog or you've worked with professional photographers developing your craft in a secondary market, you've had a chance to work through and get over some of your fears. You know how to deal with a professional photo shoot. So when you meet the model editor at *Harper's Bazaar,* you know (more or less) what to expect, and you are able to handle the situation. Spending a couple of years in the secondary markets is great for learning to get your nervousness under control.

Are You Ready for Professional Modeling?

You can tell that you're ready to move from hobby modeling to professional modeling in a local or secondary market if you're at least 15 years old and you feel confident and adept at hobby-modeling activities, such as fashion shows at the mall and test shoots for experience. You should have a certain comfort and skill level in front of the camera. Also, your body should not have changed so drastically since you started hobby modeling that you no longer possess the necessary physical characteristics to be a professional model. If you feel competent and confident in all these areas, you're ready to become a professional model in a secondary or local market.

If you're under 18, you'll need your parents' permission to pursue modeling. If you don't yet drive, you will also probably need them to drive you to meetings with agents, job interviews, and actual jobs (unless you're lucky enough to live in a city with good public transportation).

Roshumba's Rules

No matter how sure you are that you can make it as a model, it only makes sense to have something to fall back on, which is why you don't want to drop out of high school to pursue a career.

As a professional model in a secondary market, you'll need a modeling agency to represent you. Agents are the first to find out when a job is being cast. A model working alone doesn't have the resources to find out about every potential booking, nor would it be appropriate for her to call around to ad agencies and potential clients.

Agents help a model fine-tune her look so that she's marketable to local clients. They also screen clients so that a model is not sent into a dangerous situation. In addition, agents handle billings, collections, and other aspects of the money side of things. Finally, if a model decides she wants to move on to big-time modeling, an agent in a secondary or local market may have connections to agencies in fashion capitals, so she can more easily move into big-time modeling.

In Chapter 7, "Finding an Agent," we talked about how to find an agent. Although most model searches are held by New York agencies looking for models to work in the fashion capitals, the other methods of finding an agent (going to open calls at modeling agencies, attending model conventions, and mailing in photos to modeling agencies) are great ways to find an agent in a secondary market. To find modeling agencies in a secondary market, check out Appendix C, "Directory of Modeling Agencies."

In smaller markets, finding a modeling agency may be more difficult. If you don't know of any, and can't find any by word of mouth, try calling a local advertising agency and asking them which modeling agencies they work with. You may also want to try calling an agency in New York or a secondary market near you and ask if they have any recommendations.

The Least You Need to Know

➤ Chicago, Miami, and Los Angeles are the major secondary markets in the United States.

➤ Cities like Atlanta, Boston, Toronto, Dallas, and Nashville are considered local markets because the modeling opportunities are more limited.

➤ Secondary and local markets offer a lot of opportunities for models, including TV commercials and catalog work.

➤ Secondary markets may be the best choice for models with a "commercial" look.

Chapter 10

Modeling in the Fashion Capitals

Big-time modeling means modeling in the three fashion capitals: Milan, Paris, and New York. This is where the majority of models you see in magazines, in advertisements, in fashion shows, and on TV live and work most often.

Big-time modeling means that modeling is your only career, the sole way you support yourself and make a living. By industry standards, it also means that most of your work is done with well-known clients, such as *Vogue,* Donna Karan, Lancôme, and Armani. Some big-time models specialize in catalog work for famous, high-end clients, such as Saks Fifth Avenue, Neiman Marcus, and J. Crew, or do primarily advertising work for clients like Oil of Olay, Clairol, or Hanes Hosiery. Other big-time models specialize in working in runway fashion shows.

But big-time modeling also means facing intense competition, dealing with a lot of rejection, and being subject to the whims of the fashion industry. It's also about being the consummate professional, always being on time, cooperative, pleasant, and professional, and not being difficult because you're hot, or tired, or you hate the outfit you're wearing.

In this chapter, I'll give you an overview of big-time modeling and how you can give it your best shot.

The Fashion Capitals: Milan, Paris, and New York

There's no denying the fact that big-time modeling is extremely competitive. People come to New York and the other *fashion capitals* from every country, city, and small village around the world. It's in the fashion capitals that models can make the biggest bucks and get the best jobs. It's also where you're *least* likely to be able to break into the business.

Catwalk Talk

Milan, Paris, and New York are considered the three **fashion capitals** of the world because so many fashion and cosmetic companies, fashion magazines, and advertising agencies and models are based there.

Catwalk Talk

Your **mother agency** is the agency that discovered you, marketed you, and developed your career. If you've changed agencies in the course of your career, your mother agency is your base agency, located in the city you call home.

The first step to getting into big-time modeling is finding an agent. It's impossible to break into modeling in the fashion capitals without one; most clients won't even see a model who isn't represented by an agent. (Check out Chapter 7, "Finding an Agent," for more information on finding an agent.) American models generally acquire an agency in New York, which is known as their *mother agency*. Often, a model is still in school when she's signed by a New York agency; although she doesn't quit school, she does come to New York to model on holidays and vacations. Once she has finished high school, she will move to New York to pursue modeling full-time.

Often, a model's mother agency will urge her to go to Milan or Paris, especially if she's having trouble getting started in New York. The mother agency will arrange for a model to be represented by another agency in one of the other fashion capitals, and it will also take care of any necessary working papers (legal documents needed to work in places outside the country of which you are a citizen).

Each fashion capital prefers certain types of models, and each has distinct advantages that can be capitalized on and disadvantages that should be avoided. Let's take a closer look at what they are.

Milan

Milan, Italy, is often the first stop for a model who wants to launch a big-time international modeling career. Clients in Milan are known for preferring new faces with a young, fresh, untouched look, as opposed to more established models who may have been around for a while.

That's why it's the perfect place to go to work professionally when you're just starting out. (Still, it's better if you have an agency in New York that has referred you to an agency overseas. New York is American models' link to the international fashion world.) You'll have the best chance of building your portfolio and filling it with great tear sheets from internationally recognized clients (I'll tell you more about tear sheets in Chapter 14, "Tools of the Modeling Trade"). It's also ideal for building a name, image, and reputation on the runway and in front of the camera, and establishing your presence as an up-and-coming professional in the international market.

Another plus is that there are all types of work in Milan. It's full of magazines, advertising clients, and fashion designers who are willing to give newer models a chance.

Because so many of the major fashion designers are based there, and because it's such a style-conscious city, Milan also affords you the opportunity to learn the ABCs of international style. You'll be exposed to models from all over the world, as well as to people from all walks of life.

It's also not too difficult to set yourself up in Milan. Unlike agents in other fashion capitals, agents in Milan are more willing to advance money to beginning models for basic expenses and a place to live. The city has a great public transportation system. The people are willing to speak English and are friendly and open to strangers. They are also fascinated by other cultures and will want to get to know you. Also, Italian men love women from other countries, so you can expect a lot of attention!

Reality Check

Wherever there are a lot of models, there are "modelizers"—playboys whose objective is to be seen with models, have sex with models, and/ or have models pays all their bills. Before you get seriously involved with a guy, get some background from mutual acquaintances. Does he work? Does he pick up the tab at restaurants? Is he interested in spending time alone with you?

Reality Check

If you can't find an agent in the United States it may be because you aren't model material. Know that if you don't have what it takes to be a model at home you may be rejected abroad as well.

Each market has a specific type of model it prefers (although this doesn't mean other types don't stand a chance). In Milan, generally two types of models do well: ones who are curvy yet slim, with natural sex appeal, who are used by designers of sexy clothes, such as Dolce & Gabbana; or girls who are very thin, even boyish, and who have an edgy sort of look and personality that's in demand by clients who want an avant-garde look, such as Giorgio Armani.

If you haven't had any luck finding an agent in the U.S., you may want to try going to Milan on your own, to see if you can find an agent there. Before you leave, you'll need to find out what agents are there (check out Appendix C, "Directory of Modeling Agencies," or call a major agency in New York to get a list of referrals). Plan to go for a week or two to investigate the possibilities and get a sense of the market. Check out travel guides and book a hotel room before you get there.

Paris

Paris, France, is the ultimate dream of what living the life of a model is all about. Paris is the heart of the fashion industry; the industry looks to Paris for innovation and new ideas. It dictates style and fashion trends and decides the next big models, fashion photographers, and designers.

Paris is less about appealing to the mass-market consumer than working with expensive, luxury brands such as Chanel, Yves Saint Laurent, Valentino, and Givenchy.

Roshumba's Rules

Plan to go to Milan and Paris in February or in September, when the ready-to-wear fashion shows take place. It's a time when lots of models are being hired.

If Milan is about establishing yourself as a model, Paris is about building your name and enhancing your prestige: working with the most eminent designers, fashion photographers, and advertising clients. If you can establish your name in Paris, you'll gain prestige and be a part of the pulse of fashion, and your career will be made. Claudia Schiffer was a pretty German girl who broke through when she was taken on by the house of Chanel in Paris. Canadian Linda Evangelista gained fame when photographer Peter Lindberg convinced her to cut her hair. She was then featured on the cover of French *Vogue,* and the fashion industry went wild! Other models and fashion editors started cutting their hair, and the trend spread like wildfire.

It's here where you'll build a portfolio that's filled with high-class clients and where you'll increase your appeal to more well-known fashion designers, fashion photographers, and bigger advertising clients, such as Lancôme, Chanel, and L'Oréal.

In Paris, there's an abundance of magazines, fashion designers, and advertisers—all of whom are quite selective about the models they use. They'll use new models, but the girl has to have that something special, she has to be someone whom the French believe represents la creme de la creme, with class, elegance, and style.

Another good thing about Paris is that you need to find only one person to open the door for you. If one of the fashion powerhouses accepts you, others will, too. If designer Jean-Paul Gaultier thinks you're a wonderful fresh new talent and hires you for his fashion show, it's a good bet that you'll soon be appearing in the most prestigious magazines and important advertisements.

The models favored by clients in Paris are super-skinny or shapely, as well as fresh and youthful looking (if a girl is too sophisticated or world weary, clients feel like she is already developed and that there's nothing to work with). Being open-minded and free-spirited is also important, because the French abhor narrow-mindedness. Ethnic models have traditionally enjoyed a lot of success in Paris as well.

Mod Squad

When I appeared in an Yves Saint Laurent fashion show in 1987, it said to the rest of the fashion industry, YSL is using her, she must have something, so let's give her a chance. Right after that, *Elle, Marie Claire,* and Benetton all booked me for photo shoots. People from every other fashion market in the world keep an eye on what is happening on the Paris runways and in the French magazines, and that snowball effect rolled me right into New York (my ultimate goal). I worked with the most prestigious fashion designers, appeared on covers and pages of world-famous magazines, and hung out with some of the most famous people in the world.

Living in Paris can be really expensive. The city attracts people from all over the world, including many people involved in the fashion industry. Space is very limited and, therefore, expensive. In the beginning, some girls live in the suburbs, where rents are less expensive, or in model apartments (which are often very crowded). Many agencies, if they believe in a girl and feel she has the potential to make it to the top, will front her the money necessary for living expenses until she starts earning the big bucks necessary to support herself.

As with Milan, it's best if you have an agency in New York that has referred you to an affiliated agent in Paris. Again, plan to go for a short period of time, say two weeks, long enough to meet people and get a sense of the market, but not long enough so that you'll need to beg for money. A good time to go is in February and September, when lots of models are hired for the ready-to-wear fashion shows.

Roshumba's Rules

If you spend time in Paris, try to learn some French. The Parisians can be intolerant of people who don't speak their language, and even ordering a bowl of soup can turn into a nightmare!

New York

New York City is *the* place where models make the biggest bucks. Working in New York is a sign you've really made it. After building your name in Milan and establishing your prestige in Paris, New York is where you come to cash in on all that hard work. In New York, you earn the highest rates for advertisements, plus you're given the longest contracts. There's lots of catalog work, and the pay for catalogs is the highest. (In fact, if you can maintain even one catalog client at a really high day rate, you can live off that for years.) Fashion shows also pay higher rates; but the rates for editorial work are pretty much the same everywhere.

New York also offers American models an opportunity to settle down a bit from the frantic modeling lifestyle. It's a good place to build a stable foundation. If you want to get married and start a family, you can still continue to work if you live in New York. (Stephanie Seymour, Daniela Pestova, and Vendela are all married with children and still continue to work.) You can also further your education in New York, if you decide you want to go back to college. It offers many opportunities to prepare for a career after modeling, in fields such as acting, broadcasting, and retail sales.

Roshumba's Rules

You need to put in your time in Paris and Milan if you want a successful, big-time career. You may get lucky, but for the most part, you have to pay your dues in the international marketplace to make it big.

In New York, there are also lucrative opportunities in television, like the deal I have with VH1, as well as opportunities to start other businesses. For example, model Anna Bailey developed a lipstick line called Anna that's sold in major department stores; and Barbara Smith started her own restaurant, B. Smith, in Manhattan, which eventually led to her own Martha Stewart–style TV show.

Living in New York can be extremely hectic. Everybody is doing their own thing full throttle, and they don't have time for other people and their issues. Although you're in the midst of millions of people, you can feel very isolated, because everyone's going in her own direction. It's also very expensive to live in New York, especially in Manhattan. A bare-minimum, one-room apartment can cost as much as $1,500 a month. On the other hand, New York is incredibly fun and full of cultural events (theater, art exhibits, dance, and music of all kinds).

There's not one specific type of model who's most successful in New York. Because America is a melting pot, home to a variety of different types of people, it's important for the fashion market to appeal to as many cultures as possible. That's why many different types of girls are in demand. Models who have done the Paris-Milan circuit and established their names are usually the girls who do best in New York. They land the highest-paying catalog gigs and the biggest ad deals and appear in the top fashion magazines.

Once you've made it in New York, however, a model doesn't just ignore the rest of the world. In order to stay on top, it's important to maintain an international presence, to keep going back to Paris, Milan, and other cities, to replenish your tear sheets, keep a presence on the runway circuit, and appear in ads in the United States, Italy, and France. The minute you start sleeping, someone will come along to take your place.

Modeling in London and Tokyo

London, England, is an important fashion market, but even though modeling opportunities there have increased over the past four or five years, it's still not on par with Milan, Paris, and New York. London has long had a fashion industry, but it was known more for its creativity and avant-garde designs than for its viability and commercial appeal.

138

The increased international visibility of English designers, many of whom (John Galliano, Alexander McQueen, Stella McCartney) have been snatched up by old-line French couture houses, has given new credibility and appeal to the fashion industry in London. In addition, U.K. models such as Kate Moss, Alek Wek, Stella Tennant, and Kirsty Hume have given an English accent to the modeling scene.

The best reason to consider modeling in London is for the editorial work, which is innovative and cutting-edge. Say you're *overexposed* in other markets or your career has stalled. That would be a good reason for going to London—to update your look, work with people who may see you in a new light, and get tear sheets from sessions with photographers who have a different vision of you than people in other markets. Tear sheets from magazines such as British *Vogue,* British *Elle,* and *The Face* could enhance any portfolio.

Catwalk Talk

A model is said to be **overexposed** when she's been working too much in one market—she's appeared in every fashion show, magazine, and ad. Clients get bored with looking at her face and stop hiring her.

Another reason a model would head to London is for a direct (meaning arranged before your arrival) booking, or to start to establish her presence on the London runway shows. The models whose looks sell best in London are quirky, Oddball types, along with Classic English Beauties.

If you feel like you just have to get your career going in an international market and you haven't had much success in Paris, Milan, or New York, you are experiencing a work slowdown, or you just want to make some quick money, try Tokyo, Japan. You go there mainly to make money; anything else is pointless. You may get some tear sheets, but they're not that valuable in other places; in fact, they may make you look like you couldn't get work anywhere else. Japanese love Western culture, so models from Western countries are in high demand. It's a good thing to do if you're having trouble finding work elsewhere.

Generally, models don't go to Tokyo on their own, and you probably wouldn't want to. The language barrier is nearly impossible to break. All of the directions, menus, and other signs are written in Japanese. The society is very closed and isolated, which is why models usually come over under a contract that has been arranged by their mother agency in the United States. Usually, the contract is for a specific period for a certain amount of money ($30,000 for two weeks' work is a common amount). The agent also arranges for housing, a driver, and a guide, so girls don't have to deal with the problems of living there on their own. If you do accept a contract to work in Japan, be prepared to work harder than you ever have before. The Japanese are known for their meticulous preparation: For one fashion show, you could have three fittings and three rehearsals. (One fitting and one rehearsal is the norm elsewhere.)

While in Tokyo you'll gain exposure to a fascinating culture. There are nightclubs and incredible places to shop. And I suggest taking any opportunity (maybe once you've finished your job) that arises to get out of the city and travel around the beautiful countryside: It's breathtaking.

Mod Squad

Even though they're based in one of the fashion capitals, big-time models travel all the time. For example, if you have clients that are based in Texas, such as Neiman Marcus, the photo shoots may be in different locations, and you will have to travel to do all of them. Or you may work with a specific designer on an ongoing basis. Maybe she's doing a fashion show to benefit AIDS research in Los Angeles, then showing a special collection of cashmere in Paris. You would need to travel with her. Life on the road may sound like fun, but it can be lonely and exhausting. Also, you may not get to see your family and friends for months on end.

Are You Ready for the Big Time?

You'll know you're ready to give big-time modeling a shot once you have a portfolio of agency-directed test shots and tear sheets from professional jobs in secondary and local markets that show you at your best, and you feel confident and knowledgeable enough to make the move.

When you come from secondary markets, agents and clients aren't looking for who you worked with; to them, it doesn't matter if you haven't worked in New York, Paris, or Milan. They'll be looking at your portfolio to see your potential in a major market: Who you would appeal to? Would you be able to star in a major hair campaign? Are you right for the latest Versace fashion show? Could you be the next Revlon Cosmetics girl? Are you able to handle the pressure and responsibility of working with high-paying, demanding clients?

Obviously, another way to know you're ready is if an agency in a fashion capital recruits you. Maybe they spotted you in a local publication or catalog, at a model convention or search, or just walking down the street, and they feel your look is right for their clients.

Why You Should Wait to Make Your Move

Unless you get an offer too good to refuse, such as a lucrative advertising contract, I would caution you against moving into the big-time modeling stage too early, before you're 17 or 18. Up until then, you're going through a number of changes that will influence your life: Your hormones are changing, your menstrual cycle may still be irregular, you're meeting your first boyfriends. Your relationship with your family is changing, and school is becoming more intense.

At 18, you're more mature and able to handle things that come up. That's why it's better to wait until you're 18 and you can arrive as a finished "product," instead of a 14-year-old work in progress.

Supporting Yourself Until Your Career Takes Off

It's important to keep in mind that even after you've taken the plunge, moved away from home, and acquired an agent, there's no guarantee you'll be earning $100,000 right away, or even enough money to support yourself. You'll need to be able to pay your rent, telephone, gas, electric, and cable bills, buy food, clothes, and toiletries—you name it—because now you are living in an adult world.

Reality Check

Allow yourself to develop and mature before you move to a fashion capital. If you wait, you may be able to avoid unnecessary embarrassments, such as immature behavior and mistakes caused by a lack of experience. To give a career your best shot, it's better to wait until you're 18 and fully prepared, rather than start too young and be foiled by unsolved emotional and physical issues. I suggest waiting until you graduate from high school.

A Second Job

You may need to supplement your income with another, nonmodeling job. Many models get jobs waitressing or hostessing in restaurants, bars, and clubs (in fact, some hot spots hire only models), doing temporary work, working in retail (I recently saw two young models I know spritzing perfume at the Henri Bendel department store in New York), working as receptionists in beauty salons, and even walking dogs.

If you need to find a job to supplement your career, focus on getting a position that leaves your weekdays open. Most of your go and sees, test shoots, and other modeling-related appointments will be set up during business hours, Monday through Friday.

It's also key to find a job that allows you some flexibility in your schedule, so when you do book a job, you can take the time off to do it, or in case you need to travel. It's best if the job you find also somehow keeps you exposed to the fashion industry. That's why so many models end up working at major departments stores, in boutiques, and at fashionable clubs, bars, and restaurants.

Model Apartments

Many larger agencies provide "model apartments" for young models. These are apartments that are owned or rented by the various modeling agencies for use by their models in the fashion capitals. "Usually they are models who are starting out in the business," explains Karen Lee, director of scouting at Elite Model Management and the house mother of an Elite model apartment in New York City. "They are usually girls

[who] have no housing, who are going to be here anywhere from a week to several months. They are girls that we ask to come to New York, who we want to work with. They come from all over world."

Reality Check

Don't think that living in a model apartment is going to be like living a wild bachelorette life. Many model apartments have chaperones, usually a scout or booker from the agency. There are house rules, and your behavior is monitored. In the Elite model apartment in New York, there is a curfew, and "no boys, no booze, and no drugs" are allowed.

Model apartments aren't just for underage models. "Some are under 18, some are over 18," says Lee. The thing the models have in common is that they haven't yet found a place to live. Girls stay at the model apartment anywhere from one week to several months before they move out on their own. "We help them with finding their own housing after they start to get on their feet a little," adds Lee.

Many of the apartments have a dorm-like feeling. You share living spaces like bathrooms, kitchens, living rooms, and often bedrooms. Sometimes as many as five or six girls can live in one apartment.

Before you sign with an agency, ask its representatives about the availability of model apartments if you think you might want a place to stay when your first arrive.

Moving to a Fashion Capital Without an Agent

Maybe you've done the model search-convention-model school route and still haven't found an agent. If you're adventurous and don't have a problem packing up and moving to a strange new city, and you don't mind working a part-time job on the side (if necessary) to pay the bills until your modeling career gets going, you might consider moving to a fashion capital without acquiring an agent beforehand. This is especially worth considering if you think or you've been told that you have a look that is more desirable in one of the other fashion capitals. I, for instance, went to Paris because I had been told that ethnic models had an easier time breaking in there. But make no bones about it, this is a very risky move.

Roshumba's Rules

If you're going to take on a fashion capital on your own—you're moving there without having acquired an agent beforehand—consider visiting for a week or two first to get a feel for the city and its opportunities.

Before you take off, you need to deal with the fact that although you may do everything possible to break into the business, be extremely beautiful, incredibly professional, have a great attitude, and a portfolio full of pictures from a secondary market, your look may not be appealing to clients in the fashion capitals. There are no guarantees in modeling, and you may still be waitressing full-time five years down the road. But if you're determined to be a model, this might be a worthwhile risk.

The Least You Need to Know

➤ Milan, Paris, and New York are the fashion capitals of the world, and each city offers unique opportunities.

➤ London and Tokyo also present opportunities for modeling.

➤ American models generally acquire an agent in New York, who directs them to the other fashion capitals.

➤ It's best to wait until you're 18 to move to a fashion capital.

➤ Be prepared to take a second job until your modeling career takes off.

➤ Moving to a fashion capital is a risky move, but sometimes it's a risk worth taking.

Chapter 11

Advice for Parents

In This Chapter

➤ Is your teen ready to model?

➤ How you can help your teen pursue a modeling career

➤ Finding a reputable agent

➤ How you can tell if someone is trying to scam you

➤ Advice from the Federal Trade Commission and Better Business Bureau

---

If you're the parent of a teen who's interested in modeling, this chapter is for you. This chapter gives you information for guiding your teen who wants to be a model; we talk about child models in Chapter 22, "Specialty Models." Everyone wants the best for their child, and there's no doubt that modeling offers some great opportunities: to make a lot of money at a young age, travel, meet interesting people, and be exposed to art, culture, and people from around the world. At the same time, you've no doubt heard about all the pitfalls of modeling: the drugs, the predatory men, the eating disorders, the con artists, the warped values.

Even if these things don't come true, it's still scary putting a child, especially a girl, on a plane to a big city where she doesn't know anyone and doesn't know her way around. She may need to find a place to live and a job to support her before her career gets started. And of course, to you, she's still a baby.

So while letting go is never easy, this chapter has advice and tips for helping to make things go more smoothly. I offer my own advice; I asked an expert—my mother, LaVonne Joslin—for her thoughts, and I also asked an agent, Karen Lee, the director of scouting at Elite Model Management in New York, for her advice to parents from an agent's perspective.

Finally, because there are so many scams and swindles out there, I've also included information from the Better Business Bureau and the Federal Trade Commission on avoiding scams and rip-offs.

Advice from a Mother Who's Been There

First, I thought it would be a good idea to talk to the ultimate expert: my mother, LaVonne Joslin, who has stood in your shoes and knows exactly all the things you're thinking and feeling. In the following sections, she offers her expert advice.

How You Can Help Your Teen

"A parent can help her child who is interested in pursuing a modeling career by encouraging the child to follow her dreams, by letting her know it's okay to do so, by believing in her, and having faith in her talents and abilities. Acknowledge her by listening when she talks about her goals and dreams, and don't stand in her way as she sets out to pursue her career. Let her go—but monitor her activities.

"Accompany her as she goes to modeling schools, searches, contests, and other events. Help her organize transportation and arrange for someone to accompany her if you're not available. Ask her the results of these events, and listen when she talks about participating in them. I kept close tabs on all of Roshumba's activities, especially when she was first starting out."

Mod Squad

My mom says: "I first realized Roshumba was interested in modeling when she was about 16. We were living in Peoria, Illinois, and she heard that the Ebony Fashion Fair, a fashion show sponsored by *Ebony* magazine and Fashion Fair Cosmetics, was coming to town. She saved her money and purchased two tickets to the Fair, one for me and one for her. At the event, many people stopped us and asked if she was a model. During the show, I noticed that Roshumba was fixated on the models. After seeing the response of the people at the Fashion Fair to her, and watching how mesmerized she was by the whole scene, I began to take her desire more seriously."

Be Wary, Be Wise

"Be alert when you accompany your child on appointments with modeling agents, scouts, or photographers or to modeling events. Be on the lookout for any people who seem sleazy.

"If a modeling agency offers to represent your child, read the contract carefully to make sure your child is not signing anything that would tie her life up for longer than a year or two at a time. Make sure it's not going to cost her significant sums of money and that she is not required to pose nude or be in pornographic movies. Also be aware if drugs are present.

"Check with the local consumer protection agency [look in the government section of your local phone book], the *Better Business Bureau* [*BBB*] [you can find the number of your local BBB in the white pages of the phone book], or the *Federal Trade Commission* [*FTC*] [202-326-3650] to make sure the company or person you're signing with has a clean reputation, hasn't been involved with any rip-offs, and doesn't have a lot of disgruntled customers. Call the state attorney general's office [look under state government in the government section of the phone book] to make sure the agency hasn't been charged with any crimes involving either false advertising, money, drugs, or sex. [Also, check out the BBB's and the FTC's advice for avoiding modeling scams, coming up a little later in this chapter.]

"The best place to get referrals to established, legitimate modeling agencies is from fashion-related companies, fashionable boutiques, other models, major hair salons, and big New York agencies such as IMG, Next, Elite, and Ford.

"If someone is suggesting that you or your child pay a large sum of money—$500 or $1,000, say— to join the agency or to take pictures, take heed. Legitimate agencies work on commission and make money by booking models for modeling jobs; they don't make money from collecting large registration fees. Although most major agencies will arrange for test shoots for models, the fees are more nominal [Elite's test shoots average $250, and the agency will often pay for it up front]." (See Chapter 13, "Testing, Testing, 1, 2, 3: Test Shoots," for more information.)

Catwalk Talk

The **Better Business Bureau** (**BBB**) is a private, nonprofit organization with offices around the country that provides reports on local businesses. The **Federal Trade Commission** (**FTC**) is a government agency headquartered in Washington that enforces consumer-protection laws.

Is Your Child Ready for the Catwalk?

"Besides knowing that your child is getting involved with people who have her best interests at heart, it's important to know if your child is ready on a personal level to start a professional career. A few ways to tell if your child is ready to move away from home and start a modeling career is if she is self-sufficient: She can take care of her body and hygiene, she can prepare meals for herself, she can eat well and take vitamins, she's confident in public and respectful of others. Observe if she can do these things on her own.

"Other ways to tell if she's ready is that she knows right from wrong: She doesn't take drugs or drink, she doesn't get into trouble at school or with the law, and she stays away from kids who do. She wakes herself up on time for school, gets good grades, and is respectful to siblings, classmates, and authority figures. She obeys school rules and is aware of the consequences of bad behavior.

"It's also possible to tell if your child is *not* mature enough to leave home and start a career. If she cuts school, takes drugs and drinks, is mean or abusive to siblings, gets in trouble with the law, or hangs around with other kids who are known troublemakers, she will only get into worse trouble if she becomes a model. Other signs are: She can't get up in the morning for school on her own, doesn't do her homework, fails classes, and doesn't do household chores without being threatened or punished. Another indication: When she is caught doing something wrong, she always blames the other guy."

Mod Squad

Gia Carangi is one of the tragic casualties of modeling, a story that is told in Stephen M. Fried's book, *Thing of Beauty* (Pocket Books, 1994). Soon after quitting her job in her father's hoagie restaurant in Philadelphia, Gia was appearing on the covers of *Vogue* and *Cosmopolitan*. Even though she was constantly late and unreliable at photo shoots, Gia became one of the most popular models of the late 1970s. But her behavior became increasingly bizarre: After a fashion team had spent hours preparing her and getting her dressed, Gia jumped into a nearby pool, wrecking their efforts. It soon became apparent that she had a serious heroin problem. Despite efforts to get clean, Gia died of AIDS at age 26.

Some Final Words of Advice from My Mother

"Support and encourage your daughter's dreams and efforts; watch out for pitfalls like drugs, sex, being forced into nude modeling, or signing bad contracts that will tie up her career or take all her money. But equally important, don't stand in the way of her pursuing her career and realizing her dreams."

Roshumba's Advice to Parents

My advice to parents is based on my own personal experience with my parent, my observations of others whose careers grew along with mine, and my observations of younger models whom I've worked with once my career as a model was established, and whom I've met while hosting the Elite Model Look model search.

Modeling is a great career for young women both short- and long-term because it offers many advantages. Some models make a lot of money in a short period of time; they can be exposed to other countries, people, and cultures; and modeling can open the door to other careers in television, in film, and behind the scenes in the fashion industry. Because self-discipline, determination, intuition, patience, and self-reliance are the key components to being successful as a model, these qualities, when properly developed, can prepare a young person for success in a variety of fields.

The new models I've observed while hosting the Elite Model Look model search over the past three years have gone from being shy introverts to beautiful, expressive young women who have also developed a sense of self-reliance and accomplishment.

The Good, the Bad, and the Ugly

As with everything else in life, there are good aspects and bad aspects to modeling. The dark side comes into play because the fashion industry can be very decadent. Drugs are easily accessible. Sex is everywhere. Scam and con artists are waiting to take advantage of naive young women at every step of a model's evolution, from beginner to supermodel.

I've seen young, aspiring models who are just starting out get scammed into spending hundreds of dollars on unnecessary photos. I've seen models with great careers ahead of them get sidelined by too much partying. I've also witnessed established models lose everything because they got strung out on drugs, while others lost their hard-earned money because of greedy, conniving boyfriends or husbands.

That's why it's important for models to view modeling as a business opportunity and a way to open the door to a positive future, to know the risks of the fashion industry, and to avoid them. When models start veering too far off track from these goals, they often find themselves in trouble.

Parents can help their children succeed by encouraging them to follow their dreams, supporting their efforts, and monitoring their actions so they don't get hurt or taken advantage of. Read this book and encourage them to read it so they can get a working supermodel's take on the modeling experience. My mother encouraged me to follow my dreams and supported my career efforts by attending fashion shows, photo sessions, and traveling to see me when I asked her to come. Don't stand in their way by telling them they're not model material, that being a model is a stupid career goal, or by just saying no—without first giving them a chance to give it a try.

Reality Check

Some people may feel it's okay to take drugs occasionally or recreationally and that it's possible to take them without getting addicted, but why even take the chance? It has been proven over and over again by musicians, actors, comedians, models, and the everyday person that indulging in drugs is a quick trip down a dead-end street. Don't do it!

Keeping Them Close When They're Far Away

Once your child's career has taken off, you may not be spending as much time with her because she's busy working or maybe she has even left home to pursue modeling. The best way to help out at this point is to realize and accept that your child's life has changed, and don't make her feel guilty or like she made the wrong decision. Keep in close contact with her by phone. Listen to her when she needs to talk. Instead of lecturing her, share positive advice on how to handle difficult situations. If problems arise that neither you nor she is equipped to handle, find another adult or professional who can help her.

It's a good idea to set aside a special time each week to talk to your daughter once she's embarked on her modeling career in order to keep abreast of everything she's up to.

Help her manage and make the most of her career by making sure that she has a legitimate, knowledgeable accountant to handle her money; that she sets up savings accounts, trust funds, retirement funds, and makes sound investments. (Many models have lost their entire nest eggs because they let friends, boyfriends, or other nonprofessionals manage their money.) Help her find a competent lawyer to look over work-related contracts so she doesn't sign anything that is detrimental to her career and well-being. Also, encourage her to plan for a future outside of modeling.

Roshumba's Rules

When your child moves away, especially if it's overseas, set a specific time each week when you can talk on the telephone. I tried to call my mom every Saturday morning, when I knew she would be home.

Handling Sibling Rivalry

Another issue that may surface once a child's modeling career has geared up is sibling rivalry. This can be tough, especially if one child is famous and the others are not. Since I'm close to my immediate family, I was able to observe how my mother handled minor envious outbreaks. If someone felt left out or less important, my mother would explain to my sibling that God blessed everyone with a special gift and we all must find that gift and develop it. She would support and encourage my siblings' efforts with their education and respective careers as well. Overall it's best to be a wise friend and confidante whose primary interest is to make sure all your children are happy, healthy, and safe from harm, and to encourage and support them on their individual journeys.

Advice from an Agent

A good, reputable agent is essential to getting the most out of a modeling career, according to Karen Lee, the director of scouting at Elite Model Management in New York. It's key that an aspiring model find not only a reputable agent, but one that will help her carve out the most successful career possible.

Roshumba's Rules

Agents are the ones who "sell" a model. They want to make sure your look is marketable and appealing to clients. So when they offer you advice, take it. This will greatly increase your chances of having a great career.

Finding the Right Agent for Your Teen

"Models need to have an agent, because that agent is there to guide them, to help them make decisions regarding which jobs to take, to negotiate money for them," explains Lee. "To be an agent basically [means being] a manager of their career. It's important that the girl looks for a reputable agent. Parents should not be afraid to ask questions and find out if an agency is reputable.

"How do you find that out? You know that by going through the BBB [Better Business Bureau]. A better way would be to really see who that agency represents, the caliber of models they represent, and the kinds of work their girls get. Those are things that are all very important in knowing how good and reputable an agency is. If you go into a place and you see no one on the walls you've heard of or know of, or the jobs they're getting for the girls are not great work, you better think about that several times."

The Importance of Family Values

Besides making sure your child is signed with a reputable agent, it also helps a model's career if she has a good relationship with her parents. "We find many times, when the girls have supportive, positive families, it's a lot better for the girls," says Lee. "I think you have to, as a parent, be there for your child, be supportive of your child, be there to communicate with her, so that she has a family that loves and supports her, that she can talk to."

Lee also recommends that, time and money permitting, a parent go with her daughter to the city where she will be starting her modeling career. "A lot of times, if a parent can and has the money to come with the girl the first time to New York, it's always nice. That way the parent gets to see what the daughter is doing, and the daughter knows the parent is there for her."

Lee warns, however, against parents who are too overprotective or get too involved in their daughters' modeling careers. "If a parent is too involved and overprotective, then the model can't really do her job that well." The model may not feel free to express herself at a photo shoot because the parent is interfering too much, or her career may not be progressing as well as it could because the parent is trying to take over the agent's job and manage every aspect of her daughter's career.

Parents Beware: Scams Are Everywhere

Parents must also be on the lookout for scams of all kinds. Because young models don't have much experience with the world in general and the business world in particular,

Reality Check

Because a young, aspiring model's desire to launch her career may sometimes overshadow her logic, she may find herself in a situation which she isn't equipped to handle, or she may not realize she's being ripped off.

it's important that their parents or guardians be involved with their careers from the beginning. Parents are essential for asking questions, scrutinizing the situation, and reading between the lines. Trust your instincts!

In fact, modeling agency scams are so prevalent that both the Better Business Bureau and the Federal Trade Commission have released warnings about unscrupulous modeling agencies and modeling scams. I've included their reports on fraudulent modeling-agency practices, so you'll know the kinds of things you need to be on the lookout for.

Tips from the Federal Trade Commission

The Federal Trade Commission (FTC) issued a report in January 1993 for consumers on modeling-agency rip-offs that offers some guidelines about scams that still holds true. The FTC points out that it can be difficult to recognize a modeling scam because many of the advertising claims and practices resemble those used by legitimate modeling agencies. However, the following are some common advertising claims that the FTC says should make you suspicious: You can access it at www.ftc.gov/bcp/online/pubs/services/model.htm. The FTC can be reached by phone at 202-326-3650.

➤ **"No fee."** If a modeling agency advertises that there is no fee for its services, you should be wary any time you are asked to pay. Most legitimate agencies make money only by taking a commission from their models' work. An exception, however, is that you may be charged for your pictures to be in an agency book that is sent to clients who hire models. (The agency often pays for these fees in advance and takes them out of your salary once you start working.) Make sure you pay only your portion of the printing costs. But before you pay any money, ask to see a copy of the agency's previous books and the list of clients to whom they were sent. Most legitimate agencies will provide you with this information. It is a good idea to check with some of the agency's clients to determine whether they have hired any of the company's models.

152

➤ **"Earn high salaries."** Only experienced, top models can expect to receive large salaries.

➤ **"Work full- or part-time."** The hours in the modeling industry are uneven and sporadic. You will not have the flexibility to choose your own hours.

➤ **"Real-people types should apply."** Some ads encourage people of all shapes, sizes, and ages to apply for commercial modeling work that involves the sale of a product. Remember, modeling opportunities are limited even in large cities. Opportunities do exist for "real-people" models, but they are rare.

Mod Squad

One modeling agency that the FTC brought charges against claimed to offer modeling jobs for people with no experience, and that it had numerous clients who hired models. The company accepted nearly all applicants, then insisted that they needed professional photos taken by a photographer they recommended. Although the agency had 2,000 models' names on file, its commission fees in one five-month period totaled only $100. A federal court judge found that of the $2.1 million the agency had earned in a two-year time period, only $16,070 was from commissions. The remaining $2,083,930 was income from photographs purchased by would-be models who had little chance of ever getting a job through the company.

How to Spot a Scam

The FTC also recommends that you check to see if the agency you're considering working with charges you money to take their classes before you can be eligible for modeling work. A legitimate modeling agency may provide instruction on applying makeup or walking, but most do not charge you for classes. An exception to this is a modeling agency that also serves as a modeling school. A modeling school does charge for classes, but that's a separate function from finding you work as a model.

Also, an agency should realistically assess a model's chances for being a model. Are they trying

Roshumba's Rules

Even if an agent says you have what it takes to be a model, it's smart to evaluate yourself to make sure you're not being scammed. Check out Chapter 3, "Do You Have What It Takes?" to find out if you have the basic qualifications.

Reality Check

Keep copies of all important papers, such as your contract and agency literature. You may need these if you have a dispute with the agency. And be sure to get all promises in writing!

to sign your daughter because they believe they can make money for her, or because *you* look like you can afford to pay all sorts of fees?

Also, the FTC recommends that you verify the agency's credentials. Is it forthcoming about the models it represents and the clients it works with? Ask for the names, addresses, and phone numbers of models who work through the agency and clients who have used its models. Contact the models and clients to verify the information. If you can't verify them and the agency is asking for money in advance, you are better off saying no, according to the FTC.

The FTC also warns that you should be suspicious of agencies that require models to pay fees by cash or money order only, including fees for agency books. This is a strong signal that the agency is interested in taking your money, not in representing you as a model.

A Few Courses of Recourse

If you've paid money to a modeling agency and believe they are involved in a scam, first contact the company and request a refund. If you're not satisfied, register a complaint with your local consumer protection agency, Better Business Bureau, or state attorney general's office. Also, contact the advertising manager of the newspaper that ran the ad you answered. For ethical and practical reasons, the advertising manager may be interested in learning about any problems you've had with the agency.

You also should file a complaint with the FTC. Write to: Correspondence Branch, Federal Trade Commission, Washington, D.C. 20580. Although the FTC cannot represent you directly in a dispute with a company, if the Commission finds evidence of a pattern of deceptive or unfair practices, it can take action. Another way to obtain helpful consumer information from the FTC is to visit their Web site at www.ftc.gov.

Advice from the Better Business Bureau

The Better Business Bureau (BBB) advises caution when dealing with modeling agencies. Although there are ethical and legitimate modeling agencies, the BBB warns that, far too often, consumers are victimized by unscrupulous talent and modeling agencies promising money, exposure, and stardom.

Before you become involved with an agency, the BBB advises that you know exactly what the agency should be doing for you. An agency should be engaged in the marketing and booking of talent. Usually a state license is required to book work for a fee. The agent's role is to promote the talent (in this case, a model) who has contracted them for their marketing services, negotiate the most favorable contract for the talent, and collect a commission from the talent.

The BBB also advises interviewing the modeling agent as thoroughly as you would interview your doctor, lawyer, or CPA. Remember, the agent will be working for you, not vice versa. Carefully review your contract with your agent. This is your agreement regarding what the agent will do to earn the commission you pay.

To help you detect fraudulent opportunities, the Better Business Bureau warns that disreputable agencies often:

➤ Ask for up-front money, which may be called "registration," "consultation," or "administrative" fees. Legitimate agents, however, work on a commission. They don't get any money until you get paid for doing the work they have obtained for you.

➤ Pressure you to leave a check or cash deposit or sign a contract immediately. The agent may insist that you take acting (or modeling) lessons at a particular school or from a particular teacher, or may try to get you to buy expensive photographs from a particular photographer, audition tapes, or other services or materials sold by someone he or she suggests. An agent's time should be spent finding work for his or her client, not selling products and services to them.

➤ Display pictures of famous models on their walls to make you believe they are represented by that agency, although they're not.

➤ Use names that sound similar to well-known agencies. Fraudulent companies will sometimes do this to give the (incorrect) impression that they're connected to a legitimate entity.

If you have a problem or complaint about an agent or an agency, call the Better Business Bureau in the city where the company is located or the Department of Licensing and Regulation or the consumer protection agency in the city where the company is located. For the BBB nearest you or to obtain helpful consumer information, visit their Web site at www.bbb.org.

Here are 10 questions a parent should ask the agent before signing a modeling contract for her child:

➤ What kind of work do you think you'll be able to get my daughter?

➤ What other models have you represented?

➤ May I talk to other models you represent?

➤ What fees will we be responsible for paying?

➤ Who are some of the clients who have booked your models in the past?

➤ How long is the term of the contract?

➤ What individual will be supervising my daughter's career?

➤ Is that person used to dealing with novice models?

➤ What percentage of my daughter's earnings will you take as commission?

➤ Will my daughter be able to work part-time, or do you expect her to drop out of school to work?

My overall advice to parents is to be involved with, but not in the way of, your child's career. When it comes to selecting an agency, try to choose one that has been around for at least five years and has a reputation for handling the careers of well-known models.

The Least You Need to Know

➤ Parents need to scrutinize all their child's modeling activities to protect her from rip-offs, con artists, and other dangers.

➤ Carefully check out any modeling agency that wants to represent your child.

➤ Make sure your child is mature and responsible enough for a modeling career.

Part 3

Now That Your Foot's in the Door, What's Next?

Finding an agent is a model's first big hurdle. But it's only the first step on a long road. But no need to panic—everything you need to know about getting started in modeling is right here in this part of the book. First, I'll take you inside a modeling agency, explaining who everyone is and what they do, so you can make the most of their services. Next, I'll explain what test shots and portfolios are, and I'll give you some great tips for making sure that yours really stand out.

Then I'll explain everything you need to know about those "modeling musts," those essential items that a professional model can't live without. Finally, I'll tell you how to shine at go and sees (job interviews for models), so that you'll be one step ahead of the competition when it comes time for you to start booking professional modeling jobs!

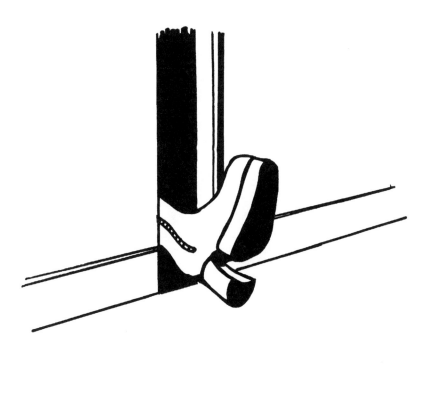

Hi! WELCOME TO
THE MS. GLAMMO
MODELING AGENCY!

Chapter 12

How an Agency Works

In This Chapter

➤ Understanding how an agency operates

➤ What an agent does

➤ What the various departments of an agency do

➤ Advantages and disadvantages of large and small agencies

➤ How to switch agencies

It's important to know how an agency works and who does what, so that you get the most out of the agency's personnel in terms of managing your career. Knowing who's who will also help you when you go to open calls and other meetings when you're in the process of trying to find an agent. You'll understand who everyone is, what their purpose is, and how they can help you. Every modeling agency has its own hierarchy, and staff members tend to be very protective of their duties and titles. You need to know the chain of command and follow it, or you can cause problems.

In this chapter, I'll give you a guided tour of a modeling agency. I'll talk about the advantages and disadvantages of small and large agencies, and tell you the right way to switch agencies.

The Booker: A Model's Best Friend

The *agents* (also called *bookers* or *model managers*) are the people at the agency who will manage every aspect of your career in the short- and long-term. When you're just starting out, they direct you to the testing photographers you should work with, decide what photos you should be taking, and determine what aspects of yourself you should be focusing on to sell.

An agent really manages the girls' careers, explains Karen Lee, the director of scouting at Elite Model Management. "Once we find a girl and decide we want to represent her, and she decides she wants to be with Elite, we work on getting the girl's book together by sending her to good, reputable photographers who will take test pictures of her. Then we put a test book together, which shows her in various ways—beauty, fashion, interesting photos, black and white, and/or color. We then send her to various clients."

Catwalk Talk

An **agent** (or **booker** or **model manager**) is the person in an agency who develops you as a model, books you for jobs, and oversees your career.

All the bookers in a department traditionally sit at one table, which makes it easier for them to communicate.

Developing the Model's Look

"Also you work on each individual girl," says Lee. "Maybe one girl needs a haircut, maybe one girl needs to learn to dress a little differently, maybe another girl needs to work on her body a little. You work on her presence, her style, her hair, her look, her book. You want a girl to look great in person—that means very natural, very much in shape, very healthy, not too skinny, not overweight."

Once you're ready to start working, the agent decides what clients you should work for. She sends you out to see a variety of clients, then interprets their reactions to you and directs you from there. The agent will soon realize that maybe you don't appeal to fashion designers booking their runway shows, but that your look is attractive to magazine editors. Or if every catalog is calling for you because you have that wholesome appeal, she may decide that your focus should be on catalogs and advertisements. An agent realizes your strengths and where you are in your career and builds on that.

Roshumba's Rules

In addition to being reputable (honest, business-like, not a scammer), it's key that the booker be an expert at doing her job. If she isn't, it could have a negative impact on your career.

Your booker will choose the photos that will appear in your portfolio and will arrange them in a certain order that will "sell" you to the client.

The Daily Details

The booker also handles the day-to-day details of your life. She schedules all your go and sees (see Chapter 15, "Go and Sees") and jobs. Clients call the booker directly, and she lets them know when you're available to work. Unless you tell her specifically that you're not available (say you need to go home and see your family, go to the doctor, or go on vacation), they will book jobs for you every day. Try to give your booker as much advance notice as possible when you need days off.

The booker also lets you know when and where a job will be, how long it will last, who the client is, how much you will be paid, and what's expected of you. If it's a lingerie shoot, they'll let you know that you need to shave and get a pedicure beforehand.

Bookers often handle some personal things as well. They can put you in touch with doctors, therapists, nutritionists, or personal trainers. They can help you find housing. They can also refer you to lawyers and accountants and any other professionals you might need.

Mod Squad

It's not unusual for me to talk to my booker at least three times a day, because things change constantly during the course of a day. Bookers are in touch with American, European, Midwestern, and West Coast clients. I might be scheduled to do a shoot the next day in a studio two blocks from my house and suddenly, instead, I'm on a plane to Paris for a shoot for French *Elle*. Depending on what's going on, if the booker is trying to reconcile a double booking (two clients want me for the same time period), or if it's a particularly busy week, like during the runway show season, I could talk to my booker up to 10 times in one day!

The Major Booking Departments

In large agencies, the agent/bookers will work in several different divisions, each specializing in a different type of model. In a small agency, the various types of models are not divided up; there is one set of bookers for all of them. Here is how a typical large agency might be divided.

The New Faces Department

This department is in charge of developing new recruits into full-fledged models and booking all their jobs in the first couple of years of their careers. The agents/bookers in the New Faces Department meet with the girls who come to all of the agency's open calls. They help choose the models the agency will represent. They help develop a brand-new model so that she has a marketable look, giving her advice on bringing out her best qualities—for instance, advising her to get a haircut, work out, get braces, or see a dermatologist. They also help new models set up test shoots with the best photographers and put together their portfolios.

They also introduce the model to the fashion industry and send her on her first go and sees to magazine editors, photographers, and advertisers. They are responsible for helping a girl make living arrangements if she's had to relocate, familiarize herself with the city, learn about public transportation and how to get around, and set up a bank account.

A girl is considered a new face, and will stay in the New Faces department until she establishes steady clientele and becomes known to industry professionals.

Your booker will give you advice on ways you can make yourself more marketable to clients, including changing your hair or shaping up your body.

The Model Management Department

The biggest department in the agency is the Model Management Department, because it handles all the models who have established their careers, but who aren't yet superstars or specialists (catalog, advertising, runway models, for example).

After a model leaves the New Faces Department, she will progress to the Model Management Department. The bookers/agents in the Model Management Department will expand on that foundation to see what type of clients are interested in her and decide how she should focus her career and what she should do next.

Overall, Model Management's responsibility is to help the model build a well-balanced career, with a range of editorial, fashion show, and ad clients, in a variety of markets. They are responsible for figuring out what clients you *should* be working with, and creating opportunities for you to meet those clients. If you haven't done any ads, for example, they may send you to see an ad agency to get feedback on what they think of you.

Having a well-balanced career is more important than you might think. The primary reason you want to have a well-balanced career is so you can get the most out of your modeling career, have the most work, and make the most money.

Many models stay with the Model Management Department their whole careers, unless they've reached supermodel status, or become specialists; in this case, the models might transfer to a department that specializes in handling their type of client, such as catalogs and advertising, which would focus on maintaining their clients, not building the models' careers.

Reality Check

Editorial modeling is great for exposure and creating a name for yourself, but it doesn't pay well; in fact, you may not be able to live off of editorial fees alone. Catalog modeling is great for making money, but it's not as well regarded, so your image and status may suffer if you do too much. Modeling in fashion shows offers fairly good money and prestige, but not as much exposure.

Catwalk Talk

Image models are models who are still relatively new (they typically have three to five years experience in the business), but they are the future supermodels. They are building toward supermodel status.

The Supermodel/Image Model Department

As you can probably guess, the Supermodel/Image Model Department handles models who are of supermodel status—women who are household names, have multi-million dollar incomes, are involved in projects outside of modeling, such as producing their own calendars, books, TV shows, exercise videos, and other merchandise.

This department also handles *image models.* These are models who are on the covers of major fashion magazines and in lots of fashion spreads, are signed to major endorsement deals, and work with the best photographers. Although they may already be making $1 million plus, they are not yet household names.

Because of the high profile of the models in the Supermodel/Image Model Department, and the caliber of their clientele, this is a separate department from Model Management. The clients are as famous as the models, and include Victoria's Secret, *Sports Illustrated, Vogue, Harper's Bazaar,* and *Elle,* along with prestigious fashion designers, such as Calvin Klein, Donna Karan, and Valentino. They may also include high-end catalogs, such as Bergdorf Goodman or the Neiman Marcus Designer Collection.

The bookers/agents in this department also have high profiles in the fashion industry. They often have a direct relationship with the most important photographers, designers, and editors.

Depending on how their careers progress, models can remain in this department until they're ready to move on to do other things or retire.

The Catalog and Advertising Department

This department specializes in booking models for catalog and advertising jobs. Catalog and advertising are the highest-paying types of modeling. Models who are nearing the end of their careers tend to do a lot of this type of work, because this is where they make the big bucks.

The main difference between the Catalog and Advertising Department and Model Management is that your career will be handled in a different way: to make sure you make as much money as possible, that you work as often as possible, and that you work for the best clients—in other words, to help you get the most out of the years you put in. The focus isn't so much on getting a variety of work or building clientele.

This department books models for the major catalogs, including Saks Fifth Avenue, Neiman Marcus, Lord & Taylor, Bloomingdale's, J. Crew, Land's End, and Tweeds. They also book models to appear in print ads in magazines and newspapers for clients such as Oil of Olay, Hanes Hosiery, Clairol, The Gap, L'Oréal, Bioré Pore Strips, Nivea, Colgate, Lady Speed Stick, and Secret.

The Runway Department

The Runway Department, as the name suggests, handles the scheduling and booking of models for runway and related work, including fittings, trunk shows, and boutique showings.

What's different about this department is that it handles runway bookings for all the models in the agency, as well as the careers of models who specialize in runway work. During the collections, it submits the composite cards of all the girls interested in doing the shows, including models from the New Faces and Supermodel/Image Model Departments, to the fashion designers presenting shows. The Runway Department does all the necessary negotiating and scheduling for all of the agency models chosen. The Runway Department also handles models who mostly do runway shows or fittings.

Mod Squad

Dalma was the quintessential runway model. She glided, not walked, down the runway. She was an expert at showing clothes well. I always watched her in awe. When she turned her body, her head would follow gracefully, and every hair would fall magically back into place. If she was wearing an evening dress with a billowy cape, it would float through the air, catching the wind. She had a incredible knowledge of clothes. She made every garment look extraordinary and made women want to have it. She finally retired from runway after an incredible 20 years. She went on to consult with Valentino on his runway shows.

The Television Commercial Department

This department handles the bookings for all the models in the agency who are hired to do television commercials, for instance, TV ads for cars (Ford, Mercedes, Lexus), beverage companies (Coke, Pepsi, Mountain Dew), and beauty products (Revlon, Finesse). They also handle related work, such as guest appearances on TV shows or even appearances in movies.

When I was booked to appear in Woody Allen's film *Celebrity,* the booking came through the Television Commercial Department, even though the rest of my bookings are handled by another department.

Specialty Departments

Many large agencies have departments that handle specialty models. These might include petites, plus-size, elegant (older), and parts models as well as male models. (See Chapter 22, "Specialty Models," for more on specialty modeling.)

The Petite Department

The Petite Department handles petite models, who are generally around 5'5", small-boned, pretty, and healthy looking, with a wholesome appeal. The clients who would book them would be petite clothing manufacturers, or the petite divisions of major fashion designers. Some examples: Sears, JCPenney, Liz Claiborne, catalog clients, as well as advertisers who might book a petite model for beauty ads (skin, hair, makeup), where size is irrelevant.

The Plus-Size Department

Plus-size models are another increasingly busy category of models. The average American woman is a size 14 and cannot identify with a size 6 model, and designers are finally catching on to this fact. Finally, there's a magazine that is devoted exclusively to plus-size women and that features plus-size models—*Mode*. In addition, advertisers and catalogs are trying to appeal to this growing market by using plus-size models. Plus-size models are larger than regular models, but they're healthy, tall (at least 5'8" or 5'10"), and toned. They may be large-boned, with broad shoulders, full hips, and full breasts, maybe a bit of a tummy. They wear a woman's size 12 to 18. Plus-size models usually have beautiful, classic facial features, and exude warmth and appeal. They're true proof that beauty comes in all sizes.

Plus-size models are booked to model absolutely everything, including lingerie, bathing suits, sportswear, and evening dresses. They appear in magazines, catalogs, and advertisements.

The Elegant Department

Elegant models are usually older models; the minimum age to enter this department is about 35. A model might work through this department for the rest of her life.

Elegant models have become very popular over the last few years. As baby boomers have aged, designers want to use models that appeal to this huge group of consumers, and they have found that 50-year-old consumers just don't identify with 14-year-old models.

Elegant models used to work only part-time, but now they can model full-time. They have a range of clients, including runway, advertising, and editorial. Most of their work, however, is modeling for catalogs.

The Parts Department

Many large agencies have Parts Departments that represent models who specialize in leg, hand, and foot modeling. These women probably would not be regular model material—maybe they're not tall enough—but they have at least one standout "part," such as beautiful hands, gorgeous legs, or perfect size-6 feet.

Hand models model jewelry and nail products, anything where an advertiser would want to focus attention on the hand. Leg models model hosiery, footwear, shaving products, and body creams. They need to have long, lean, toned legs with no scars, bruises, tattoos, or scratches. Foot models model shoes, socks, foot-care products, and toenail polish. They wear size $5^1/_2$ to 7 medium-width shoes and have a medium to high arch, without any bunions, toenail fungus, crooked toes, badly proportioned toes, or calluses.

The Men's Department

Some small agencies handle men exclusively, while some larger agencies have a Men's Department. In either case, a men's agency or department specifically focuses on the development and marketing of male models, from beginners to established models.

Male models walk the runway for major menswear designers, including Joseph Abboud, Paul Smith, Prada, Gucci, Ralph Lauren, and Calvin Klein. They also appear in men's magazines, such as *GQ* and *Esquire*. They appear in catalogs, including J. Crew, Benetton, Saks Fifth Avenue, and Macy's. Finally, they appear in ads for soft drinks, men's clothing, cars, men's grooming products, and sports products.

Other Agency Departments

Modeling agencies have other departments that are common to many other types of businesses. But it's important to know what they are and what they do, because each one will have an effect on your career as a model.

➤ **The Accounting Department.** The Accounting Department deals with all incoming (from clients) and outgoing (to you, among others) money. When you work a job, you need to have the client sign a special voucher acknowledging that you did indeed work. (Every model is issued her own voucher book with the agency logo on it.) You then turn that voucher into the Accounting Department, and they bill the client for the work you did. The bill includes the model's fee, the agent's fee, and any other fees that were negotiated.

➤ **The Promotions and Publicity Department.** This department is in charge of promoting the agency's name and image in the business community. It ties the agency's name in with charity events by providing models for the event for the sake of name exposure. This department also handles press inquiries about the agency, and often, individual models.

➤ **The administration.** The administration includes the presidents, vice presidents, and department directors of the agency. They handle the running of the agency, the hiring and firing of bookers and other personnel, and renting and remodeling the agency's office. They plan for the agency's future and troubleshoot any internal or external problems. The administration, in particular the CEO, has the final say about everything affecting the agency and the models it represents.

➤ **The receptionist.** One of the key people in the agency, and someone you'll have a lot of contact with, is the receptionist. She greets all the visitors, answers all phone calls to the agency, and routes callers to the correct department. She answers general questions about the agency and deals with all the messengers who are constantly dropping off and delivering packages.

Roshumba's Rules

Make friends with the receptionist of your agency, because your portfolio will be passing through her hands on a daily basis as it's sent out to various clients.

David vs. Goliath: Small and Large Agencies

When you're first starting out, there are several advantages to going with a small agency. There's a lot less competition, so you're not competing against so many girls in your own agency. The bookers in a small agency may work harder for you when you're getting started, because they may not have as many high-profile, big-name models who are bringing in the big bucks. They may need to get you jobs to ensure a steady stream of income and keep the agency going. Also, many agents/bookers in a small agency may have a personal financial sake in the company, so they have a vested interest in making sure you succeed.

One of the downsides of being with a small agency is that each individual model manager has a lot more responsibility than someone at a larger agency. The manager may be responsible for scouting new models, developing them, organizing their books, sending them to see clients, booking the models, and following up. He or she may be doing everything involved with managing the models, promoting and running the agency, even balancing the checkbook and negotiating with the landlord, which can be overwhelming. This may take away from the time she's able to devote to you.

In addition, if you want to focus on one area, say, building a strong editorial career, a small agency may not have contacts with all the editorial clients, because the agency is also trying to service advertising, catalog, and fashion-designer clients as well. The agency can't focus on just one thing, whereas in a larger agency, there are specialists for each type of modeling.

When you're starting your career, the advantage of a large agency is that they have the manpower to take care of all your individual needs. You can also grow with a larger agency, starting your career there—working with the New Faces Department, which develops new models. New Faces will tend to have more knowledge of model development and have special relationships with the clients who tend to hire new faces.

When you're ready to move from New Faces to the Model Management Department, you won't need to switch agencies if you're with a larger agency. Also, there will be more than one person looking out for you, in addition to your own personal booker. There are a number of bookers in the department who are all getting a lot of requests. Even if you're not working with a particular booker directly, if a request comes in to her for someone who looks like you, she'll recommend you.

Once you've developed, grown, had a full career, and decide you want to focus on a specific area, such as runway or catalogs, a large agency will have a special department to meet your needs, and you'll be able to move there without switching agencies.

Larger agencies have the financial and manpower capacities to hire in-house as well as freelance model scouts, and most large agencies also sponsor model searches and other scouting events. All this may make it easier for you to get signed by a larger agency in the first place. Finding a smaller agency to represent you may take a little more legwork on your part. Larger agencies may also be able to provide a place for you to live, because a big company has the money available to afford model apartments.

One disadvantage of a large agency is that even though there are a lot more bookers who specialize in what they do, there are also a lot more models. As a result you end up competing not only with models from other agencies, but also with your own agency mates. Also, if your career is not progressing the way the agency had hoped, you may get lost in the shuffle because they have so many girls to think about. They might not take the time to focus on your weak areas and help you improve.

Roshumba's Rules

If you're new to modeling or very young, a small agency may be the best choice for you. It is less intimidating for girls who need a lot of attention, hand-holding, and confidence building.

Reality Check

Smaller agencies are much more vulnerable to going out of business than larger ones because their volume of business is lower, so they don't have the same financial stability as a larger agency. In fact, two of the smaller agencies I was represented by have since gone out of business. Unfortunately, sometimes models don't get paid when agencies go bankrupt.

Another disadvantage is that even though there are many people working to fulfill all your needs, you have to take the time and be able to build relationships with all of those people, instead of just the one booker you have to deal with at a small agency. If you're young, or your people skills are not that strong, that may be difficult for you.

Is This a Match Made in Heaven?

An agent shouldn't look at you as a commodity only—something that can be marketed and sold. The agent should be interested in you as a person. Whether the agency is large or small, you should get the feeling that it's interested in representing you. You also want an agent who maintains a certain level of professionalism, has ethics, and treats you with respect.

You want an agent who won't lose interest in you, one who will work hard to sell you. At some point, everyone needs an extra push. You may have difficulty getting started in the business and have trouble landing those first jobs. Or maybe you start off well, but a year or two later, things slow down. You want an agent who looks at you as a human being first, and a career second. You have to have a personal relationship, so you know the agent won't give up on you as soon as you hit a rough spot in your career.

The best way to tell if an agency is right for you is if, after about three to six months, the agency has started you working. If you're not working after six months, either you're not marketable or your agency doesn't know how to market you.

Switching Agencies, Staying Friends

Before you switch agencies, find out if there's something you need to improve first. If you leave an agency and *you're* the problem, you're going to run into the same situation at the next agency. Ask your booker if there's something you need to improve either physically or mentally. But if you've been with the agency for three to six months and you feel like you're not being serviced properly, the agency may be the problem. Other reasons to switch agencies include:

➤ You're having problems getting paid for the jobs you do.

➤ You're not being sent out to see clients.

➤ You're not being pushed or marketed.

➤ You don't get along with your booker.

If these problems can't be resolved, and the agency can't find anyone else for you to work with, it may be time to switch.

Before you head for the door, however, first talk to your booker, and let her know that you're not satisfied with what's happening with your career. You've taken her advice, gone on appointments, and still nothing is happening. Or maybe she's not sending you out on go and sees at all. Whatever the reason, your career has stalled. Let her know you're not happy.

After you've had this talk, give her about two weeks to make changes and to show you that she's making an effort to improve the situation. If she doesn't do anything, you'll probably want to move on. But before you make a move, make sure you've contacted another agency.

You should have two or three agencies lined up before you leave your current one. You can find out about other agencies by word of mouth from other models. Look at various agency's books to see what models they handle. Once you've narrowed it down to two or three agencies, call each one, introduce yourself, and ask for a meeting.

At the appointment, explain what you want to do, the problems you're having with your current agency, and why you want to leave. Let the agency know what you think you should be doing. Meet with two or three agencies so you can compare them, gauge their reactions, and see how enthusiastic they are about you. If they listen intently to what you're saying, study your book, study you, and get a feel for your potential, these are strong signs they're interested in you.

Once you have two or three strong possibilities, let your current agency know you want to change. Approach your booker, tell her you really thought about it, but that you think a change will be best for everyone involved. Tell her what date you will be changing, and ask her if she will have all of your pictures, composites, and portfolios ready to give to you (after all, you paid for and own these). Also, make sure you get your final paychecks.

Although you may be tempted to tell the agency staff exactly what you think of them, it's better to make friends, not enemies, in the process of leaving. Be respectful and polite—even though you didn't get what you wanted out of the relationship, they did take time for you. It's not a good idea to burn bridges because the agency might try to alienate your clients. Instead of telling clients you switched agencies, they might tell your clients that you're pregnant and quit modeling or went on safari for six months!

Most of the time, agencies will give you the money they owe you. But it's always a good idea to have it set up so you get paid on a regular basis, say every two weeks, so they never owe you a lot of money. If you owe money to the agency for composites, portfolios, or Federal Express or messenger expenses, the agency may hold onto your money until you've paid them back. The agency pays

Reality Check

If someone is making threats, saying that you'll never get work if you don't have sex with him, don't believe it. No professional agency conducts business like that, so this person probably couldn't help your career anyway. Tell the supervisor of the person who threatened you, or if the harasser is the big boss, leave that agency immediately.

Roshumba's Rules

In addition to telling your agent in person or on the phone that you're switching agencies, it's also good to put it in writing for legal protection. Just write her a letter and mail or fax it to her.

these fees in advance for you. When your client pays for a job you've done, the agency will deduct monies they've paid in advance for you from your paycheck.

The agency will be at the center of your life as long as you are a model. The more you know about how an agency works and the better you cultivate relationships with the agency staff, the easier your career will flow.

The Least You Need to Know

➤ Your agent/booker is responsible for all aspects of your career, including development and day-to-day management.

➤ Depending on the stage of your career, you may be handled by the New Faces, Model Management, or Supermodel/Image Model Department, or by a specialty department.

➤ There are many behind-the-scenes people in a modeling agency who play a key role in your career.

Chapter 13

Testing, Testing, 1, 2, 3: Test Shoots

In This Chapter

➤ Familiarizing yourself with the camera: test shoots for experience

➤ Getting the shots you'll want

➤ Practice (posing) makes perfect

➤ Your calling card: test shoots for your book

Test shoots are special photo shoots that models do before their careers get started. There are two different kinds of test shoots. The first type is called "test shoots for experience" and are done by models who don't yet have an agent. They are usually done with novice photographers who want to gain experience working with models and perfecting their craft. These are not pictures you want to show to agents; you just want to study them and learn from them.

The second type is called "test shoots for your book." Once an agency has agreed to represent you, your agent/booker will arrange for you to have a photo session with a reputable photographer. The agency usually pays for these photos up front (the cost of them is deducted from your first paychecks) and the photos from the session are arranged in your book (which is also called a portfolio—that photo album you bring to clients that contains photos that show you at your best). The agency will give you a professional portfolio with the agency name and logo on it. The cost of the portfolio will be deducted from the money you make.

In this chapter, we will discuss both types of test shoots in depth, what you should expect from each, and how you can make the most out of them.

Your Debut in Front of the Camera: Test Shoots for Experience

As the name suggests, *test shoots for experience* are done for the experience. They don't help you get an agent, and they don't help you get clients. They help you learn how to pose and move naturally but effectively in front of the camera, so you don't look uncomfortable, stiff or afraid, or like you're "modeling." Instead, they'll help you learn how to look (and feel) natural and comfortable. Test shoots will help you figure out the best angles of your body and face, get comfortable in the environment of a photo studio, and learn to take directions from a photographer. They can also help you get used to bright studio lighting.

Catwalk Talk

Test shoots for experience are done for the sole purpose of helping you familiarize yourself with working in front of a camera. They are done in collaboration with inexperienced photographers who want to gain experience working with models.

The Price of Experience

Test shoots for experience should cost you little (no more than $100 for film, processing, and prints) or nothing. Paying more is a waste of money, because the only purpose of these photos is for you to see how you photograph and to learn from looking at the pictures. If someone wants to charge you more than that for a test shoot for experience, just say no: Either he's not the right photographer for your needs (you don't need an experienced pro), or he's trying to scam you.

It's also not worth it to hire a makeup artist and hairstylist for a test shoot (unless they want to test, too, and are willing to work for free). If you're really not confident about your ability to style your own hair, get your hair done at your local salon; it will be a lot cheaper than having a stylist come to the shoot. If you're not handy with makeup, go to a department store and get one of the salespeople to give you a free makeover.

Roshumba's Rules

Don't spend a lot of money on test photos for experience. You should not waste your money, because when you get an agent, he or she will set up professional test shoots with experienced photographers.

Finding the Right Photographer

To find a photographer to do a test shoot for experience with you, inquire at local hair salons; they often have books filled with pictures of hairstyles, and they may be in touch with the photographer who took them. Also, ask the managers of stores in the mall if they know anyone who test-shoots models for experience. Another great place to check is the photo club or yearbook staff at school; often aspiring student photographers are eager to find models to shoot. You could also sign up for a photography class yourself, where you're likely to meet other novice photographers (and it's not a bad idea to gain some expertise behind the camera).

Giving It Your Best Shot

Before you begin the test shoot, you'll want to talk to the photographer and get an idea of the image he's trying to get. (Because it's your test shoot, you may want to work on a concept together, whether it's a spring day in the park or studio shoot with special props.) Let him know what you want to accomplish—maybe you want to imitate a fashion story you saw in a magazine—but also open yourself up to his ideas, so he can help you make the most out of the session.

Find Your Best Look

Before you do a test shoot for experience, practice posing in the mirrors in your house. This sounds silly, but it's a great technique for figuring out your best angles, whether you look better smiling or pouting, and which stance best hides a figure flaw.

Start by trying out some of the poses you see in catalogs and fashion magazines. See if you can imitate the poses and expressions of some of your favorite models. Try imitating the sexy pout of the Victoria's Secret model Heidi Klum. Do you look like you're pouting, or do you look like your lips are chapped?

Next you might want to try the intense, animalistic stare of supermodel Helena Christensen. In photos, her gaze is so unwavering it seems like she's looking right through you. See if you can do that stare, and critique yourself: Do you look like your eyes are looking through someone's soul or does it look like you're about to tear up?

Or try lifting one eyebrow like supermodel Christy Turlington. Can you do it? Do you look chic and vampy ... or do you look like you have a bad headache?

If you have long hair, play with it, flip it back and forth, work your hands through it. See what kind of creative hair poses you can come up with. If you look at a magazine, you'll see that professional models are often asked to play with their hair. If your hair is a selling point, learn how to make it move so it attracts attention. Models with beautiful hair luck out because they are often selected to appear in lucrative advertisements for hair-care products.

Reality Check

Don't worry if you can't pull off every single one of these looks. Everybody has something they can do, but not everyone does everything, and every look doesn't work for everyone. Niki Taylor, for instance, is almost always pictured smiling, and would probably be much less appealing with Kate Moss's trademark pout. Figuring out what works on you will give you a big head start once you're in front of the camera.

Roshumba's Rules

Looking at your reflection in the mirror is a good way to try to figure out which model type you are (see Chapter 5, "Which Look Are You: The Seven Basic Model Types"). Start by putting on your favorite music and posing and dancing around.

Also, check how you look in several different mirrors throughout the house: Notice how you look in each different kind of light and which light looks best on you.

See how your body looks in various poses in front of the mirror as well. Pull out one of those lingerie or bathing suit catalogs, look at what the models are doing, and try their poses yourself. Stand with your hands on your hips, or try lying on your side, supporting the weight of your head with your hands. Does your body look similar to the models in the catalog? If not, look for ways to disguise any flaws.

Shot by Shot: Photos You'll Want

There are three basic types of shots you'll want: pictures of your face and your body and shots that show your personality. Here are the photos you'll want to capture in your test shoot for experience.

Face/Beauty/Head Shots

First you'll want to focus on beauty or head shots—close-ups of your face. In these photos, you'll want to experiment with different facial expressions—happy, pouty, sexy, intense, aloof—to get an idea of what you look like with a smile, with a soft, sultry look, or with an intense stare. Trying different expressions will give you an idea of the range of emotions you can project, and which expressions best suit your personality and facial features.

Catwalk Talk

When a photographer wants your head or body to face the camera, that's called a **straight-on** shot. A **profile** shot is a photo of the side of your face or body.

Catwalk Talk

Another popular shot is the **three-quarters angle,** which means you're facing slightly off to the side, halfway between the straight-on and profile shots.

Also, take pictures of your face at different angles: *straight-on* and in *profile*. Throw your head back and laugh, tilt your head up, tilt your head down, thrust your jaw out.

Even though the pictures will focus on your face, you want to move your body as well, to see how that affects the way your face looks. Turn your body sideways, but move your head to look straight at the camera. Lie on your back, to see how the weight of your face shifts when you're prone. Turn your body straight to the camera and poke out one hip, then turn your head to the *three-quarters angle,* but look straight at the camera and make big doe eyes.

You'll want to have three different kinds of head shots taken: natural (wearing very little makeup), enhanced (wearing a medium amount of makeup), and glamour (wearing a lot of makeup).

For the natural photos, you don't want to wear a lot of makeup because these shots are meant to give you an idea of how your skin and facial features look in their natural state. At most, you'll want to apply just a little liquid foundation, brow powder, mascara, and lipstick in a natural color. You'll want to pull your hair back off your face. (For more information on applying makeup, see Chapter 27, "The Outer You.")

Try posing with a range of expressions on your face: laughing, happy, sultry, serious, intense. Try moving your head and body in a variety of positions as well.

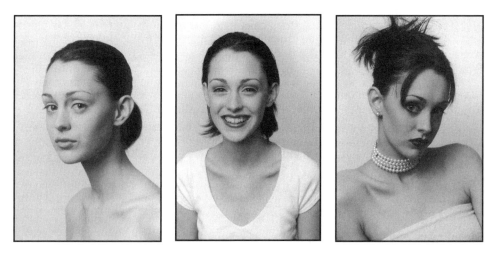

When you're doing test shoots for experience, you'll want to try out three makeup looks, from left to right: natural (with very little makeup), enhanced (with just enough makeup to make your features stand out), and glamour (the to-the-max Dynasty look). Also try out a variety of expressions—pensive, happy, pouty—to see which ones suit you best. Photographer: Kwame Brathwaite. Model: Laura McLafferty.

Enhanced Beauty Shots

In the second set of photos, you'll want to wear a medium amount of makeup, just enough to enhance your natural features, a little more than you wore in the natural shots. Apply some more blush to your cheeks, line your upper lash line with an eye pencil, line your lips with a lip pencil before applying lipstick, and/or use a powder eye shadow to enhance your brows. Your eyes will stand out more if you add a darker-colored shadow in your eye's crease. You may also want to experiment with slightly darker or more dramatic makeup colors. Your hair can be worn parted straight down, slicked back, or in any other simple style.

For these shots, you'll again want to see how you look with a range of expressions on your face: happy, sultry, serious, intense. You'll want to try moving your head and body in a variety of positions as well.

Dramatic Test Photos

These are the glamour shots: You'll be wearing intense, dramatic makeup (bright red lips, smoky eyes, deep blush), and your hair will be done up (now's the time to try out a bouffant or other dramatic style). All in all, you'll look like you're going to the black-tie event of the year.

These shots will give you an idea of how you look wearing a lot of makeup, how you feel with it on, and how your skin reacts. Some people look like the most gorgeous supermodels in the world wearing a lot of makeup; others look like they've been playing with their mom's makeup kit.

For this look, you'll want to apply foundation all over your face for a smooth canvas on which to work. Next, apply powder to set the makeup. You'll definitely want to apply dramatic eye makeup—a smoky eye shadow on the lid, a darker color in the crease of the eye, liner along the upper lash line, at least three coats of mascara, and/or false eyelashes (if you know how to apply them).

Accentuate your cheekbones by applying blush on the apples of your cheeks and along your cheekbones. If you're skilled with makeup application, you may also want to contour your cheeks by applying a slightly darker shade under your cheekbone. Choose a bold lip color; first line lips in a matching color, then use a lipstick brush to fill in. You may even want to put a gloss over your lipstick for a more dramatic look.

Your hair can be a true 'do: Try teasing it, spraying it, putting it in a French twist or pin curls, blowing it up into a bouffant—whatever suits your hair. And don't forget the jewelry: big earrings, rhinestones, jeweled collars, and sparkly bracelets.

Again, try a range of poses, to see what your features look like when you're soft and pouty looking, or sultry and sexy looking, or have a big, broad laugh or pleasant smile. Take a few shots in profile, three-quarters, and looking straight at the camera, and with your head tilted up and down.

Body Shots

For the body shots, you'll want to pose in a simple one- or two-piece bathing suit. You can also wear a leotard, a body-conscious dress (such as a spandex dress), shorts and a tank top, panties and a T-shirt, or body-conscious lingerie.

You want to familiarize yourself with what your body looks like without a lot of clothes on. This will allow you to clearly see your body in the photographs; the purpose of test body shots is to learn about your body's lines, proportions, and best (and worst) features: Do you have long, bony arms, or a long, elegant neck? Do you have a rounded tummy or wide shoulders? Test pictures can help you learn how to pose in ways that enhance your best features and disguise your worst. For instance, by arching your back, pushing your chest and butt out, you can accentuate a sexy, curvy body.

Wear whichever style of makeup most complements your face—natural, enhanced, or dramatic—or choose the one that you feel most comfortable with.

When you're posing for body shots, make sure that your whole body is working. You don't want to have a big, brilliant smile while the rest of your body looks limp. A good example of this is the advertisement for the Clinique fragrance Happy. In both the print ads and the TV commercials, every part of the models' bodies expresses happiness—from their beaming smiles to their energized body positions and kinetic movements—their whole bodies look happy!

During your test shoots for experience, you'll want to practice the T-leg pose, with one foot in front of the other. (Turning your hips to the three-quarters angle while facing the camera with your shoulders and head is a great way to camouflage wide hips and thighs.) You'll also want to move around as much as possible: Try turning your body to the side for a full profile shot, as well as sitting and kneeling on the floor. Photographer: Kwame Brathwaite. Model: Laura McLafferty.

Here are some body poses you'll want to capture in your shots:

➤ The T-leg, the classic beauty pageant pose, with feet together, one pointing straight ahead, and the other pointing outward

➤ Facing the camera with hands on hips

179

Reality Check

Even though many women's hips are larger than their shoulders, you don't want the photograph to show this. One way models often disguise this imbalance and make their shoulders and hips seem like they're actually the same width is to turn their hips to the three-quarters angle, but keep their shoulders and head facing straight ahead to the camera.

Catwalk Talk

A **contact sheet** is a large sheet of photographic paper that has mini prints of all the pictures that were captured on one roll of film by the photographer.

➤ Hips facing three-quarters, shoulders and head facing the camera straight on

➤ Full profile, with body and head turned sideways

➤ Sitting on the floor sideways with legs bent and arms behind you, supporting your weight

➤ Kneeling on the floor sideways with your hands on your knees and your head facing the camera

➤ Lying on your side, with your arm bent and your head propped up with your hand

Personality Shots

The third type of photo you'll want to take during a test shoot for experience is a personality shot. When you look at the *contact sheets* of these shots (a large sheet of photographic paper that has mini prints of all the pictures on it), you'll be able to discover what you're capable of in front of the camera, which will help you figure out what type of model you are and what moods you're best able to project.

When a camera is turned on a person, her whole attitude changes: One person becomes closed and withdrawn, another gets aggressive and strong, and still others get silly. Personality shots will give you an idea of who you become when the camera is on you. You want to learn who that is and enhance it, because it's your true persona and the key to the image you'll project as a model. Personality photos also teach you what style of clothing suits you best—athletic wear, high-fashion styles, masculine-tailored clothing, or simple, casual clothes.

For these photos, you'll want to experiment with different types of clothing, makeup, even wigs—let your imagination guide you. Most likely you'll collaborate with the photographer on the looks you want to use. Some ideas: an elegant evening dress, a punk rock look (tight black jeans, leather jacket), or business wear (suit and stockings). You may also want to try playing with different types of wigs, high heels, fishnet stockings, and other fun, costume-y items that allow you to create a character.

For your personality photos, try a variety of poses: in motion, standing completely still, and sitting down.

Looking at Contact Sheets

Usually a photographer will get back contact sheets, not individual prints. When you get them, study them closely and evaluate each one. Look at your facial expression in every photo. Do you look totally fake and stiff in certain poses, comfortable and natural in others? In which photos do you look best: with natural, minimal makeup or dramatic, intense makeup? In which pictures does your hair look its best? What hairstyles most flatter your face? At what angle does your face look its best: straight-on, in profile, tilted up, or tilted down? Does your nose look broad when you face the camera? Do you have a gorgeous profile? Do your eyes look bigger with your head tilted down? Do you look better smiling, pouting, or being serious?

In the body shots, study how your body looks. What poses best complement your body? What body parts look big and which look slim? Does your body look comparable to the models in the Victoria's Secret catalog, *Sports Illustrated,* or *Self* magazines? If not, figure out poses that better complement your figure, or you may need to work on your body to get it in better shape.

With the personality shots, check to see that your entire body is involved in the pose. For instance, you don't want to have your hands defiantly on your hips, your head cocked, but your eyes lifeless and without expression. Evaluate how well you create the image and if the image looks comfortable on you.

Which personality photos do *you* like best? Does the shot of the strong, energetic leader, the soft sex kitten, or the active woman running and jumping appeal most to you? Whichever photo appeals to you most, practice posing in the mirror to build on the part of you that you feel the most comfortable projecting.

Roshumba's Rules

If your nose is broad, avoid poses where your head is tilted down looking straight at the camera. Instead, turn your head to the three-quarters angle and use your eyes expressively to attract attention away from your nose.

In all three categories (head, body, and personality shots), study in particular your favorites and your least favorites, so you can learn the best things to do, and the things to avoid doing. Critique yourself, and learn from the mistakes you made in the test shoot. Also have someone else critique you—parent, friend, boyfriend—for an objective viewpoint. When you move on to the next step of modeling—professional test shoots for your book, or even a real photo shoot—you will have a big head start on learning what to avoid and what to play up.

Picture Time

You may want to—although it's not necessary—have some of your favorite photos printed (transformed from contact sheets to prints). But remember, this is just for fun, not to help advance your modeling career. Having more than two photos printed of each different category is really not necessary unless you want to give them away as Christmas presents. You're just learning from these photos, they're not something you're going to be showing or giving away to a professional modeling agent. Also, there's no need to purchase an expensive portfolio. An inexpensive photo album is all you need because when you get an agent, they will provide you with an agency portfolio.

Reality Check

In general, you don't want to show your test shoots for experience to an agent. Perhaps you didn't photograph well because of bad lighting, or you look five pounds heavier in the pictures because you weren't familiar with your body and didn't know how to pose. But an agent might think it's because you don't photograph well, when in fact, it's because you were working with an inexperienced photographer.

Catwalk Talk

Test shoots for your book, as the name suggests, are done so you'll have photos to put in your portfolio, which you take to potential employers to give them an idea of your look and personality in pictures.

Test Shoots for Your Professional Portfolio/Book

The second type of test shoots are test shoots for your professional portfolio, which are usually referred to as *test shoots for your book*. These are very different from test shoots for experience. Test shoots for your book are not done until you have an agent, who will set them up for you.

Your Calling Card

Test shoots for your book give you experience in front of the camera, but that's not their primary purpose. The real reason you do them is to have photos to put in your portfolio, or book. Your book is shown to potential clients when the agency is booking a magazine shoot, fashion show, or advertisement. It gives clients an idea of what you look like and how well you photograph.

Unlike test shoots for experience, test shoots for your book won't require much of your input. You don't have to find the photographer or decide which photos to take. Your agent will arrange all of this.

Calvin Wilson, the director of New Faces at Elite Model Management in New York, explains how test shoots for your book work. "We find a girl from a convention, walking down the street, an open call, or an agency referral, and we bring her to New York. She needs pictures to go around New York [to show to clients in order to get jobs]. Some girls, you take a few Polaroids (which are shot by the agents in their offices) and send them to people and they'll book them directly. But 9 times out of 10 a girl needs a test [photo shoot with a professional photographer]."

"We have *testing photographers* we work with constantly. Before the test, we try to figure out what [type] the girl is going to be, more editorial, more commercial, more all-American, and we gear the test that way. We do a test shoot, then we get all the pictures back together." The best ones are chosen, put in the model's portfolio, then she is sent out to meet with clients.

At What Cost Beauty?

The aspiring model is responsible for paying for the test shoot. But in most cases, the agency will pay for it in advance, then deduct the money from the girl's first paycheck. Elite's testing photographers are paid $150 for each test; they are also reimbursed for the cost of film processing and prints. The total is usually about $250.

Catwalk Talk

Testing photographers often act as assistants to major working photographers. They are aspiring to become working photographers in their own right.

Emotional Rescue

One major goal of the shoot is to show your range as a model. "There are so many different types of girls that are out there, we try to capture each girl's personality in the photos," says Wilson. "To me, that's the most important. It's hard to sell a girl unless you can see in the pictures some sort of personality is showing through.

"We try to get a whole range of emotions, whether it's crying, laughing, anger, or fear. We always try to get them laughing, which is almost next to impossible because no one wants to do that. They hate their laughs, a lot of them. They don't think that's modeling. It doesn't look like Cindy Crawford, it doesn't look like Kate Moss. A lot of girls like to be sexy, serious, lips pouting, that's what they think a model is." But this isn't always the image the agent is trying to build on a model, especially a very young one.

Generally, however, almost all shoots involve some beauty shots (up-close portraits), showing what the girl looks like naturally, without much makeup. There are also usually some body shots (pictures that show your body). Unlike test shoots for experience, however, you wear normal clothes, not a bathing suit, for these. Another difference between test shoots for experience and test shoots for your book is that the personality shots are not a separate set of pictures; they are done in conjunction with the beauty and body shots.

Shooting on Location

Most test shoots for your book take place on location, which means they are shot outside of the studio. They can take place just about anywhere: in a park, in a café, at the beach, in an amusement park, on a terrace overlooking the city. (Usually, models don't travel too far outside the city for these shoots.)

Although it may not seem like "real" modeling, most test shoots for your book take place on location. "Often a girl doesn't know what to do [in a photo studio]," says Wilson. "There are only so many poses she's got in her repertoire. If you have them

183

actually doing something—say, flying a kite—it gives them something to [focus on, so they] forget about taking the picture. I've seen shoots done everywhere: underwater, in trees, with animals, with kites, with hula hoops," says Wilson. "For one shoot, someone did a whole thing of having [a girl] fly a kite, then they had big giant balls, a hula hoop, a remote-control car—it was a whole story."

No Advance Preparation Necessary

Unfortunately, there's not too much a model can do beforehand to ensure that her test shoot is a success. "I think it's something you're born with," says Wilson. "Models are kind of their own race, their own class, they have a special genetic makeup. For the best models, it just comes naturally. You can't teach someone how to be sexy, it just has to happen. You can't teach someone how to giggle on command, it's something they just have to do. With experience, you get better at it.

"I always tell girls to practice in front of a mirror, trying to get different kinds of emotions, like fear, anger, sadness, happiness. But it's really hard to practice what you're going to be doing at the shoot because you never know what you're going to be doing … The best thing is to be well-rested, go there with a good attitude, to work well in collaboration with the photographer to get pictures that you want," says Wilson.

Hit Me with Your Best Shot

After the test shoot, the photographer looks over the pictures and picks out the best shots. He discards any that aren't top-notch—maybe the lighting is poor, the pictures are out of focus, the model's hair is hiding her face, or she's just not looking her best.

Reality Check

Legitimate agencies will send aspiring models to photo shoots with specific photographers they have selected. Unfortunately, this is very similar to a scam many unscrupulous agencies and con artists use on new models: They will tell a girl that before they can represent her, she first needs to set up a photo session with a specific photographer who charges an exorbitant fee. The unscrupulous agent, meanwhile, gets a big kickback.

Then the photographer sends the photos to the agent, who picks the ones he wants to include in the girl's book. The girl is generally not involved in deciding which pictures will be chosen. "We decide [which photos will be included in the portfolio]," says Wilson. "Sometimes the girl will come by and say, 'Can I see?' But usually they trust our decisions. We want to get the pictures that are going to make the girl look the best. We're not trying to jeopardize anything."

To avoid getting scammed, Wilson recommends checking with the Better Business Bureau to see if any complaints have been listed about a specific agency, especially if you haven't heard of it (see Chapter 11, "Advice for Parents"). "If you haven't heard of something, ask around, look it up in the Yellow Pages, ask to talk with people who have worked with them. Ask them to give you a list of clients you can call. Also, if you have to pay a lot of money to get pictures, that's not a good sign. Normally we'll advance the [money for the] pictures." (At Elite, test shoots generally cost about $250.)

Once your book has some great test shots in it, you're ready to get the rest of your modeling materials together, which I discuss in the next chapter.

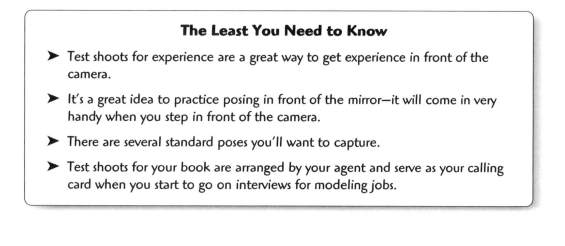

The Least You Need to Know

➤ Test shoots for experience are a great way to get experience in front of the camera.

➤ It's a great idea to practice posing in front of the mirror—it will come in very handy when you step in front of the camera.

➤ There are several standard poses you'll want to capture.

➤ Test shoots for your book are arranged by your agent and serve as your calling card when you start to go on interviews for modeling jobs.

Chapter 14

Tools of the Modeling Trade

> ## In This Chapter
>
> ➤ Selling yourself: the model's portfolio and composite card
>
> ➤ The voucher system of getting paid
>
> ➤ Keeping track and in touch with datebooks, answering machines, and cell phones
>
> ➤ Promotional materials the agency uses

Writers have their laptops; tennis players have their racquets; ballerinas have their toe shoes. Like all these other professionals, models have certain materials that are absolute necessities for their careers.

Once you've found an agent to represent you, you, too, will need to acquire these model must-haves. They include photos, tear sheets, composites, and portfolios; these items show clients the work you've done and the work you're capable of doing. You'll also need vouchers, which are how you'll get paid, and a datebook, to let you know when and where you need to be at any given time. Models rely on answering machines, beepers, and cell phones to keep them up to date on all their appointments and bookings.

In this chapter, I'll explain everything you need for a modeling career.

Shooting Stars: Photos and Tear Sheets

Because models are usually hired on the basis of their looks—an advertiser wants a girl with long hair for a shampoo campaign, a magazine wants a sexy blonde for its Valentine's Day issue—photos are an essential part of a model's professional materials.

Catwalk Talk

Tear sheets are pages torn from a magazine, newspaper, or other periodical. A model tears out any pages on which she's pictured and puts them in her portfolio.

Photos are needed for a model's portfolio, for composite cards (two-sided cards with several pictures of one model on them), for the agency's book, and for the agency's head sheet, which is the agency's composite card. (We discuss portfolios, composite cards, agency books, and agency head sheets later in this chapter.)

Depending on the stage of a model's career, photos for her portfolio, for composite cards, and for the agency book and the agency head sheet come from two major sources: Either they are taken at a test shoot for your portfolio, or they are *tear sheets* (pages torn from a magazine, newspaper, or other periodical), from an advertisement or editorial photo shoot you appeared in.

Whenever a model does a job, tear sheets are removed from the magazine or catalog for which she worked and placed in her book.

If a model is just starting out and hasn't worked yet, she would use the photos from her test shots for her portfolio (see Chapter 13, "Testing, Testing, 1, 2, 3: Test Shoots," for more information). Once a model starts working, however, her test shots are gradually replaced by examples of her professional work, or tear sheets.

Your agency will get tear sheets for all the work you do. Often, the magazine or catalog company will send them copies, or the agency may subscribe to the publications themselves. It's also a good idea for the model to have her own copies of her tear sheets. Your agency may be able to give them to you, or you may want to buy one or two copies of the magazine.

There are several reasons you should have your own set of tear sheets. Once your career gets going, you may find that you have acquired agencies in several different cities, and you may need extra tear sheets because you'll need to keep a current portfolio in every market. Also, if you decide you want to change agencies and something gets lost in the shuffle, you have your own archives to fall back on. Keep at least five perfect copies of all of your covers, tear sheets, and advertisements just in case one of your agencies is missing something. They're also great to keep as souvenirs!

It's acceptable to make color laser copies of your tear sheets and test photos for your portfolio.

Beauty Book: Your Professional Portfolio

Your portfolio or book is basically a photo album that contains select test shots and tear sheets. The portfolio is a leather- or quality vinyl-bound album that has see-through sleeves inside. It can vary in size but averages around 12" × 15". It's provided by the agency to all its models, and it has the agency's name, address, phone number, and logo on the cover.

Different agencies have different styles of books. Some are leather bound; others have high-tech plastic covers. Portfolios have pockets on the inside covers where composites (see the section on composites later in this chapter) and extra photos can be placed. You keep one copy of your portfolio, and your agency keeps two or three copies, so they can be sent out when requested by clients.

You bring your portfolio with you whenever you go on go and sees at magazines, with advertisers and photographers, and/or for fashion shows; your agency sends it out when clients call to request a specific type of model.

The purpose of a portfolio is to keep your photographs neat and organized, to tell your individual "story," and to give clients a sense of your best features and personality. Your portfolio may open with a head shot; on the next page, there may be a lovely body shot; on the next, shots that reveal your personality. Others may spotlight your best features, such as hair, legs, or skin. When you're first starting out, your portfolio may contain from six to 10 photos; more will be added as your career progresses. An established model's portfolio could have up to 20 shots. But you don't want to include too many pictures, which can overwhelm the client.

You may be wondering why you need to bring a portfolio with you to a go and see. After all, you're standing in front of the clients, why do they need to look at photos of you as well? The reason you need a portfolio is that you may walk into a go and see in jeans and a T-shirt, because the client wants to see you in your natural, unmade-up, unstyled state. But the client also needs to know how well you photograph, whether your features are enhanced or lost in photos, what kind of personality you project, and how you move in pictures. That's why a portfolio full of great photos is so important. Also, although you may not always be available to go on a go and see, your agent may send your portfolio to the client to give them an idea of your type.

This illustration shows a model's portfolio. As a model gets more experience, her test shoot photos are replaced by tear sheets from actual jobs.

Your agent will select the pictures to be used in your book and will arrange them in a particular order that best markets your individual assets. Although you may not like the pictures she's chosen or the order they appear in, don't change the pictures around on your own. Often the agent has had a conversation with the client beforehand, and she's sold you in a certain way; she wants the book to show you in that way. So don't change the pictures around without at least discussing it with her first.

How often your portfolio is updated will depend on your progress as a model. If you have five magazines stories coming out, your entire book may change practically overnight. (On the other hand, if there is one image that is just a classic, it might remain in your book for 10 years.)

Even supermodels need to have up-to-date portfolios. Although people in the fashion industry may be up on all your most recent accomplishments, you may get a call from a client who's not necessarily familiar with your most recent appearance in the pages of *Vogue*. When you send your portfolio to that client, it's best if it contains your most recent work.

It's also key to update your portfolio whenever you undergo a significant physical change; for example, if you cut your hair or after you've had a baby. Even though you may be the hottest supermodel, changes still need to be documented in your portfolio.

A supermodel may also have a separate portfolio containing all the magazine covers on which she's appeared, as well as a publicity or press clippings book containing all the interviews she's done.

Reality Check

Your book is your calling card to the client; it represents who you are. If it's messy, sloppy, or dirty, it's annoying for the client and reflects badly on you. A neat, clean, organized book sends the positive message to a client that you are reliable and professional. Make sure you keep your portfolio clean and in order. To keep the inside sleeves clean, moisten a cotton ball with water, then wipe off each sleeve. Also make sure all photos are neatly aligned.

Mod Squad

I actually have three different portfolios, which is common for models who have worked as much as I have. I have a regular fashion portfolio, with images of my magazine and advertisement work. It contains beauty, fashion, and personality shots and is sent to editorial, advertising, catalog, and fashion designer clients. I also have a cover book, which contains all the magazine covers on which I've appeared. So if someone wants to do a documentary on my career, my cover book, which documents my evolutions as a model, would be more useful than my fashion book. I also have a book of my press clippings, which includes all the interviews I've done.

Although your agent is the one who organizes your book, you can still make it stand out by keeping it clean, neat, and organized. You'd be surprised at the condition of some models' books: They are littered with old slips of paper with appointments scrawled on them, candy wrappers, pens—you name it.

Models carry their portfolios with them whenever they go on job interviews.

A Picture's Worth a Thousand Words: Your Composite Card

A *composite card*, which is more familiarly called a *comp card*, is an $8^1/2$" × 6" card. Each agency has its own trademark comp card style for all its models, so the size may be larger or smaller, depending on the style the agency has chosen. The comp card contains an arrangement of up to six photos of the model in different poses. There are usually one or two pictures (usually at least one is a head shot) on the front of the card. On the back are three or four more photos, including a body shot, personality shot, and one showing some of the model's outstanding attributes: beautiful hair, a lovely smile, or incredible legs. The composite also lists the model's measurements, including height; weight; bust, waist, and hip measurements; dress and shoe sizes; and the agency's logo, name, address, phone, and fax numbers.

Catwalk Talk

A **composite card,** also known as a **comp card,** is a $8^1/2$" × 6" card that features several different shots of a model. It is given out to clients so they can get an idea of the model's look.

Roshumba's Rules

Keep your comps in good shape: Make sure they don't get bent, crumpled, or dirty. They should look neat and professional, not like the homework your dog ate in third grade.

Composites are standard, necessary tools of the trade for models. You will need to take yours with you when you go on go and sees, auditions, and castings. Clients use comp cards when they are selecting models for fashion shows, advertisements, magazine shoots, and TV commercials. The comps help them remember the model they meet once she's left their offices. Sometimes, a client may be seeing hundreds of faces in one afternoon, which is why they need comp cards to remind them of all the people they've met. A comp card is like a sales brochure for the model's look and style.

The agency that represents you will put your comp card together for you. (There's never any reason for a model to have a comp card before she finds an agent, so don't worry about this until you have an agent.) Your assigned model manager (also known as your booker or agent) will select the photos that show you at your best and/or embody the image that is being promoted to clients.

The agent will select the photos from the best of your test shoots and tear sheets. She'll then arrange the photos for the comp card, add the necessary statistical information, and arrange for the comp cards to be printed. You can be a part of this process if you like, but it's not mandatory. I suggest that you do take part in the selection and arrangement of your photos, however, because it will help you become involved with the management of your career. You can also learn a lot about how the agency sees you, how it is marketing you, and what is currently in fashion.

Comp cards are given out to clients to give them a quick idea of a model's look and image.

Generally, 100 to 200 composite cards are printed at one time. A model, not the agency, pays for her comp cards. The cost is often deducted from her salary once she starts to work. Usually, a model may be charged anywhere from $100 to $300 for comps, depending on how many copies are printed and how many photos are included.

Comp cards need to be updated and changed on a regular basis, at least once a year, and sometimes as frequently as every three months. In the first five years of my career, I was doing so many magazine shoots that I was changing my comp card every season (every three months). Later, when my career was established, I would go for up to a year without changing mine. Still, if a comp is more than a year old, clients may get the feeling that you're not in demand, that you're not doing anything new. Evaluate your comp card on a

Reality Check

Although it's a good idea to get involved with the selection of pictures for your comp card, don't be too adamant about your likes and dislikes. If you're just starting out, your agent may see you differently from the way you see yourself, and it may be that a photo you don't like may be crucial for promoting a certain image of you to the industry.

193

regular basis, and talk to your agent about it periodically to ensure that all the photos are current and reflect what you look like at the moment. As with your portfolio, you'll need to update your comp card whenever your appearance changes. Old, outdated photos may cause a client to think your new look is not selling.

Besides being a model's stand-in for a business card, comp cards are used to label the rack holding all the garments a model will be wearing in a fashion show. This helps the designers and stylists at a fashion show keep the clothing organized. Also, when a client, such as a fashion magazine or an advertiser, is planning a photo shoot that will include multiple models, all the models' composites are put together to determine if their looks complement each other.

Clients may also use comp cards for inspiration for a photo shoot. If a client has a new collection of clothing and they haven't figured out a creative way to shoot it, they may look at comp cards for ideas. Say there's an energetic shot of you on a trampoline on your comp card: That could be a great inspiration for the client in finding a way to shoot their collection.

Roshumba's Rules

When you're a beginning model, don't freak out if you don't like your composite. You're probably not going to be used to seeing yourself as a product, as an image that *is* being sold to clients.

Because you need to take them with you whenever you go on job interviews, comps are kept in a pocket on the inside cover of your portfolio, which you also need to take with you on go and sees. It's customary to keep about 10 composites in the pocket of your portfolio. You may want to keep about 20 more at home so you can replenish your supply as necessary. The rest of the supply is kept at the agency, which sends them out to clients when they request to see a specific model or a particular type of model. Whenever you run out, stop by the agency and pick up some more, or ask your agent to send you more.

She Works Hard for the Money: Model Vouchers

Instead of punching time cards or filling out time sheets, models are paid through a *voucher* system. Vouchers are issued to a model by her agency, usually in books that contain 20 or so vouchers. The model takes the voucher with her to the job, where it's signed by the client, confirming that she worked. Then the model submits the signed copy to the agency's accounting department, which bills the client and pays the model.

Your agency's vouchers have the agency's name and address printed on them. There are also blank spaces that the client is responsible for filling in: the client's name, address, phone number, the photographer's name, the contact person in the client's billing department, and the client's signature.

The model fills in her name, the date the work was performed, the amount of the modeling fee, any extra costs such as travel fees (if the model is to be paid for flying to a location), and miscellaneous fees for such things as special haircuts, manicures, pedicures, or bikini waxes, and overtime fees.

Each voucher form has an original and two copies. The model tears off the clients' copy and gives it to them at the end of the shoot. She also tears off the agency's copy and mails, hand delivers, or faxes it to the agency's accounting department. The model's copy stays in the voucher book. It should be retained until full payment has been received for the job done.

Your voucher book should be taken with you to every job. You should have the vouchers signed on the spot because they are truly your only legal document that proves that you worked and should be paid. The voucher states the legal and binding terms of the relationship between the client, model, and the agency. Once it's signed by a client, it legally binds them to the stated terms and rates. Whenever a problem arises regarding payment, terms, or fees for a specific job, a model should consult with the agent who booked the job.

Vouchers are used for almost all types of modeling: advertisements, editorial, catalog, and fittings. The only exceptions are runway shows, because things are just too hectic, and TV commercials, which usually involve a contract that's negotiated beforehand.

Catwalk Talk

Vouchers are forms issued by a modeling agency to all its models that are used for billing purposes. The client signs the voucher at the end of a job, which verifies the model worked and should be paid.

Reality Check

Many models don't bother with getting vouchers signed, and instead leave their finances up to the agency. But I personally am a stickler about getting vouchers signed. If any problems arise after the shoot is over, that piece of paper is concrete documentation of the time you worked and the amount you're owed.

If you forget to get your voucher signed at the end of a shoot, you could do a couple of things. First, you could trust that the client will be honorable and pay you for the work done. This option is best used when it's a client you know well and work for often. The second alternative is that you could go back and get it signed the next day. Hopefully, the client's offices are located in the city where you're based, or maybe the same team is still working in the studio. Thirdly, you could mail it to them and ask them to sign it and send it back. And finally, you could fill out your part of the voucher, sign it, and send it to the Accounting Department of your agency, and they'll take care of it.

Keep your voucher book in your handbag or backpack, because you'll need it every day, especially when you're working a lot. It's important to keep it in something you know you'll be carrying with you all the time. When work is sporadic, keep it in a file drawer with other important papers.

Keeping in Touch

Other modeling musts include answering machines, cell phones, and pagers. Although you probably don't need all three, you will need an answering machine at the very least, and a cell phone and/or a pager are great extras.

Because so much of a model's time is spent running around going on go and sees or working away from home, it can be almost impossible for an agent to keep in touch with a model. She may need to talk to you several times a day to let you know about newly scheduled go and sees and jobs. For instance, your agent may have heard from a client you already met with who wants you to come by their offices later in the day for a fitting because they want to book you for a shoot the next day.

That's why having an answering machine (or voice mail) that you can check regularly is so important. It's also great if you have a cell phone, which your agent can use to reach you, or a pager, which lets you know when someone is trying to get hold of you.

Roshumba's Rules

Because you'll be using your answering machine or voice mail for work as well as personal messages, keep your outgoing message short, sweet, and professional. Simply state your name and ask the caller to leave a message.

Although the cost of cell phones and pagers is decreasing all the time, if you're just starting out, you may want to economize by using public phones to check your messages on your answering machine.

If you're on a go and see, and you haven't had a chance to check in with your agency for several hours, it's okay to ask to use the client's phone to call the agency. Just keep your call brief and professional, and let your agent know that the client allowed you to use their phone. The client is doing you a special favor, so be sure you don't take advantage of them. This is not the time to call your girlfriends to gossip, your boyfriend to tell him you miss him, or your parents (long distance) to say hello. Also, if the client is obviously frantically busy, don't ask to use their phone.

The Essential Datebook

Models rely on their datebooks to keep their lives organized, and many modeling agencies give agency datebooks with their logo on it to their models every year. (Often, they're the agency's Christmas present to its models.) You can also buy your own datebook. The best type is the kind in which each day has its own page. You need room to write down as many as 15 appointments per day, all the details about each one, as well as any personal engagements, which is why the day-per-page format is preferable. Try to select one that's not too bulky, because you'll be carrying it around a lot, and if it's too heavy, it can be a pain—literally. A good size is 5" × 7".

Most agency datebooks also include an address book section, where you can keep track of addresses and phone numbers of your bookers, photographers, and clients, and other important names and numbers. If you're buying your own datebook, look for one that includes a section for addresses and phone numbers. Keeping track of things like this can also be done with vouchers.

Your datebook also has a couple of important long-term uses. It's good for keeping track of how much you're owed for jobs, which helps you make sure you're getting paid the right amount for the work you're doing. Also, it can help you make sure you're getting the same amount when clients hire you again. If I worked for J. Crew six months ago and they paid $5,000, and now they want to pay me $4,000, I'll know that they're cutting my rate, and I'll be able to ask my agent to check into it.

Another use for datebooks: At the end of the year, if you want to send out Christmas cards to all the clients you've worked with that year (I always think this is a nice idea for showing clients how much you appreciate their hiring you), you don't need to bug the agency for all the names and addresses of people you've worked with. They're all there in your datebook!

Roshumba's Rules

At the end of every month, I write myself a little note in my datebook. I evaluate the month, making notes about things I want to change or improve and things I want to talk to my agent about.

Calling All Models: Agency Promotional Materials

Just as an individual model has her portfolio and composite cards, an agency has its own promotional materials. Most agencies have two different types of books. The first, the in-house *agency book,* stays in the agency's office. It is the agency's own portfolio; it contains several pictures (either tear sheets or test shots) of each of the models the agency represents. Depending on the size of the agency, each department—New Faces, Model Management, Runway, Catalog, and Advertisement—may have its own book. The agency is responsible for putting together the agency book and for all costs involved in its production and maintenance.

The agency book is used when clients come into the agency to see all the models the agency represents in one fell swoop. For instance, there may be a Japanese client who is interested in hiring models to do shoots in Japan. He would set up an appointment at the agency to look at the agency book, which would give her a quick overview of many different types of models.

The agency also has a *promotional book,* a bound book that is sent out to clients and photographers.

Catwalk Talk

An **agency book** is an in-house portfolio that contains pictures of all the models that the agency represents. An agency's **promotional book** is a bound book of models' photos that is sent out to clients and photographers. The agency **head sheet** is a poster that features pictures of all its models.

It contains several pictures (either tear sheets or test shots) of all the models the agency represents. Every year or so, the agency will print a new promotional agency book and send it out to clients. Clients use it as a quick reference whenever they're looking for models to hire. Models pay for their own page in the agency promotional book—the agency will let you know what the charge is and the payment procedure.

The agency also regularly prints what's called a *head sheet,* which is a poster-size agency composite with every model's head shot on it. Like the agency's promotional book, the agency head sheet is sent out to clients and photographers. It's updated more frequently than the agency book, however, because it's less expensive to have printed. Models may have to pay their share of the cost of the agency head sheet, but sometimes the agency itself will take care of the expense.

The agency head sheet contains pictures of all of an agency's models.

All of these tools of the trade are necessary to keep your modeling career running smoothly and efficiently. Although they may seem foreign to you now, they'll soon become must-haves once your career gets going.

The Least You Need to Know

➤ A model's portfolio and composite card are used to help sell her and her look to clients.

➤ Model vouchers, which are signed by the client, allow models to get paid.

➤ Datebooks are essential for helping models keep track of their appointments.

➤ Answering machines, cell phones, and beepers help models keep in touch with their agents and new job developments.

As a model, you'll be trying out many different makeup looks to see which ones suit you best. This photo shows just a minimum of makeup—some foundation, mascara, and a little lipstick—just enough to look good on camera.
(Photo courtesy of Hosea L. Johnson.)

This photo shows a medium makeup look. I'm wearing some blush, eye liner, and lip liner, yet I don't look too "done."
(Photo courtesy of Hosea L. Johnson.)

This photo shows a glamour makeup look. My eyes are done up to the max, my lips are a vivid, bold pink, and my cheekbones have been contoured. A dramatic accessory, like this shawl, heightens the illusion of sophistication.
(Photo courtesy of Hosea L. Johnson.)

A big part (an hour and a half, at least) of any model's day is getting her hair and makeup done, as I am here, before going onstage to host the Elite Model Look model search. Sitting in that chair for a couple of hours a day is not as fun as it sounds at first!

(Photo courtesy of Roshumba Williams.)

Here's how I look onstage at the Elite Model Look after 45 minutes with the hairstylist, an hour with the makeup artist, and 20 minutes with the fashion stylist. Before you start comparing yourself to any model, know that there are a lot of people behind the scenes who help her create that look.

(Photo courtesy of Roshumba Williams.)

As the name suggests, a headshot is a closeup of a model's face and head. A photo like this can be your official headshot in your modeling portfolio. (Photo courtesy of Antoine Verglas.)

ROSHUMBA

This photo shoot took place on the warm, sunny beaches of Jamaica. Because the trend right now for magazines, advertisement, and catalogs is for outdoor photography, many shoots happen in sunny climates, to take advantage of the beautiful weather, which means models must travel continuously from shoot to shoot. This is a good pose (in or out of water) to try out when you're doing your test shoots for experience.

(Photo courtesy of Adrian Buckmaster.)

This shot, which was taken for a calendar, really plays up my image as an Amazon, one of the seven distinct model types.

(Photo courtesy of Adrian Buckmaster.)

This is another shot taken for a calendar. Notice the position of my arms and the way my body is turned slightly to the side (which is known as the three-quarters angle). This is a great pose for de-accentuating wide hips or thighs.

(Photo courtesy of Adrian Buckmaster.)

As a model, you'll be called on to pose in all sorts of crazy ways. This shot, the classic runner's crouch, emphasizes the athletic nature of the outfit I'm wearing.
(Photo courtesy of Adrian Buckmaster.)

Shown here is the classic T-stance (also known as the beauty-contestant pose). Models use this pose a lot for every aspect of modeling—in photos, on the runway, during fittings. Try it out when you do your test shoots for experience.
(Photo courtesy of Adrian Buckmaster.)

This shot is a great example of posing for catalogs: You can clearly see the outfit and how it fits, and I have a huge smile on my face (which, hopefully, the viewer will read as "she's so happy in that dress," and then be inspired to order it from the catalog). *(Photo courtesy of Charles Tracy.)*

The photo here is for an editorial fashion spread. This picture is more about creating an image of glamour and allure than it is about showing the outfit—which is typical of editorial work. *(Photo courtesy of Charles Tracy.)*

I'm posing with five regional winners of the Elite Model Look model search in this photo. These five young women are wearing the ideal clothes and makeup for models looking for an agent. Their T-shirts are close-fitting, but not too tight; their skirts allow the judges to see their legs but aren't too short or clingy. Their makeup and hair is simple and complimentary. (Photo courtesy of Roshumba Williams.)

Aspiring models from all over the country enter model searches like the Elite Model Look in the hopes of finding an agent. These six national finalists winners will now go onto compete in the international contest. The prize? A lucrative modeling contract with the Elite modeling agency. (Photo courtesy of Roshumba Williams.)

Here I'm having fun playing the "biker chick" on a Harley-Davidson motorcycle at a promotional event at Planet Hollywood. Models are often called upon to play a variety of roles, depending on what the job calls for.
(Photo courtesy of Kwame Brathwaite.)

Chapter 15

Go and Sees

In This Chapter

➤ What are go and sees?

➤ It's all in the preparation

➤ Overcoming a case of the jitters

➤ What to expect at a go and see

➤ How to stand out: tips from an expert

You've come a long way, baby: You've found an agent, you've done your test shoots, and you've assembled all your model materials; now it's time to go out and find a job. Unfortunately, legitimate modeling jobs aren't listed in the want ads, and landing a modeling job involves more than filling out an application.

Getting a modeling jobs involves a lot of legwork—literally. Your agent will set up job interviews, which in the modeling business are referred to as "go and sees." You can go on as many as 15 go and sees in one day.

Although a lot of your success at go and sees depends on your physical attributes, your personality and demeanor also count a great deal. That's why it's important that you know what goes on at a go and see, so you can be prepared, which will enable you to stand out—in a positive way—from the dozens of other models the client may be meeting.

I also asked the model editor of *Mademoiselle* magazine, Nikki Suero-O'Brien, for her expert, insider tips on succeeding at a go and see, and I'll share them with you in this chapter.

Go, Girl: What Are Go and Sees?

Once a model's portfolio and composite card are ready, her agent/booker will set up appointments for her to go on go and sees and *castings*. You may meet with any number of people on a go and see: the model editor and/or the fashion editor of a magazine, photographers, catalog clients, advertising clients, and/or executives from advertising agencies.

Although some go and sees will be for specific jobs, another purpose for them is for you to introduce yourself to the fashion industry and get to know as many people as possible—any one of whom could be a possible future employer. You may be sent to meet with a photographer, who then may refer you to a model editor trying to book a job, or maybe the photographer himself will keep you in mind for a future job. You may see a fashion designer who's not hiring any models at the present time, but whom your agent wanted you to meet so she'd consider you for future runway shows.

One of the most important aspects of go and sees is for clients to see you up close and personal. Although a model may have a book full of wonderful test shots, clients want to know what she's like in person, what makes her stand out from the pack. Sometimes models photograph different from how they look in person due to the lighting, the makeup, the pose, or just some intangible quality that makes them photogenic.

During a go and see, clients are looking for a model's unique, individual qualities: Is she at ease with strangers? Do unfamiliar situations totally freak her out? How does she make people feel when they are around her? Does she come off as a haughty princess, a gregarious best friend, or a sweet, naive little girl? Do her eyes sparkle when she speaks, does her body language suggest ease, not tension? Is she fun and bubbly, sexy and sultry, or quiet and moody?

Your agent will set up your go and sees as much as a week or as little as a day in advance. Every evening you must call in to the agency to get all your go and see appointments for the following day, including the client's name, street address, suite or floor number, and any special requests the client has.

Catwalk Talk

Castings is another word for go and sees. In America, a casting usually refers to a go and see for a TV commercial. In Europe, the term is used more often for all types of go and sees.

Roshumba's Rules

Make sure you write down all the facts regarding your appointments in your datebook so they don't get lost. It's annoying for agents when they're forced to repeat information about appointments more than once.

It's very important to be outgoing and talkative on go and sees, which will help the client get a better idea of your personality.

The Model Maze

I won't sugarcoat it: Go and sees can be a draining, depressing experience. I've had to go on up to 15 a day, so I know how hard it can be: You're running from place to place all day long, getting on and off the subway, often getting lost or getting caught in bad weather. Also, you're undergoing that nerve-wracking experience of meeting someone for the first time all day long, so you're constantly feeling tense and fearful. On top of all that, you know in advance that your chances of being rejected are high.

Despite all these obstacles, the most important thing is to stay cheerful, always be yourself, and let your natural personality shine through, because every client is looking for something unique and individual in each model.

My First Go and See

My first go and see came just one day after I had gotten my agent in Paris. My booker assembled a temporary composite card for me (which is common when you're first starting out, especially in Europe, where business practices tend to be more informal). When I stopped by the agency to pick up my temporary composites, the agents told me that they were going to send me to see a few clients.

The haute couture runway collection shows were coming up, and they hoped I would be able to find a job doing fittings for the shows, or maybe book a show. I was sent to several design houses. One of them happened to be Yves Saint Laurent, who needed a *fittings model.*

Walking into the mansion where Saint Laurent's design business is housed was overwhelming. It was so large and elegant, it felt like something from a grand old movie. I rang the buzzer and was buzzed into a marble entryway with a golden staircase. The receptionist was an extremely elegant, utterly intimidating French woman.

She directed me to the room where all the models were waiting to meet with Saint Laurent. He has a lot of unique rules for the models he works with, so I was required to put on a special white coatdress, black sheer stockings, and high heels before an assistant came out to get me. He led me into Yves's workroom, where I was dressed in a garment that was being prepared for the upcoming couture show.

Catwalk Talk

Fittings models work in a designer's studio. They try on the unfinished clothes; the designer then makes any changes in the garment so it fits perfectly.

Finally, I was brought in to stand in front of Yves and was asked to walk back and forth. He looked at me in the clothes, then simply said, "Thank you." I had no idea what he thought—whether he loved, hated, or didn't care about me. Later that day, however, one of his assistants called my agent and told him Yves wanted to book me. (Usually, a client won't give you any clues as to what he thinks of you, although you can usually get an idea from the amount of time he spends with you and his general reaction to you.)

Mod Squad

On some go and sees, the client will reject you before you even get all the way in the door. The worst reaction I ever got was during a season when the designers were using only blondes. I had barely gotten my foot in the door of one designer's offices when the people at the front desk called out, "No black girls!" It wasn't a racist thing, it was just the way fashion was at that moment. In fact, the very next season, exotic girls were hot. The very same client called and requested me. I said to my agent, "I thought they didn't work with black models." His reply was: "That was just last season!"

Go and Sees Never Go Out of Style

Go and sees are done by models at all stages of their careers. Even models who have been working for seven or eight years and have established clientele still do go and sees. One reason for this is that a model's appearance might change: She may gain or lose weight, cut her hair or grow it out, go from brunette to blonde and back again. A go and see gives the client the chance to see what the model looks like at that moment.

Fashion—and the "in" models—change as well. What was in style last season may not be in this season, so a client who wouldn't give you a second glance three months ago can be suddenly booking you every day.

Also, the people who hire the models are always changing jobs and new people take their places. For instance, even though I had worked for *Sports Illustrated* for four years, when they got a new model editor, I still had to meet her, so she could get to know me. (It's true, however, that the number of go and sees a model goes on decreases as her career becomes more established. For one thing, you'll already have met many clients, and for another, you may be so busy working, you won't have the time.)

But What Should I Wear?

It's totally acceptable to wear casual clothes on a go and see, and they're preferable from a comfort point of view. Jeans, a short skirt, a T-shirt, a sweater or denim jacket, and comfortable shoes (even sneakers) are perfect. Avoid wearing clothes that are too tight or baggy. Makeup should be clean and simple or none at all. Remember, agents and clients want to see what can be done to you, not what you've done to yourself.

Don't wear high heels if you're spending your day doing go and sees. You're going to be on your feet a lot, and high heels will just add to your misery. For runway go and sees, you may want to put a pair of high heels in your bag, in case the client wants to see you walk in heels.

This model is wearing the ideal clothes for a go and see: She looks comfortable and casual, yet her figure is evident under the slim-fitting T-shirt and jeans.

205

With her huge oversized top, big, baggy pants, and messy hair, this model may have a difficult time getting booked because she's hiding her assets.

Countdown to a Successful Go and See

The night before a go and see, figure out how you're going to get there (whether you can walk or if you need to take public transportation, and if so, what subways or buses you'll need to take). Also plan what you're going to wear. You may also want to think of a few topics you can chat about with the client (but leave room for spontaneous conversation).

Be sure to get a good night's sleep. Take a shower or bath the night before or that morning. Try to eat some breakfast or at least drink some juice before you leave for the day.

A lot of models carry backpacks when they have a day full of go and sees. When you're spending that much time away from home, you'll need to bring a lot of things with you, and it's just easier and more comfortable to carry them in a backpack.

Here are some things you'll want to bring with you on go and sees:

➤ Your datebook (of course!)

➤ Your portfolio

➤ A stack of comp cards (see Chapter 14)

➤ A subway, bus, and/or street map

➤ Snacks

➤ A bottle of water

➤ A sweater or jacket, in case it gets cold

➤ Any toiletries or medications you may need, such as contact lens solution or allergy medicine

➤ Makeup, if you wear it, such as light liquid foundation, powder, lip balm, or natural-colored lipstick

➤ A magazine or book to read while you wait

➤ A pager or cell phone

➤ High heels, if you're going to see runway clients

Overcoming Nervousness

Whenever I go on a go and see, I always feel a little nervous and jittery. I know I'm being critiqued; I know I'm dying to book the job they're hiring for; and I know I'm competing with many other beautiful girls (and often, they may be sitting right next to me).

It's only natural to feel insecure at go and sees. So that my attention isn't so focused on everything that can go wrong, I always bring something with me to read, such as a magazine or book. Reading serves the dual purpose of giving me something to do besides stare into space and think about how scared I am, and it shows the client I have interests outside modeling, that I'm into learning and bettering myself, that there's more to me than meets the eye.

Roshumba's Rules

A great book can be a useful conversation piece when you're meeting with the client. For example, if you're reading a best-seller, you can ask the client, "I'm reading this great book, have you checked it out?"

Another way to keep yourself feeling calm during a go and see is to ask the receptionist if you may use the bathroom while you're waiting for the client to come out and meet with you. In the bathroom, drink some water and splash some on your face. Another good trick is to take 10 deep breaths, exhaling fully from your diaphragm each time. Sometimes, if I'm really jittery, I'll go into the stall and run in place to get rid of all my nervous energy.

I also keep repeating some positive affirmations to myself while I wait. For instance, if there are many other beautiful girls in the room, I might repeat to myself, "Beauty is only skin deep," over and over to keep my confidence up.

The most important thing about go and sees is to just do them—do your best at each one and keep your focus on moving ahead and booking jobs. Don't get caught up in clients' negative reactions, because the client who rejects you today because your look is not right for her may turn around and book you for a major ad campaign when the look of fashion changes six months down the road.

The Early Bird Catches the Worm

Try to arrive at the go and see at least five to 10 minutes early. Give the receptionist at the client's office your name and ask her to call the contact person and tell him you're there. Depending on the layout of the offices, the client may ask you to come into his private office or come out and talk to you in the reception area.

The client will definitely want to look at your portfolio. He will also probably ask you various questions: Have you modeled before, what type of modeling you like best, what you see yourself doing in the future. *What* you say isn't as important as saying *something*. The client just wants to get an idea of your personality and how confident and self-assured you are. Be yourself, and allow your personality to shine through. Avoid giving one- or two-word answers to every question you're asked. Instead, be friendly and talkative and try to share some (positive) personal things with the interviewer. That's the only way personality will come through—if you open up and share some part of yourself.

Roshumba's Rules

As clients look at your portfolio, study their faces to try and judge their response to the various photos. Their reactions can help you get an idea as to how good your portfolio is.

Show the client you're interested in his work by asking about the job you're being considered for or about any upcoming projects. Many of the people you'll be meeting interview models all day long and are friendly and easy to talk to. Many (especially at magazines, clothing companies, and advertising agencies) are young, artistic, and interested in meeting with other young, artistic people.

In addition to chatting with you to get a feel for your personality, the client might ask you to walk or move around, and you may also be asked to try on a garment. From start to finish, a go and see can last anywhere from five to 25 minutes.

Insider Tips from *Mademoiselle*'s Model Editor

Nikki Suero-O'Brien, who has been the model editor of *Mademoiselle* magazine for 10 years, explains the go and see process from her perspective and what *model editors* are looking for.

"Once I see what the story is about, whether it's about little black dresses or bathing suits, I then work with the fashion editor and the photographer, and together we come up with ideas for models for the shoot," says Suero-O'Brien. "I'll have my input of girls I've seen that I thought were great and sometimes the photographer may request a specific girl.

"Every single day, I see five to 20 girls. Sometimes it's a general go see [meaning] the modeling agency calls and says, "We'd love you to meet this girl." Sometimes it's us calling them saying, "I'm looking for a girl with great hair for a hair story, a brunette with curly hair." We deal with all the agencies, from the mega to the tiny. You never know where you can find your little superstar. She can be with a little agency.

"I do go and sees by appointment. The models come in and sit down, and I'll take a look at their book, see what their pictures look like, see what they look like in person. I'll ask them questions, where they come from, a little about their background, schooling, how long they've been in the business, how they like the business, how they like New York, just to get a feeling as to what they're all about.

Catwalk Talk

The **model editor** books all the models featured in a magazine, including those used in fashion stories, beauty pieces, and all the other features in the magazine.

"From there, I'll take Polaroids of her. I have thousands of them. They help me in casting. It's hard to remember all those girls! Sometimes a model will come back four to five times before she gets booked on a specific job.

"I prefer to see them in a short little skirt, in winter it's obviously difficult. That way you can see what her legs look like. Also, something formfitting, where you can see her stature, the structure of her shoulders, her legs. The worst thing a model can do is walk in wearing a huge skirt, a wide balloony dress, or the hip-hop look.

"Once I see a girl who is the [*Mademoiselle* type], I'll introduce her to the fashion editor, the editor in chief, and to the creative director of the magazine (who's in charge of the visual look of the magazine).

"The type of girl we're looking for is dictated in part by the story, but the type will be similar. A *Mademoiselle* girl—she's fresh-looking, she's between 15 and 23, she has a great personality, she's bright, social, interesting, not necessarily a Classic Beauty, although we like the Classic Beauties as well. She has something that's quirky and interesting about her, someone with a great smile that shouts exuberance and happiness.

"Personality is also critical. I've had so many beautiful girls come here, and they'll sit in my office and not say a word. You're looking at their portfolio, and their eyes are just roaming around. They'd rather be anywhere than there. You have to get a certain energy, because if I'm not getting it here [in the office], then she's not going to do it in the studio with a photographer in front of a camera.

"Confidence really comes into play. It comes through in the way she expresses herself, in the way she communicates, her stature when she walks through the door. Even if she's petrified, at least she gives the illusion—and it's all illusion, all image in this business—that she's happy to be there, she loves what she's doing, she feels great about herself, and that she communicates that in her style, her language, her wardrobe.

Reality Check

According to Nikki Suero-O'Brien, model turnoffs include: "Someone who's obnoxious—you have to be confident, but nice, not obnoxious—someone who's not friendly, someone who's not well-kept (in the sense of grooming). Someone who doesn't like you today but may love you tomorrow—and vice versa."

"She comes in standing tall, elegant, slightly cocky with some attitude. That certainly attracts attention. You know she'll be able to carry it off in a studio. When you think of the money that's going into those shoots, the thousands of dollars, she's got to be able to pull it off in a studio," Nikki concludes.

The good news is, the more go and sees you do over the years, the more comfortable you'll become with them. You'll learn what to expect and develop a technique or routine for getting through them successfully.

But all the hassle and tension will all seem worth it when your agent tells you: "*Mademoiselle* finally confirmed, you'll be doing a eight-page fashion story about the best new clothes for fall!"

The Least You Need to Know

➤ Go and sees are job interviews for modeling jobs.

➤ Wear simple, comfortable clothes on go and sees.

➤ Prepare the night before for go and sees, and bring your portfolio and your composite cards with you.

➤ It's important that you can converse with the client; your personality could be the deciding factor in helping you get a job.

Part 4

Oh My God, I've Booked a Job, Now What?!

Booking your first modeling job is equal cause for excitement … and panic. But don't worry, you'll be calm, cool, and collected once you've read all the information and tips I have for you in this section of the book. First I'll tell you, step by step, everything you need to do to prepare for the job. To insure that you'll be comfortable once you arrive at the photo studio, I'll explain who everyone at the shoot is, including the photographer, the client, the hairstylist, makeup artist, fashion stylist, and the various assistants.

Finally, I'll take you through a day shooting in a photo studio versus a day shooting on location outdoors. Once you know the advantages and disadvantages of both, you'll be able to give it your best shot!

Chapter 16

... AND I EXPECT TO FIND
FRESH MILK AND COOKIES IN
MY TRAILER AS STIPULATED
IN MY CONTRACT....

Preparing for Your First Modeling Job

In This Chapter

➤ The who/what/were/when of your first job

➤ The ABCs of high maintenance

➤ Getting photo-ready

➤ Beauty and grooming countdown

➤ Staying cool, calm, and collected

Booking your first job can be the most exciting day of your life, the most frightening day of your life, or (most probably) both. Whatever you feel, there are certain things you'll need to know to make your day go as smoothly as possible. As always, knowledge and preparation are your most important secret weapons in ensuring that your first day on the job is a success.

In this chapter, I'll talk about what you need to do to get ready for that first shoot: what you should do the day before the shoot, the night before, and that morning, so when you walk in the studio, you can be confident and ready to give it your best shot.

What You Need to Know Before the Shoot

Whether it's your first job or your thousandth, it's a good idea to make certain preparations the day before. The first thing you want to do is get all the necessary details from your booker about the job.

First and foremost, you'll want to find out the location of the shoot (be sure to get the exact street address, the cross streets, as well as the suite number), the call time (the time you are required to arrive at the photo shoot), and how long it will last; the client's name, the name and phone number of the contact person for the shoot; and how much you'll be paid.

You'll also want to know any special requests the client has. If it's a *lingerie* or *bathing-suit shoot,* for example, you may need to get a bikini wax (a procedure in which excess pubic hair is removed), or the client may ask that you get a manicure or pedicure. Write all this information down in your datebook, not on a little piece of paper or the back of an envelope that can easily get lost.

Agents hate it when they have to give job information to a model more than once because of the model's irresponsibility. Also, writing all your appointments down in your datebook is just a good habit to get into in any case. That way, you'll always know where you're supposed to be, when you're supposed to be there, and what you need to do to prepare for it.

Besides helping you to keep all the necessary information in one place, writing appointments down in your datebook helps you plan ahead. Say you look in your datebook and see you're booked for a bathing-suit shoot on Friday, and two days before then, you have an afternoon free. You'll know that you should go get a bikini wax as long as you have some free time.

Catwalk Talk

A **lingerie** or **bathing-suit shoot** is a photo shoot for an ad, magazine story, or catalog in which the model wears lingerie (a bra, panties, slip, teddy, or other underwear) or a bathing suit.

Or maybe you realize from looking at your datebook that you're flying to the Caribbean for a shoot in a week; you'll have plenty of time to make any necessary preparations, such as getting out and packing your summer clothes, and buying sunscreen and other necessary toiletries. If all your appointments are written on sticky notes crumpled in the bottom of your backpack, you won't be able to plan ahead with the same efficiency.

Also, writing appointments in your datebook will help you always keep track of how much you're owed for the work you've done.

Roshumba's Rules

Writing down all your appointments in your datebook will help you at the end of the year, when you want to send Christmas cards to all your clients; you'll have everyone's names right at your fingertips.

In addition to getting the where, who, what, and when from your agent, you'll also want to get as many details as possible about the client, the shoot, and the team that will be working with you. Ask your agent who the photographer and hair and makeup people on the shoot will be, so you can familiarize yourself with their names. If you remember something about those people from doing your homework—perhaps you enjoyed a photo spread the photographer just did—you'll be able to compliment him on it.

Also, find out who the client is and what they do, what type of shoot it will be (whether it's a fashion shoot, in which case the focus will be on clothing, or if it's a beauty shoot, which may focus on the skin, the hair, makeup, or the body). This will give you an idea of what you're getting yourself into and what the client is expecting from you, so you can get into the mood of the shoot beforehand.

Also ask your agent for any feedback, comments, or compliments the client gave her about work you've done in the past. Maybe the client loved a particular shot in which you resembled a certain actress. This will give you a good clue as to what the client liked about you, which will in turn allow you to give them what they want at the shoot. Or if they liked a particular picture in your book of you running on the beach, you'll know they want to promote an image of health and athleticism. You can apply this information at the shoot.

Roshumba's Rules

If the client says something like they loved that test shot in which you looked like Sophia Loren, rent one of her movies before the shoot to get a feel for what they're talking about.

Are You Photo-Ready? The Day Before the Shoot

The evening before your first big shoot is not the time to start thinking about getting your hair trimmed, your legs waxed, and a manicure and a pedicure. Good grooming is an essential part of your job as a model. You'll want to stay on top of these things, so you don't need to panic and try to fit everything in the evening before a shoot.

Well-manicured nails are a model must.

Regular Maintenance

You should get your hair trimmed every two to four weeks, depending on how fast it grows. You should get a manicure and pedicure on a weekly or biweekly basis. Your legs, bikini area, and underarms (some people prefer shaving their underarms) should be waxed as often as necessary (it's a good idea to get this done several days in advance, as they can cause breakouts). Some models also like to get a facial or a massage every couple of months. If you don't know a good salon in your city, ask your agent to recommend one. Many agencies have arrangements with certain salons, allowing their models to get discounts on beauty services.

Clean-shaven legs are mandatory, because you never know when you'll have to model a skirt, shorts, or a bathing suit.

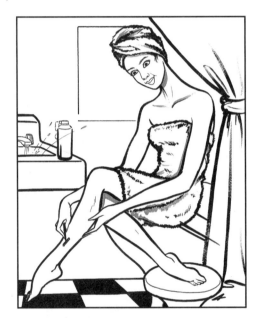

If you color your hair, make sure that your roots don't need a touch-up, or that your roots don't need to be straightened (in the case of African American models).

'Twas the Night Before the Shoot...

Either the night before the shoot or the morning of, make sure to shower or bathe so that your body is clean, fresh, and odor-free. Applying deodorant is also essential. The hairstylist and makeup artist will be working in close proximity to your body, and the fashion stylist will be pinning you and helping you take clothes on and off. You don't want them to be exposed to anything unpleasant, including body odors and armpit hair (believe it or not, some models go to work with bad body odor).

Another reason that it's so important to shower and apply deodorant is so you don't perspire in the clothes and leave any body odors on them. The garments used in a fashion shoot for a magazine (and sometimes for ads and television commercials) are

216

generally borrowed from the designer in return for a *fashion credit* in the magazine. But clothes are lent with the understanding that they will be returned clean and odor-free.

Also avoid wearing strong perfume and really greasy body cleaners. These things also stain and leave odors that could ruin clothes. Instead, try using fragrance-free or lightly fragrant nongreasy products.

Also apply your favorite body lotion after showering, whatever makes your skin look and feel good.

Catwalk Talk

In return for being allowed to borrow clothes from designers for fashions shoots, the magazine will identify the designer in the magazine's **fashion credits,** a listing of which designer created which garment.

Good Hair, Bad Hair

Your legs and underarms should always be freshly shaved or waxed whenever you're shooting. You may get to the studio and discover you have to shoot in a tank top; the client won't appreciate it if you have a jungle growing under your arms. Your personal hygiene will affect everyone on the shoot, so it's best to be clean and well-groomed at all times, even if the client doesn't specifically request it.

You also want to have clean hair when you arrive at the shoot. The hairstylist won't take too kindly to greasy, dirty hair, hair that's full of dandruff, or hair that's not well maintained. Before the shoot, you should shampoo and condition your hair—but skip the styling products; the hairstylist will apply any that are needed.

Ready, Steady, Go!

It's also a good idea to pack up what you'll need the night before so you're not rushing and forgetting important things. You'll want to bring your voucher book, a book to read during downtime, any special makeup requirements (for instance, if you have sensitive skin and need special foundation), any prescriptions you need, contact lens solution, your datebook, and your cell phone or pager, if you have one. You can also bring some of your favorite CDs to play in the studio. Pack it all together in a backpack, tote bag, or large purse.

It's also fine to bring a personal tape or CD player. But if it has bulky earphones instead of tiny earplugs that fit inside your ears, don't use it while you're getting your makeup and hair done. Earphones interfere with the hairstylist and makeup artist's work. If yours has earphones instead of earplugs, save it to listen to during lunch and other downtimes. Otherwise, it's okay to listen to except when it interferes with your actual work.

Another essential thing you should do the night before is plan the easiest and fastest route to take to the shoot. Check out a street map or public-transportation map to make sure you know where you're going and the best way to get there. If you're not sure, or are new to the city, ask your agent for her suggestions.

I also suggest that before you go to sleep you practice your poses and facial expressions in the mirror so they'll feel natural to you when you step in front of the camera. It might be a good idea to spend some time looking through your portfolio, so you can get a feel for why the client may have booked you for the job. If your agent told you that the client mentioned a specific picture that they liked, study it and try to figure out what they liked about it.

Reality Check

Don't think you have to run out and buy an expensive designer outfit for your first shoot. As your career progresses and you start to make money, your wardrobe can become more elaborate. Also, you'll no doubt start to develop a personal sense of style from being around people in the fashion industry so much. But in the beginning, it's best to keep your dress simple.

Dress for Success

You should also plan what you're going to wear, check it to see how it looks, and lay it out for quick dressing in the morning. Try to keep it simple—clean and neat jeans, T-shirt, and sneakers are fine.

Another reason it's smart to dress simply when you're just starting out is because right now, your focus of attention should be more on learning how to make your image more marketable. Dressing up could be distracting—for you and for the client. But if you are the type of model (a Chameleon or an Oddball, for instance) who has a strong personality and a strong sense of personal style that contributes to your image as a model, by all means, let it shine through in your style of dress.

Goodnight Moon, Hello Star!

You'll also want to get a good night's sleep so that when you arrive at work you will feel rested and energetic, without any bags under your eyes, with fresh, glowing skin and the necessary energy to get the job done. Don't celebrate your first job by going out for a big night on the town the evening before the shoot. Lack of sleep makes a model cranky, irritable, short-tempered, tired-looking, and less enthusiastic than normal—in other words, the sort of model no one wants to hire.

Remember, models are selected for the sexy, healthy image they project; that tired and worn look doesn't sell very well. Feeling tired will be reflected in the pictures as well, which will not enhance them or accentuate your beauty.

The Best Way of Waking Up: The Morning of the Shoot

On the morning of the shoot, make sure that you eat a good meal before you leave for the job. There is usually breakfast served at the shoot, but if you think you may be too nervous to eat in front on a bunch of strangers, eat something beforehand. (Otherwise, it's fine to eat at the studio, where breakfast is usually provided by the client.) You don't want to eat something too heavy, but you want something substantial enough to give you the energy necessary to help you stay alert and focused, which will allow you to do the best job possible.

If you're hungry, chances are you'll be concentrating on your empty stomach, not on how to do your best job as a debut model. If you're not accustomed to eating in the morning, at least try to drink a glass of fruit juice, so you'll be able to perform at work. A rumbling stomach is embarrassing—especially since people will be working so close to you!

Skipping breakfast is not a good way to keep your weight under control. You won't have enough energy to get through the day, and you'll be a lot more likely to overeat at the next meal.

The morning of the shoot, you should also shower (if you didn't the night before) and wash your face as usual. You should apply a light moisturizer as well, if you're shooting indoors. If you're working outdoors and there is a possibility of your getting sunburned, apply a moisturizer with sunscreen.

Also, be sure you brush your teeth the morning of the shoot. Remember that you will be spending the day in an environment where you will be in very close and intimate contact with people you will probably be meeting for the first time. The makeup artist will be working on your face, and it won't be appreciated if you have bad breath. Also, as a model, you want to take care of your teeth; a winning smile will play a large part in the success of your career.

Roshumba's Rules

Definitely have a cup of coffee if you always drink it, but this isn't the morning to drink your first-ever cup of coffee. It may totally throw your body's chemistry off and make you feel extra-hyper.

First-Job Checklist

The day before:

➤ Make sure hair, nails, and toenails are photo-ready.

➤ Get a bikini wax, if necessary.

➤ Write all the details about the shoot in your datebook.

➤ Exercise or take a yoga class to relax.

The night before:

➤ Call your parents for moral support.

➤ Shave your underarms and legs.

➤ Plan what you're going to wear.

➤ Pack your bag.

➤ Figure out the best route to the shoot.

➤ Practice your modeling poses.

➤ Get a good night's sleep.

The morning of the shoot:

➤ Take a shower or bath.

➤ Wash your hair.

➤ Apply deodorant.

➤ Brush your teeth.

➤ Apply moisturizer or sunscreen.

➤ Eat a light breakfast.

Building Confidence and Reducing Stress

Now that we've talked about your body, let's talk about your mind. It's normal if you're a little bit nervous or excited about your big debut. Here are some tried-and-true tips for staying calm.

The night before, it's a good idea to talk to your parents for some much-needed moral support, to hear some encouraging words, and to build your confidence. I would wait to talk to your friends, however. You will probably be nervous enough, and you don't want to add to that tension by talking to your friends, who, although they may have the best of intentions, may increase your expectations—and your nervousness—with their enthusiasm.

Reality Check

Before you tell people about your first shoot, you should know that many things can happen to prevent the photos from being published. Sometimes it may be due to bad weather, or perhaps the model wasn't quite right for the image the client was after. Other times, the client just changes her mind. I usually wait until I know a photo will definitely be published before I tell people.

There are also things you can do to help you overcome minor jitters and find your center. When I'm nervous or feeling off-balance, I bring my yoga books with me to read on the way to the shoot or take a yoga class the evening before. I may also attend a service at church or a spiritual center. Other times, I take an aerobic class or do some other physical activity to release excess energy and tension. Meditating is another way to calm your nerves. Taking a relaxing bath, watching your favorite television show, or listening to some mellow music can help, too.

Finally, try to keep everything in perspective. Although your first job is important, know that it's just one step on the ladder of success, not the whole ladder, so treat it as such and keep minor mishaps in perspective.

One job, no matter how glamorous, does not make a modeling career. Just because you may be working with one of the most famous photographers in the world, or are being paid a large sum of money to pose for an advertisement, doesn't mean you've got it made and that now it's time to act like a diva. Be humble and grateful that you're being given a chance to work. Try to make friends and build relationships with the entire team, including the client, photographer, hairstylist, makeup artist, fashion stylist, assistants, and other models on the shoot. These relationships may come in handy in building and maintaining your career.

The night before your first big job, you'll want to relax as much as possible. Yoga always helps me; you may also want to try going to the gym or meditating.

Panic Attacks

Minor jitters are natural before your first job. But if you find that the thought of your first job gives you a *panic attack*—a feeling of extreme anxiety, fear, and stress—and makes you want to throw up, or makes you so nervous you break out in hives, you're experiencing way more anxiety than is normal in this situation. If it's at all possible, try to get through the job in order to protect your professional reputation. But know that you will need to seek help immediately if you want to continue modeling.

Although these extreme reactions may stop after you've worked your first few jobs, you're better off trying to work through them with a medical professional as soon as possible. The first step is to let your parents and your agent know what's going on. Your agent will appreciate your candor and professionalism in dealing with this problem. She may also be able to refer you to a doctor who can help you deal with it. (Your best bet is to talk to

Catwalk Talk

A **panic attack** is an extreme reaction to a situation that wouldn't be cause for abnormal distress for most people. It's characterized by an extreme sense of anxiety, fear, and stress.

221

your regular doctor first, who will probably refer you to a psychologist or psychiatrist.) Don't be embarrassed; you're not the first model to suffer from this problem!

Even if your career gets a shaky start due to your anxiety, it's not the end of your career. Once your condition is straightened out, you may go on to work at the top of the fashion heap.

Hopefully, though, panic attacks won't be a problem for you. And you can decrease the tension and anxiety level by preparing thoroughly for your first shoot, following the advice I've given in this chapter.

The Least You Need to Know

➤ Write down all the details of the shoot in your datebook.

➤ Make sure your hair, skin, and body are photo-ready.

➤ Get a good night's sleep before the shoot and eat breakfast before you leave.

➤ Stress is normal; try to find positive ways to deal with it, such as exercising, listening to mellow music, or meditating.

➤ If you suffer from extreme anxiety before a shoot, get professional help to deal with the problem.

Chapter 17

Who's Who at
the Shoot

In This Chapter

➤ Wooing the client

➤ Wowing the photographer

➤ Working with the creative team

You're about to walk in the door of the photo shoot to begin your modeling career. You've done all your homework, you're freshly showered and shampooed, and you're eager to get started and make a splendid debut in front of the cameras. Your first day will be even more successful if you know and understand who's who at a photo shoot.

In this chapter, I'll explain who all of the people at a shoot are, what their roles are, and give you special tips on how to woo them, establish a solid working relationship with them, and make them want to work with you again and again. A team (photographer, model, hairstylist, and makeup artist) that works well together to produce outstanding images may be hired by a client again and again.

Impressing the Boss: The Client

Clients come in all different shapes and sizes and work in all different aspects of the business. The type you will encounter will depend on the type of shoot you're doing—whether it's for a magazine, a catalog, or an advertisement. The client can range from the young, super-chic *fashion editor* at a top magazine to a business-like catalog client, to a hip advertising agency executive.

On a magazine shoot, the client will be the fashion editor. On a catalog shoot, the client can be the art director or an in-house representative of the catalog company, or a freelance person who's been hired to produce the catalog. At an advertising shoot, the client will be the person who works for the company that produces the product being

Catwalk Talk

On a magazine shoot, the client is the **fashion editor** (also known as the fashion stylist or the sittings editor). She selects the clothes to be photographed, arranges the shoots, and makes sure the magazine's vision is being captured.

Catwalk Talk

The area in a photo shoot where the pictures are actually taken is called the **set**. The cameras, lighting, and any necessary backdrops or props are positioned on the set.

advertised; and, also, the advertising agency that came up with the idea for the shoot and is responsible for producing the ad will usually have at least one representative on the *set*.

A client's job on the set is to oversee the entire shoot itself, making sure the team is there, that they're staying on course, and accomplishing what they need to get done. The client also has final approval of the hair, makeup, clothes, lighting, and poses.

The important thing to know about clients is this: No matter who they are, you want to get on their good side by being polite, friendly, and attuned and responsive to their needs and personality. Above all, no matter who the client is, be professional and respectful.

Magazine Clients

The client on a magazine shoot is the fashion editor. She is usually very fashion-savvy and well-dressed. She probably worked very hard to rise through the ranks of the magazine, from intern, to assistant, to associate, to senior fashion editor. She may attend international fashion shows every season, or she may have worked directly with fashion designers at one time or another. Sometimes, however, her natural fashion savoir-faire has been the key to her progress up the ladder.

This type of person is really into the who's who of the fashion industry. She may own all the newest clothes—the latest Prada bag, the coolest Gucci shoes. Compliment her on the way she looks and how she dresses, and share your own personal likes.

Another way to really get on the fashion editor's good side is to acknowledge her talent and respect her power. You can compliment her on her work by saying something like, "I loved your business-suit piece in the June issue; it was so new and fresh." Fashion editors appreciate being acknowledged for the work they do. Also, be sure to thank her for giving you the chance to appear in the magazine.

Catalog Clients

Catalog shoots tend to be business-like and no-nonsense compared to magazine shoots, because a catalog is more interested in selling garments than in creating illusions. They have a strict schedule of what they have to get done and how many pieces they need to shoot in a day. The format of a catalog shoot is a lot more rigid, they shoot a lot more garments, and the days are busier and more pressed than other shoots. Catalogs are usually catering to an audience that is a bit more down-to-earth than the audience of a fashion magazine.

When it comes to work, catalog clients tend to be more low-key and business-oriented than some of the other people you may work with. Their primary focus is on the business of the day. They want to work with models who know what they're doing, who are grounded, and who have a strong sense of self, because those are the types of customers they're trying to appeal to.

Advertising Clients

Advertising clients are trying to appeal to the world at large. The atmosphere in the studio may reflect that excitement and creative energy. You want to tune into the mood of the shoot, giving them what they're looking for, and helping them generate that excitement. To do this, get as much information as possible in advance from your agent about the product, the image the client's trying to create, and what they're looking for from the model. This will help you do your best job at the shoot itself, so you can help them get across the image that they need for their pitch.

Advertising shoots tend to be a little looser and more casual than catalog shoots. Because people in advertising tend to be very creative, hip, and modern, you, too, can showcase your creative, humorous, or artistic side.

Roshumba's Rules

When you're dealing with the representatives from a catalog, be professional and mature in your demeanor. You don't want to be as chit-chatty and informal as you would be with a magazine editor.

Scenes from Behind the Camera: The Photographer

The photographer is the person with the camera, but he's not there to just mindlessly snap pictures. He has a lot of input into the format, imaging, and the story behind the photo shoot. Often, a photographer is selected because of his style of photography, whether it's realistic, fantasy based, or somewhere in between.

The photographer is the heart of the photo shoot. He's as important as the model because he's the one who captures the image. The model can pose and do what she's told or what occurs to her, but it's up to the photographer to capture that perfect image.

For instance, if *Vogue* wants to do a photo shoot featuring the latest swimsuits for its January issue, they don't just call in a random photographer and say, "We want to shoot swimwear, come on down and bring your camera." The magazine's editors and art director will sit down and discuss with the photographer the story they want to tell and the look the photos should have.

The photographer may suggest different types of locations—such as models in bikinis on motorcycles in a small town in California for biker-inspired bathing suits, or a shoot in the middle of a remote Moroccan town with models in bikinis on donkeys.

The photographer will also suggest types of film and style of photography for the shoot, the poses that can be used, and the hair and makeup styles.

The photographer and the model must communicate throughout the photo shoot. The photographer may offer advice, yet the model must also know how to move.

The photographer must also inspire the model and be open to inspiration by the model. That's why the relationship between the photographer and the model is so important, and why they really have to be in sync.

Mod Squad

Linda Evangelista did several famous photo shoots with photographer Steven Meisel in which she changed her appearance drastically in each picture, going from a blonde, Marilyn Monroe-inspired starlet in one, to a dark-haired Spanish flamenco dancer in another, to a redheaded Eva Peron diva in a third. This was a classic example of model and photographer inspiring each other, of a model acting as a muse for a photographer. Meisel was able to envision Linda in each of those guises, and she was able to fulfill his vision through her poses. Their working relationship, which was also a close personal friendship, spanned many years and resulted in many indelible images.

Once all the film for the day is shot, the photographer's day continues, because he's responsible for the developmental process as well. He has to be sure that the pictures are developed to the specifications and liking of the client. He must communicate with the photo lab he's working with to make sure they understand the look and image he's trying to capture. If the technicians at the lab don't process the film correctly, hundreds of rolls of film can be ruined and tens of thousands of dollars can be wasted.

Because it takes a while for a model to develop posing techniques, your best bet until then is to listen to the photographer's directions. And that sometimes means putting your ego in check so you can understand and learn what he's asking you to do. Sometimes when a girl is working with a photographer, and he's telling her to move her arm a bit to the left, tilt her head down, move her feet closer together, it can be tedious and annoying, especially if you feel like you already know what you're doing. Just know he's not picking on you and trying to imply that you're a bad model. Rather, the photographer's trying to capture you at the best angles and in the best light, depending on the lens and lighting he's using. His main goal is to get the best pictures possible.

When you're working with a photographer, be polite at all times, even when things don't go as planned or the shoot starts to get hairy. Sometimes, everything on a shoot can start getting out of whack, especially if it's at an outdoor location. You may be scheduled to shoot at a gorgeous beach location on the beautiful island of Bermuda, but then it starts to rain and the shoot is spoiled!

The model can help the situation by being open to the idea that the concept of the shoot may need to change. Maybe the story idea will change from a sunny beach shot to a picture of a model in the rain, which means she may need to get wet. Be open and willing to make adjustments whenever needed. Also, have a sense of humor and try to enjoy yourself. Just look at each shoot as a learning experience, and know that there's something to be learned each and every time.

Roshumba's Rules

It's crucial to listen to what the photographer is telling you to do. Even if you don't know how to move in front of the camera, you can listen and learn to follow directions.

Many times, if a model has never worked with a photographer, he may want to meet the model before the shoot, to get a feeling for her temperament and personality, and to explain the concept he has in mind for the shoot. Even if a photographer has seen pictures of you, he won't have a true sense of what you really look like until he sees you in person.

All in all, you want to try to make the photographer your friend. One photographer could make a model's whole career, if the two of you get along well and inspire each other. During the first three years of my career, I worked with Oliviero Toscani nearly every single day, shooting magazine stories for *Elle* and *Grazia,* and advertisements for Benetton, Sisley, and Esprit. Working with this one photographer paid my rent (and more) for years.

Mod Squad

I remember one shoot that was especially harrowing. *Sports Illustrated* was shooting in Barcelona, where they had rented a huge stadium for a night shoot. Three other girls and I were being shot in gold bikinis. We were shooting in November, when Barcelona is still pretty warm—a light sweater is all you usually need. But that night, there was a freezing sleet storm. We could use the stadium for only one night, the photographer had rented all sorts of special equipment, and the other models were leaving the next morning. So we went out and posed in a sleet storm. That was a true test of a model's professionalism.

Backstage with the Creative Team

When you're working with any member of the creative team, whether it be the hair-stylist, the makeup artist, or the fashion stylist, you want to be friendly, polite, open to her ideas, and cautious about expressing your personal dislikes. The fashion industry is relatively small, and more likely than not, you will be working with these people again. If you leave on a good note, you will start on a good note at the next shoot. You want to start to form strong relationships, which will contribute to the workings of a great team.

Reality Check

Feuding with any member of the team on a shoot could have negative repercussions on a model's career. You never know, the same team may have worked with the client for years, and you may be the new kid on the block. And if the hairstylist or makeup artist tells the client that you're difficult, there's a good chance the client won't book you again.

At all times, you need to remember that you're there so these people can create an image with you. Your physical self is a canvas that they'll be using to create the illusion that is needed for the particular photograph. No matter how it's sugarcoated or what grand illusion you've been told, the truth is that you are a product, and ultimately your personal likes and dislikes about hair, makeup, and clothes don't matter. So avoid expressing any negative opinions, unless someone wants to do something that can physically harm you.

The Hairstylist

On most shoots, your hair is done first, before your makeup is done or the fashion stylist gets you dressed. The hairstylist usually has a separate room in the photo studio (which she may share with the makeup artist). The stylist may wet your hair and apply various hair products to it to give it the texture she wants it to have. Then she may blow dry it straight, curl it with a curling iron, or put hot curlers in it, decorate your hair with jewels or hair accessories, or create any other look the client and photographer have decided they want. It often takes 45 minutes to an hour and a half for your hair to be done. The hairstylist may restyle it every time you change clothes. For one photo, she may blow it straight, for another, she may curl it, for a third, she may put it up in a chignon.

The hairstylist also comes with you onto the set to make sure your hair always looks its best. For example, if your hair starts to fall in your face, she pulls it back. She brushes your hair periodically to keep it looking freshly styled. She may also direct you to work your hair so it looks its best, say, by telling you to run your fingers through your hair.

When you sit down in the hairstylist's chair, know that first and foremost, you're working with an artist. Be respectful of the fact that she came up with this creation with the photographer and the client. You always need to remember that you are there to be the object of their creation, not to express your personal opinions. Besides, she wants the project to come out as good as possible; she's going to style your hair so that it complements you and is appropriate for the picture. So don't be too critical or judgmental while she's working.

Roshumba's Rules

Often hairstylists are very sensitive, especially when it comes to their work. You don't want to offend them or deflate their egos. Just sit back, relax, and let them do their thing. Look at it as an opportunity for you to experiment and see how different styles look on you!

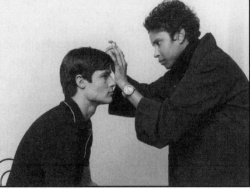

Patience is a virtue for models: They'll spend up to an hour and a half being prepped by the hairstylist before a shoot.
Photographer: Kwame Brathwaite. Models: Laura McLafferty and Ryan Kopko.

If a hairstylist asks you, you can suggest ways that make you feel comfortable—but only if she asks. The only time you should speak up is if the hairstylist is doing something that can damage your hair, for instance, she applies gel to your hair and then wants to use a curling iron on it. But instead of freaking out and totally rejecting what she wants to do, try to offer a positive alternative that will protect your hair and allow her to pursue her vision. For instance, you can say, "My hair's very fragile at the moment. I love your idea, but if you could avoid over blow-drying it or using a curling iron, I'd really appreciate it." When it comes to her actual artistic expression, however, you should let her do her thing.

The Makeup Artist

After the hairstylist has finished with your hair, the makeup artist will apply your makeup. She will prepare your skin with toners and/or moisturizers, then apply all the necessary makeup to your face. Foundation is applied first, followed by concealer, any necessary *contouring,* and loose powder. Then she begins to "paint," with eye liner, eye shadow, brow enhancer, blush, lipstick, and mascara. If body makeup is called for, she'll apply that as well. Depending on how elaborate the makeup look is, it can take the makeup artist anywhere from 45 to 90 minutes to do her job.

Catwalk Talk

Contouring means shading a model's face with darker foundation in order to enhance her facial features by creating the illusion of high cheekbones or a slender nose, for example.

If different makeup looks are required for subsequent photos, the makeup artist will redo the makeup each time. Generally, though, once your foundation is on, the basic makeup is set for the day. But with the various changes of clothing, the makeup artist may add some eye shadow, change the blush, or apply a new lipstick. When an entirely different look is called for, she may take off all the makeup and start over again. (See Chapter 27, "The Outer You," for more information on makeup.)

Even if the basic look doesn't change, the makeup artist checks your face before every picture to make sure your makeup looks fresh and beautiful. She also watches you as you work on the set, and if touchups are needed, for example, if you're sweating, she will blot your skin or apply some powder.

Here, the makeup artist applies the finishing touches to the model's makeup.
Photographer: Kwame Brathwaite. Model: Laura McLafferty.

Makeup artists are just that—artists—so respect their talent and artistry. They tend to be a bit more receptive to your input, though, especially when it comes to your skin and how it reacts to various products. If you're a successful model, you will be wearing makeup every single day of your life, and that can take a toll on your skin. They will usually do what they can to be gentle on sensitive skin.

Even as you make suggestions, you always want to be respectful of their talent and of the time they have taken to create a beautiful makeup look. You don't want to insult them or hurt their egos. They're not there to make you look bad; they want to make you look as good as possible—within the confines of the shoot.

The Fashion Stylist

The fashion stylist is in charge of all the clothes that will be used in the photos. His job may include visiting all the clothing designers' showrooms and selecting the clothing, shoes, and accessories that will be used for the shoot. He is also responsible for all the logistics of borrowing the clothes from the designer, arranging for their transportation from the showroom to the photo studio, and making sure they are all returned to the right place. He also must make sure all garments and accessories are returned in the same condition in which they were borrowed, which means they are clean and fresh, with no stains, dirt, body odors, rips, or tears. Once the model has put the garment on, the stylist will pin the clothes if they don't fit properly, make any other necessary adjustments, and accessorize the outfit as needed.

Roshumba's Rules

Once the fashion stylist has dressed you, you should try to avoid any body movements that can wrinkle the clothes. Don't sit down, and be very careful about folding or bending your arms.

Therefore, the best thing a model can do to make the fashion stylist her friend is to do everything she can to respect the clothes and keep them clean, unwrinkled, and properly hung up. A model should always arrive at a shoot freshly showered so that body odors aren't transferred to the clothes. (See Chapter 16, "Preparing for Your First Modeling Job," for more information on preparing for a shoot.)

You also need to be extra careful when putting clothes on and taking them off if you have makeup on, so it doesn't rub off on the clothes. In addition, don't smoke once you're dressed in the clothes for the shoot, because you don't want to burn them or leave them with a smoky smell. Also, don't spray perfume once you're dressed; you'll leave the scent on the clothes. Don't eat either; stains can happen. Be thoughtful of the stylist: When you take off the clothes, hang them up neatly.

Even though the garment might not appeal to your personal taste, any negative remarks about the clothing or outright refusal to wear something reflects very badly on you. Remember, it's not your job to like the clothes, it's your job to wear them, so don't complain about what you have to wear.

It's a good idea to talk to the fashion stylist to get any information about what is special about the garment, why the client is featuring it, or if it's part of a larger fashion trend. He might also give you some clues as to how you can best show off the garment's special features.

You should also chat up the fashion stylist to get to know him better on a personal level. You can talk about fashion trends (stylists are often very interested in fashion), or share other personal stories.

The Assistants

Often times, the professionals at a shoot—the client, the photographer, the hairstylist, the makeup artist, and the fashion stylist—will bring along assistants to help them. Many of these assistants are aspiring professionals themselves; they take care of some of the more mundane aspects of the professionals' jobs. It's important that you establish good working relationships with the assistants at a shoot, to ensure a smooth shoot and because they are the photographers, hairstylists, and makeup artists you may be working with in the future.

Whenever you come into contact with any one of the assistants on a shoot, keep in mind at all times that she plays an important role. While you want to acknowledge her presence and treat her politely and cordially, you don't want to be overly friendly or extremely personal. As a model, you need to do a tightrope walk between being friendly to the assistants and being overly intimate. The lion's share of the attention must be directed to head people—the client, the photographer, the hairstylist, the makeup artist, and the fashion stylist.

Now that you know all the people on the shoot, you'll have the confidence to make an auspicious debut.

The Least You Need to Know

➤ Your relationship with the client may vary, depending on whether you're shooting for a magazine, a catalog, or an advertisement (although you should treat all of them with professionalism and respect).

➤ The photographer is in charge of every aspect of the photo shoot, so it behooves a model to cooperate with her.

➤ The creative team, consisting of the hairstylist, makeup artist, and fashion stylist, are there to make you look your best, and deserve your respect and cooperation.

v.s.

In the Studio and on Location

In This Chapter

➤ Modeling 101: working in a photo studio

➤ Shooting on location, in town and out of town

➤ Leaving on a jet plane: supermodel travel tips

In the last chapter, we talked about all the essential people at a photo shoot and the role that each of them plays. Now that you know who the key players are, you're probably wondering what a day at a shoot is *really* like.

There are two basic types of photo shoots: those that take place in an indoor photo studio and those that take place on location. A location shoot refers to any shoot that takes place outside of a photo studio: in a park, on a beach, in a café, in a bank, or wherever. The kind of shoot you're doing will determine what your day on the set is like.

In this chapter, I'll take you through a typical day shooting in the studio and a day shooting on location, and explain the pros and cons of each one. Along the way, I'll give you some tips about shoot etiquette that will ensure that you're a success no matter where you're shooting.

Behind the Scenes at a Photo Studio

A studio photo shoot takes place in a photo studio that is rented for the day. (Occasionally, photographers have their own personal studios, but more often a studio is rented for the day.) The usual *call time* for most photo shoots is 9 A.M. (most end at 5 P.M.). You are expected to be there on time. Most of the other professionals on the set (hairstylist, makeup artist, fashion stylist) will also arrive at 9 A.M., although some may come earlier to prepare for the day.

Catwalk Talk

The **call time** is the time a model is expected to arrive at the job. It's the time the work of the day should begin, when the model and other team members go on the clock—that is, start getting paid.

Roshumba's Rules

I always try to arrive at the studio 5 to 10 minutes early, to ensure that I won't be late. Arriving early also shows the client that you take your work seriously.

The client may also come in early to make sure that everything that needs to be there is there, such as the clothes and any props, and that the team is there on time. The photographers' assistants may also come in early to start setting up the lights and camera.

The photographer, however, may come in from one to two hours later, because he's not needed until then. The model will be getting her hair and makeup done and the photographer's assistants will be setting up the lighting, camera, and set.

Breakfast is almost always provided by the client. Usually it consists of coffee, juice, bagels, muffins, fruit, smoked salmon, cream cheese, and preserves. It's usually laid out buffet-style; feel free to help yourself.

Your First Stop: Hair, Makeup, and Wardrobe

Eat your breakfast quickly, because the hair and makeup people will be waiting for you to finish so they can get started. Although it's acceptable to eat and drink in the hair chair, it's considered rude to eat and drink while you're in the makeup chair. The makeup artist needs to focus on your face, and chewing is very distracting.

Makeup and hair are most often done in the same room, which is usually separate from the shooting area. The hair and makeup chairs are often set up side by side, facing a big mirror. The makeup chair is usually a high director's chair, while the hair chair is lower, like the ones in a hair salon.

Hair is usually styled first, so that the various gels and spritzes the hairstylist applies don't ruin the makeup. Unless you're otherwise instructed, you should arrive at the shoot with clean, shampooed hair that's neatly trimmed. Don't glop lots of products on your hair or try and style it yourself. It should be clean and ready to work with.

When your hair is finished, it's time to move over to the makeup chair, where the makeup artist works her magic. This is when the look starts to come alive, and the studio starts to buzz with energy. Often, the team starts chatting, telling stories, maybe reminiscing about another shoot, or talking about the future. If the team hasn't worked together before, everyone gets to know each other. Often there is a CD player in the hair and makeup room, and music is constantly playing. If there is no music playing, you can put on whatever you like (many models bring their favorite CDs with them); the music is there to set the mood for the model.

After your hair and makeup are done, you will often have a little break of 5 or 10 minutes. This is a great time to go to the bathroom, because you may not be able to go once you're dressed.

Next, it's time to go into *wardrobe*. In some studios, this can be in the same room as hair and makeup, but usually it's a separate room to give the model some privacy to change.

The fashion stylist's assistant will give you everything you need to wear, from any special undergarments to shoes, and show you where to get dressed. She may help you put on a garment to make sure you don't get makeup on it.

The stylist will check you once you're dressed to make sure everything fits right, that the color looks good on you, that all the buttons are buttoned, and that there are no rips, tears, or stains. If something doesn't fit, she will clip or pin it (in the back, or wherever it won't show in the photo) so it looks like a perfect fit on the model. She may suggest different shoes, or another color hose, or different earrings.

Once you're dressed, don't sit down, don't eat, don't smoke—don't do anything that will wrinkle, stain, or damage the clothes. Also, try to avoid bending your arms, which can crease the sleeves. To avoid leaving footprints on the set, often you won't put on the shoes you'll be wearing for the shot until you get onto the set itself. In the meantime, you may be given temporary shoes.

Catwalk Talk

Wardrobe refers to both the clothes you'll be wearing and the area where you get dressed. It's where the fashion stylist works and where the model changes from her street clothes into the clothes for the shoot.

Roshumba's Rules

I suggest you wear a flesh–colored thong panty and a flesh–colored bra to a photo shoot. These are versatile enough to work with most garments.

Lights, Camera, Action: On the Set

When you go out onto the set, usually the entire team will accompany you—the head hairstylist, makeup artist, and fashion stylist. The photographer and the client will also be there. Once you're on the set, final touchups will be done: The hairstylist may re-spray your hair, the makeup artist may apply more powder and touch up your lipstick, and the fashion stylist may adjust your clothing.

After that you'll probably be asked to practice a few poses to give the team an idea of what you plan to do. You will also pose for a Polaroid, so the photographer can check the lighting, and the other professionals can check your hair, makeup, and clothes to make sure everything looks perfect. At this preliminary stage in the shoot, the photographer and client may tell you what image they are looking to capture.

The hairstylist and makeup artist accompany the model onto the set, so they can touch up her hair and makeup whenever necessary.

Finally, the shoot begins. Despite all your preparations, it's natural to feel unsure and frightened the first time you step in front of the camera. If you've done your homework, studied other models, practiced posing in the mirror, and done test shoots, you should have some ideas. If it doesn't seem to come naturally, try to take as much direction as you can.

Reality Check

Some models have such huge egos that even though the poses they are doing are not what was envisioned by the client and photographer, they refuse to take direction from the photographer, much less ask, "Is this what you want?" It's the question-and-answer process, however, that allows you to get feedback from the photographer and the client.

The most important thing is to stay calm, don't get frustrated, and listen to the photographer. If you're not sure about a specific pose, ask the photographer: "How does this look in profile?" "What do you think about my jumping or running?" Asking the photographer questions lets the rest of the team know that you're open to direction.

After each roll of film is shot, there is a short break to allow the photographers' assistants to change the film. It's standard for a photographer to shoot from 3 to 15 rolls of film for each look change (each different outfit).

Depending on how elaborate the shot is, you could be posing anywhere from 20 minutes to an hour. Shoots can go more slowly if there are special details in the clothing that need to be captured (maybe they're photographing something with a lot of details on the back that needs to be shot in a special way), or if problems arise (say a button hole won't stay closed).

After the garment has been shot to the photographer and client's liking, the model heads back to the dressing room to change clothes. Her hair and makeup are checked and retouched as needed, then she returns to the set, and the whole process is repeated.

On an editorial shoot, you'll shoot anywhere from 4 to 10 garments, with the average being around 6. On a catalog shoot, the number of garments shot is much higher: I've shot as many as 20 outfits in one day. The average, however, is about 12 pieces. Advertising shoots can vary, depending on the type of product.

Midway through the shoot, there's a break for lunch. Again, lunch is generally catered and there is usually a wide variety of choices. But you're free to order something different or bring your own food if you're on a special diet.

After lunch, the hair and makeup people will again touch you up, then you'll put on another garment, and shoot again. When it's the last shot of the day and everything is finished, the photographer or the client will say, "We're *wrapped.*"

Before or after you put your own clothes back on, politely ask the client or the client's assistant to sign your voucher. It's also nice if you thank them for the day, and tell them you hope everything turns out as they hoped. But don't go overboard and beg for another job: Your work and attitude will speak for themselves.

Sometimes, you will be hired to do a studio shoot out of town, which is a shoot in a studio in a city other than your home base. Out-of-town studio shoots are very similar to studio shoots in your home base. The biggest difference may be in the call time. This is to take into consideration the travel schedules for both the models and the clothes, which may be flown in for the shoot from another location.

When you're shooting out of town, keep in mind that you may not be able to find everything you're used to being able to easily get. If you have special dietary or other needs, plan ahead and bring whatever you need with you.

Catwalk Talk

When the photographer or client says "We're **wrapped,**" it's the official word that the shoot is over, that the work of the day has been completed, and that the model and the team can pack up and go home.

Reality Check

Keep in mind that studios in places outside of New York, Paris, and Milan may not have the experienced staff and other resources that those in the fashion capitals may have. The people who are managing and running the studio may not be as savvy about catering to the needs of a fashion team, because they're not as experienced in dealing with professional photo shoots.

In-Town Location Shoots

There are two types of location shoots: in town (which take place in your home base) and out of town. In-town location shoots often take place in a park, a busy area of town, such as Times Square in New York, or architecturally significant places such as the Duomo cathedral in Milan. Sometimes, locations are chosen for the ambiance that they lend to the shot; examples include a picturesque local street, a cozy café, even a beach.

Most location shoots take place outdoors, but not all. It's also considered a location shoot if you're shooting evening gowns for *Harper's Bazaar* at the Ritz Hotel in Paris, or business suits for a catalog in an architect's office in Atlanta.

Often location shoots have odd hours. This is because of the restrictions imposed by shooting permits, which are often necessary for location shoots, especially in big cities, and more important, because of lighting requirements of the shoot. Generally, photographers don't like to shoot in the middle of the day, when the bright, glaring midday light looks harsh in photos. The light in the early morning and early evening is much more complimentary. Often, you'll have a 4 or 5 A.M. call time because once the light is gone for the day, it's gone.

Another reason you may get an odd call time is if you're shooting in a busy location, say a grand old railroad station. Since it can be nearly impossible to shoot with huge crowds of people around, you may be asked to come in very early in the morning. Other times, the call time may be 11 P.M. for a night shoot, when the photographer wants to capture a glamorous nighttime look.

Mod Squad

One particularly glamorous night shoot I did was for French *Elle*. We were shooting couture evening gowns, and the editor wanted to shoot them in an especially alluring setting; they chose the magnificent Place de la Concorde in Paris. Special makeup was used that would glisten in the night lights. In addition, the photographer used a special light, a "sun gun," to give a unique look to the pictures. The biggest challenge on the shoot was the lighting; we had a much longer wait time than usual between every shot. As odd as it felt to be shooting at that hour, it was fun, because there was a kind of a party atmosphere at the location.

The call times for a location shoot also take into consideration the fact that many more things can go wrong to delay a location shoot than a studio shoot. There may be parking problems, bad weather, or trouble getting the model to the set. These contingencies are all taken into consideration when call times are scheduled.

For the majority of in-town location shoots, specially outfitted Winnebago trailers are used for all the preparations for the shoot. The Winnebago is the place where the hairstylist and makeup artist work, where the clothes are prepared, and where the model gets dressed. This is also where you eat, socialize, and wait between shoots, and where the bathroom is.

Whenever you're working in a Winnebago, know that space is limited. Don't bring a lot of stuff with you, and don't leave it strewn about the whole trailer. Also, once you've gotten your hair and makeup done, stay out of the way of the team, because they need space to work. Try to be more patient than usual; with such close quarters, it can be tedious and annoying with everyone on top of each other.

Once she's ready, the model waits in the Winnebago until she's called to the set by the photographer or his assistants. They are on the set getting ready and keep in contact with the Winnebago via walkie talkies.

Roshumba's Rules

Because of the logistical problems involved with location shoots, it's especially important that you arrive on time. If you arrive even 15 minutes late, you will inconvenience the whole team and may wreck the whole shoot.

Normally the Winnebago is parked a few yards away from the set, although the location could be a couple of blocks away because of parking restrictions. In this case, you would need to walk from the trailer to the location. If it's any further than that, there will probably be a car to transport you.

Just as a studio shoot, an eight-hour day is the norm on location. Despite the more complicated logistics of a location shoot, you can usually get the same amount of work done. Also, both breakfast and lunch will be catered.

Out-of-Town Location Shoots

The second type of location shoot is an out-of-town location shoot. A client may decide to do a shoot away from home to capture a special ambiance. For example, if the client wants to capture the image of sunny skies and beautiful beaches, they may decide to shoot on a Greek island. Furthermore, because the fashion capitals (Paris, Milan, and New York) are cities that have cold, rainy winters, clients often travel to sunnier, warmer locations when they want to shoot outdoors, especially during the winter months.

Like in-town location shoots, the average location photo shoot away from home may have an odd call time. Generally you'll start very early in the morning, primarily for the sake of lighting and crowd control. It may also be that the location is available only during certain hours. Often, though, you get a long lunch break (from one to three hours) during the middle of the day, when the harsh lighting looks the worst on the model's face. You may be shooting later than 5 P.M., however, because the best light is also complimentary in the early evening.

Depending on where the shoot is taking place, you will usually travel from your home base to the location the night or day before the shoot to make sure you arrive in time. You probably won't be asked to arrive any earlier than that, because the client is responsible for paying for you and your expenses from the time you arrive for the shoot.

Days on location tend to be extremely relaxed if everything goes smoothly—the weather cooperates, the sets are all available, and the models and the rest of the team all show up. When everything runs perfectly, a location shoot can seem like you're on vacation. On the other hand, if the elements don't cooperate and things don't go according to schedule, a location shoot can be your worst nightmare! Maybe the clothes, models, or other members of the team don't arrive or are delayed. The weather may not be agreeable, the hotel may not be accommodating, someone may get sick, or someone may be in a bad mood. Maybe there's no crowd control and no real security on the set. The camera may break. The things that can go wrong are endless.

Even though none of these things is the model's fault (assuming her attitude is positive and she doesn't cause any unnecessary disturbances) and no one is blaming her, she may be affected by the tense, pressurized atmosphere of a shoot gone wrong. Just be sure that you remain professional, cooperative, and willing to work to the best of your ability at all times.

Another disadvantage of location shoots is that sometimes models may be asked to do things that can cause them some physical discomfort. For example, you may be asked to pose outdoors in a wool suit on a steamy day in July, or to wear a bathing suit on a beach when it's only 40 degrees. These sorts of discomforts come with the job, and you should do your best to be accommodating.

Roshumba's Rules

If you're on a location shoot where everything that could go wrong has gone wrong, the best thing you can do is to focus on the work. Be a professional: Don't complain, and don't take anything personally.

Another disadvantage of shooting on location, especially in a foreign country, is that people don't always know the etiquette of a photo shoot. Crowds may gather to ogle or harass the models, and even when there is security, it can be an uncomfortable situation that can fray the nerves of everyone on the set.

On a location shoot, all your expenses are paid, including hotel, meals, and transportation. However, you are responsible for paying for anything you take from the mini bar, any long-distance telephone charges, and any pay television.

When you're required to travel to a shoot, you will probably be paid for the time it takes you to get from your home base to the location. Depending on where you're going, your travel fee could be the equivalent of one day's pay, half a day's pay, or whatever the agent negotiates. (Sometimes, however, you may not be paid a travel fee at all.)

Mod Squad

I remember one *Sports Illustrated* swimsuit-issue shoot in a foreign country where model Paulina Porizkova had to climb up on top of a light tower to pose. When the guys in the town where we were shooting found out Paulina was actually up there, they circled the set and started screaming her name. Although they probably meant no harm, it was a very scary situation at the time, being surrounded as we were by a threatening, screaming mob. We kind of got the feeling that even though there were a couple of security guards, the whole thing could get out of hand and a riot could erupt at any moment.

Super Travel Tips for Supermodels

The number-one rule of traveling for a modeling job is to pack as lightly as possible. Whenever possible, you should try to carry on your bag. Airlines lose baggage all the time, and it's an awful feeling to arrive at a location and not have the things you need to make you as comfortable as possible. Also, it makes a model look like a prima donna if she shows up with five suitcases for one week.

Another reason to pack lightly is that often you will have to leave for the airport directly from the shoot, so you'll need to bring your baggage with you to the location. You'll want to have the smallest amount of luggage possible, so you don't have to lug tons of stuff around.

If you're going to be away for only two or three days, everything you need can probably fit into a carry-on bag. If your trip is longer than that, however, you will probably need to check it.

When you're packing, keep in mind that you'll need to bring only the clothes you will wear from your hotel to the shoot (as well as maybe an outfit or two to wear out at night). Once you get to the shoot, you'll take off your own clothes and put on whatever's being photographed.

Roshumba's Rules

I would advise against using very high-end, brand-name luggage (unless it's a carry-on). Expensive luggage is an inviting target for theft. Instead, I recommend good-quality, rugged bags (wheeled bags are the best), but nothing too flashy. And always lock any bags you check!

It's best to keep your wardrobe as simple as possible: Jeans, leggings, T-shirts, and sweaters are your best choices. Bring a fresh top to wear each day, but it's okay to "recycle" bottoms; you can wear the same pair of jeans two days in a row. Also pack something slightly dressier that you can put on if you go out at night, such as a slip dress or a nice pair of pants and a lightweight sweater.

It's also a good idea to pack clothes you can layer. Although the average temperature may be 80 degrees where you're going, the weather can change suddenly, and it's great if you can slip on a long-sleeve shirt and a sweater over your tank top. Bring a couple pairs of socks and two or three pairs of comfortable shoes (running shoes, sandals, and a pair you can wear out in the evening are sufficient).

You may also want to bring workout clothes and a swimsuit. Many of the hotels you'll be staying in have gyms and pools, or you may have the opportunity to go jogging.

I also always suggest bringing your own personal alarm clock, because you can't always depend on wake-up calls from the hotel staff. If you have to leave at 5 A.M. for a location that's an hour away, you don't want to inconvenience the client by being late. To make sure I'm up, I like to arrange for a wake-up call *and* set my alarm clock.

Here is a checklist of some other items you may need:

➤ Your composites

➤ Your portfolio, if it's not too large

➤ Voucher book

➤ Your passport, if you'll be traveling to a foreign location

➤ Your driver's license or other valid ID (for airport check-in)

➤ Prescriptions

➤ Vitamins

➤ Makeup, if you like (lip color and mascara is all you'll absolutely need)

➤ Body lotion, facial cleansers, hairstyling products, contact lens solution, any other special toiletries you'll need

➤ Sunblock

➤ Insect repellent, depending on where the shoot is and the time of year you're going

Reality Check

Even in the nicest hotel in the world, you still want to take precautions to ensure your personal safety. When you're in your room, make sure you lock the door and put the security chain on. As soon as you've checked in, call someone at your home base to let them know you reached your destination safely and give them the phone number of the hotel.

Reality Check

There are many stories of the traveler who sets down his bags to make a quick phone call, and someone walks away with them while he's on the phone. Or someone's wallet might be swiped out of an open purse before she's even aware anyone is nearby. Always stay alert and protect yourself and your belongings.

➤ Aspirin, along with other medicine such as allergy medicine, if necessary

➤ Food, if you have special dietary needs

Before you leave, find out the best way to get from the airport to your hotel, so you'll know if you're being taken on an unrequested sightseeing trip. Before you get in a taxi, you'll want to know how long it will take and how much you'll have to pay.

The most important thing you can do when you're traveling is to stay aware and alert. Be especially aware of con artists and thieves.

By following these helpful tips, you can ensure that your career will be a successful one, no matter where in the world you're shooting.

The Least You Need to Know

➤ Studio photo shoots are the most controlled and have the least hassles.

➤ Photo shoots on location are more exciting and creative, but there are more logistical problems to be overcome.

➤ Models should travel light and always be alert to potential dangers.

Part 5
There's Something for Everyone

As you've no doubt realized by now, there are many different types of modeling, from walking down the runway in a fashion show, to a photo shoot for a magazine cover, to a television commercial for a consumer product. I'll discuss print modeling, which includes magazine and catalog work, and the advantages and disadvantages of each. I'll also talk frankly about nude modeling, and why you may—and may not—want to consider it.

Next, I'll talk about the exciting world of runway modeling, why it's important for your career, and what are its drawbacks. I'll also discuss the big-bucks realm of modeling for advertisements, and its pros and cons.

Finally, I talk about specialty modeling, which includes nontraditional models such as plus-size models, ethnic models, classic (older) models, male models, and child models. And because not everyone meets the stringent qualifications to be a fashion model, I'll discuss opportunities for real-people models, including character and parts modeling.

Print Work

Print work, which includes modeling for magazines and catalogs, is the foundation of many models' careers. In this chapter, we'll discuss the advantages and disadvantages—in terms of the pay, career advancement, and prestige—of print work. If you want a career that is both long-lasting and lucrative, it is vital that you understand about the different types of print work, the types of models who are booked to do it, and the pros and cons of each.

In addition, in this chapter I'll discuss the ultimate reward for a model: appearing on the magazine covers, as well as nude modeling, and what you need to consider before you take it all off.

Editorial Work and What It Means to Your Career

As you learned in Chapter 2, "The World of Modeling," editorial work includes fashion spreads, which are photos that are "spread" across two pages of the magazine. These types of stories often showcase the latest style trends—the newest look in coats, the must-have shoes for spring, or the new suits for fall. The other major type of editorial story is beauty-related, which means anything having to do with skin care, hair care, makeup, or cosmetic procedures, such as facials and massages.

With editorial fashion shoots, there's equal emphasis on showing the clothes and creating a beautiful photo, such as this one I did several years ago.
Photo: Charles Tracy.

More than anything else, magazines determine what's in style at any given moment. Because of their format (featuring large photographs) and frequency of publication (generally on a monthly basis), magazines are able to capture the look of the moment and chart its evolution from month to month (as well as allowing the image to be captured for eternity). Live media (runways shows and television programs), on the other hand, are more fleeting.

Magazines also establish the visual standards—the style of photography, the types of models, the graphics—for the fashion industry at large.

Because of the creative license they enjoy, magazines are the launch pad for many new and innovative ideas. Magazines are where new fashions and ideas come alive, whether they involve clothing, makeup, hair, or lifestyle trends.

If fashion designers decide that bellbottoms should be revived, for instance, that idea won't take hold in consumers' minds until a magazine features them in a story. Bellbottoms can be in every store and every catalog, but few people will buy them until they see them on some fabulous model in *Elle* or *Glamour* or *Seventeen*. Once they have been given the stamp of approval by a magazine, consumers realize that bellbottoms are back in fashion and are much more likely to go out and buy a pair.

Mod Squad

Each magazine tends to use models who embody its idea of the ideal woman. *Vogue,* for instance, uses models who exemplify the modern, style-conscious woman. For almost a decade, Christy Turlington, Claudia Schiffer, and Linda Evangelista—three models who exude sophistication, class, worldliness, luxury, and decadence—dominated the pages of *Vogue.* When a recession hit in the early 1990s, however, that image was no longer marketable, and there was a backlash against their high-style look. Kate Moss and the grunge look came in, along with the idea of paring down and living a more bohemian lifestyle. Once the recession ended, and the economy grew stronger, Christy, Claudia, and Linda came back bigger than ever to dominate the pages of *Vogue.*

Eyes on the Prize: Editorial Modeling

Editorial work is done primarily by big-time models in the fashion capitals (New York, Paris, and Milan) because that's where the majority of magazines are based. Models in secondary markets (Chicago, Miami, and Los Angeles) may appear in magazines that are headquartered in those cities, but it's unlikely they would be hired to appear in a well-known magazine in a fashion capital. Editorial work for models in local markets is even more limited, because there are so few magazines located in those cities. Your agent is your best source for finding out about opportunities for editorial modeling outside the fashion capitals.

Even in the fashion capitals, it's only a lucky few models who will ever appear in a magazine. Editorial work is the big prize for a model, the most prestigious assignment she can get. When you were back in your bedroom at home dreaming about your future career, you were probably dreaming about editorial work, appearing in *Vogue* or *Seventeen.* But this is not to say that only models who appear in magazines can have successful careers, because that's a little like saying a musician is successful only if he has five number-one hits. That's great if it happens, but it's not the norm.

Even for models who do get lucky and are booked to appear in magazines, this is usually just a phase that happens early in their careers. During this period, they're known as editorial models, because they are appearing in so many magazine stories. (Some lucky few are known throughout their careers as editorial models.) If you're appearing in numerous magazines every month, it says to the fashion industry and to the marketplace at large that you're hot, that your beauty has been accepted as the current standard, that you embody the look of the moment. It also (usually) sets the stage for a successful career overall. Once you've appeared in a magazine, the rest of the industry—fashion designers booking runway shows, advertisers, catalogs, as well as other magazines—will also want to use you, because magazines establish the standards that others follow.

Editorial models also set the standards for other models, and for other women. If a new face comes around who's being accepted and promoted as the look of the moment, many models as well as real people will try to adapt that look, whether it means that they imitate that model's haircut, hair color, or trademark makeup look.

Mod Squad

I was very lucky in my career in that I was able to appear in numerous magazine stories. As is typical of many models, I went through a phase in the first five years of my career in which I was considered an editorial model. As often happens, once one magazine started using me, numerous other magazines soon started calling wanting to book me. The more work I did for French *Elle,* for instance, the more I was in heavy demand by every other fashion magazine. Once I had established my presence in magazines, I soon found myself being booked for advertisements, TV commercials, and fashion shows. This "snowball" effect is very characteristic of the career path of successful editorial models.

Why Editorial Is Important for Your Career

Being a successful editorial model will benefit all aspects of a model's career. If a model is featured on the covers and in the pages of numerous magazines, her career is made. She will be able to demand the highest day rates and enjoy the incredible perks that go with a high-flying modeling career, including great travel opportunities (all-expenses-paid trips to fabulous locations, where she'll stay in the best hotels and eat at the best restaurants, and invitations to the coolest parties and gala events).

When you establish yourself as an editorial model, it says to the fashion industry that you are the current standard of beauty. Consequently, for those in the industry to be considered current and in style, they should hire you to appear in their magazines, as well as in fashion shows, advertisements, and catalogs.

Models who become known as editorial girls usually eventually make the most money. Editorial itself doesn't pay well, but the payoff comes with the exposure and prestige editorial offers, because you will be in demand

Catwalk Talk

A model's **day rate** is the amount of money she makes in one day. This rate is determined by her agent, based on a model's popularity and status in the industry at any one time.

by all facets of the fashion industry. As a model's visibility in the editorial arena goes up, so does the demand for her services and her *day rate* for catalog, advertising, and fashion shows. She could even find herself in line for lucrative endorsement deals like Elizabeth Hurley for Estée Lauder or Cindy Crawford for Revlon. (Still, a model who doesn't do editorial can still make significant amounts of money from catalog, TV commercial, runway, and other work.)

This is a good example of an editorial beauty shot I did, as the focus of the photo is on the makeup, hair, and skin (as well as the attitude), not the clothes.
Photo: Charles Tracy.

Another advantage of editorial is that it's the best way to build your portfolio when you're just starting out. Editorial is more creative and daring than other types of work. You get to experiment with different types of looks and work with the best people in the industry. It's also a great opportunity for you to express yourself creatively and to really give the world a look at what you can do. Editorial tear sheets demonstrate that a model has personality and range, that there's something special about her. A portfolio featuring a lot of editorial tear sheets will inspire clients, which will help you land more jobs. Catalog pictures, on the other hand, feature more mundane poses, less interesting hair and makeup, and are usually taken in more everyday locations. They won't show off the model's personality or range in the same way editorial tear sheets would.

The Disadvantages of Editorial

Although overall, the advantages of editorial far outweigh the disadvantages, there are a few cons to doing lots of editorial. The main disadvantage is that it doesn't pay well. (You probably can't pay your rent if you're just doing editorial—the day rate averages $200, even for covers.) For many young people, $200 may sound like a lot of money, especially if you live at home with your parents and they take care of all your major expenses. But if you live on your own in a fashion capital and are responsible for paying everything from rent to light bulbs, $200 is not a lot of money, even if you work every day.

Another disadvantage is that although an editorial model's career is more prominent on the way up, it's also more noticeable when a model is on her way down. Often, it happens that when an editorial model first starts working, she may find herself working for the best, most prestigious magazines—*Vogue, Elle, Harper's Bazaar, Mademoiselle, Allure, Glamour, Marie Claire, Seventeen,* and *Cosmopolitan.*

Magazines thrive on change, and eventually will start booking someone else—the next hot model. You may find your career shifting from a point where you're in constant demand by all the top magazines to not being booked by them at all. You may find yourself forced to accept less prestigious bookings. And if you spent three years being featured in *Vogue,* and then all of a sudden, you're nowhere to be seen, the industry realizes that things have changed, that you're not as "in" or as valuable as you once were. Because your success as an editorial model was so visible, everyone in the fashion industry knows when your career starts to downshift.

Cover Girl: The Pinnacle of a Model's Career

Appearing on a magazine cover such as *Vogue, Harper's Bazaar, Elle, Allure, Mademoiselle, Glamour, Seventeen, YM, Cosmopolitan, Rolling Stone, GQ,* or *Details* is the icing on the cake for a model. It means that out of all the people in the world who could have been selected to sell that magazine, you were the chosen one! Landing a cover is the industry's way of honoring you as a valuable commodity.

The picture on the cover sells the magazine, because often people don't have a chance to look inside the magazine or read any of the articles before they buy it. What motivates them to purchase it may be simply the image on the cover.

There are several reasons a model may be chosen to appear on a cover. Perhaps you're the new It Girl in town and the magazine wants to feature you. Maybe you embody the look or style prevalent at that moment, or it may be that you are so classically beautiful that some editor fell in love with your face and put you on the cover.

Usually you won't know if you'll be appearing on a cover when you're shooting it. Because the cover is such an important element of the magazine, editors generally don't make any guarantees that any of the photos from one particular session will definitely wind up on the cover until they've had a chance to see them. Instead, they'll book a model for what's called a *cover try.*

In addition, a cover image may have been shot for a story that was originally intended for the inside of the magazine, but which happened to come out so well that the editor decided to put it on the cover.

Surprisingly, despite their high visibility, covers don't pay well. Usually a model will earn the standard editorial rate, $200 a day, and nothing more. But the benefits are far greater than any day rates. A beautiful cover shot for a well-known magazine can give your career a huge boost.

First of all, once you appear on one cover, cover frenzy could break out, and every other magazine could want to put you on its cover. Landing a cover also means that you've broken through to the upper echelon of modeling, that you're a member of a very elite club. If you happen to find yourself in the position of being a cover girl, enjoy it: You're at the pinnacle of your career. You may also find yourself in high demand by the rest of the fashion industry, including fashion designers who want to use you in their runway shows, top-tier advertisers who want your face for their new campaigns, as well as catalogs that want you to model their new spring lines. Also, your day rate may increase substantially, and you may find yourself being sought after for TV commercials and even movies, all because of one great cover!

Catwalk Talk

A **cover try** is a photo shoot that's done to try and get a picture that's good enough to appear on a magazine cover. The photo itself must be striking and the model must look her best.

Mod Squad

Before she was an actress, Cybill Shepherd was a very successful model and cover girl in the late 1960s and early 1970s. Her career was launched when she won a Model of the Year contest held by a New York modeling agency. She quickly became one of the top models, appearing on numerous magazine covers. Movie director Peter Bogdanovich spotted Shepherd on the cover of *Glamour* and fell in love with her on the spot. Soon after, he cast her in *The Last Picture Show*, one of the most successful films of 1971. Shepherd went on to star in many other films, and in her own series, *Moonlighting*, and the *Emmy*-winning sitcom, *Cybill*.

The major drawback of covers is that if you don't look your best on them—if you look out of shape, unhealthy, tired, or in any way less beautiful than normal—it can have a serious, negative impact on your career. The cover photo is highly visible: It's not buried inside the magazine where people might flip past it, or part of an eight-page story where the impact of one bad photo will be mitigated by seven beautiful ones.

I remember one model who appeared on the cover of *Top Model*. She was a very successful model who was just peaking in her career; she was in demand for advertisements, editorial work, and fashion shows. But on this cover she looked really tired, she had circles under her eyes, her skin didn't look healthy; on top of all this, the lighting in the photo was really bad. After that cover came out, her career took a nose dive, and she's never recovered her previous standing in the industry.

Another disadvantage of covers is that they can cause you to become overexposed (meaning people are tired of your image because it's been seen too much) much more quickly. If you've appeared on the cover of every major magazine for a year or two, the industry generally will get tired of your look, which (through no fault of your own) could lead to a career slowdown.

There's nothing special you can do to land a cover; it's really the luck of the draw. It usually just happens that a number of elements fall into place at the right time: Maybe you have the perfect California-girl look and the magazine wants to feature California style, or you have an exotic look that works well with that season's Thai-inspired clothes.

A magazine's advertisers can also influence the cover choice. If an advertiser buys a lot of ad pages in a magazine, they may ask that their spokesmodels be considered for the cover. Other times, when a model becomes a celebrity in her own right, a magazine may feature her on the cover. Sometimes, magazines have to fulfill various types of quotas with their cover girls; for instance, maybe they have to feature an ethnic model on the cover every six months or so in order to appeal to ethnic readers.

I didn't know I was shooting my first cover until it came out on the newsstand. It was for French *Elle*. At the time, I was working with the photographer Oliviero Toscani constantly. I was appearing in every *Elle* (Japanese, English, French, American) every single month. My look—the energetic, pretty, ethnic girl—was catching on. One time, we were doing a photo shoot featuring the clothes of the designer Azzedine Alaia. There was one photo in which I happened to look especially great, and the powers that be at *Elle* thought that everything about it was perfect—my facial expression, the way my body was posed, the clothes, the lighting, the hair and makeup—so they put the picture on the cover.

Roshumba's Rules

If your modeling career progresses to the point at which you do appear on the cover of a magazine, be sure to keep copies of the covers. I have a portfolio that contains all of mine. Other models frame theirs and hang them in their homes as souvenirs. Keeping copies is a great way to remember your career, and they can be useful for future projects, such as your autobiography or a model profile on TV.

I was also chosen to appear on the cover of the 1998 holiday issue of *Time Out New York*. This time it was because of my celebrity status: I was selected to do it because of everything that had been happening in my life, including a thriving modeling career, being a veejay on VH1, and appearing in Woody Allen's *Celebrity*. There was also an interview inside the magazine in which I was asked about my favorite places to shop. (I guess they figured since I was a supermodel, I was an expert on the subject.) When a model is chosen to appear on a cover because she is a celebrity, the magazine is trying to capitalize on the fact that she's well-known and popular and that her visibility in the public eye is already high, which they hope will translate into newsstand sales.

The Lucrative World of Catalog Modeling

Modeling for catalogs is one of the most lucrative types of modeling. Catalog modeling includes modeling for catalogs published by specialty houses such as J. Crew, Spiegel, and Tweeds, and department stores such as Neiman Marcus, Saks Fifth Avenue, Filene's, and Dillard's. One department store may do a dozen or so different types of catalogs, including those featuring designer, bridge (designers' secondary lines, such as DKNY and Anne Klein II), and moderate merchandise, as well as ones with seasonal themes, such as Christmas and Mother's Day. Catalog modeling also includes *look books,* such as those published by fashion designers or fashion companies, such as Esprit, Benetton, and Versace.

Catalog work is not fancy or creative—I like to call it bread-and-butter work. The purpose of a catalog is to sell merchandise, and the purpose of a catalog shoot is to show the merchandise at its best. The buyers for the catalog have already spent millions of dollars purchasing the clothing being featured in the catalog. They don't want to jeopardize that investment, so the focus of the catalog is on making those garments look their most appealing to customers. The model, photographer, hairstylist, and makeup artist are all chosen for their ability to make the clothes look appealing and desirable.

Catwalk Talk

Look books are photo albums put together by clothing companies so consumers can look at all of that season's styles in one place. Look books can be in-store photo albums or printed brochures that are mailed out to customers.

The Advantages of Catalogs

Catalogs can offer a very lucrative, steady source of work for a model. First of all, there are many, many catalogs. They also pay very high day rates, up to $50,000. In addition, they're extremely loyal: You can find yourself working for a single catalog steadily for many years, if the client likes you and finds that the garments that you model sell very well.

Catalogs are not interested in following the latest trend—they don't want to use just the hottest new girls. The models they choose appeal to the average consumer in the mass market, not just to a small clique of fashion-industry professionals. In addition, for the many models who aren't famous and who haven't done a significant amount of editorial work, catalogs offer a way to make a really good living. The day rate averages about $3,500 but can range from $1,000 to $50,000 for top models.

I've done a lot of catalog work and always will. I've probably appeared in every fashion catalog imaginable, including Neiman Marcus, Saks Fifth Avenue, Filene's, Dillard's, Rich's, JCPenney, and Sears. Catalog companies discovered that whatever I put on, even if it was a hot pink muumuu, it would sell. It always made me feel good when clients would say, "That dress you wore in the spring catalog sold out." It let me know that I was doing a good job. That's one real advantage of catalog modeling: It's the only area where you can tell if you are having an impact, where your impact as a model is measurable. I always found that extremely gratifying.

Not only did catalog work pay a lot of bills, it kept me exposed in the international marketplace. All my catalog work helped me build my clientele and appeal in a way that I wasn't able to do through magazines, even though I had a strong editorial presence.

Building Your Mass Appeal

Whenever clients held focus groups, my image always garnered a strong positive response from customers. I found that by appearing in so many catalogs, my appeal to "real" women grew stronger.

Many women have stopped me in airports to tell me, "I got that jogging suit you wore in the JCPenney catalog." (I think I even helped establish the jogging suit as leisure wear. Before I started modeling them, they were considered athletic gear. But I appeared in so many catalogs wearing them that they soon became a fashion statement that everyone was wearing.)

This is a picture taken for a catalog. I'm posing in a way that lets the viewer see as many details of the clothes as possible.
Photo: Charles Tracy.

Catalog modeling increased the number of people who knew my face. It helped me relate more to a mass audience and taught me how to appeal to them. It kept me grounded, because I was modeling for real people. And that experience definitely helped me in the next stages of my career. Even when people see me on TV, they always say, "She's so human," and I know that came from doing so much catalog modeling. Part of that is because most catalog clothes are real clothes for real women, not size-2 catsuits that only fashionistas and a few celebrities will be wearing.

The one downside of catalog work is that the shoots themselves are not that exciting. The focus is on getting as much work as possible done and showing the clothes to their best advantage, not on telling a story or creating an illusion. Also, models are not allowed to be as creative with the poses because certain movements may not make the clothes look their best.

Keep It on or Take It Off?

Nude modeling is a very sensitive subject. Every individual has her own opinion on what's tasteful, what's vulgar, and what's immoral when it comes to nudity.

In the United States, nude modeling is generally considered to be kind of taboo; for the most part, it's seen as stepping over the line of decency. In Europe, however, the nude human body is considered beautiful, and no one blinks an eye when models appear topless in tasteful magazines, advertisements, and TV commercials. In ads for body lotions, breast creams, or cellulite treatment, the model may even be completely naked. Europeans are just more open about the human form; they recognize that everyone is born naked, so what's wrong with the human body? Of course, there's a difference between the pictures they're talking about, which are done in a beautiful, tasteful way, and photographs of women spread-eagle on a pool table in a porn magazine.

If you decide you don't want to model nude, that's absolutely fine. Industry professionals will understand and respect your decision, whether it's for religious reasons, you feel nudity objectifies women, or you're just not comfortable with your body.

If you do decide you want to model nude, that's fine, too. But be very careful about the jobs you accept. What's most accepted are artistic nudes—beautiful, aesthetically pleasing photos that evoke a mood and explore the body's form and line. Most often these types of photos appear in a women's magazine or advertisement, in an art magazine, or in a photography book or exhibit, more often than not in Europe.

The second type of acceptable nude is for a tasteful men's magazine such as *Playboy,* which is considered more respectable than most of the other men's magazines. Although the models are baring all, they're not shown in a vulgar, exploitative way. *Playboy* also has a history of featuring legitimate models in its pages, including Stephanie Seymour, Cindy Crawford, and Elle Macpherson; it's considered the "okay" naughty magazine.

Reality Check

Once you cross the line into the world of actual *pornography,* you will no longer be looked at as a high-quality, marketable model, and you may find yourself unable to book other types of jobs.

257

Playboy is as far as I would go with nude modeling; the other magazines tend to fall more into the pornographic category—actual sexual acts are featured, the photos are much lewder and more indecent—and you want to stay away from that.

Nude modeling has several advantages: It shows the world that you have a perfect, beautiful body. Doing a feature in a magazine such as *Playboy* can help launch your career in a different direction and lead to high-end gigs for quality clients such as Victoria's Secret. Anna Nicole Smith couldn't get arrested until she appeared in *Playboy*. Soon after, she became a model for Guess?, appeared in magazine stories, and was offered movie deals.

Roshumba's Rules

Because it's a vulnerable, touchy situation, the model has a lot more say over the set on a nude photo shoot. You can request that only the photographer be present, and that wish will be respected.

I personally have done artistic nude modeling in Europe. I was working with a Swiss photographer who was assigned to do a profile of me; he suggested we do series of semi-nude black-and-white shots. But if you choose to model nude, be selective. Some conservative clients may feel that girls who do nude modeling are not wholesome and won't book them for jobs.

Nude modeling shoots are somewhat different than ordinary ones. Usually, there's a closed set, meaning access to the area where shooting is taking place is strictly limited. The only people who are permitted are those directly involved (the photographer, the client, the hairstylist, the makeup artist). Also, special care is taken to cover you up between shots.

If an opportunity to do a nude photo shoot arises, talk it over with your agent and family to decide if it's something that will benefit—or hamper—your career.

Because of the variety and amount of work available, print work can be the cornerstone of many model's careers. Understanding the pros and cons of each type can help you once your career gets started.

The Least You Need to Know

➤ Modeling for magazines is the most prestigious type of modeling, and models who are lucky enough to do it end up having the most successful careers.

➤ Although rare, appearing on a magazine cover is the pinnacle of a model's career.

➤ Modeling for catalogs can be a lucrative and steady (if less than thrilling) source of work.

➤ Nude modeling offers advantages, but it is a very personal choice.

Chapter 20

The Exciting World of Runway Modeling

In This Chapter

➤ The three categories of designer runway shows: haute couture, ready-to-wear, and resort

➤ A fashion show from casting to final bows

➤ Fit models

➤ In-store and trunk-show modeling

Of all the types of modeling, runway is one of the most exciting. For one thing, it's a live performance, and it's thrilling to strut your stuff in front of a crowd. There's also the excitement of being part of the presentation of the latest designs from a fashion designer. Finally, the atmosphere backstage is festive and exhilarating.

In this chapter, I'll talk about the different categories of runway shows, and about other related types of modeling. I'll give you an insider's look at a model's involvement in a fashion show, from go and see to final curtain. Finally, a runway expert, Ellen Harth, the president of Elite Runway in New York, will share her expert knowledge and advice about this exciting world.

Are You Ready to Work It?

You've no doubt seen footage on TV of models strutting up and down a long narrow stage (called the runway or catwalk) dressed in the newest fashions. Runway shows allow fashion designers to present their latest creations to the press, executives of clothing stores from around the world, and wealthy customers. For these fashion shows, the designers hire a squadron of models to wear the clothes and walk up and down the runway in them.

At a traditional runway show, the model walks up and down a narrow stage that juts out into the audience.

Although it's generally only the top fashion designers' shows that are showcased on television and in the press, there are many other types of fashion shows that hire models, including local events at malls and stores around the country. These shows are known as consumer fashion shows. (While a few wealthy individuals may attend designer fashion shows of famous designers, they're mostly attended by fashion industry professionals, such as store buyers and the fashion press.)

Consumer fashion shows take place at malls and stores around the country. The purpose of consumer fashion shows is to give local shoppers an idea of the newest design trends and styles; hopefully, the audience will then buy the fashions they see on the runway. Generally, local models are booked for these shows.

When it comes to designer fashion shows, there are three different categories of shows, each featuring a different type of garment: haute couture, ready-to-wear, and resort.

The Exclusive World of Haute Couture

Haute couture shows (which are called *alta moda* in Italy) are the most exclusive and prestigious. They take place in Milan and Paris twice a year, usually in January and

Catwalk Talk

Haute couture clothes are ultra-expensive clothes that are custom-made to fit the few women wealthy enough to afford them. They are made of the most expensive, luxurious fabrics, with exquisite details and hand-sewn seams.

July. In order to decide which styles she may want to order that season, a woman will attend a show featuring the designer's couture collection. She will then order the garments she wants. Couture clients are a very elite group that includes movie stars, millionaires, and royalty.

Designers' couture collections focus mainly on evening wear, but they also include dresses and suits for day. Couture garments start at around $10,000 and can cost up to $500,000, such as the diamond-encrusted wedding dress Christian LaCroix designed for the wife of a sheik. Because there are few customers for these types of clothes, and because presenting a couture collection is expensive, only a few design houses do couture, including Chanel, Christian Dior, Givenchy, Christian LaCroix, Yves Saint Laurent, Versace, and Valentino.

This glamorous ball gown is a classic example of a haute-couture garment.

The High Style of Ready-to-Wear Shows

Ready-to-wear (known in Europe as *pret-a-porter*) is the largest category of fashion shows. All designers do ready-to-wear. Ready-to-wear includes most types of clothes: shirts, sweaters, jackets, pants, skirts, shorts, suits, dresses, evening wear (fancy dresses, gowns, cocktail dresses), and coats.

There are ready-to-wear shows in Milan, Paris, and New York as well as in secondary markets, such as

Catwalk Talk

Unlike couture garments, which are custom-made, **ready-to-wear** clothes are mass-produced. Nearly all the clothes you see at the local mall fall into the ready-to-wear category.

Germany, Spain, England, and Japan. Ready-to-wear shows take place twice a year, usually in September and October (when spring designs are presented) and in February and March (when fall clothes are shown). Normally, the schedule runs as follows: The Milan designers show their designs, then about two weeks later, the runway shows in Paris take place; two weeks after that, the New York designers show their latest.

This stylish tailored suit is typical of ready-to-wear clothing.

Catwalk Talk

Resort wear is casual clothing that was traditionally worn at resorts in warm-weather climates by socialites escaping cold winters. It includes T-shirts, shorts, skirts, jackets, as well as swimwear and sports-specific garments (for tennis, golf, and sailing).

Resort Wear

The third category of garments shown in designer runway shows is *resort wear*. This is much a smaller category that features clothing that is made for warm weather and transitional times of the year. The emphasis is on leisure and casual wear, such as shorts, T-shirts, casual sweaters, jackets, long, flowing dresses, and bathing suits. Resort shows are presented in New York (and in some secondary markets), and they take place in January and July.

Tennis, anyone? This sporty outfit is characteristic of resort wear.

Walking the Runway to Fame: The Pros of Runway Modeling

Runway modeling is one of my favorite types of modeling, whether I'm appearing in a couture show for Yves Saint Laurent or walking the runway in a ready-to-wear show in New York. First of all, it's exciting, because it's a live performance, a time when I can let my personality really shine. I also get a tremendous sense of freedom from walking up and down the runway; I really get a feel for the power and excitement of being a model.

Appearing in a designer runway show is great exposure, whether you're a novice or an established supermodel. All of the heavy hitters in the fashion industry go to runway shows. They take note of which models are participating, because it's a barometer of who's hot at that moment. Many new models' careers have been launched on the runway.

It's also fun because of all the excitement that surrounds the *collections* every season. Backstage, you meet a lot of people you wouldn't have the opportunity to meet by doing only photo shoots. There are always lots of parties and restaurant, art gallery, and club openings. People also plan special celebrations around runway shows because they know all the important people in the fashion industry will be in town. For instance, Ralph Lauren threw a big party to launch his newest fragrance during the New York ready-to-wear collections. The gala opening of Giorgio Armani's flagship Madison Avenue store took place during the collections.

How much a model earns doing runway depends mainly on the caliber of the client. Some of the models in the Victoria's Secret runway show, for instance, can earn up to $30,000 for a show that lasts less than 30 minutes! Doing fashion shows in the fashion capitals of Milan, Paris, and New York also pays well, although the amount that can be earned will vary according to how famous the model is and who the designer is. Famous designers pay more than lesser-known ones. A famous designer might pay a top model up to $20,000 to appear in his show.

Most models, of course, even in the fashion capitals, make a lot less than this. A few hundred dollars is more the norm. But if you do many shows within a short period of time, you can end up really making a lot of money doing runway shows.

Even if you're just appearing in a hobby modeling show in the local mall for which you're not being paid, runway modeling is still very fun. (For more information on runway opportunities for hobby models, see Chapter 8, "Modeling for Experience (Hobby Modeling).")

Catwalk Talk

The **collections** refers to the collective showing of designers' new fashions in one particular city. The New York collections take place when all the top New York designers show their latest designs for the season.

The Fast Track to Exhaustion: The Cons of Runway Modeling

The biggest disadvantage of doing a lot of fashion shows is that they're extremely draining. Every fashion show you do could involve one or more go and sees, up to three fittings, one or more rehearsals, plus the actual show. Even if you're not doing that many shows, you could work more hours than you would the whole rest of the year. Doing the collections can be so overwhelming that a lot of models get sick because they're run down emotionally and physically. Their skin breaks out, their hair gets fried from being styled so many times, and they are completely exhausted.

One season, in my second year of modeling, I did 32 shows in five days in Paris. It was great, but to this day, I still cannot believe I managed it. I was doing up to five shows a day, plus fittings, rehearsals, and go and sees. Then I had to repeat the process in New York and Milan. I think I must have been crazy!

From Go and See to the Final Curtain

The grueling process of go and sees or castings (which is what go and sees for fashion shows are called in Europe) for designer runway shows in the fashion capitals generally starts about 10 days to two weeks before the shows take place. You often feel like herded cattle at these, because there are so many models there. Young women come from all over the world—Africa, Iceland, China, Russia—to give modeling a shot and to try to get booked for a fashion show. Not only is it a great way to launch a career, but you can buy a house with the money you make doing shows. Thus the shows are an irresistible lure to women from all over the world.

During runway season, you could do up to 15 go and sees a day. Often there are 50 girls ahead of you who are also waiting to be seen. Some are dismissed outright, because they are just not right for that particular designer. Others are invited in to walk, show their books, maybe try on a few outfits, and meet with the designer. This can take from 20 to 30 minutes per model.

Often when you're just starting out, you're using public transportation to get from one go and see to the next, so you're always having to stop and check your map to figure out where you're going—it's all extremely stressful. And you have to repeat the process in each market, Milan, Paris, New York.

These days, the models who are most likely to get booked for a runway show are those editorial models who have appeared in the pages of *Vogue, Harper's Bazaar,* and *Elle,* according to Ellen Harth, president of Elite Runway, the Elite modeling agency's runway division. "It used to be that print [editorial] girls only did print and the show girls only did shows. That got changed a long time ago. The more you do for *Harper's* and *Vogue* and those magazines, the more shows you'll do, because it means that you are what is happening today."

Still, often a designer will take a chance on hiring a model who has little or no experience or magazine clips (tear sheets).

After the go and see/casting, if a client is interested in you, they will call your agent. The client may *confirm* you, or they may put a hold, which is called a *tent,* on you. Usually they have to make up their minds and confirm you 24 to 48 hours before the show, or they may have to pay you even if they don't use you.

Once you're booked for a show, you are scheduled to go in for a fitting, which is when all the garments that you'll be wearing in the show are altered to fit your body. For ready-to-wear clothes, there is usually just one fitting session. For couture, there may be up to three, because the garment is custom-fit to your body.

Usually your agent sets up the appointment for the fitting. It can last from half an hour to three hours, depending on how many garments you'll be wearing in the show, how complicated the designs are, and what design problems arise with the clothes. (The average number of garments a single model might wear in a ready-to-wear show is five. The most I've ever seen a model wear—and the most I've ever worn—is 10 outfits.) Elaborate designs, such as evening dresses with details such as feathers, lace, or embroidery, will take longer to fit.

Couture requires more fittings because the designer must first make a facsimile of the garment in muslin, an inexpensive white cotton fabric. At the first appointment, you try the muslin on so it can be fitted to your individual body. The muslin is then used as a pattern for the actual garment. At

Catwalk Talk

If the client definitely wants to book you, you are said to be **confirmed.** If the client likes you but isn't ready to commit, they put a hold or a **tent** (short for tentative) on you.

the final fitting, any last-minute adjustments are made to the actual garment, and any necessary accessories—shoes, belts, shawls, capes—are added.

Dress Rehearsals

In addition to fittings, fashion shows generally involve only one rehearsal, which can take place a day or two before the show, or even the morning of the show, if it is scheduled in the evening.

Mod Squad

The only people who do more than one rehearsal are the Japanese designers, such as Rei Kawakubo (the designer of Comme Des Garcons), Issey Miyake, and Yohji Yamamoto, who show their designs in Paris (and sometimes in New York). They can do up to three rehearsals for one show. I think the reason for this is that the Japanese, due to their culture, are absolute perfectionists. They may hold three rehearsals on three different days, or three in one day. In that case, the show may be scheduled to take place at 5 in the afternoon, but the model will be booked to arrive at 9 A.M. The whole day will be spent rehearsing and preparing.

The rehearsals are coordinated so that they don't take place during any other shows. Usually all the shows in one city take place in one location (although that is changing in some cities), and rehearsals are scheduled when no other shows are taking place. The reason there are rehearsals for fashion shows is so that the designer can get a feel for the run of the show, making sure the garments appear in the correct order, that the clothes compliment each model, that a new model fits in with the regulars, and that the music is appropriate. If the designer is pushing a new style, he would open or close the show with it.

It's rare for the designer to do a full hair and makeup rehearsal because of the cost of paying the hair and makeup team and the models for the extra time. The house models (models who are used by the designer in-house for fittings), however, may be in full hair and makeup. All the models will be dressed in the clothes, assuming the clothes are finished and available, alterations aren't still being made, and the clothes have already been sent over from the showroom.

At a rehearsal for a fashion show, you'll usually run through the show once, albeit with a lot of stops and starts. During the rehearsal, any kinks are worked out so everything flows smoothly. Generally, rehearsals can take about an hour, sometimes up to two hours.

It's kind of an unspoken rule that supermodels don't have to attend fashion show rehearsals. Designers know these women are professionals, that they already know what they're doing, and they're frantically busy with all the shows they're in. Models are paid for fittings, rehearsals, and fashion shows or on an hourly basis. Or a flat fee may be negotiated for the model's time.

It's Show Time!

Often designers will request that you arrive two to three hours before the show starts in order to get your hair and makeup done and to get dressed. That way, there's time to make sure everything is perfect—the lost earring can be found, the broken high heel can be mended, the unfinished seam can be sewn.

As you've probably seen on various TV shows, backstage at a fashion show is a frenzy of activity. The hair and makeup team, which could number up to 16, are working. There is champagne and a buffet table laid out, where everyone is welcome to help themselves to something to eat or drink. Models are sitting around chatting or getting their hair and makeup done, people from the design team are making last-minute alterations, and TV cameras and TV, newspaper, and magazine journalists are interviewing the designer and the models.

About 15 minutes before the show begins, the models get dressed in the first outfit they're going to wear. The designer goes around making final adjustments to the clothes, the hair and makeup artists check all the models to make sure everything looks perfect, and the choreographer reminds them one last time about any special things they may need to remember.

All the models line up, the music starts, and then the *featured model* walks out in the first outfit, followed down the runway by all the other models.

Once you've walked the runway and returned backstage, you have to run back to your rack, because you may have only one and a half to three minutes to change your outfit, shoes, stockings, accessories, and whatever else goes with it, look perfect, and get back out. Your rack is where all the clothes you'll be wearing in the show will be hanging. That way, everything is in one place, so you can change quickly. Each model also has her own dresser to help her get out of one garment and into the next.

Roshumba's Rules

Despite the crazed atmosphere backstage at a fashion show, it's best to stay calm and not get caught up in the craziness. Read a book, listen to music on a personal tape or CD player, or chat with friends. This allows you to remain professional and focus on doing a great job.

Catwalk Talk

The **featured model** may be the designer's favorite model or a famous supermodel. She's usually the first and/or the last model to appear, and at the end of the show, she walks down the runway on the arm of the designer.

Dressers can be people who work at the designer's company, students from a design college, interns who are trying to get into the industry, or professional dressers. Once you're dressed, you dash past the fashion designer and the hair and makeup team, who may make quick adjustments or give you little tips.

Mod Squad

One of the most outstanding runway models of all time was Pat Cleveland, an African American model who appeared in every major fashion show in every city—Milan, Paris, and New York—for years during the 1960s and 1970s. "She was like a ballerina," remembers Ellen Harth, president of Elite Runway. "She was built like a dancer—very lean and thin, wiry, with the most adorable smile. She just floated and she could twirl like nobody on this Earth. She was so exciting to watch." At that time, the models in fashion shows moved in a more dramatic, theatrical way, not the straightforward, simple moves common in shows today. "Pat was perfect for that time," says Harth.

Reality Check

It often happens that you absolutely fall in love with something you wear in a fashion show. But never just take something. For one, it's stealing, and for another, the designer may need it for a photo shoot or to show to store buyers in the showroom. One famous model swiped a pair of shoes from a show, and the incident was reported in the tabloids.

Fashion shows generally last about an hour, and at the end, all the models file out onto the runway, where the featured model appears on the arm of the designer, who takes a bow.

After the show, models may dash out if they have another show to do, or they may stick around for the post-show celebration. Usually, champagne and hors d'oeuvres are served, and throngs of well-wishers and journalists crowd backstage to congratulate the designer on the collection.

If there's something you wore in a fashion show that you would love to own, tell the designer or a member of the design team during the fitting how much you like it, and ask if there's any way you could get it. You can also ask your dresser, who can ask the team for you. Often designers will be happy to give it to you once they're finished with it.

The designer takes a bow at the end of the show, often on the arm of the show's featured model.

Beyond the Runway

In addition to fashion shows, there are several other types of modeling that come under the category of "runway."

Sizing Up Fit Models

Fit models work closely with the fashion designer, trying on all the garments so they can be adjusted and fitted correctly.

There are two types of fittings models, according to Ellen Harth. The first type of model is the sample model. A sample model must be a perfect size 6. Although she generally won't appear in the designer's fashion show, all the garments that will be worn by other models in a designer's runway show are fit on her. "Because there's such close contact between her and the designer, there has to be a real rapport between them," says Harth. Sample models usually work for several designers, and in the weeks leading up to the collections, they can be frantically busy.

After the show has taken place, another fitting is done, which is called the duplicate fitting. At a duplicate fitting, all the size 6 garments that were worn in the fashion show are resized and remade into a size 8. The duplicate model must be a perfect size 8, because the size 6 garment will be remade to fit her body. This is necessary for the manufacturing process, because this duplicate sample serves as the standard from which all the other sizes will be made.

Not only is it essential that sample and duplicate models remain at the same weight and size, but they also need to be knowledgeable about clothes. "You must know when something is off by an eighth of an inch, because an eighth of an inch, when graded up or down, becomes a quarter of an inch," a mistake that is compounded as the sizes get much bigger or smaller, says Harth. The duplicate must be perfect, because any mistake will cause all the other sizes to come out wrong. If a duplicate is done incorrectly, a customer may try on a garment in her size and find that it's too big in the waist or too tight on the thighs, in which case she won't buy it. This is why the duplicate needs to be a perfect size 8—and to know when a fitting is not being done correctly, something that comes with experience.

Catwalk Talk

Showroom models work in the designer or manufacturer's showroom. Her job is to model the garments for visiting clients such as department store buyers.

Sample, duplicate, and showroom models don't gain the fame and recognition that other models do, but their careers last much longer than other models'—some work up to the ages of 35 or 40. Although the rates they earn aren't that high, there is a lot of work, so this can be a very lucrative type of modeling. This is an area where size, shape, and proportion are more important than anything else; sample models must have a perfect size 6 body, duplicate models must be a perfect size 8. She has to keep her body in perfect shape, and she cannot gain or lose weight.

In-Store Modeling

With in-store modeling (which is also called informal modeling), the models are dressed in the clothes from the store; they walk around and let the customers see the clothes up close as they shop. In-store modeling is done by hobby models, as well as models in secondary and local markets and the fashion capitals. In fact, one of my first jobs was doing in-store modeling at a boutique in Peoria, Illinois. It's a great way for hobby models to get experience. It's also great if you're the type of model who enjoys meeting people. The pay scale depends on the caliber and location of the store and can range from nothing to several hundred dollars.

Trunk-Show Modeling

Trunk shows allow designers to take their designs directly to consumers all over the country. For instance, a bridal store may invite bridal designer Vera Wang to do a trunk show. She would then bring her newest wedding gown collection to the store to do a fashion show. Locally hired models would try on the gowns for the customers, who can then try them on themselves once the show is over. The audience may also be given the opportunity to meet the designer. Trunk shows tend to be informal, as opposed to grand staged presentations.

Trunk shows are advertised in the newspaper, on TV, or on the radio, so that the interested general public knows to attend. Trunk-show modeling is available in all large, many medium, and some small markets. Sometimes the designer attends personally, other times a member of the design team or some other employee of the company attends, depending on the size of the market and how important that market is to the company. The pay scale for trunk-show modeling is generally middle of the road, approximately several hundred dollars per day.

It's fortunate that runway modeling is available in almost all areas of the country, as well as in the fashion capitals, because it really is one of the most fun and most exciting.

The Least You Need to Know

➤ There are three categories of designer runway shows: haute couture, ready-to-wear, and resort. A different type of clothing is shown at each one.

➤ Doing a lot of runway shows can be grueling, because they involve many go and sees, fittings, rehearsals, and shows, all in a short period of time.

➤ Fit models are a specialized category of runway models; this can be a lucrative specialty for a model with a perfect size 6 or size 8 body.

➤ Trunk shows and in-store modeling take place all over the country and offer great opportunities for live modeling.

Chapter 21

Advertisements, Endorsements, and TV Commercials

In This Chapter

➤ Modeling in print advertisements

➤ Lucky ladies: landing an endorsement deal

➤ Lights, camera, action: modeling in TV commercials

Advertisements, endorsements, and TV commercials are some of the most lucrative jobs a model can land. Although you can make a lot of money working for catalogs and doing fashion shows, modeling for advertisements, endorsements, and TV commercials allows you to make it in a much shorter period of time. In addition, it can help you extend and broaden your career by introducing you to large new audiences and showing you in a whole different light to clients.

In this chapter, I'll explain how modeling for advertisements, endorsements, and TV commercials works, the types of models who get booked for them, and how you can maximize your chances to cash in on these great opportunities.

Modeling for Advertisements

Doing advertisements is extremely important to your career, because it says—not only to the fashion industry but to all of corporate America—that you are a marketable product, that you have the power to inspire people to buy the products you represent. Ads represent a whole level of power that is different from editorial work. You may appear in fashion magazines because you embody the hot new look, but that says nothing about your marketability, your ability to sell things.

Doing advertisements can take your career into the realm of being a viable, marketable product. It can give your career longevity, because clients realize you're not just the flavor of the month but a force to be reckoned with.

Mod Squad

Without advertisements, my career might have been over seven years ago. After the moment passed when I was the hottest model, appearing in all the magazines, I'd have been gone. I think advertisements took me from being an exciting, exotic fashion girl into being a viable, marketable product. Major corporations put time, energy, and money into me because they believed I could sell products. Over the years, I've done tons of ads for clients such as Oil of Olay, Maybelline, The Gap, Anne Klein, Benetton, Esprit, Yves Saint Laurent, Paco Rabonne, Samsung, Sprite, and Hanes.

If your face and image can sell an everyday product like a bar of soap, that's an incredible talent. If you're smart and your agent is smart, you could really rack up substantial sums doing ads for a variety of clients.

Advertising work includes any work that is done for a print ad (TV commercials will be covered separately, later in this chapter) that will appear in magazines, in newspapers, on billboards, and/or in brochures. The contract with the client specifies the amount of time they can run the ad (three months is common), and in what format, such as magazine ads and billboards, among others. If they want to use the ad for a longer period of time or in any other format, they have to pay another fee.

Catwalk Talk

Conflict of interest is when a model appears in two advertisements for similar products, thus undermining her ability to sell either one. An example would be a model who appears in both Revlon and Maybelline ads.

It's rare that one model will be booked to appear in ads for more than one company that makes the same product. Once you've done an ad for Colgate, for example, it's extremely unlikely you'll be hired to do an ad for Crest, because it's seen as a *conflict of interest*. Often, in fact, the contract will state that during the term of the contract, you can't appear in ads for a similar product. You can, however, do ads for different products, and it's okay if they all run simultaneously.

The Types of Models Who Get Ad Work

Models who land advertisement bookings often have physical attributes that relate to the product. This is particularly true of beauty ads, which include advertisements for hair- and skin-care products and makeup. If it's a body cream, the model will have beautiful, flawless skin, without any bruises or scratches or tattoos. If it's a hair ad, she'll have healthy, beautiful hair. Until recently, the models in ads for hair products all had long, flowing, and usually blonde tresses. Now, hair ads feature models with styled hair—bobs, pixies, shags—in all different colors. This is a reflection of what's happening in society, where the majority of consumers work and their hair is cut in business-friendly styles.

For fashion ads, on the other hand, designers usually select a model who is either the It Girl of the moment or one who embodies what's happening in fashion, depending on what look the designer is trying to sell that season. Other times, especially in smaller markets, the advertiser will choose a model whose look appeals to local consumers.

Real-people models are also often chosen to appear in advertisements. (For more information, see Chapter 23, "Real-People Models.")

Mod Squad

Models whose personalities are wholesome and appealing, who look like the girl next door, are also in demand for advertisements. Niki Taylor, for instance, with her happy, healthy, blonde good looks, is one of the most popular models among advertisers. On the other hand, those skinny, pale, sickly "heroin-chic" models may be very successful in magazines, but have a hard time getting booked for ads. Occasionally, an Oddball type will be so popular clients will clamor to use her anyway: baby-faced African model Alek Wek appeared in luxury jewelry ads, and androgynous model Kristen McMenamy appeared in Versace ads. For the most part, though, Classic Beauties, Amazons, and Athletic-Girl-Next-Door types dominate advertisements.

Getting Booked for an Advertisement

Like all other modeling jobs, advertising jobs start with a go and see that is set up by your agent. Before you go, your agent will tell you what it's for and that they'll want you to be exclusive to them for three months, meaning you won't be able to appear in an ad for one of the client's competitors during that period.

The go and see is similar to any other one (see Chapter 15, "Go and Sees," for more information); you want to arrive on time and to be as friendly and personable as possible. Depending on who the advertiser is, you should dress as simply as possible, in jeans and a T-shirt or sweater. If it's an ad for a fashion designer, you could wear something more fashion-forward (although it's by no means necessary). If it's for an advertisement that involves a body-conscious product, the client may ask you to wear a bathing suit underneath your street clothes, so they can get a good look at your figure. They will also probably take a Polaroid of you in the bathing suit.

Clients may request that you wear a two-piece bathing suit such as this one underneath your clothes when you go on castings for television commercials so they can see your body. Photographer: Kwame Brathwaite. Model: Laura McLafferty.

If the client decides they want to book you for the ad, they will call your agent and state the terms of the contract—the amount you'll be paid, the time period in which the ad will run, and the format of the ad.

The major reason you would refuse is if the money isn't good enough, especially if it's early in your career. Often, once you appear in an ad for one product, even if it's just for a short period, more likely than not you'll never be hired to represent a competitive product. For instance, if you do a shampoo ad in the first or second year of your career, that means for the next eight or so years that you're working as a model, there's a strong possibility that you'll never represent another shampoo product again. You and your agent need to decide if the money being offered is ample compensation.

Another reason you might decide against doing an advertisement is if it's for a product that's not considered to be high-end or reputable, such as a feminine-hygiene product. Once you do an ad for a product like that, you might find yourself stuck at that down-market level and unable to secure advertising deals for more prestigious companies.

In general, try not to do ads for products that will end up limiting your career. This means steering clear of feminine-hygiene, cigarette, and alcohol ads, which are all considered down-market advertisements. Once you do those, it says to the industry that you couldn't get anything better, and it's unlikely you'll be considered for more prestigious jobs (ads for cosmetics or clothing, for instance) in the future.

Modeling for an advertising job can be very creative work, although other times it can be very tedious; it all depends on the individual job. You may be shooting only one or two clothing changes (as opposed to doing 12 different "looks" when you're doing a catalog shoot), but you could find yourself in the uncomfortable position of hanging off the Eiffel Tower for the whole day so the photographer can get the shot he wants. I once did a job for a body-wash advertisement in which I had to pose for three hours in a "waterfall" that was constructed in the studio.

Generally, though, advertisers pamper the model and treat her well. They often provide a car service to and from the location, and they have nice catered lunches. The whole day is about you. They want to make you feel your best, so that good feeling will be reflected in the ad, and (hopefully) in sales.

Reality Check

When you're asked to wear a bathing suit on a go and see, don't wear a suit that will get more attention than you. Your best bet is a solid-color, two-piece suit. Avoid thongs and patterns, which are too distracting. Wearing a bra and panty instead of a suit is too intimate, and therefore not appropriate. A one-piece, on the other hand, hides too much.

Why Endorsements Rate a Model's Stamp of Approval

To land an endorsement is to hit the lottery. With an endorsement, a company signs you on to represent their products and their company for a relatively long period of time for a sizable amount of money. For example, L'Oréal might hire you to endorse their hair-care, makeup, and skin-care products for three years at a rate of $1 million a year. But you may be required to work only a relatively few number of days—20, perhaps—to earn that money. Granted, only a few models—less than 1 percent—ever land endorsement deals, but it can happen!

When a company signs a model to do an endorsement, they're not just thinking about how pretty she is, they're thinking how she will affect their bottom line: Will sales increase or decrease? Will they gain or lose customers? Will the price of their stock go up or down? It's not just about being fun and fabulous on the cover of *Seventeen,* it's a whole other level.

Landing an endorsement deal means that not only are you considered to have an extremely valuable, desirable image, but you are also an integral part of a major corporation. An endorsement deal means that your image is pleasing to people and that you have what it takes to be the face and voice of a major corporation. Showing your image is how the company communicates its message to the public. You have the power to affect the value of the company's stock on the stock markets, and that in turn can affect millions of people.

Some models who've landed endorsement deals include:

➤ Christie Brinkley (Cover Girl)

➤ Cindy Crawford (Revlon)

➤ Linda Evangelista (Kenar)

➤ Paulina Poritzkova (Estée Lauder)

➤ Isabella Rossellini (Lancôme)

➤ Niki Taylor (Cover Girl and Liz Claiborne)

➤ Christy Turlington (Maybelline and Calvin Klein)

➤ Vendela (Elizabeth Arden and Almay)

➤ Roshumba Williams (Clairol)

One of the reasons models make so much money when they endorse products is because usually it's the most successful models who land endorsement deals, and they can command sky-high dollars. Also, an endorsement is considered an exclusive deal, meaning the model cannot represent competitive products. A model with a Revlon deal can't represent Estée Lauder, for instance, because they're both cosmetic companies.

Roshumba's Rules

A spokesmodel will often be required to make appearances on behalf of the company at business meetings and charitable events. If you're being considered for an endorsement, make sure your behavior is always poised, professional, and mature.

If a model has more than one endorsement deal, each product she represents must be in a different category, as well as equally reputable. For instance, if a model is representing Maybelline, you won't see her doing feminine-hygiene endorsements, which are considered less respectable. She can, however, endorse a brand of high-end cell phones, and a well-known clothing company, because none of these businesses competes with the other and they are all considered high-end products with the same level of appeal.

The reason why an endorsement contract would prohibit a model from representing a less reputable product is that when a model endorses a product, she represents both the product and the image of the company; she's their spokesperson. And a blue-chip company doesn't want its spokesmodel appearing on a late-night TV ad hawking miracle knives or pocket fishing gear, because it reflects badly on that company.

Endorsement deals also have clauses that govern personal conduct, because your behavior is a reflection on the company. If you're the spokesperson for a major cosmetic company, and you lose your temper with your assistant and throw a bottle of perfume at her, and the story winds up in the tabloids, that not only makes you look bad, it makes the company you represent look bad.

Also, during the term of the endorsement deal, your contract may specify that you can wear only the clothes of the designer whom you're endorsing (if it's a fashion company) or the makeup of the company that signed you (if it's a cosmetic company). These are minor restrictions, but you should be aware of them.

Mod Squad

For three years, I was the spokesperson for Clairol Balsam Color. I appeared in all their ads during that period. Once I had worked with them for a while, they found that I could do more than just pose, that I could hold my own in business situations. Because I could discuss the product intelligently, I was asked to represent Balsam Color in interviews with the press. They also asked me to make appearances on their behalf at the Essence awards (an award show sponsored by *Essence* magazine honoring people in the entertainment industry), in-house business meetings, and charity events. For me, what was even more important than the money I made was the wonderful opportunity it offered me to represent a major corporation and become accustomed to being a spokesperson.

If you want to land a major endorsement deal, you need to keep your reputation clean from the moment you start working as a model. You don't want to be known as the girl who parties too hard, who's impossible to work with, or who's always having public spats with her boyfriend, because that sort of behavior is a red light to major corporations handing out endorsement deals, no matter how beautiful you are.

Major endorsement deals can secure you financially for the rest of your life, but they're given out only to models with the best, most professional reputations. If your image is tainted, whether it's physically (you don't take care of yourself, so you don't always look your best), socially (you're known to be difficult to work with), or psychologically (you're rumored to be a heavy drinker), you are really just hurting yourself. Before a major company spends millions of dollars on an endorsement deal, it wants to make sure it's working with a credible, reliable, reputable person.

Roshumba's Rules

If you have an endorsement deal, try to keep your image fresh by keeping up your editorial work and adding more things to your life, such as preparing for a career after modeling or going back to school.

Although the advantages far outweigh the disadvantages, there is a downside to doing endorsements. When a model lands an endorsement deal, she's the hottest model in town, because she's endorsing a major company and making a lot of money. Many other models (and people in general) will be saying to themselves, "I wish I had her job." But once the endorsement deal expires, she could be thought of as old news. For the rest of her career, she could be known as the *old* DKNY model, or the *old* Estée Lauder model. By that point, many models have been in the business a long time and are ready to retire. But if not, it can be hard getting clients to think about her in any other terms other than as the former spokesmodel for some other company.

A few models, however, discover that once an endorsement deal lapses, other companies are clamoring to use them. When Bridget Hall's Ralph Lauren contract expired, she started appearing on every magazine cover and in every fashion show. Vendela also went from an endorsement deal with Elizabeth Arden to one with Almay products.

On Camera: Modeling for TV Commercials

TV commercials offer you a way to reach a much broader audience and become more recognizable than magazine work or even print advertisements. With a magazine, people have to go out and buy the magazine to see you. Besides having much larger audiences, TV requires no effort on the consumer's part—he or she doesn't even have to turn the page—so you're being exposed to a much broader audience.

Another advantage of doing TV commercials is that you're being seen in a whole different medium. You're coming across live and in full color into people's living rooms, which gives consumers a chance to see your personality in a way that's not captured in a still ad. This could help you land other clients, too, when they see how well you can project in a TV ad.

In addition, TV commercials pay very well, too, because you may also earn *residuals* as well a fee for your modeling services.

When it comes to TV commercials, you can't really predict who's going to be selected to represent what. It's a medium that's very different from print ads. With print ads, there's a lot more leeway; you can always air brush a print ad to look completely different. On TV, however, flaws cannot be hidden. If a model doesn't have what the client or consumer is looking for, it can't be air brushed in; you can't fake it. This is why directors of TV commercials are so notoriously picky when it comes to choosing people for the commercial: Once they've selected someone, that's it. There's no faking it if the person isn't right. Therefore, clients try to pick people who are extremely consumer-friendly, who customers will like, and to whom customers can relate.

Catwalk Talk

A **residual** is a payment an actor or model receives every time the commercial she appears in is broadcast. For a national commercial that gets heavy play, this could be a significant amount of money.

Catwalk Talk

A **casting** is the television industry's term for auditions for television commercials. Usually, you'll meet first with the casting director, who narrows down the number of possible candidates for the client.

It's also essential that the viewer believes the model really uses the product. If a size-0 model is selected to star in a Jell-O pudding commercial, no one will believe it. Or if a 15-year-old model is cast as the mom of three, it won't create a believable image. When it comes to TV commercials, it's all about believability. When you go to a *casting* for a TV commercial, the client will ask you a lot more questions than you'll be asked on other go and sees, such as, "Do you like pudding? Did your mom make Jell-O?" The camera will pick up on any credibility gaps.

For TV commercials, models compete with other models, as well as actresses and real people. It's more a question of whether you embody what the client is looking for; it doesn't matter who you are. Even the most beautiful girl in the world could be turned down if her personality—her essence—doesn't capture what the client is trying to sell.

Still, because there are so many different types of products, all sorts of models can find themselves cast in TV commercials. Not only are they booked to sell the obvious— clothes, cosmetics, accessories—they're also used to sell other consumer products from cars to soap. You can get the quirky young woman selling Diet Coke, the wholesome teenager selling Noxema, or the androgynous model selling Lee Jeans.

Your regular agent probably won't be handling your television commercial bookings. Most agencies have in-house TV commercial departments that handle TV commercial bookings for all the models in the agency. If the agency doesn't have its own TV department, it may have an agreement with an outside company that handles TV work for all the agency's models. (If your agency doesn't have a TV department, ask your agent if you can sign up with an agent who specializes in television.)

You will probably find yourself being sent out on TV commercial auditions from the time you sign with the agency. Usually when a casting director calls the agency looking for *talent,* she may say something like, "I'm looking for a redhead with long hair with a country-girl sort of look." If the agency just signed a brand-new, 13-year-old redhead, she will be going out for the commercial, along with any older, more experienced redheaded models.

The pay for TV commercials can be really good. Not only will you be paid for the actual shoot, but you will make more money every time the commercial runs. (The rate will be negotiated by your agent.) If the client decides to rerun the commercial after the initial cycle, they have to pay you additional money. Every time they run it, you receive a fee. Furthermore, they have to pay you additional sums if they use the ad past the time frame designated in the initial contract, if they use it outside of the United States, or if they use it in another medium (for example, on the Internet).

Catwalk Talk

Talent is the word that's used to refer to the models, actors, or other performers working at a still photo shoot, on a TV commercial or movie set, or at a live performance.

The ABCs of TV Commercial Castings

Castings for TV commercials are quite different from other go and sees. First of all, you usually don't need to take your book. You will need to bring your composite, though. At the first meeting, usually just the casting director and the assistant will be there. They'll ask you to stand in front of a video camera so they can tape you, in order to see how you look on a live camera. You might be asked to walk around. They may film your body from the left, from the right, and straight on, then do close-ups of your face from every direction.

If there's dialogue involved in the commercial, you may be asked to read it. They may also ask you to do something completely strange, such as pretend you're eating the most delicious piece of chocolate cake, or imagine you're on a desert island, and you'll need to try to act that out. It can make you feel pretty stupid. What's even more disconcerting is that generally, you get no feedback whatsoever from the client.

TV commercial auditions can be very embarrassing and uncomfortable. My only advice for getting through them is to try to remember we've all been there and try not to freak out too much. Instead, try to be yourself and enjoy the moment. Hopefully, you'll learn something new, such as which angles best suit your body and facial expressions on a live camera.

One way to make yourself more marketable for TV commercials is by learning how to deliver dialogue—learning how to talk on camera. This skill, which you can learn in broadcasting, acting, or commercial classes, will make you much more marketable and allow you to appear in a wide variety of commercials. Acting classes in general will help you learn to be more comfortable and expressive on camera.

Shooting a TV commercial can take anywhere from one day to two weeks, depending on the concept, product, location, and what is needed from the model. TV commercials can be filmed in a studio or on location, such as a big house, a beach, or a restaurant. The setup of a TV-commercial shoot is different from the setup of a still-photography shoot because the cameras have to be able to move.

Also, there are usually a lot more people involved in a TV shoot. In addition to the commercial's director, who usually worked with the advertising agency to come up with the concept, there's the camera operator and one or two of his assistants. Then there are numerous union

Roshumba's Rules

One way to make a good impression at a TV casting is to ask a lot of questions: "What are you trying to sell in this commercial?" "What image do you want to capture?" "How can I stand out?"

Roshumba's Rules

If you're working on a TV commercial, find out when you're needed on the set, and make sure you're dressed and ready in time. Schedule your personal phone calls and snacks around the shoot. The cost of shooting a TV commercial is so high, you don't want to do anything to cause a delay.

workers who set up the lights and cameras and do whatever else is needed to create the set and keep it running smoothly. There's also the hairstylist, makeup artist, clothing stylist, and all of their assistants. The clients themselves will be there, as well as the art director and other personnel from the ad agency. Craft service employees will be there to provide the food for everyone.

TV commercial shoots are much more structured and time-conscious than print photo shoots. Everyone is on the clock, and if the shoot goes into overtime, the budget can quickly skyrocket.

TV commercials challenge you to express and sell yourself in a totally different way. Your best bet is to talk to the director, the camera person, and the art director to get a better understanding of what they are looking for, what image they're trying to project, and what they want from you, and to keep asking questions throughout the shoot to make sure you're giving them what they need.

The Downside of Commercials

The biggest disadvantage of TV commercials is that they require exclusivity from the model, meaning that if you're doing a TV commercial for one product, and somebody wants to book you to represent a similar product, you won't be able to do it, even if they want to pay you more.

Also, the actual work of filming a TV commercial can be a lot more draining. It often requires much more energy than other types of modeling work, and you may be required to do a lot of things you're not used to. Because the technical aspects of filming are so complicated, there tend to be many more logistical problems, which can make shoots more of a headache.

Whenever you have a chance to appear in an advertisement or TV commercial, or are asked to endorse a product, congratulations! This is a sign your beauty and marketability are highly valued by the industry.

The Least You Need to Know

➤ Modeling in print advertisements can pay well and offer a way for a model to develop her mass-market appeal.

➤ Landing an endorsement deal is as lucrative—and as rare—as winning the lottery.

➤ TV commercials are a good way to learn how to work in front of a live camera and can be quite profitable.

Chapter 22

Specialty Models

In This Chapter

➤ Big is beautiful: plus-size models

➤ Beauty over 35: elegant models

➤ The explosion of the male-model market

➤ The changing face of ethnic modeling

➤ Opportunities for child models

In addition to the Christy Turlingtons, Cindy Crawfords, and Elle MacPhersons of the world, there are many other beautiful models who come in all sorts of sizes, shapes, sexes, and ages. There are beautiful size-14, plus-size models, gorgeous male models, fabulous ethnic models, and adorable child models.

In this section, we'll discuss the types of work each of these models does, the qualifications to get involved, as well as how you can get started in the exciting world of specialty modeling.

Big and Beautiful Plus-Size Models

The market for plus-size models (generally defined as models who wear a size 12 and up) has boomed in the last 10 years, mainly because the fashion industry has finally realized that the average American woman wears a size 14 and couldn't relate to super-skinny regular models. Plus-size models are booked to model the same type of clothes that regular fashion models model, including lingerie, bathing suits, sportswear, and evening dresses. They appear in magazines (*Mode* magazine is devoted exclusively to plus-size women), catalogs, runway shows, and advertisements.

Plus-size models are larger than regular models, but they're healthy, tall (between 5'8" to 5'10"), toned, and well-proportioned. They may be large boned, with broad shoulders, full hips, full breasts, and maybe a bit of a tummy. They may wear a woman's size 12 to 20 (but most wear 14 to 16).

Plus-size model Natalie Laughlin strikes a sexy pose.
Photo: Fadil Berisha.

Until recently, plus-size models tended to have an older, more matronly look. Now they tend to be much more fashion forward. "Prior to [the debut of *Mode*], it was just catalog work, the kind of work where they looked older and matronly. It wasn't body conscious," explains Corynne Corbett, the executive editor of *Mode* magazine. "Now it's all about the body and showing the body a little bit more. Even people who do full-figured ads, like Lane Bryant, are doing a more fashion-forward type of advertising."

Today, you'll find plus-size models of all types, including Classic Beauties, Athletic Girl Next Doors, Oddballs, and Exotics.

Plus-size models do a lot of catalog work, and they have a growing presence in television commercials and commercial print (advertisements), according to Corbett.

Plus-size models are also doing more editorial work. In addition to magazines like *Mode*, "there are European magazines that are booking some of our girls," says Corbett. Even regular fashion magazines such as *Glamour*, *Seventeen*, and *YM* are featuring plus-size models in stories.

Mod Squad

Plus-size model Natalie Laughlin (pictured on the previous page) is often referred to as a self-made model. After building her portfolio in Miami and London, she moved to New York to try and get her career going, to no avail. Then she wrote a letter to a number of fashion magazines, trying to encourage them to focus on women size 12 and up, who represent 60 percent of the population. *Glamour* magazine ran a fashion spread and article on Natalie, which received unprecedented response. "That article gave my career a huge boost, and then everybody wanted to look at me," she says. "Being a plus-size model gives you a lot of freedom and confidence. It's a real boost to get paid quite a bit of money to be big when all your life, all you wanted to do was be small. As a plus-size model, you're not just a model, you're a role model. You're changing people's ideas and attitudes about what's considered beautiful and sexy and acceptable."

In New York, Wilhelmina, Click, and Ford are the agencies with the largest plus-size divisions. In local and secondary markets, most agencies aren't large enough to have a separate division for plus-size models, so plus-size models are handled by an agency's regular bookers.

"New York is where most plus-size models work," explains Laughlin. "But before they come to New York, most work in smaller markets, such as Miami, Atlanta, Chicago, Seattle, Toronto, and L.A., to build their books. But you have to be patient—it doesn't happen overnight.

"For any model, especially a plus-size model, testing is really important," advises Laughlin. "Test constantly for your book. Unfortunately, you usually have to spend some of your own money, because photographers don't want to test with you, because they don't want to show plus-size models in their book (although that's changing). But by testing, you can find that freedom within yourself to move. A lot of plus-size models, when they start out, are inhibited by their bodies, and they feel uncomfortable in moving. Also, really practice moving in front of a mirror in the morning. When you are in front of the camera (whether it be for a job or for a test), create an idea in your mind of the attitude you want to project—this may come out of a made-up story or emotional relationships.

"Staying in shape is also important," she says. "Being a plus-size model doesn't mean you're not in shape. It's really important to exercise. You have to eat right, drink lots of water, and get enough sleep."

Because there's no uniform size for plus-size models, plus-size models sometimes wear padding (breast pads, hip pads), explains Laughlin. "So if the clothes don't fit on your body correctly, you use the pads to fill you out."

In general, there aren't open calls and model searches for plus-size models looking for agents. To find an agent, an aspiring plus-size model's best bet is to send snapshots of herself to agencies that handle plus-size models. See Chapter 6, "Getting Started," for information on taking snapshots, and see Chapter 7, "Finding an Agent," for information on sending them to agencies.

The Elegant Department

Elegant models—fashion models over 35—are another category of models that have become very popular over the last few years. As baby boomers have aged, advertisers and fashion designers have moved toward using models who appeal to this huge group of consumers, and they found that 50-year-olds just don't identify with 14-year-old models. Therefore, a whole new category of models who are 35 and over has emerged.

Catwalk Talk

An **elegant model** (also known as a **classic model**) is a model who's over the age of 35. Elegant models are usually former "regular" models who have returned to the business, such as Cheryl Tiegs, Patti Hansen, and Carmen.

Although elegant models usually don't work full-time, many have viable careers and can support themselves on their modeling incomes. They have a range of clients, including runway, advertising, and editorial. Most of their work, however, would be modeling for catalogs. Catalogs use older models, because they need to appeal to a variety of people, and they're not so trend driven. Elegant models may also appear in specialty ads for designers who are trying to incorporate people of all ages. In addition, they may do product endorsements, especially for cosmetic products such as wrinkle creams that are geared toward older consumers.

Mod Squad

Beautiful Rosie Vela is an example of a fashion model who made a comeback as an elegant model. Vela appeared on the cover of *Vogue* 14 times in the late 1970s and early 1980s. After she quit modeling, she focused on her music career until she got a call from Calvin Klein, asking her to appear in his 1994 fashion show. Appearing along with several other elegant models including Beverly Johnson, Patti Hansen, and Lauren Hutton, she created a sensation. Maybelline subsequently offered her a lucrative cosmetic advertising contract to represent its Alpha Hydroxy Moisture Lotion. She was once quoted as saying that she felt more beautiful than ever, even though she no longer had a 17-year-old's butt.

Elegant model Dianne DeWitt is living proof that models are beautiful at any age.
Photo: Martin Brading.

Elegant models may transfer from other departments without any break, or they may have been models who took time off from modeling and have gotten back into the business. Other elegant models are just starting out in the business for the first time. Elegant models can include any type, from Classic Beauty to Amazon, Exotic, and Athletic Girl Next Door.

Like their younger counterparts, elegant models are tall and slim, with well-proportioned bodies. They must have striking features, beautiful skin, teeth, hair, and nails. It's very important for elegant models to stay slim, youthful, and attractive and to keep their skin in its best condition. They shouldn't look unnaturally young, but should look youthful, the best their age can look. They may need to take more vitamins, use special moisturizers and skin treatments, work out more, watch their diets more carefully, and avoid smoking.

In general, there aren't open calls and model searches for elegant models looking for agents. Most elegant models have experience in the business and use their contacts to establish themselves as elegant models. If you've never modeled, but think you have what it takes to be an elegant model, you should send snapshots of yourself to agencies that handle elegant models. In New York, certain large agencies (Wilhelmina, Ford) have elegant model divisions. The Bryan Bantry agency in New York handles many elegant models, the majority of whom are former cover girls who are making a come-back. In smaller markets, elegant models may be handled by an agency's regular bookers, not by a special division. Call some of the agencies near you to find out if they handle elegant models; if so, you'll want to send snapshots of yourself to them to see if they'd be interested in handling you. See Chapter 6 for information on taking the right kind of snapshots, and see Chapter 7 for information on sending them to agencies.

Male Models

The male model market has exploded due to the rise of models such as Mark Vanderloo, Tyson Beckford, and Marcus Schenkenberg, all of whom have become celebrities in their own right.

Male models walk the runway in the major menswear fashion shows twice a year in Milan, Paris, New York, and London, explains M.L. McCarthy, casting director at Urban Productions in New York. They appear in shows for major men's designers, including Giorgio Armani, Gucci, Prada, Joseph Abboud, Paul Smith, Ralph Lauren, and Calvin Klein. They also appear in men's magazines, such as *GQ, Esquire,* and *Details* in the United States, *Uomo Vogue* in Italy, *Vogue Homme* in Paris, and *Arena* in London.

Male model Ryan Kopko is too sexy for his shirt. Photo: Kwame Brathwaite.

Male models also do a lot of catalog work, including J. Crew, Bloomingdale's, Neiman Marcus, Saks Fifth Avenue, and Macy's. Finally, they appear in ads for men's clothing (Ralph Lauren, Donna Karan, and Calvin Klein are the biggest names), as well as for soft drinks, cars, men's grooming products, and sports products.

Mod Squad

Mark Vanderloo is one of the most successful male supermodels. A native of Holland, he got his first modeling job when he accompanied a model girlfriend to a shoot one day, and the photographer called him into action. After that, however, Vanderloo thought his modeling career was over. He was tending bar near his hometown in Holland when he was signed by Wilhelmina; four months later he made a sensational debut on the runways of New York during the menswear fashion shows. He has since appeared in all the major men's magazines, as well as in ads for Hugo Boss, Calvin Klein, Donna Karan, Armani, Valentino, Trussardi, and Guess?.

Male models must be tall, generally at least six feet. "There are exceptions to the rule, but between six feet and 6'2" is the rule," says McCarthy. "Basically, they need to be able to fit into a size 40-regular to a 42-long jacket. You have to be lanky, you have to look good in clothes, with great, clear skin. With male models, it's not so much about beauty and perfection, it's about interesting personalities, too. That's something that's really important these days, versus the 1980s, where it was about beauty and being perfect looking. Of course, classic, good-looking guys are never going to go out of style. Those are the money makers, but there is also a whole breed of more exotic, offbeat, funky-looking guys, who are skinnier, with longer hair."

Like top female models, male models travel constantly, doing the fashion shows and photo shoots all over the globe. Like female models, when they're not traveling and working, they have to keep themselves looking their best. "You can't be gaining weight, eating poorly, and having your skin break out," says McCarthy.

In New York, IMG is the biggest agency that handles men. Other agencies include Wilhelmina, Ford, Major, ID, and Boss Models. Like female models, male models do test shoots and assemble a book once they've acquired an agent. It usually takes longer for men to launch their careers, because there's not the amount of work that there is for women, according to McCarthy. In smaller markets, agencies generally will have a men's division.

Roshumba's Rules

Male models generally start their careers slightly later than female models—at 18 to 20—but can work much longer, conceivably until their mid-30s. Some male models in their 40s are still working regularly.

In general, there aren't open calls and model searches for male models looking for agents. To find an agent, an aspiring male model's best bet is to send snapshots of himself to agencies that handle male models in the city where he wants to work. See Chapter 6 for information on taking snapshots, and see Chapter 7 for information on sending them to agencies.

Ethnic Models

Ethnic modeling is one of my favorite subjects. Within the past 10 years, the definition of who is an ethnic model has changed drastically. Before, an ethnic model was considered anyone who wasn't "all-American" looking, with blond hair and blue eyes. Now the all-American model can be blond-haired and blue-eyed, a brunette with brown eyes, or a redhead with green eyes. So basically this means that today, an ethnic model is anyone who isn't considered Caucasian, meaning anyone of Spanish, Asian, or African descent.

Ethnic models are not a separate category, in that they are not handled by separate agencies or departments; they are handled by the same bookers and agents as all other fashion models. But if you are an ethnic model, it will affect every aspect of your career, in both positive and negative ways.

Being an ethnic model can be an advantage or a disadvantage, depending on the situation. I would have to say now, with the emergence of advertising that is really about appealing to specific consumers, it can be to your advantage to be ethnic in a lot of cases. For a long time, you could have eight white girls and only one ethnic girl in an ad; magazines would put only one ethnic girl on the cover every year at best. Now, however, that has shifted drastically. Advertisers have finally realized that ethnic consumers spend a lot of money every year on clothes, beauty products, and everything else. So now, they hire ethnic models to represent those products. For instance, most of the mass cosmetic lines feature ethnic models (for example, Halle Berry does the Revlon campaign). Ralph Lauren hired Tyson Beckford to appear in the Polo ads, Victoria's Secret uses Tyra Banks, and many other products also use ethnic models in their advertising. Also, instead of being exposed just on billboards in ethnic neighborhoods, ethnic models are used in mainstream advertisements, in major fashion magazines, billboards in Times Square, and in catalogs such as J. Crew.

The disadvantage is that the amount of work available to ethnic models is still limited compared to the work available to white models. This also means that ethnic models can have a more difficult time getting their foot in the door and their careers launched. (But because ethnic women have a tendency to age more slowly, they can work a lot longer!)

The other disadvantage is the model herself. I've been approached by many ethnic models who have huge chips on their shoulders. They have a fear that they won't work because they are ethnic and that they won't relate to whites.

But I think if you're model material, if you have a good attitude, and work hard, you have as good a chance as anybody else. But you need to forget about all those negative attitudes; those will not help you as a model. If you want to be bitter, do it on your own time, but know that when you work as a model, you'll be working with people of many different backgrounds and ethnicities who are just there to do their best job, not to be abused, disrespected, and accused of something that happened that they weren't directly involved in. I would recommend just doing your job and focusing on building a fruitful career.

Roshumba's Rules

One area in which ethnic models are accepted more easily is runway shows, especially in Europe. If you find your career is not taking off, this may be a good route to try.

Child Models

Every mother of a cute kid has wondered if her child has what it takes to be a child model. Patti Abbott-Claffy, president of Jarrett-Claffy Management, a talent management firm in Philadelphia, which launched Brooke Shields' modeling career (among many others), shares her insider secrets on breaking into the business.

These photos of child models Christiana Anbri and Stephen Schmidt give the viewer a sense of their friendly, outgoing personalities.
Photos: Art Lynch.

293

Child models do magazine work (both for children's magazines and adult magazines that focus on families), advertisements, endorsements, TV commercials, and industrial work (training videos for corporations, corporate manuals, and brochures, particularly in the booming health care and pharmaceutical industries).

Because it's such a specialized field, child models are handled by agencies specializing in children.

Before a child reaches the age of about five, there is not a tremendous amount of work for child models, except for the occasional job for a baby. This is mostly because working with very young children is so difficult. Once a child wears a size 5 clothing, the amount of work increases tremendously, assuming the child is mature and cooperative. "They're able to get the cooperation at age five," explains Abbott-Claffy. "That has a lot to do with it."

Looking younger than her age has many advantages for a child model. Christiana Anbri is a very successful child model who does a tremendous amount of print and TV work. Even though she's $8^1/_2$, she still wears a size 5. And she also just lost her very first tooth. "What they get with that is a really intelligent child, who's more disciplined, a child who can really withstand more pressure and longer hours, yet she looks five," says Abbott-Claffy.

For catalog and fashion modeling, being a perfect size (a child who fits perfectly into a child's size 5 or 6) is an advantage. For commercials, industrial work, and editorial, it goes by age range (seven to nine, eight to 10), not by size. Between the ages of 12 to 14, it's harder for children to work, because they're at an awkward age—they're no longer a child, but they haven't reached teen maturity.

Also, it can be difficult for a child to work after she loses her baby teeth, before her adult teeth are in. Generally, there are two options, according to Abbott-Claffy: Wait it out, or get flippers. Flippers are a removable dental appliance that fit over the teeth to make it look like the child still has all her baby teeth intact.

Catwalk Talk

The **P&G child,** which stands for the Procter & Gamble child, is a common industry term that refers to a child with perfect, all-American features. Mikey from the Life cereal commercial is a classic P&G kid.

Years ago, only classic, all-American *P&G children* could get bookings. "Now we get calls on just about all types," says Abbott-Claffy. "Exotic is in, racial mixes are definitely in. The child that you choose generally jumps out at you when you're meeting them in the first two minutes, personality wise, looks wise, the way they use their eyes when they speak to you," she explains. "That, coupled with discipline. You have those who are precocious and adorable, but you can't get them to pay attention. Their attention span doesn't allow them to focus and follow directions yet. It's the combination of a sparkling personality and terrific listening skills plus the ability to follow directions," that makes for a successful child model.

Because the parent must accompany the child to all go and sees and auditions, it's key that parents understand what they're getting into. "I not only interview the child, but if I have an interest in the child, I sit down and talk to the child to find out whose main desire this is," says Abbott-Claffy. "It should be fun for the child. If it's not fun, I don't want to participate. You don't want a child who doesn't love it, because you have to love it to put in the time, or the child will get stressed and eventually crumble from the pressure. Also, I don't want to see a child responsible for making their parents happy."

Being the parent of a child model is a huge investment of time. "Being available, particularly for print and commercials," says Abbott-Claffy, "is one of the most important things. Sometimes you get a call in the morning for a booking that afternoon. If you don't have the time to really put into it, the child won't be able to work. If you do have the time, you're ahead of the competition. It seems those moms who can drop everything and have talented children, they seem to book more. Also, you must have the type of family life that allows that. Many of the families that work a lot have the grandparents involved."

It's also important that parents not pressure children, and that they find success in the small victories, and not emphasize bookings over everything. "I believe you should treat each audition, each interview, as being successful," says Abbott-Claffy. "The idea that your child can go in there and represent themselves, they've done what 98 percent of the population hasn't done. Most seven- and eight-year-olds could not walk into an interview and introduce themselves. The self-esteem you can gain, if you treat each time as a success, whether or not you book the job, is great."

Although a few children will make enough as child models to finance their college educations, this is not the norm. In general, the money you will make will be "the icing on the cake," as Abbott-Claffy calls it, not a major source of income. According to Abbott-Claffy, "The top kids do [make enough to pay for college], if all the factors are there. But it can become a full-time job for mothers for really successful, in-demand children. There are children whose college is paid for, but it's not common. Those who hang in for the long run seem to be more profitable."

The hourly rate for print shoots runs from $50 and up. An average is $75 an hour. Starting out, a child model may accept a lower pay rate in order to get the experience.

Con artists waiting to take advantage of naive parents who want to get their children into

Reality Check

If your child isn't feeling well, call and cancel the appointment. "Yesterday I met with a little girl who wasn't feeling well," says Abbott–Claffy. "She was very cute, but she was acting shy. Her mother said she'd been really sick, and that she wasn't normally like this. We really liked her look, but we can't risk our reputation by having that happen [on a job]."

modeling abound. To give you a heads up about bad business practices, here are standard operating procedures for finding an agent and getting your child started as a child model.

To find an agent, send informal snapshots to the agencies you're interested in working with. Don't spend a lot of money on professional portraits. "I prefer they don't have professional pictures done before they [see me]," says Abbott-Claffy. "A lot of times, the parents think they've got what I'm looking for and it's not at all what I'm looking for. A good department store photo showing the personality that costs $20 is all we need. A snapshot that mom took of the child by herself, especially in outdoor light, is also perfect. We don't like to get those Christmas pictures with friends and family, the kind of snapshot that is really busy. It should be just the child, and not with a hat pulled down or anything so you can't see what they look like."

The only money you should pay an agency is a commission on fees your child earns for working. Although some agencies will charge an interview fee, an evaluation fee, or a consultation fee, it should never be more than $25 to cover administration costs, according to Abbott-Claffy. Charging registration fees, or any kind of fee just for representing your child, is not legitimate.

Once the agent has agreed to represent the child, professional test pictures will need to be taken that will be used for the child's portfolio, head shot, and comp card. "I give them recommendations of photographers, and they go to whomever they want to," says Abbott-Claffy. It should never be outrageously expensive, because children change so quickly that photos need to be retaken often. You shouldn't pay more than a couple hundred dollars. If someone is coercing you into using only one photographer, especially one who is charging outrageous fees for taking professional photos, beware!

Eventually, the test photos will be replaced by tear sheets in the child's portfolio. "That's when the book becomes more of a thing to have on hand," says Abbott-Claffy. "[The client] can see how the child can work and their appeal and range." Starting out, however, the child can work with just a comp card and a head shot.

The only other legitimate charge an agency will make is for the agency book, which contains pictures of all the children the agency represents. It usually comes out every year or so. "The talent is responsible for paying for it," says Abbott-Claffy. "It can run from $100 to $200. That is a worthwhile investment, because that book is put in front of so many people, and they may book directly from the book (without a go and see)."

With these guidelines in hand, you'll be well-equipped to give your child her best shot at being a child model.

Roshumba's Rules

There's a great difference between a portrait photographer and a photographer who shoots for modeling and commercials. In a photo taken by the portrait photographer, the personality doesn't necessarily come through.

The Least You Need to Know

➤ Plus-size models (fashion models who are generally size 12 to 16) are an increasingly busy category of models.

➤ Elegant models (fashion models over the age of 35) have also become busier than ever.

➤ Male models have gone from obscurity to celebrity, thanks to the popularity of male supermodels.

➤ There are plentiful opportunities for ethnic models with the right attitude.

➤ The field of child modeling can be a lucrative, fun-filled opportunity if parents avoid the many pitfalls.

Chapter 23

Real-People Models

It's true—in a fashion magazine, the models are mostly tall, thin, with good hair, skin, and teeth. But if you didn't happen to be born that way, there are still modeling opportunities for you. Models who don't meet the stringent requirements for fashion models outlined in Chapter 3, "Do You Have What It Takes?" fall into the category of "real-people" models. Although modeling opportunities for these types are much fewer than for fashion models, they still exist.

One major source of work for real-people models is parts modeling, where just one part (hands, legs, feet) appears in the photographs. The second major source is character modeling, where models portray real people (young moms, concerned pharmacists, grandfathers, and so on).

In this chapter, we'll discuss the modeling opportunities for real-people models.

Do Real-People Models Need Agents?

I would like to dispel the myth that a real-people model doesn't need an agent. In my opinion, all models need an agent or someone representing them. One of the main reasons is that agents are the first to find out when a job is being cast. A model working alone doesn't have the resources to find out about every potential booking, nor would it be appropriate for her to call around to ad agencies and potential clients. Also, agents screen clients so that a model is not sent into a dangerous situation. Finally, agents handle billing, collections, and other aspects of the money side of things. The only type of models who don't need agents are retail models, because they are hired directly by the stores.

In large agencies, real-people models are handled by *commercial agents,* as opposed to fashion-model agents. (In smaller agencies, especially in smaller markets, one agent may handle both.)

Depending on what type of modeling you're interested in doing, the way you go about acquiring an agent will be different. In each of the following sections, we'll discuss the best procedure for each type.

Catwalk Talk

A **commercial agent** handles models who don't fall into the traditional fashion-model category. They are called commercial agents because they book models for commercial work (print ads, TV commercials) as opposed to editorial or artistic work.

Parts Models

A parts model is a model who specializes in modeling certain body parts, such as legs, feet, hands, or back—basically any part of the body but rarely the face. Some may model one or more of those parts. They can be hired to do a variety of work—editorial work, advertising, TV commercials, and catalogs.

Parts models generally don't meet the requirements to be fashion models—maybe they're not tall enough, or don't have the right look—but they have at least one standout part, such as beautiful hands, gorgeous legs, or perfect feet.

Aside from having the physical qualifications of a great part, an aspiring parts model needs to have plenty of patience and the ability to keep her part still while photographers adjust lights, backdrops, and props to get ready to shoot.

Reality Check

If you're considering parts modeling, keep in mind that you need to take amazing care of your parts. Although this may sound simple, it can have a major effect on your lifestyle. For example, many hand models wear gloves constantly, even on hot summer days, to protect their hands from sun and wind damage. You also can't do dishes (some people might like that!) or play sports.

Here, a hand model enhances the look of a fancy evening purse.

Parts for Parts

Although jobs aren't as plentiful for parts models as they are for fashion models, there is a fair amount of parts modeling available. Just think about all the ads and commercials you see for sandals, nail polish, jewelry, hair ornaments, hosiery, and more.

➤ Hand models model jewelry and nail products, or anything where a magazine, advertiser, or catalog would want to focus attention on the hand. Their hands may also occasionally double as the hands of regular models. A hand model's hands should have a perfect shape—long elegant fingers, well-manicured nails and cuticles, no sun damage, and no scars.

➤ Leg models model hosiery, footwear, shaving products, and body creams. They need to have long, lean, toned legs with no scars, bruises, tattoos, or scratches.

➤ Foot models model shoes, socks, foot-care products, and toenail polish. They need to wear size $5^1/_2$ to 7 medium-width shoes. They need to have medium to high arches, without any bunions, toenail fungus, crooked toes, badly proportioned toes, or calluses.

Clients often want to hire many different types of parts. Aside from the obvious male and female, there are glamorous-looking hands where the nails are a bit longer and polished the color of ballet slippers, for example. There are "mommy" hands that look a bit stronger and more capable, and there are surgeon's hands that appear smooth and steady.

Body parts modeling jobs, as well as all other types of modeling jobs, are available in any market, small or large, where advertising is created. Even the smallest of cities have cable systems that sell local ads and need talent to help sell products. Although it's the

301

major markets that get the bookings for the big national ads, think about the advertising circulars you get in your mailbox and with the Sunday newspaper. Chances are they were created by a local ad agency, who hired the models from a local agency.

Some established parts models in the fashion capitals can have full-time careers, depending on the type of work they're doing and their success in booking clientele on a regular basis. Once they have built a name for themselves as a parts model, they can find themselves in steady demand, and they may even work over and over for the same clients. In secondary and local markets, however, the work is more sporadic, and it may be difficult to have a full-time career as a parts model. Still, it can be a good source of extra income.

Parts modeling pays more in the larger markets, where the big national ads are booked. And once a model is established as a great foot model, for instance, she can command higher rates.

Finding a Parts Agent

As I mentioned earlier, all types of models, even parts models, need to be represented by a modeling agent. Several large agencies in the fashion capitals, such as Ford and Wilhelmina, have divisions set up for models who specialize in parts modeling. Like regular models, part models have portfolios and composites of their work; when clients call looking for a hand or foot to use in an ad or magazine story, the model's portfolio is sent out to that client.

Because parts modeling is a small, rather specialized field, there aren't model searches or open calls for aspiring parts models. Instead, call an agency that represents parts models and find out what their preferred procedure is for seeing new models—whether you should send in photos, drop by the agency, or make an appointment. First, you will need to have snapshots taken of your part.

Roshumba's Rules

It's fine if these snapshots of your part are taken by a friend or family member who's handy with a camera. Spending loads of money having professional pictures taken is a waste of money when you're first starting out.

If you're a foot model, you would want to have several pictures taken of your feet perfectly groomed with no color on your toes. Also take some shots of your feet with your toes polished in a colored nail polish and makeup added to your feet to smooth out their color and texture. Also, do a shot of your feet in high heels (without stockings). Take several pictures of each "look" from a variety of angles.

A leg model should take several pictures of her (makeup-free) legs in different poses—some where she's barefoot, some wearing high heels, some wearing tennis shoes. Take some photos straight on, some in profile, some with the feet in the model-T pose (the classic beauty pageant pose, with feet together, one pointing straight ahead, and the other pointing outward).

A hand model should take photos from several angles of her well-groomed (moisturized, nails filed neatly) hands with unpolished nails. Then she should polish her nails in a natural-colored polish and take pictures of them from several angles. Try to find natural-looking poses, and feel free to use a prop, such as a flower or champagne glass.

If you do decide to get your photos taken by a professional, ask the photographer to show you a contact sheet (a piece of photographic paper with numerous tiny prints of every shot on a role of film on it), not prints. It's more economical to choose the photos you like and then get them blown up (8×10-inch or $9^1/_2 \times 11$-inch is a good size) or if you're not working with a professional photographer, it's okay to get film developed at the 4×6 size at a drugstore. Have the photos printed at the 3×5 size, select the shots you like, then get them blown up before sending or taking them into an agency. (If the agency asks that you send the photos in, make sure you get a couple of sets of duplicates made up; ask that they be returned if the agency is not interested.)

Parts models generally get started a little older than regular models; between the ages of 18 and 20 is common. As long as your part stays beautiful, you could model for up to 20 years or more. The work can be very intense and tedious; you often have to hold an uncomfortable pose for a long time until the photographer gets the shot. It also doesn't have the same hype that regular modeling does. Yet it can be a long, lucrative career for someone with fantastic legs, standout feet, or lovely hands.

Character Models

Character modeling is available in almost every market and is often more accessible than fashion modeling. Character models portray real people in all areas of advertising and TV commercials, as well as in industrial training films, music videos, and as retail models. Think about any career or field of interest and there is probably a publication or TV program that targets that audience. And where there is a magazine or a TV show, there are advertisements. A character model can be a florist, a health care worker, a concerned teacher, a jubilant grandmother, the harried office worker who needs to send an overnight package, the young mom with laundry woes, and the police officer with a pounding headache.

One of the great things about character modeling is that experience, height, weight, and classic features are rarely factors in determining whether or not a model is hired for a job. Most important is that he or she has the right look for the job. Kate Moss may have all the modeling experience in the world, but if the job is a print ad for a hospital that features a typical-looking female doctor, it would be difficult for her to fit that bill.

Character models have to be skilled at expressing different emotions through their facial expressions. If a director told you to look competent,

Roshumba's Rules

Just because character models are more like real people than their supermodel counterparts doesn't mean that they don't have to have that special sparkle that sets all models and actors apart.

would you know how to position your head and facial muscles? Character models benefit from having strong acting skills. For one thing, being a good actor enables you to make various expressions. Also, because television commercials are such a huge source of jobs for character models, models with acting skills work more because they can do television commercials as well as print work. If you're interested in pursuing character modelling work, consider taking acting classes or on-camera classes (classes that teach on-camera techniques, speaking, working your best angles, and character development and projection) to develop those essential acting skills.

Like all types of models, character models have agents. When a job is being cast, the client will call the agent with a description of what type of model the client is looking for. The agent will then call all of the models she represents who fit that type. Character models generally have comp cards with three or four pictures representing different looks (see Chapter 13, "Testing, Testing, 1, 2, 3: Test Shoots," for more information on comp cards) or a straight *theatrical head shot* with a resumé printed on the back. Theatrical head shots are generally taken by professional photographers. Once you have an agent, she can tell you whether you need a comp card or a theatrical head shot and refer you to a good photographer, but once again, don't pay for expensive photos before you have an agent—it's a waste of money.

Catwalk Talk

A **theatrical head shot** is an 8 × 10- or 9¹/₂ × 11-inch inch photo of an actor's or model's head and face. They are given out to casting agents on auditions to help them remember the models they've interviewed.

Although character models generally don't make as much as fashion models, this still can be a lucrative area. A lot depends on what kind of jobs you're doing. As with fashion models, print advertising bookings pay better than editorial bookings. Television commercials also generally pay well.

If you're interested in becoming a character model, you should call some of the reputable modeling agencies in your area and find out which ones have a commercial division. They may request that you drop a Polaroid in the mail, or they may make an appointment for you to visit them.

The Real-People World of Television Commercials

There is no other area of modeling that offers more opportunities for real people than the area of television modeling. The need exists for every age, type, and ethnicity. Household products need homemakers to help sell them, copier machines need business people, bologna needs cute little kids, and the guy who gets sand kicked on him at the beach needs to look kinda nerdy! Even men who look like Santa Claus (or women who look like Mrs. Claus) can find work doing holiday commercials.

Television work is available just about everywhere, in cities large and small. Locally produced commercials, like those you see for car dealerships and other local retail and service establishments, all provide work for local models. (Usually these commercials don't have the budget to fly models and actors in from around the country.) As is the case with advertising print work, though, the bookings for large national commercials will take place in the big cities. (One more reason to support your local drugstore, hardware store, and boutique!)

Bookings for television commercials are generally handled by specialized agents who handle only TV; many large agencies have TV departments. (In some smaller markets an agency may not have formal departments but still handles all types of bookings.) If you know anyone who does TV commercials, call and ask who represents him or her. Otherwise, call the reputable agents in your area to find out who handles this kind of work. If and when you are invited for an interview, be prepared to be auditioned on camera.

Training and developing one's acting skills are of utmost importance. Hopefuls should sign up for acting workshops and try to surround themselves with the best possible teachers. Would you rather be a well-trained actor or compete against one? Auditioning is also something you can perfect; the more auditions you go on, the better you'll get at them! Good actors are constantly working on improvement.

Reality Check

Unless the part calls for someone with a specific accent (like an English accent on a British Airways safety video), accents can impede rather than help your career. Could you picture someone with a New York dialect (think Joe Pesci) representing British Airways? Well, neither can casting agents. The ideal situation is to have some voice training so that you are able to turn accents off and on.

Industrial Training Films

Industrial training films and corporate videos are used to train people for a specific career or even throughout one particular company. When a new worker is hired at the big bank downtown, for instance, he may be shown a video outlining various work-related procedures. When a new customer service representative is hired at a consumer catalog company like Victoria's Secret or J. Crew, she may be shown a video that will help answer customer's questions and concerns. Even the guy you bought your car from probably watched a video that taught him how to negotiate with you. In all of these cases, the actors/models who were used physically resemble the real people you would find working in these and many other fields.

Catwalk Talk

A **sample reel** is a videotape of all of an actor's or model's on-camera work, including television commercials and industrial training films. Think of it as a portfolio spotlighting an actor's/model's best clips.

Actors/models are also used for what is basically a cross between a training film and a commercial (almost like an infomercial) that often run in housewares stores like Bed Bath and Beyond and Linens 'n Things. In videos such as these, products are demonstrated on continuous-loop videos that play on stands near the merchandise.

Any area of the country where there are manufacturing or commercial hubs would have use for training videos, which makes it a great area for aspiring models outside the fashion capitals and very large cities.

The pay for training videos is a fraction of what a national commercial spot would offer. It could be as little as $50 plus a free lunch. But this is a good foot in the door and a good opportunity for a model or actor to get video footage of herself so that she can begin putting together a *sample reel* of her work (and that is valuable!).

To get involved with industrial training films, you need to have a commercial agent who can send you out on auditions.

Music Videos

Music videos are another source of employment for real-people models. Some music videos just show the band and exclude all outsiders; others don't show the band or artist at all and rely heavily on talented models and actors to tell the story. Go figure. The point is, there are numerous opportunities for all types of people to appear in music videos.

Think about the chubby little girl tap dancing in Blind Melon's "No Rain" video, or the odd-looking 20-something girl licking the ice cream cone in Soundgarden's "Black Hole Sun." There was a time when only beautiful vixens graced music videos (remember Christy Brinkley in "Uptown Girl"?). Now, the process goes more like this: The director of the music video and the band members collaborate on an idea for what the video will be like visually. With concepts often being unusual, calls have gone out for some pretty unusual-looking people. Next thing you know, agents are getting a call for a thin, barefoot, grandma type who will be seen stalking through the woods in a wispy white nightgown. Voilà! If you fit that bill, you could find yourself appearing in a music video, no matter how "un-MTV" you may seem.

Although bands often rely on friends and relatives to appear in their videos (Liv Tyler appeared in one of dad Steven Tyler's Aerosmith videos with actress Alicia Silverstone), some parts are cast in a traditional manner through modeling/acting agents.

Because bands choose to film videos in cities around the country, it's hard to predict which markets offer the best chance for music video work. 'N Sync's "I Want You Back" was filmed at Universal Studios in Orlando, Florida. Luscious Jackson's "Naked Eye" could have been shot in any big-city airport. The location and finished effect desired is what determines where a video will be shot. Country-music videos are often taped in areas of the country that rely heavily on that type of music (Nashville and other southern locations). Videos for rap tunes are often filmed in urban settings. Sometimes the models are hired locally, other times they are cast in New York or L.A. and flown to the desired location. But when a video is being cast locally, this can be a great chance for a real-people model.

The average beginning budget for a high-quality music video is about $250,000, but they have been created for much more and much less. How much of that is actually spent on talent depends on the budget, how major a role you play, or whether or not you were just used as an extra. A good commercial agent will negotiate the best possible deal.

Retail Modeling

All kinds of "real people" are involved in retail modeling, which generally requires the model to hand out free samples, coupons, or information to customers in an upscale retail store. These types of jobs are given to all types of real-people models: retirees, homemakers, and students. Unlike the other types of real-people modeling I've discussed, however, bookings for retail modeling generally aren't handled by modeling agencies, but are hired directly by the store or the manufacturer.

Occasionally, however, a modeling agency might get a request for retail models. One exception would be a "street-corner" campaign put together by a major manufacturer, such as the one recently held in Chicago for Pantene where identically dressed models handed out free hairspray on Michigan Avenue, a busy shopping area. If you're interested in getting involved in retail modeling, your best bet is to contact retail stores directly, especially ones that hire models to give out samples or spray perfume on a regular basis.

Whether you have a great part, or embody the look of a specific character type, you may be able to find work as a real-people model.

Roshumba's Rules

Retail modeling is a great way to break into modeling if you've not yet acquired an agent. This is because most retail models are hired directly by the store's personnel department.

The Least You Need to Know

➤ People who don't fit the height, weight, age, and other requirements for fashion models can find work as parts models and character models.

➤ Real-people models are used in print advertisements, television commercials, industrial training films, and music videos.

➤ Retail modeling doesn't require an agent.

Part 6
Career and Personal Management

Once a model has gotten her career off the ground, she'll want it to keep building momentum, so she can get as much out of the business as possible. In this section, you'll get a complete overview of what you need to know to intelligently manage your career once you get it up and running. I'll give you advice (as well as tips from other experts) about how to manage and maintain your career, so that you work as often as possible, make as much money as you can, and have a career that lasts for a good long time.

The first thing I'll discuss is how to establish and maintain clientele, balance your workload, and find your niche in the modeling world. I'll also talk about personal management, how to deal with fame and the downsides of modeling (drugs, alcohol, partying, bad boyfriends, eating disorders). Forewarned is forearmed: If you know what to look out for, you'll be a lot less likely to fall prey to one (or more) of these traps.

I'll also discuss how to manage your money, why you need a qualified accountant, how to set up a savings plan, and how to spot scams. Finally, I'll talk about planning for your future; the career span of a model is often relatively brief, and it's vital that she starts planning for the future sooner rather than later.

Cathy's
game plan
1. FAME
2. FORTUNE
3. RECORD DEAL
4. MOVIES
5. WORLD
   DOMINATION

Chapter 24

Managing Your Career

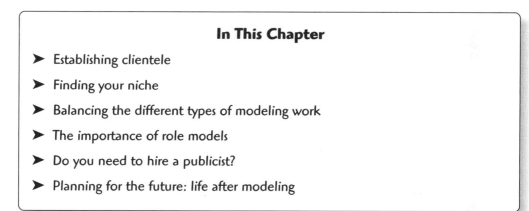

In This Chapter

➤ Establishing clientele

➤ Finding your niche

➤ Balancing the different types of modeling work

➤ The importance of role models

➤ Do you need to hire a publicist?

➤ Planning for the future: life after modeling

You've come a long way, baby! By this point, you've found an agent, persevered through many go and sees, and survived your first few photo shoots. But it takes careful planning, strategizing, and managing to get as much as you can out of a modeling career, to ensure that you make the most money and work for the best clients you can, work consistently, and have the kind of career that evolves, grows, and lasts for more than a few years.

In this chapter, I'll explain how you can make the most of the work you've done to get a career started: how to establish clientele, find your niche, make the most of the clients you have, and find and nurture new ones. I'll also talk about finding role models, the pros and cons of hiring a publicist, and planning a career after modeling.

Nice and Steady: The Beauty of Establishing Clientele

Just as a car salesperson establishes clientele—meaning she develops and builds relationships with customers who come back to her again and again whenever they need a new car—so, too, successful models establish clientele. Like the car salesperson, you can derive great benefits for your career by developing and building relationships with certain clients and certain *teams*.

The ideal situation is to have several clients and several teams with whom you work all the time. First of all, working for specific clients means steady work and thus a reliable source of income. Also, once you've established clientele, they will call just you and book just you; you don't need to spend time running around on go and sees.

Catwalk Talk

In modeling, a **team** refers to the behind-the-scenes people who work together to help the model look her best. This includes the photographer, the hairstylist, the makeup artists, the clothing stylist, and all their assistants.

Reality Check

The disadvantages of having a work relationship evolve into a friendship is that if something happens in the personal relationship—maybe you don't see eye to eye on something—that personal rift could end up affecting your work. If things are really bad, the client may no longer book you because the situation is so uncomfortable.

For a long time, *Elle* magazine was my home. I was an "*Elle* girl" for three or four years. I did photo shoots for them every month. I became really close friends with *Elle*'s creative director, Regis Pagniez. Whenever *Elle* or Regis would host or attend private parties, charity events, and famous dinners, I was always invited. Although Regis has since retired, he is still a very dear friend, whom I know I can count on to this day.

Working for one client also allows you to become familiar with a certain style and format of shooting, with the members of the team, and with a certain group of models. The more you work with one team, the better your work can become. As hard as you try, you can't reach your potential or do your best work at a one-time-only job. But the more you work together with the same team, the more you learn, and the more you are able to break through the barriers of unfamiliarity. You inspire them, and they inspire you, and all of your work becomes better.

Although you obviously want to establish clientele for professional reasons, it's also great to have a chance to establish personal relationships and friendships in what can be a very lonely business. This is more important than it may sound, because once you're a part of the fashion world, you may find it difficult to build relationships with ordinary people. They often don't understand your world and your lifestyle, which is why it's so great if you have the opportunity to develop relationships with people in the fashion world who understand and can relate to your problems and everyday existence.

As great as it is to establish clientele whom you work with frequently, you have to make sure you don't neglect to pursue new clients as well. If you don't continually replenish your list of clientele, you could find yourself stuck with just one client. So even though you may have strong relationships with a few clients, you should always keep trying to form and nurture relationships with new ones.

The Niceties of Finding a Niche

After you've been working for a year or two, you will start to get a feel for the type of clients who like your look and book you most often. Sometimes new models find that they're in demand for a lot of editorial work. Or maybe catalogs and advertisers are attracted to a model's all-American appeal and are booking her for jobs consistently. Evaluating who hires you regularly will give you a feel for how the industry perceives you and what your "niche" is.

It's good to have a niche. A niche allows you to establish a place for yourself within the modeling industry. A niche can make it easier for you to find work; once clients get used to seeing you do a certain type of work, other clients start to think, "She worked for the competition's fashion show/catalog/magazine, she'll be great for our fashion show/catalog/magazine."

Almost everyone falls into one category or another, depending on the type of work they do. They can be an A-list editorial cover girl, a consumer-friendly catalog-advertisement model, a youthful junior model, an elegant runway type, or a voluptuous lingerie and bathing-suit model. Obviously, there's a lot of crossover, and almost everyone has experience in more than one area; for instance, many editorial models also appear in fashion shows and in advertisements.

Mod Squad

When I first started modeling, I was categorized as the exotic runway model, and so I made sure that I went to every runway casting and met everyone having to do with runway shows in every single market—Milan, Paris, Germany, Spain, London, and New York. Eventually, I started doing more magazine work, and soon I had evolved into the spunky editorial-advertising model. For the next five years, I did editorial, advertising, and runway modeling. My career continued to grow and branch out, and I was booked to appear in *Sports Illustrated* for four years in a row, which took my career into the realm of supermodel. After that, I moved into the high-end catalog and advertising niche.

Also, in the course of your career, you may see things begin to change and evolve. Most junior models, for instance, eventually outgrow their niche and move on to a different segment. But overall, your niche is that one aspect of the industry where you seem to have the most frequent bookings at any one particular time.

Once you've figured out what your niche is, you want to focus on getting as much work as possible in that niche; that's the key to developing and profiting from having a niche. If you're a model in a fashion capital who finds herself being booked primarily for runway shows, you'll want to make sure you're going on go and sees for every type of fashion show (couture, ready-to-wear, and resort) in every market, focusing on doing the shows in Milan, Paris, and New York. If you're a bathing-suit model, you should make sure you're meeting every bathing-suit and lingerie client you can.

Once I figured out what my niche was, I made sure I saw as many clients in that niche as possible. For instance, when I had moved into the editorial arena, I asked my agent to make appointments for me with every single magazine. If I heard about one I hadn't been to see, I would ask my agent to do some research, find out if they were booking any jobs, and set up a go and see for me.

Roshumba's Rules

If you go on a go and see for a client in your niche and they don't book you the first time, try to go back at least one or two more times; maybe your luck will change.

The bottom line is you want to figure out what your niche is and then make it work for you. Every year or so, you should re-evaluate the work you're doing to see if your niche has evolved and changed. If it has, you'll want to re-focus your energies and start establishing new clients while maintaining your old ones. Finally, remember that your agent can be key in helping you figure out your niche and how you can maximize its potential.

Balancing Editorial, Advertising, Runway, and Catalog Work

The flip side of finding and developing a niche is maintaining a good balance of work. It's great to have a niche, but it's also important to try to work in as many different aspects of modeling as you can. Models often make the mistake of doing only one type of work: All they ever wanted was to appear on a runway in Paris. That's great, but they need to focus on having a fabulous career, not just one fabulous moment.

For one thing, modeling in different arenas helps you build exposure, and, also, every aspect of modeling feeds off the others. Somebody may see you in a fashion show and love your look and book you for an advertisement. Somebody else may see you in an ad and want to use you in their catalog. Working in a variety of areas also gives your career more longevity than is possible with a single-minded focus.

Ideally, you will be doing some editorial work (to keep your image fresh and your face in front of the fashion industry), TV commercial and advertising work (to make money and to broaden your audience in the mass market), runway work (to solidify your place as a fashion model), and catalog work (to pay the bills and establish long-term clientele).

Another reason to work in as many aspects of modeling as possible is that the fashion industry is notoriously fickle: What's hot today and who's in at this moment could all change tomorrow. So if a client stops booking you because they found a new model, you'll want to have another client or another aspect of modeling to fall back on. Not only will you expand the possibilities of your career, you'll learn new skills, meet new people, and at the same time grow as a talent.

Just to give you an example of what I mean, at one point in my career, I was doing every fashion show, which meant that all my time was spent doing fittings, rehearsals, and shows. I loved it, but I was in danger of being stereotyped as a fashion-show model. Although I enjoyed the work, I knew this would severely limit my career and the amount of money I could make.

Reality Check

Although it may be tempting, don't get lazy and focus on only one type of work. Even though it may be easier in the short term, a single-minded focus won't be to your benefit. Always make sure you're being sent on go and sees for a variety of jobs, including fashion shows, TV commercials, catalogs, and advertisements, especially early in your career.

I talked to my agent about this and told her I didn't want to do just runway, that I also wanted to see magazine clients. Soon after this, she started sending me out on go and sees with fashion editors. But the fact that I was a success on the runway definitely helped me get booked for editorial jobs. The agent would tell them, "Roshumba's doing the Yves Saint Laurent show, why don't you consider her for the Yves Saint Laurent story in the magazine?" Knowing that I was working for a prestigious designer, fashion editors would give me the chance and book me for an editorial shoot, which led to a lot more editorial work.

Although not everyone will be able to work in all aspects of modeling (or even in more than one), it's very important that you at least give it a try (unless you just want to try modeling for a year, then quit). If you want to have a modeling career that spans several years, however, you must work in as many aspects of the business as you can and make yourself as marketable as possible.

That's why a good relationship with your agent is key, so that you make the right decisions and take advantage of all the opportunities that present themselves. Because once they're gone, they're usually gone for good.

Super Role Models

There are two kinds of role models, both equally important. First of all, there are career role models. I define career role models as people you want to pattern your career after.

A career role model can give you an idea of the path you should take to see your career develop and grow to its fullest potential. If you want a career like Linda Evangelista, for instance, it would be a good idea to try to find out as much information about her as possible—how she started out, the photographers and clients she works with, who her agent is, what her style in front of camera is like. Then you'll want to try to duplicate or better what she did by adding your own personal touch.

Mod Squad

One of my major career role models is Cindy Crawford, whom I especially admire for her career-management skills. Not only did she reach the pinnacle of modeling—appearing on countless magazine covers and landing a coveted cosmetic contract with Revlon—but she also managed to get hired for TV endorsements for non-fashion-related products (Block-buster Video, Pepsi). In addition, she branched out into broadcasting, and put MTV's *House of Style* on the map. She found a manager (the William Morris Agency) who helped her take her career to the next level: They helped her negotiate a major contract with ABC to do her own specials. Finally, she disproved the notion that models can't have a career after a certain age.

Depending on the role model you chose, you may want to follow closely in her footsteps—going on go and sees to meet the photographers she worked with, asking her agent to represent you, adapting her style in front of the camera and on the runway. Obviously, you don't want to be a carbon copy of anyone; you just want to follow in her career path.

Besides finding role models who can be career guides, it's also a good idea to have personal role models. These role models can come from anywhere; they can be people you know personally, or people who are famous. It can be your mother, a model you admire for her professional reputation, for being wise, for working hard, and for being a force to be reckoned with. For me, my personal role models are my mother and grandmother.

My mother was my first image of a beautiful, glamorous women. She has been my main role model. She made sure her six children were always healthy and well cared for, and she looked great doing it. She could have been a lot of things and done a lot of things with her life, but she chose to raise her children. She overcame amazing odds to raise six healthy, positive, viable individuals. To this day, she's incredibly optimistic. She just knows how to take a bad situation and shine light on it; she can find laughter and joy in the darkest moments in life. She also taught me three key things: to say please, thank you, and excuse me.

Not only did my grandmother give birth to and raise 13 children, she later cared for a number of her grandchildren as well, including me for a time. She never shrank from any challenge, but would do her best to work things out. My grandmother, and the people who came before me, put a lot of effort into making me what I am. Whenever my ego gets out of joint, all I have to do is think about my grandmother breast-feeding twin babies, while pregnant with her fifth child, with two kids hanging at her knees. That puts all my problems in perspective.

Besides picking positive role models, it's also good to select role models you don't want to imitate, such as people who really wasted the opportunities their careers gave them by partying too much, getting caught up in situations where they exposed themselves to physical harm, or by being abusive to clients and coworkers.

Extra, Extra: Finding a Publicist

Once you've established clientele, secured a niche, and worked in all areas of modeling, you may be ready to take things to the next level. Maybe you want to try to get into acting, broadcasting, or another field in which you'll be in the public eye. A *publicist* can be very useful in helping you make that transition.

Basically, your publicist tries to promote you, your name, and your image as a celebrity as well as a model. (Anything that would be considered an actual modeling job, however, would still be handled by your agent. An interview in *Allure* about your favorite moisturizer would be handled by your publicist; also, you would not be paid. A fashion photo shoot for *Allure* would be handled by your booker and you would be paid.) A publicist can help you grow from being known as just a model to being recognized as a supermodel, celebrity, and personality in your own right.

A publicist would try to get you included on such things as *People* magazine's list of the 100 Most Beautiful People of the Year. He would let the gossip columns of the local papers know about parties you attended. He would get you booked for appearances on various radio and TV talk shows, both nationally and locally.

Catwalk Talk

A **publicist,** who is also called a public relations specialist, handles all your contacts with the press. This can include magazine and newspaper interviews and mentions, photo shoots, and appearances on radio and TV shows.

Some modeling agencies work with outside public relations companies that represent all the models in the agency, while others don't, in which case, the model managers may handle all publicity requests for their models. The disadvantage of relying on the agency's public relations company is that they're usually handling all the models in your agency. That could mean they're trying to publicize too many models, which can work against you. Agents don't mind if models work with independent publicists as long as the publicist does not interfere with scheduling or negotiations of day-to-day modeling jobs.

Once my career got to a certain level, I found it to be a very worthwhile investment to have my own public relations specialist (as opposed to relying on the agency's publicist). First of all, I like people who specialize in what they do. I like having the personal touch, and I don't want to compete with other models for the attention of the agency's publicist.

I got a publicist in the third year of my career, because at that time, I felt I had accomplished enough to talk about to the press. Before then I was working, but I wasn't doing anything so spectacular that I felt I needed a publicist to promote it. By the third year of my career, however, I had established clientele, I had done all the runway shows, I had worked for French *Elle* for three years, I had worked for *Sports Illustrated,* and I found that more and more, people were requesting me for interviews.

Magazine, newspaper, and television reporters would call and say something like, "We want to interview Roshumba for a segment on models and trends," or "We want Roshumba's advice for upcoming models," or "We want Roshumba to be on the committee for a charity event." I realized that I needed a publicist who could handle all these requests, sort the good ones from the bad, and help me build my name as an individual and a celebrity.

Roshumba's Rules

Not every model needs a publicist; it depends on the type of career you have. If you just want to make money and get out of the industry after five years, you probably don't need one.

Roshumba's Rules

Make sure the publicist you hire is knowledgeable about the modeling industry. I know of many models who spent a fortune on publicists but who got very little press, because they didn't hire the right publicist.

My publicist has booked me for appearances on late-night talk shows, including *Late Night with Conan O'Brien* and *Late Show with David Letterman,* and radio spots, including the Howard Stern show. She has arranged interviews for stories about me in *The New York Post,* the *New York Daily News,* the *Chicago Tribune,* and *People* magazine. She's also arranged for me to appear on the celebrity pages of *Harper's Bazaar, Vogue, Cosmopolitan,* and *In Style.*

The biggest disadvantage of hiring a publicist is that her services don't come cheap; they can range from $1,000 to $5,000 a month. A lot of people don't want to spend that much money.

To find a publicist, ask your agent if there is anyone that he recommends. If your modeling agency retains its own public relations agency, models who want personal representation may get discounts on the fee.

Another way to find a publicist is if you happen to notice that one of your favorite models is being featured in a lot of magazine and newspaper articles and getting a lot of publicity outside of being a model, find out who her publicist is. You can also ask other people in the industry, including other models, photographers, stylists, and editors, who the best people are when it comes to model publicity.

It's a good idea to find a publicist who knows the modeling field. Most public relations people specialize in one type of publicity, such as film, music, fashion, or medicine. Especially when you're just starting out, you want to work with someone who knows what's going on in the fashion industry and who will have the contacts necessary to get your name and image out there.

Another thing to watch out for is publicists who are so desperate to get you any notice they can that they book you for tacky appearances to do things that are not on the same level your career is on.

You may want to reconsider your decision to retain a publicist if you reach a point in your career where paying for one becomes a financial burden. If you're spending money on a publicist instead of socking it away in your savings account, it's probably time to reconsider having one. Also, if you decide you're not interested in establishing celebrity status, there's no reason to hire a publicist privately.

Planning for a Future Beyond Modeling

Usually by the third to fifth year of her career, a model has established clientele, secured a niche, and done a variety of types of modeling. But unfortunately, like athletes, models have a limited career span, which is why it is so important to start making plans for your post-modeling future in the third to fifth year of your career.

The first step is to ask yourself what you want to be doing in five years:

➤ Do you want to have made enough money so you can just quit the business, get married, and have a family?

➤ Do you want to use modeling to segue into another career as a magazine editor, a fashion writer, a fashion designer, an actress, or a broadcast personality?

➤ Do you love modeling and want to keep doing it as long as you possibly can?

Whatever choice you make is great, but you need to map out a game plan so you can accomplish your goals. During this process, whatever you decide you want to do, you should talk to your model manager about your plans, to make sure she knows what you're up to so she can help you. Your decision about your future will affect how she will promote you and structure your career, so that she makes sure you get what you want out of the business.

If you decide you want to just make money, you'll want to concentrate on doing fashion shows, catalogs, and ads—anything that will pay you a decent day rate. Hopefully, you may also get lucky and land an endorsement deal as well.

If you decide you want modeling to segue into another career, this is the time to educate yourself for that next phase by taking acting or broadcasting classes, going back to school to pursue a degree, or whatever else is necessary to prepare for that next phase of your life.

If you want to model as long as you can, you should start developing client loyalty by developing a personal relationship with your clients, making sure you participate in any private dinners they have, and maybe giving dinners for them. The fashion industry is very cliquey; for a career with longevity, it's a good idea to become a part of a clique. At a certain point, you may want to transfer to the elegant models department (see Chapter 22, "Specialty Models," for more information on elegant models).

Reality Check

The process of planning for your future can be very difficult. At the same time that you're trying to take classes or pursue various other interests, you'll still be modeling full-time, and it's not a good idea to turn down too many jobs. When I started to prepare for my future, instead of signing up for classes that would force me to cancel jobs, I worked with a coach and took classes on weekends, which made scheduling easier.

If you're part of a successful team consisting of a photographer, a makeup artist, a hairstylist, and a fashion stylist, you could work together for years. You could become a vital part of a functioning, profitable family. Especially with catalogs, if everyone is delivering what the client and their customers want, it's rare that that team will be split up, unless there's a change in management at the catalog company.

Victoria's Secret, for example, has used the same team for years because that team gets the job done; in other words, they sell the merchandise. The behind-the-scenes team and the models work so well together that they sell millions of dollars worth of clothes a year. The customers are familiar with the models; they even know them on a first-name basis.

The Final Curtain: Leaving the Business

Hopefully by the time your career is coming to an end, you will have figured out what you want to do with your future, and you've already started doing it. It's much better to walk away from the modeling business than to have the business walk away from you. The end can come anywhere between the eighth and fifteenth year of your career, but in general, most models have 10-year career spans.

Roshumba's Rules

When your career slows, between the eighth and fifteenth year, this may be the first time in your career that you'll have the time to pursue a college degree, if that's your ambition. Once you start attending school full-time, it may be almost impossible for you to travel for modeling jobs.

The conclusion of your modeling career can come in several ways. Your agent may tell you to consider retiring, that the natural cycle of your career has come to an end. Or maybe for the past year, your bookings are down to one a week, and even that's not always guaranteed.

I personally think that it's better to retire yourself than to be asked to leave. If you want to continue modeling, transfer to your agency's elegant division, or find an agency that handles elegant models. Even if you're not working every day, if something comes up, you will still have representation.

Mod Squad

You may also be inspired by the success of many ex-models. Many models, including myself, have gone into broadcasting: Willow Bay, Cindy Crawford, Rebecca Romijn-Stamos, Joan Lundun, and Emme. Andie MacDowell, Kim Basinger, and Rene Russo are busy, accomplished actresses. Cybill Shepherd and Brooke Shields have enjoyed success with their own network sitcoms. Beverly Johnson wrote a beauty book, and Iman developed her own line of cosmetics. B. Smith owns a successful Manhattan restaurant and has her own TV show. Vendela is a good-will ambassador for the United Nations. Kathy Ireland has designed her own line of sportswear, and Cheryl Tiegs developed a line of eyeglasses. Elle Macpherson designed a lingerie collection.

This is also a good time to seriously pursue acting, if that's your ambition. Again, this may be the first time you have to seriously dedicate the necessary time and energy into learning your craft, going on auditions, and trying to find an agent.

If you want to start your own business, this can be the time to do it. (Depending on what the business is, you may be able to start it earlier—sometime after your fifth year in the business.) Most self-owned businesses, especially service businesses such as restaurants, health clubs, and nightclubs, are so time-consuming that you probably can't manage running them while pursuing a modeling career.

Whatever path you decide to take, you can always look back with pride and fond memories on your glamorous, exciting years as a model.

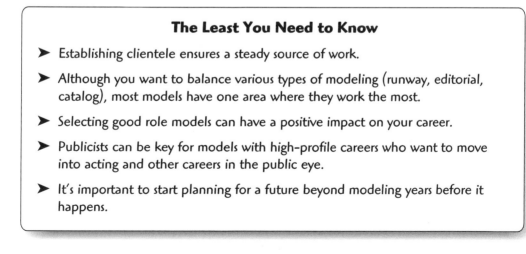

The Least You Need to Know

➤ Establishing clientele ensures a steady source of work.

➤ Although you want to balance various types of modeling (runway, editorial, catalog), most models have one area where they work the most.

➤ Selecting good role models can have a positive impact on your career.

➤ Publicists can be key for models with high-profile careers who want to move into acting and other careers in the public eye.

➤ It's important to start planning for a future beyond modeling years before it happens.

Chapter 25

Personal Management

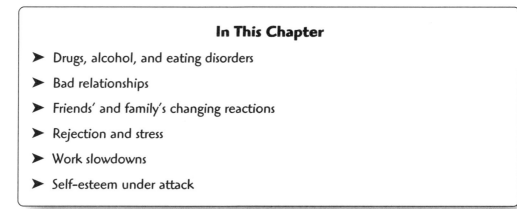

In This Chapter

➤ Drugs, alcohol, and eating disorders

➤ Bad relationships

➤ Friends' and family's changing reactions

➤ Rejection and stress

➤ Work slowdowns

➤ Self-esteem under attack

Staying emotionally and mentally healthy is just as important as managing your career wisely. The emphasis on physical beauty in the modeling industry and the continual rejection models have to deal with can take an enormous toll on a young person's self-esteem.

I've survived 10 years in this business, and I've seen it all—the rejection, the stress, the exhaustion, the drug and alcohol problems, the bad relationships, the work slow-downs. Although many models fall victims to these problems, many others manage to reap the benefits of a modeling career without self-destructing. In this chapter, I give you the benefit of my experience in the modeling business, so you'll be prepared for any obstacle that comes your way.

Downsides of Modeling

We've all heard the stories of how great the perks of modeling can be: the money, the clothes, the parties, and the travel. But there are two sides to every story, and the other side of modeling can be pretty frightening. Not every model falls prey to drugs, alcohol, overspending, eating disorders, and bad relationships, but many do. Here's the real scoop on the dark side of modeling, and how you can avoid being a casualty.

Just Say No to Drugs

The modeling world is a world full of excesses. Yes, drugs are around, and, yes, models do take them. For a very long time, industry professionals denied this. But in the past five years, the fashion industry has acknowledged their existence and the fact that they are frequently used and abused by many people. Even though drugs are so readily available, most models don't use them; it's not a given you'll start using drugs or become an addict if you pursue a serious modeling career.

Models who get into drugs tend to be young, just starting out in the business, rather insecure and looking for a way to either ease their fears, control their weight, or fit in with the cool crowd. Drugs are also not too hard to come by when you're a model. They're available in photo studios, backstage at runway shows, in nightclubs, and on street corners. On top of that, it is possible to have them delivered to almost any location.

I'm not going to preach to you and tell you what to do and what not to do. I just want to warn you that drugs destroy. They can take away everything that you have worked so hard to earn. Not only will they rob you of all your material possessions, because an addict will sell everything or steal anything to get her fix, but they will also take away your health, beauty, youth, and dreams.

Reality Check

Some people may feel it is okay to take drugs occasionally or recreationally and say that it's possible to take them without getting addicted, but why even take the chance? It has been proven over and over again by musicians, actors, comedians, models, and the everyday person that indulging in drugs is a quick trip down a dead-end street.

Alcohol Abuse

Drinking alcohol is one of the indulgences that is very easy to get caught up in and addicted to, especially because it is everywhere in the fashion industry and it is accepted as one of life's necessities. Models are regularly offered champagne before fashion shows, even if the show is at 9 A.M. This is because of the party atmosphere surrounding fashion shows and because it is supposed to take the edge off and calm the models' nerves.

A glass of champagne is fine. But imagine if a model does three to five shows a day in all the major markets—Milan, Paris, and New York—for six weeks straight and she drinks champagne at each show. In addition, she may have wine with both lunch and dinner, then drink a couple of cocktails at a party each night. That adds up to a great deal of alcohol consumption.

Models may not notice how much they're drinking, and no one in the fashion environment will think it's abnormal to drink socially. But the truth is all these "social drinks" could lead to a serious drinking problem. Many models and other fashion industry professionals do have problems with alcohol. So be aware of the possibility that drinking too much can happen very easily in the fashion industry, and even though it may seem acceptable, it's not, and in the end it could destroy or damage your career—not to mention your health.

Shopping 'Til You Drop

Working as a model exposes you to the finest things in life, including designer clothes, accessories, and luxurious jewelry. When I first started modeling, I knew nothing about Chanel, Prada, and Gucci. But after working with many of the designers of these garments and accessories, and meeting other models, fashion editors, agents, and photographers who owned these products, I found myself wanting to have them, too. For a while, I went crazy, buying everything in sight—clothes, shoes, bags, and jewelry—until one day, my accountant said to me, "Roshumba, it's okay to have nice things, but take it easy; you don't need to own the world." Remember, a modeling career is short-lived and when your money is gone, it's gone, so spend in moderation.

You may want to follow my accountant's advice as well, because I have seen many of my fellow models make a lot of money in a very short period of time, then throw it all away on luxury items. These include first-class airfares, tons of clothes and jewelry, and expensive apartments. At some point, the models panic when they realize that their modeling careers are coming to an end and they don't have the finances to maintain their luxurious lifestyles, haven't saved any money, and have no plans for the future. So, as soon as you can, develop a financial management plan. (See Chapter 26, "Money Management," for more on managing your money.)

Roshumba's Rules

As hard as it may be, especially when you're around beautiful, expensive things all day, try not to over shop. It's okay to have some of the finer things in life, but you don't need 10 of everything.

Dieting and Eating Disorders

Although dieting and eating disorders are associated with modeling in many people's minds, the majority of models are naturally thin and don't suffer from eating disorders. But for those models who don't have a healthy relationship with food and/or are not naturally thin, who are genetically big-boned or full-figured, staying model-slim may be an enormous challenge. Unless you plan to have a career as a plus-size model (which offers limited work), you will need to maintain your weight so that you are able to wear a sample-size dress.

But diet pills, crash diets, fad diets, purging (vomiting), fasting, and other gimmicks are not the answer to staying slim. Maybe you will lose weight initially, but these take a toll on your looks in other ways; not only that, but once people stop these practices, they tend to regain the weight—and then some—very quickly.

Catwalk Talk

Anorexia is an eating disorder whose sufferers eat little or nothing because they think (erroneously) that they are fat. **Bulimics** consume huge amounts of food, then purge it by vomiting, abusing laxatives, or exercising excessively.

Reality Check

Don't freak out if you suddenly find you've gained a few pounds. It's true that your agent and clients may notice, and you may be asked to lose weight. But try to deal with it calmly and sensibly, so you don't endanger your physical or mental health. Step up your exercise program, consult a registered dietitian, or start a reputable weight-loss program such as Weight Watchers.

Excessive, overzealous dieting can also sometimes trigger eating disorders in certain people. People with eating disorders, which include *anorexia* and *bulimia,* are obsessed with food, weight, and appearance to such an extent that their health and daily lives are negatively affected.

Anorexics literally starve themselves, eating and drinking little even though they suffer terrible hunger pains. Even when they are bone-thin and way underweight, they think they are overweight. They have a terror of gaining even the smallest amount of weight. Anorexia can damage vital organs such as the heart and brain. In addition, monthly menstrual periods may cease, nails and hair may become brittle, the skin may dry out and turn yellow, and the body may become covered with soft hair. Ultimately, it could kill you if untreated.

Bulimics consume huge amounts of food and then rid their bodies of the excess calories by vomiting, abusing laxatives, or exercising obsessively. Because this "bingeing and purging" is done in secret, and because many bulimics feel terrible shame about their actions, bulimia can be hidden from others for years. Still, it takes a terrible toll on the body. The acid in vomit wears down the outer layer of the teeth, causing them to become discolored. Scars can form on the hands from being cut by teeth due to pushing down the throat to induce vomiting.

Eating disorders often develop as a means of dealing with emotional pain, low self-esteem, stress, traumatic events, and stringent diets. Early treatment is the most effective, so if you think you have a problem, get help now! Ask your agent or family doctor for a referral to a psychologist, social worker, or psychiatrist who treats patients with eating disorders.

Boyfriends Who Aren't Your Friends

The fashion industry is flooded with all sorts of sexual overtones. When people of the opposite sex see models in advertisements, especially where they're selling things with sexual overtones, illusions are created that say models are sex objects and many people in the mass market may believe that models are easy or loose.

But in their private lives, most models are not sexually promiscuous. Many are married, in committed relationships, or are so busy with their careers that they just don't have time. Still, there are others who throw caution to the wind and have sex with everyone they can. Some are trying to sleep their way to the top, some are trying to desperately fill a need, some are lonely and far away from home, some haven't yet realized they don't have to sleep with everyone who asks them, and some are just naturally sexual.

If you find yourself in a position where you are being pressured sexually by any man, be he a photographer, an agent, or a fan, and you are not comfortable or interested, let him know that you are a professional, are in a relationship, or are just not available for anything that is not work related. Tell him you would appreciate it if he would respect your wishes and treat you as a professional.

For those women who are on a mission to sleep with everyone from here to Timbuktu, know that this is not a good thing. First, it's dangerous, because of the threat of AIDS and other sexually transmitted diseases. Also, if you get the reputation of being someone who sleeps around a lot, it could turn off your clients, agents, and other industry professionals, which can have serious professional repercussions and cause you to lose everything you've built. I'm not going to tell you what to do in your personal life, but know that there are consequences to this type of behavior.

I've mentioned modelizers a couple of times already—men who hang around and date models exclusively. Many modelizers just like the idea of dating a model, but aren't interested in the real person. If a man is dating a model just because of her beauty, eventually he is going to have to realize that there's a real person there, with physical flaws, insecurities, and other shortcomings. It's at this point that most modelizers flee the relationship, because they're interested in the external image, only, not the whole human being.

Reality Check

Don't use sex as a way to fill a void in your life. If you're feeling lonely, get a pet, make some friends, or call your family. If you think you may have an emotional problem, get professional psychological help as soon as possible. Know that you can have a very successful, happy, and fulfilling career without sleeping with anyone you're not totally in love with or committed to.

Roshumba's Rules

Before you get involved with anyone, ask yourself, does this person have a life of his own? Does he work? What has he ever accomplished, and why is he so willing to be your Boy Friday?

Another type of modelizer is the sensitive, available guy who hangs around at every model-related event. Watch out! This is the guy who is probably the most dangerous modelizer of them all. His shyness and sensitivity may appeal to many models who are away from home for the first time, a little lonely, and rather insecure. He may also be appealing because he will go out and escort models at a moment's notice, walk their dogs, pick up their dry cleaning, and do whatever errands are necessary. Don't be fooled by his niceness; this type can be a leech.

Unfortunately, I have had many model friends get caught up in relationships with this second type of modelizer. From the beginning of the relationship, the model paid for everything—the rent, the food, all the clothes for the two of them, and exotic vacations. These guys were so financially dependent on the models they couldn't even afford to buy a candy bar. In addition, they were emotional drains because they didn't have a life or any interests of their own.

Because the guy had no life or ambitions of his own, he would end up trying to run or manage hers. He would make sure he was also invited to every fashionable dinner and party along with the model, would develop relationships with the model managers, interfere with her bookings, and negotiate what she should and shouldn't be doing with her career. When the model's career started to come to an end, along with all the perks that went along with it, the guy would lose interest, dump her, and be off to the next model, leaving the woman broke and emotionally drained.

Now don't get me wrong, not all sensitive, shy, accommodating guys are modelizers. Many are just wonderful men who possess these qualities. But the way to make sure you are not getting in with a bad type is to make sure the guy's ambition is not just to be around and date models and live a fun, glamorous lifestyle at the model's expense. Check out if he works and can support himself, see if he has career goals and accomplishments and his own apartment. Can he take you out to dinner, is his career a priority in his life, and most important, do you feel safe, secure, and mentally, emotionally, and financially supported when you are with him? If not, he may be using you, in which case you don't want him to be a part of your life.

Mod Squad

Many models have been caught in relationships with physically abusive boyfriends. These brutes have a tendency to beat up their girlfriends whenever they are enjoying a big career triumph. One successful model I know was beaten by her boyfriend every time she appeared on a magazine cover, whenever there was a big party in her honor, or whenever something good would happen in her life. She would show up at her agency with a huge black eye or walk into a shoot with bruises all over her body. He was so threatened by her success that he felt obliged to re-assert his power and dominance by beating her up.

Bad relationships can drain you emotionally and physically. In extreme cases, they can even take a toll on your career. A bad relationship is one that makes your life worse, not better, in any way, shape, or form. Maybe it's with someone who wears you down mentally with his neediness; it could be someone who disregards your wants, needs, and feelings, or someone who is emotionally abusive or resentful of your career. He may encourage you to self-destruct by using drugs, skipping work, or being disrespectful to clients; or he may try to run your life. Others may be physically abusive.

Many models are very young and may not have that much experience with serious relationships. But let me tell you, no matter how cute he is, how charming he is in public, how much money he makes, or how much you fear being alone, a bad relationship is not worth it.

Get up your courage and tell the person that the relationship is no longer a healthy situation for you to be in anymore, that you're moving on with your life. Hopefully he will respect your request to stay out of your life. If he doesn't, even though it sounds cold, you may have to hang up on him when he calls or change your phone number. If he won't leave you alone, the next step may be to go to the police and take out a restraining order.

If someone is physically abusing you, leave him immediately. Don't wait around for him to reform, because it hardly ever happens.

Handling Family and Friends and Their Changing Attitudes

This subject is actually a little painful for me to talk about because once my career took off, my picture could be seen in all the magazines and on television, and my income increased, I found that I had less and less in common with the people I grew up with. Still, I hope my experiences in this area can help you.

While I was off in Paris appearing on magazine covers and in designers' runway shows, my friends, family, and other associates (the Chicago-based models, hairstylists, makeup artists, and designers who were still living in Illinois) were all still living "ordinary" lives. Many were still in school, working at "regular" jobs with entry-level salaries, using public transportation or driving used cars for transportation, eating at McDonald's, and going to movies as their main form of entertainment. Most of the people who were the foundation of my life were happy for me, but there was also a lot of envy and resentment about my new fame and success.

Some friends were jealous because I had made it and they were still struggling with no break in sight. They took my joy and happiness as a slap in the face.

Reality Check

When your best friend from childhood is struggling to earn a college degree and can barely afford to move away from home, and you're making a lot of money and appearing in fashion shows, catalogs, and magazines, that will create an imbalance in the relationship and may provoke jealousy. Your best course of action is to understand what they're going through and to be patient; don't push your success on them.

Eventually, my new lifestyle, as well as all the traveling that goes along with modeling, took me away from those old friends. At the same time, however, I was making new friends in the industry with whom I had more in common.

With my family, things were different. I came from a family with six children. My mother spent her life doing all she could to raise happy, healthy, viable, God-centered human beings. We went through many ups and downs together, but we always remained a close-knit unit. As we grew older, each of us discovered our own unique talents and began to pursue our own paths. Although my mother did her best to support and encourage each child's efforts and successes, sibling rivalry was inevitable, even in a family as close as ours.

My relationships with my sisters and brothers were still close and loving, but the constant talk about my modeling career did take its toll, and I do believe it created a distance between my siblings and me.

When it comes to handling your personal relationships with your family and friends once your career has taken off, I suggest that you keep everything in perspective. Know that if your modeling career is a success and you begin to make considerable amounts of money, jet-set around the world, and spend your time hanging out with other models and celebrities, your relationships with the people you grew up with are going to change. Some people are going to be happy and supportive, and others will be envious and intolerant. But in any case, the differences in your ways of life will mean that you have less in common.

The way to deal with these shifting relationships is to be humble, patient, and respectful of other people's feelings. Even more important is keeping your ego in check. Try to take an interest in their lives; don't always be lording your success over them by talking about how much money you make or which famous people you've met. If people feel they need to distance themselves from you because of their own phobias and insecurities, so be it. Just make sure you're not alienating people with your attitude and egomania.

If conflict does occur between family members once your career takes off, it will probably be based on something other than envy. It may be more about the fact that you don't spend as much time together as you used to or it could be based on unresolved childhood issues.

In this case, try to keep them close. Invite them to visit you in the city where you live, and make an effort to be there for their special events, such as graduations and weddings. Just love them for who they are and what they are, but don't alienate them with a big ego and a bad attitude. Don't sacrifice your career for them, because deep down inside, they don't expect you to do that. Your life is yours, and their lives are theirs.

Dealing with Rejection

Probably in no other business in the world will one human being receive so much rejection as in the modeling industry. Even supermodel Claudia Schiffer was initially rejected by the French modeling market because they said she looked like a milkmaid. She was considered to be someone who would never make it above second-rate catalog work. Finally, someone saw her in a different way, and the fashion world fell in love with her Brigitte Bardot beauty in a Guess? Jeans ad.

So if you decide you want to become a model, get ready! Plan to have doors slammed in your face, and hear very blunt criticisms of your body and features (her butt's too fat; her boobs are too small; no Asian girls; her jaw's too square). But if you really want to have a modeling career, swallow your pride, grab your portfolio, and hit the pavement. The truth is, there is something for every type of model, because every client is looking for something different.

Hopefully, you will quickly get past the shock of learning how cold and cruel the modeling world can be. Keep in mind that you're not being critiqued on the inner you, but on your "product"— your face, body, hair, skin, and so on. Although it's not a great feeling in any case, it helps if you know if wasn't meant as a personal insult. Believe me, I've heard people slander models' race, physical attributes, height, weight, eyes, nose, ears … you name it. Generally clients are polite and don't say anything negative, but sometimes, the comments are absolutely scathing.

Roshumba's Rules

Rejection and criticism never feel good. When I first started out, I took each negative comment as a slap in the face. After a while, though, my skin toughened when I realized it wasn't personal.

The smallest thing—maybe something you've never even noticed about yourself—can be cause for a client not to book you. Perhaps they're looking for a girl with really skinny calves to sell a shoe that wraps up the leg, and your calves are just medium. Or maybe the client is shooting a collection of dark-colored clothing and they feel the clothes won't stand out against your dark skin. You can't help any of these things, there's nothing you can do to change them, so don't let them upset you. Just move on to the next go and see, where the client may be looking for someone with just your shape of calves or just your color of skin. Always remember that whenever a client evaluates you, it's always in terms of what they need to sell the product, as well as their own personal tastes.

Reality Check

What you definitely *don't* want to do is curse at clients, scream at them, criticize them back, or show them any disrespect, even if they rudely rebuff you or say something insulting. If someone rejects you, say "Thank you for your time," take your book, and walk away.

Fortunately, your agent is there to act as a buffer against harsh criticisms and mean-spirited rejections. A good agent will usually sugarcoat a client's words. If a client has some constructive criticism, however, and mentions something that you can improve on—your teeth need to be straightened, you need to gain a few pounds, you need to let your hair color go back to its natural state—your agent may pass along the message.

Don't deal with rejection in a negative way, by overeating to soothe the hurt; using sex to validate yourself and make yourself feel wanted; or drinking or taking drugs to numb the pain. Because even after you've binged on ice cream, slept with someone indiscriminately, or gotten drunk, the rejection will still be there in the morning. Not only that, but it will be compounded by the extra weight you gained, a hangover, a drug addiction, and maybe finding yourself pregnant or with a sexually transmitted disease.

Roshumba's Rules

When you're feeling rejected, talk to your agent. A good agent can be your own personal cheerleader. She'll tell you, "Okay, you didn't get this one, but I know you'll get the next one; keep your chin up."

Instead, talk to some uplifting friends who always make you laugh or feel good about yourself. Or call your parents, who will tell you they love you no matter what those people said.

Because rejection in the modeling industry is so constant, I have all these little tricks to cheer myself up. I'll rent the movie *Clueless;* it always makes me laugh to watch Alicia Silverstone and her buddies rule Beverly Hills. I might read a book of positive affirmations with sayings such as "The sun may not be shining today, but it will come out tomorrow" or "There's a pot of gold at the end of every rainbow." Focusing on these messages always inspires me to go out the next day and try again.

Under Pressure: Dealing with Stress and Exhaustion

Whether you're appearing in a dozen fashion shows in three days, flying somewhere new every night, or just running around town trying to accomplish everything you need to get done, modeling can a be a stressful, exhausting job.

Probably the most stressful time of all is fashion-show season. If you happen to be a model who does the shows in the fashion capitals, you will most definitely get burned out doing all the go and sees, fittings, rehearsals, and the actual shows (and you might have to squeeze in a couple of photo shoots as well). Other times of the year can be equally stressful. Right after the fashion shows, the industry tends to be super busy because that's when all the magazines and catalogs start shooting the next season's clothes. The weeks before Christmas can be stressful, too, because the whole industry is trying to get as much done before the holidays as possible.

Here are some stress busters that may work for you:

➤ **Stay organized.** This is the time when your datebook becomes more important than ever; if you know everything you need is in there, you don't ever have to worry about where you're supposed to be next. I also try to keep my apartment (when I'm in New York) or my hotel room neat and organized. It only adds to my stress level when I have to sort through a lot of stuff to find one little thing.

➤ **Exercise.** If I'm tense, tired, or stressed out, I have found that working out will give me more energy and relieve stress; as an added benefit, I'll also be toning my body. I personally think yoga is an especially great way to alleviate stress.

➤ **Take care of your health.** During runway-show season, or whenever I'm really busy, I also make sure I take some good vitamins to keep me healthy; I take vitamin C, echinacea, and an immune system builder. I also find that drinking as much water as I can helps me feel better, too.

➤ **Get enough sleep.** Try to get as much sleep as possible. This is easier said than done, especially when you're leaving the house at 5 A.M. and you don't get home until midnight, night after night. I'm fortunate in that I can sleep anywhere—in the noisiest hotel room, backstage at a fashion show, in the back seat of a cab, on planes. I try to catch naps whenever I can.

➤ **Cut down on stress factors.** Try to eliminate other stress factors in your life. If I'm working hard, I try to postpone dealing with boyfriend problems, family issues, and needy friends.

If you are really getting burned out and can't hack it, you may be overworking yourself and you may want to consider cutting down your workload. A beautiful, stress-free model who works only five days a week is better than a cranky, overtired model with circles under her eyes and broken-out skin who works seven days a week. In fact, in the long run, exhaustion could take its toll on your career; people may stop booking you because you're so tired, you don't look your best.

Talk to your agent and let her know that you're tired and burned out, and ask her if there is any way your schedule can be reworked so that you can have a couple of days off to rest. Agents are usually sensitive to that. If a girl is working non-stop, they realize she does need a break.

Roshumba's Rules

Whenever you do get a chance for a break, it's great to bring your favorite music along with you and listen to it on a personal stereo or CD player, which can be really relaxing.

Situation Wanted: Dealing with Work Slowdowns

At various stages of your career, it's only natural that you experience work slowdowns. When you're first starting out in the modeling business, it may seem like not much is happening with your career. Even though you've done numerous test shoots and been on a million go and sees, the bookings are only dribbling in.

Don't panic! This happens to just about everyone. The best way to deal with this is to stay optimistic. Realize that you're the new kid in town and that it may take a while to make yourself known. Also, remind yourself that if an agency signed you, someone believed that you had the potential to become a model.

Roshumba's Rules

Until your career gets started, focus on making yourself a better model by doing as many test shoots as possible and by getting to know your agent and the other staff at the agency better.

Once a week or so, drop by and talk with the agents, both your own and the others in the agency. While you're there, introduce yourself to the managers who run the agency. Keep it light and friendly. This shows you're optimistic, that you're gung-ho, which will renew their faith in you.

Make sure, however, that you're not being a pest, that you're not spending all your waking hours hanging around the agency moping and pouting. If your career isn't taking off the way they expected, it's frustrating to your agent, too. If you go in moping and crying, and they're depressed already because things aren't clicking, it might turn them off completely.

In the meantime, try to make some new friends; invite other models, makeup artists, or test photographers you meet at go and sees or on jobs to have coffee, go to lunch, see a movie, whatever. Develop some interests outside of modeling. If you haven't yet graduated from high school, this is a good time to focus on getting your diploma. If you're new in town, take this opportunity to learn the city; take rides on the subway, take long walks, and learn your way around. Also, explore some of the local cultural institutions—museums, landmarks, galleries, theaters. Because once your career takes off and you do get busy, you will probably have very little time to enjoy these things.

Finally, if you're sitting around poor and broke, consider getting a job. Many models get jobs waitressing or hostessing in restaurants, bars, and clubs (in fact, some hot spots hire only models), temping, or working in retail stores. See Chapter 10, "Modeling in the Fashion Capitals," for more information on the best types of jobs for models.

At other points in your career, you may find that several regular clients are no longer booking you. Don't be bitter or angry about shifts in your career. Recognize that change is a natural part of being a model, and move on to the next chapter. The best way to deal with this is to recognize that it is inevitable and even natural, and to get busy going to see new clients. At this point, you need to talk to your agent and really focus on seeing other clients. Now's the time to go on a new round of go and sees and establish a new set of clientele.

Self-Esteem Under Attack

Especially at the beginning of your career, your sense of self-esteem and self-worth will be subject to an enormous amount of abuse. When you're just starting out, you'll probably feel like a fish out of water the whole time, a square peg trying to fit into a round hole.

Everything you do—go and sees, photo shoots, traveling around a new city—will be new to you. You weren't born on the runway or in front of a camera lens, so of course you can't know everything you're supposed to do. You may often feel awkward, lost, or just way out of your league.

The best way to handle this is to accept that all these things are new and foreign to you and realize that it will take time to learn everything a model needs to know. Accept that you're going to make mistakes and that you may be asked to do things over and over until you get them right.

Mod Squad

When I was trying to get my modeling career off the ground, I had a full-time job in the medical field. Even though I was having trouble booking modeling gigs, the medical job was a great self-esteem booster. Not only was I helping people, but I also knew I had something to fall back on if modeling didn't work out. Another thing I always loved doing was coloring in coloring books. Whenever I was down and distracted, I would get out my crayons and color Mickey Mouse and Snow White! Something about seeing all those colors calmed me and made me feel happy, because I was focusing on something other than the fact that I wasn't modeling.

Try to develop other things in your life that are important to you outside of modeling—hobbies such as basketball, dancing, singing, theater, or crafts. Make those things a priority. They'll serve as a reminder that you're good at many things, and they'll help you get over those rough patches at the start.

The worst thing you can do is sit at home and dwell on all the bad things that happened and everything you did wrong. Go out, date, see friends, and have fun!

All in all, it's true, modeling can be a very cold-hearted, harsh business. The rewards are great, but so is the toll it can take on your emotional self. That's why it's so important to know what you're getting into, so you can develop coping mechanisms to insulate yourself from the harshness of the modeling world.

The Least You Need to Know

➤ Drug and alcohol abuse, overspending, eating disorders, and bad relationships can all derail a modeling career.

➤ Your new modeling career may change the attitudes of old friends and family members toward you.

➤ Constant rejection is an intrinsic part of the modeling game; learning not to take it personally is the best way to deal with it.

➤ Successful models learn to deal with stress and work slowdowns in positive ways.

Chapter 26

Money Management

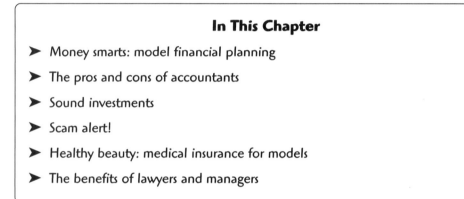

In This Chapter

➤ Money smarts: model financial planning

➤ The pros and cons of accountants

➤ Sound investments

➤ Scam alert!

➤ Healthy beauty: medical insurance for models

➤ The benefits of lawyers and managers

This is perhaps the most important chapter in this book. So many models have gotten caught up in living above their means, thinking their careers will last forever and that they'll be bringing a check home all their lives. Others get caught up with con artists who promise them huge profits and end up stealing their money. Still other models make bad investments or get involved with bad boyfriends who just want an easy means of support.

But after 10 years or so of hard work as a model, you don't want to find yourself working as a checker at a grocery store because you lost all your money or you didn't save anything, and all you have to show for all your hard work is a five-year-old Prada bag.

Read this chapter and learn everything you can about handling your financial affairs so you can take control. Or else, believe me, those dollars will be there one day and gone the next if you don't know how to handle money and don't keep an eye on how you spend and invest it.

A Model Plan for a Financially Sound Future

When a model starts out, especially if she comes from a family where she hasn't had to deal with money management, she may not have a real grasp of money—what it takes to earn it and how to handle it. Maybe her parents just gave her money whenever she needed it.

When they're starting out, many models are very young people who often suddenly find themselves making more money in a week than they could make in a year at the local Burger King. Because they're very young and often rebellious, they don't want anyone telling them what to do. Once their careers take off, they may not realize that although they're making a lot of money really fast, it can disappear as quickly as it comes in, and once it's gone, it's not coming back!

Roshumba's Rules

Follow the one-third plan: Pay your bills with one-third of the money you earn, have fun with one-third, and put one-third in a savings account. Even if you don't follow this plan exactly (at the beginning of your career, you may not be able to afford to save one-third of your salary), make sure you save at least a portion of the money you make.

Some models earn a lot of money right from the beginning of their careers. Once they start working and the money starts rolling in, they quickly discover shopping at all the most expensive shops, flying on the Concorde, going on expensive vacations, and taking care of boyfriends and friends. They'll buy every new Prada bag and pair of Gucci shoes, never saving or investing a cent.

Three to five years later, they're no longer earning top dollar, and they're no longer quite as in demand. Suddenly, they realize they have a very luxurious lifestyle and no way to keep it up. They may have an expensive apartment, vacation homes, and cool sports cars, but they didn't plan how they would maintain these things once they stopped making the big bucks.

The moral is: Plan ahead from the very first paycheck.

Planning for the Future, Right from the Start

The day you get your very first paycheck, you should open a checking and a savings account. (Ask your agent for the name of a local bank that has a good reputation.) Later on, you'll want to open an investment account as well. A checking account is necessary because it allows you to write checks to pay your bills and other expenses. A savings account is great, because you can deposit money that you're going to keep, not spend.

It's vital that models learn to manage their own personal finances.

Mod Squad

In the first three years of my career, I took savings to an extreme. I hadn't yet learned anything about luxury, about five-star hotels and champagne and caviar, and I was so shocked at how much money I was making that I just put it all in the bank. I kept tabs on every penny that came in and went out. But within those first three years, I had managed to purchase two apartment buildings in Chicago, so that if my career suddenly ended, I would always have a place to live, a source of income (from the tenants), and something concrete to show for work I did.

Model Investments

It often happens that models make a lot of money in the first few years of their careers, then a medium amount of money, and finally very little as their careers come to an end. This is just a fact of life for models, and it's far less devastating if you continue to adjust your lifestyle according to your income level.

When you find your career slowing down, that's the time you really want to start socking away every cent into savings, because soon, you may not be earning anything at all. Start by limiting your expenses as much as possible. You don't need to go out to dinner every night; instead, save money by learning to cook. Hopefully, by the time your income starts to decrease, you will have acquired a lot of luxuries you want to keep, such as a home, furniture, and a car.

Roshumba's Rules

While you're still making top dollar, it's a good idea to buy a home where you can live once your modeling career is over. Just make sure you'll be able to maintain it on a diminished salary.

Roshumba's Rules

When it comes to your money, speak up, be involved, and tell your investment counselors yes, no, maybe later. Read *Money* magazine, *The Wall Street Journal,* and *Fortune* on a regular basis to find out more about the financial world.

When it comes to your investments, be serious and conservative. Get involved with an investment professional who's been in business a long time and has a good track record and upstanding reputation. Work with an established financial company that can give you sound advice as far as stocks and other investments go.

It's a good idea to invest in well-known, stable companies. Whenever I got a big check, I would buy stocks in blue-chip companies such as Coca-Cola or Campbell's Soup. Even if the market crashes, everyone is still going to drink Coca-Cola and eat Campbell's Soup, so the chances of losing all your money are lessened. Even if you can't afford to buy the pricier safe stocks, invest in mutual funds that have these stocks in their holdings.

Only after you've saved a good amount of money should you invest in a riskier, less well-known stock, where you might make a lot of money or lose a lot. But remember the old maxim when investing in these types of stocks: Don't invest more than you can afford to lose.

Make sure you get monthly statements that let you know what's happening with your money. Insist on documentation for all your stock purchases, retirement accounts, and other investments.

Scam Alert

Many con artists know that models are an easy target for scams, and they lurk around the industry in the hopes of finding their next victim. They've lured in many models with their get-rich-quick schemes. Some con artists may set up investment companies where they buy risky stocks using models' money. Others want to open their own businesses, such as health clubs, nightclubs, restaurants, and resorts.

To a young model who is inexperienced in dealing with large amounts of money, these plans may sound like good investments. Some of them may be, but I think it's a much

340

better idea to buy stock in a company such as IBM that you know is going to be around for a while. Giving money to such people can mean a quick trip on the road to financial ruin. Steer clear of the happy-go-lucky guy or gal who is fashionable and fabulous and asks you for money.

Mod Squad

Just last year, a friend of a friend approached me and asked me to invest $50,000 in an eyeglass company he wanted to set up. If I had not been financially aware, I might have done it, because he was very enthusiastic and convincing. It now turns out, though, that this guy is bankrupt and in debt to the IRS and no eyeglass company has ever materialized. He was probably just using the scam of setting up an eyeglass company in order to get my money to pay his bills. If I had invested in his company, I'm sure my money would have been long gone by now.

Don't think you can spot con artists just by looking at them. Most of them aren't the slimy-looking "good fellas" you'd imagine. Usually, they're clean-cut, well-spoken people who look like they know what they're doing. The guy who wanted to start the eyeglass company, for instance, was someone who hung out in my immediate circle and seemed to be a reputable individual.

Remember, if it sounds too good to be true, it probably is. If someone tells you that if you invest in his restaurant you will double your money in six months, grab your wallet and run. Only a minuscule number of investments yield those kind of returns, so you should be very suspicious if someone promises that you'll double your money.

Another big source of scams is modelizers, playboy types who are obsessed with models and often prey on them financially. Make sure any man in your life has his own job, career plans, apartment, and money. See Chapter 25, "Personal Management," for more on these predators.

Many modelizers ask their model girlfriends for money to set up new businesses, such as restaurants, clubs, and gyms. Even in the unlikely event that the venture is a success, you have no security and no recourse if something goes wrong. If you've given him most of your money, and then the relationship breaks up and your money is still tied

Reality Check

Run for cover if someone tries to get you to co-sign a loan for him to buy an apartment, car, or other luxury item. If that person defaults on the payments, *you* are liable. If he can't afford it on his own, he doesn't need it.

up in his company, that can be a very messy situation. The bottom line: Any man who asks you for money is not a man you need in your life.

Even when you get married, you should still follow the same rules—until you've passed several major anniversaries. Too many models find that those great guys they married quickly turn into total money grubbers, especially when the relationship sours.

Even if the guy makes more money than you, you should always have a prenuptial agreement when you get married. As bad as divorce is on a personal level, it's a lot worse when you have to give him half of everything you own, pay his debts and taxes, and pay him alimony when you split up. And believe me, it does happen!

Mod Squad

I know several prominent models who have been burned financially in divorce court. When one highly paid model split up with her husband, he got to keep the million-dollar house she had paid for, plus she had to pay him alimony. Another model got married and had children right away. When she and her husband got divorced, she had to pay him off to stop him from harassing her. Another model was dating a guy who talked her into buying an apartment. She put up all the money and paid all the bills, but he had co-signed the loan, so when they split up, he was entitled to half, even though they'd been dating for only a short period.

Charge It! The Credits and Debits of Credit Cards

Because models are on the road so much, they definitely need to have a major credit card. Although the client will pay for your hotel room, you are responsible for extra things such as telephone calls, pay-per-view movies, and snacks and beverages from the minibar. When you check into the hotel, you will need a credit card to secure the telephone and other necessities.

Credit cards are also important in case of emergencies. For instance, you may find yourself stranded in a foreign country, and the client may need you to buy a plane ticket yourself (they'll reimburse you later) because there isn't time for them to purchase one and have it delivered to you. Other times, you may need to rent a car, which requires a major credit card. Also, you may want to go shopping and you don't want to be carrying large amounts of cash around, especially when you're on the road.

At the same time, credit cards can be very dangerous. When you hand that credit card to the salesclerk, it can give you the false impression that you're just signing a paper and then walking away with something for free. It's a great convenience, but you have to be careful not to abuse it, because when the bill comes, the credit card company wants its money. So before you charge anything, make sure you already have the money to pay the bill at the end of month.

Mod Squad

I knew one model who had three or four credit cards. She would run one up to its $25,000 limit, wouldn't pay the bill, then run up another one to its limit. That happened with three or four cards. With the accrued interest, she probably owed several hundred thousand dollars. Then her career slowed down, she stopped earning the big bucks, and none of the credit card companies would extend her credit or issue her another card. On top of all that, she owed thousands of dollars in back taxes. Despite having had a busy, successful career, she ended up completely broke because of her "just charge it" mentality.

The One Certainty in Modeling: Taxes

When most people receive a paycheck, their employers withhold a significant amount of money for income and Social Security taxes, which the employer then pays to the government on the worker's behalf. When a model receives a check from her agency, however, no income or Social Security taxes have been deducted from the check. This is because the model isn't an employee of the agency; she is an independent contractor, meaning that she is self-employed, someone who works for herself, not for a company.

Because no taxes are withheld from her paychecks, a model has to pay her own federal and state taxes on a quarterly basis. This means that she has to set aside a certain percentage of each paycheck so that she'll have enough money to pay her taxes four times a year. Because the tax laws are so complicated and change all the time, most models have accountants who figure out how much they owe every quarter. Your accountant will let you know how much you need to pay each quarter, but you'll write the check to the IRS.

The one thing you don't ever want to blow off is paying your quarterly taxes. Don't get behind in your payments, because the IRS will come after you in a big way, and that's one of worst things that can happen to you financially. They will assess you penalties and interest on the amount you owe, so your bill can quickly skyrocket. In extreme cases, they can also put a lien (a freeze) on all your accounts, so you won't be able to spend a cent without their approval.

If you can't pay your taxes on time, talk to your accountant, who can try to set up a payment schedule with the IRS.

Calculating Why You Need an Accountant

No matter how financially savvy they may be, most models benefit from having an accountant. (And if you're no math whiz, you'll definitely want to get one.) Tax laws are always changing, and you need someone who's really knowledgeable when it comes to doing taxes for models. For one thing, models have write-offs other people don't have, including makeup, certain clothing items, manicures, pedicures, car services, and taxis. Basically, this means that they can deduct these expenses from their income, so that they don't have to pay taxes on them.

It's very important that your accountant be legitimate, professional, and trustworthy. You hear about many scams involving celebrities who wanted to focus only on the artistic aspects of their career, leaving accountants, friends, spouses, or managers to handle their money. Too many of them find out years later that their accountants have lost all their money through incompetence and bad investments. When huge sums of money are flying around—and if you're earning it and they aren't—people often feel entitled to more than they're being paid.

Also, writing your own checks and paying your own taxes makes you more responsible and involved with your personal finances, which ultimately is to your advantage. You're the one who earned it and put it in that checking account, so you should be the only one who can take it out. Only you know how hard you had to work to get it.

In addition to taking care of taxes, accountants can help you keep track of how much you're earning, saving, and investing. They can give you advice on savings and investments and tell you whether this is a smart time to invest in Wall Street, or whether it's better to keep your money in a less risky money-market account. Accountants can give you tips on quality stocks to buy and refer you to professionals who can help you invest your money wisely, such as money managers,

Reality Check

Some models give their accountants power of attorney, which gives them the power to sign the models' name on checks. This ensures that all your taxes and bills are paid on time, but I think giving anyone that type of power over *your* money is crazy, because it's a power that can be abused very easily, and you'll be the one who's thousands of dollars poorer.

Reality Check

Don't make the mistake of spending every cent you earn. You will be modeling in your prime years, the same years during which your peers will be going to college, getting their first jobs, and developing professional skills that will pay off later. Since you won't have that education and those skills to fall back on, it's vital that you save some money.

money-management firms, and stock brokers. They also try to get you to evaluate your expenditures, so that you're not spending mindlessly or foolishly (see Chapter 25) and you're saving and investing as much as you need to for the future.

Your accountants can also counsel you on setting up a retirement account (Keogh, SEP, or IRA). The rules for these often change, and an accountant who keeps up on the latest revisions in the law can help you maximize your investments in these.

Accountants will also help you get more value for the money you *do* spend, and advise you to spend money on things you can use as tax write-offs, such as exercise classes and fax machines. They may also encourage you to buy an apartment as opposed to renting one. They may even suggest a location or neighborhood that will offer optimum value and a price range that you can afford.

The best way to find an accountant is to ask your agency for a referral. Or maybe your family has one they've used for years. When you're looking for an accountant, you want to make sure it's someone with whom you can develop a long-term relationship. You'll want to be able to talk to your accountant about money matters, taxes, investments, retirement planning, and ways to avoid or delay paying taxes, so be sure it's someone you can relate to.

Financial Rx: Medical Insurance

It's probably the last thing you'd think of buying when you get that first paycheck, but it's one of the most important. Medical insurance isn't as much fun to buy as a Calvin Klein jacket, but it is one of the smartest investments you can make.

Although it's a remote possibility, if a medical emergency were to happen, it could quickly wipe out all your savings because of the high cost of medicine in this country. Unlike most people who get medical insurance through their jobs, models don't, because they're considered self-employed.

Ask your agent, other models, or other industry professionals if they know of any good medical plans. Also, once you do a TV commercial, you may be eligible for the medical insurance plan of the TV actors' union, the Screen Actors Guild. (You are required to earn a certain minimum amount to qualify.)

Roshumba's Rules

Although it's costly, you may also want to consider getting disability insurance, which provides you with an income in case you get hurt and can't work for a significant amount of time.

The Big Guns: Lawyers and Managers

Although your agent can handle most standard contracts, when it comes to any contract that is very detailed or complicated, you will probably need to hire a lawyer. Lawyers are necessary whenever you're negotiating an endorsement deal or a TV or movie contract. In general, these contracts contain language that only lawyers can really understand.

Lawyers can also negotiate difficult situations or disagreements between you and the client, which spares your having to deal with a negative situation. A good lawyer can also suggest ways for making the most out of contract opportunities.

It's best to have a lawyer who has experience in negotiating contracts for artists, especially if she's a specialist in the field of books, calendars, TV, modeling, or performing. Your agent or other industry professional can probably recommend a good lawyer who has experience working with other models.

If and when your career starts branching out to the point where you're not just doing modeling, but also TV, films, and endorsement deals, as well as developing your own product lines, you might want to consider getting a manager. Many models end up having managers because they can be lifesavers for very successful or very busy models, especially those who want to break into show business.

Reality Check

Be careful of managers who start forcing on you ideas of what you should be and what you should do when you are not comfortable with their ideas, or managers who schedule activities that conflict with your modeling career.

Roshumba's Rules

The way to tell if a manager is a good one is to ask her who else she manages. If she represents people you're aspiring to be like, such as successful actresses, that's a good sign.

When you have many different things going on—modeling for TV commercials, runway shows, and magazines, going on acting jobs, producing a calendar, starting a regular broadcasting career—you may end up having four or five different agents. It can be a little hectic having to keep everything organized, in addition to doing the actual work. A manager is great when you get to the point where you're having a hard time managing your schedule and all your activities yourself.

A manager can coordinate your whole schedule, so you have only one person to deal with. In addition, she can help you develop your career outside of modeling and help you grow as a talent. It's good to work with one person who can help you make the most out of all the things in which you're involved.

A manager can also help you plan a second career. She can help you in the decision-making process when it comes to deals and contracts, refer you to lawyers and accountants, and suggest ways you can enhance your career. Finally, she can act as your confidante, best friend, and sounding board.

Finding a manager can be a bit tricky. Most likely, your agent will not be very helpful, because he may be concerned about someone invading his territory. Your best bet is to ask other models or professionals in the field you want to get into, whether it's TV, broadcasting, or movies. Also, your film or TV agent, accountant, or lawyer may be able to refer you to someone.

Good managers always make you feel that you're their first priority. They take your phone calls or get right back to you. They're always on top of your schedule. They encourage you to better yourself, to take acting classes or see certain movies, and they keep you informed of what's happening in the field you want to get into. You get the impression that they're constantly seeking new opportunities for you, that one of their first priorities is making sure you are accomplishing what you want.

Six months to a year after you start working with a manager, evaluate the relationship: How successful has she been in helping you accomplish career goals? If she's not getting the job done, she may not be so good for you.

Also beware of control freaks. It's good for them to be interested and dedicated to your career, but when it crosses the line to fixation and obsession, that can be very scary and definitely not worth it.

Hopefully, you will read and re-read this chapter many times, to ensure that you reap all the financial benefits for all the blood, sweat, and tears you put into your modeling career.

Reality Check

A bad manager never takes your call when you telephone. You hear about castings and potential jobs that you weren't sent on and big industry dinners you weren't invited to. When you do speak to the manager, he has no news of opportunities for you to further your career. Also, he fights with your modeling agency or suggests that you leave the agency before he's brought anything to table.

The Least You Need to Know

➤ Smart models start saving and investing from their very first paycheck.

➤ Paying taxes on time and using credit cards responsibly are key for a model's financial security.

➤ Most models benefit from hiring an accountant.

➤ Certain models will need to hire a lawyer and/or a manager as their careers take off.

Chapter 27

The Outer You

In This Chapter

➤ Making healthy food choices

➤ A model exercise program

➤ Makeup tips for your most beautiful look

➤ Keeping hair, skin, nails, and teeth picture-perfect

Because a model depends on her looks for her fortune, it's vital that she knows how to take care of herself so that her physical appearance is always at its best. Not only is grooming mandatory—getting frequent haircuts, hair coloring, manicures, pedicures, facials, and dental cleanings—she will also need to eat healthfully and exercise.

In this chapter, I'll describe everything a model needs to know and do to keep herself looking picture-perfect. I'll also let you in on some of my secret tips that have helped me to look my best over the years.

Model Meals

Mmmm, food. If I had a nickel for every time I've been asked if models eat, I would probably be the richest woman in the world. Not only do models eat, but many of them eat things that are extremely fattening—hamburgers, French fries, and ice cream. Victoria's Secret model Laeticia Costa, for one, is known for her chocolate fetish.

Although many models may indulge in eating fatty foods, it's usually done in moderation. For the most part, models have healthy diets, not only because they have to but because it is the nature of the business. The fashion industry in general is very health conscious. Magazine editors, photographers, hairstylists, makeup artists, and fashion designers make up the majority of the people in the fashion world. They tend to be an international group, and they bring with them many cultural and social differences as well as different (often healthier) eating habits.

America is really the only country where so many people eat such enormous amounts of food nonstop, 24 hours a day. In other countries, such as France and Italy, the focus is on sitting down and enjoying a meal. Dining is looked at as a special time, a time to relax, let go, and socialize. For breakfast, usually just coffee and a croissant or a breakfast bread is eaten, not bacon, eggs, hash browns, and toast, which are loaded with fat and calories. Lunch is usually a balanced meal, consisting of meat or fish, vegetable or salad, bread, and a light dessert. Usually, nothing else is eaten until dinner.

Dinner is a repeat of lunch as far as a type of food: meat, fish, or poultry, vegetables or salad, bread, and a light dessert. (In Italy, the diet differs in that pasta is a big part of each main meal.) This may sound like a lot of food, but the proportions are small to medium—especially compared to the enormous amounts of food that Americans often consume.

The quality of food is also very important. Lean cuts of high-quality meat, super-fresh fish, fruits, and vegetables, and whole grains are the staples of the diet. Lots of love, planning, and attention go into meals and the eating process. For the most part, these eating habits have been adapted by the fashion industry as well. When meals are catered on photo shoots, a great deal of attention is paid to the preparation of the food.

Reality Check

While it's true that people believe models are superhumanly thin, I think that many of them don't realize that models, especially during the prime years of their careers, are usually very young—between the ages of 16 and 25. At this age, it's quite normal to be thin, so actually, models aren't so abnormally thin, if you take their ages into consideration.

Caterers take into consideration not only the meal's nutritional value, but also people's special eating habits. For instance, there is usually a vegetarian selection. Meats, poultry, and fish are grilled or baked instead of fried, and vegetables and salads are abundant.

Mod Squad

Many models are vegetarians, and I, too, went through a period of about five years when I was a vegetarian. At first, I ate nothing that came from an animal, which included milk, cheese, eggs, meat, and fish. Instead, I consumed mostly whole grains, beans, vegetables, and fruit. This change was too drastic and did not agree with my body. I felt tired, my skin lost its glow, and I lost a lot of body fat; it did not look good. So I added eggs and fish to my diet, which I found was the perfect balance for me. It also made it much easier to find things to eat when I traveled.

I have never been a big eater, even when I was a little girl. My mom always encouraged me to watch my figure. She was really adamant about my siblings and me eating balanced, nutritious meals. When I grew up, this habit stuck with me. I made sure I watched what—and how much—I ate. My diet consists mainly of grilled fish, seafood, and salads, but I do have a weakness for potato chips and cookies, and I occasionally indulge in other treats like pizza and ice cream.

For the person who is in good shape and has the perfect weight for her age and height, I suggest she eat balanced meals and not snack too much in between, or eat too many fatty foods or breads.

This is the diet I follow. You should make adjustments for your caloric needs, your age (our caloric needs decrease as we get older), your activity level (athletic people require more calories to maintain their weight), and your own personal tastes.

Roshumba's Rules

If I go over my ideal weight of 120 to 125 pounds, I cut out breads, dairy, fried foods, and desserts. As long as I don't overindulge in these foods, I'm able to maintain my ideal weight.

Breakfast:

➤ 1 or 2 eggs, boiled or poached (scrambled or fried are okay occasionally), OR 1 cup yogurt, OR $^1/_2$ cup cottage cheese

➤ 1 or 2 slices whole-grain toast, OR 1 small muffin or bagel, OR 1 cup oatmeal

➤ Fresh fruit or juice, and tea or coffee

Lunch:

➤ 3 to 4 oz. grilled fish, seafood, (lean) meat, or poultry

➤ Salad and/or vegetable

➤ Grains or beans ($^1/_2$ cup rice, pasta, or couscous, or 1 slice bread)

➤ Fresh fruit

➤ 1 cup yogurt (optional)

Dinner:

➤ 3 to 4 oz. grilled fish, seafood, (lean) meat, or poultry

➤ Salad and/or vegetable

➤ Grains or beans ($^1/_2$ cup rice, pasta, or couscous, or 1 slice bread)

If you had fish for lunch, have poultry or meat for dinner, and vice versa.

I find these meal plans work very well for me in helping me to maintain my model figure. Each person is different and portion size plays a big role in the number of calories that are consumed. (In restaurants, it's not uncommon to be served a half-pound hamburger, or a 20-ounce baked potato—which alone may contain almost a day's worth of calories!) Also, eating desserts and in-between-meal snacks can affect this plan, so it is up to each individual to adapt the plan for themselves.

If you have an unhealthy relationship with food that is causing you to be overweight or underweight, you may need to work on improving your attitude toward food. If you suffer from an eating disorder such as anorexia or bulimia (see Chapter 25), consult a medical professional to help you work these things out. A modeling career will only exacerbate these problems, not make them better.

Reality Check

Avoid quack nutritionists who have no academic background in nutrition. Instead, make sure anyone you consult has a university degree in nutrition and is an R.D. (registered dietitian). R.D.s are professionals certified by the American Dietetic Association.

If your eating habits aren't healthy—if your diet consists mainly of fried, processed, and fatty foods, or if you eat a lot of sugar—think about changing the way you eat. As a model, you may find it very difficult to maintain your weight if you eat a lot of unhealthy junk foods. A dietitian or an organized eating plan such as Weight Watchers can help you establish a better relationship with food and improve your eating habits.

Model or not, it's much more important that a person be happy, healthy, and accepting of herself the way she is than to have any one particular body type. But if you are not satisfied with your eating habits and want to lose weight, my proposed eating plan could work for you as well. *The Complete Idiot's Guide to Total Nutrition* (Alpha Books, 1999) is another good source to check out if you're interested in nutrition and eating healthfully.

Model Moves

For hundreds of years, people have sought ways to take care of and improve their bodies. By far the best way to improve the condition of your body is through good old exercise. If done properly and on a regular basis, exercise not only makes you look good, it also makes you feel good.

The exercise programs that I have done over the years include:

➤ Afrobics, a combination of African dance moves, aerobics, stretching, and toning

➤ Yoga, a series of postures incorporating stretching, breathing, meditation, and chanting

➤ Tae Bo, a martial art that is a combination of stretching, toning, breathing, punching, and kicking

➤ Calisthenics, such as sit-ups, squats, and stretching

➤ Belly dancing, my favorite of all!

Mod Squad

I love to exercise, although I'm not really into going to the gym. I find the environment of a gym to be very impersonal and rather competitive. I prefer working out in the privacy of my own home. I love working out to videotapes that incorporate stretching, toning, and aerobics. When I wake up in the morning, the first thing I do is slip a video into the VCR and work out for a half an hour, five days a week. I choose workouts that are designed to burn calories and fat and tone and tighten my muscles. Sometimes I alternate these with yoga, depending on my mood or what I feel my body needs.

Although models are often naturally thin, most of them do exercise. It is important to establish some sort of exercise routine that will keep your body toned and in shape, alleviate stress, and burn calories. Develop your own regimen of moderate exercise that includes cardiovascular work (exercise such as walking, running, swimming, or biking, which gets your heart pumping); strength training (workouts such as weight lifting or calisthenics that increase your strength and tone your muscles); and stretching (which keeps your muscles flexible). Try to exercise at least four times a week.

Most models work out regularly to keep their bodies toned and strong. Photographer: Kwame Brathwaite. Model: Laura McLafferty.

The Stress on Tresses

Those luscious locks may be your ticket to big money. Hair advertisements can be a very lucrative source of money for models with beautiful, healthy hair. But whether or not your hair is your crowning feature, you'll want to make sure yours is in top shape.

First of all, make sure you keep your hair clean, well conditioned, and well groomed. You will need to get a quarter to a half an inch trimmed off your ends every two weeks to a month to get rid of split or damaged ends and keep your cut in tiptop shape.

If you color or highlight your hair, get your color redone at least once every month, or as soon as roots start showing. Even though it's expensive to maintain, it will cost you a lot more if clients don't book you because of your unsightly roots.

Reality Check

Be extremely cautious about who you let color your hair. You don't want to end up with a bad color job, which could stop your career in its tracks. Ask your agent for recommendations, or ask other industry professionals if they know who colors the hair of famous models. Try to stick to the same colorist every time, which limits the possibility of a hair disaster.

Roshumba's Rules

Try not to be a trend junkie, meaning don't try every new cut and color that comes along. It's okay to try something new once in a while, but remember, classic, healthy hair sells better than any trend.

If you're working every day, hairstylists are probably applying buckets of hair products to your hair on a daily basis. That's why you want to make sure that you keep your hair as clean as possible. Because many hair products contain alcohol, which can dry out hair, I try to wash my hair as quickly as possible—usually as soon as I get home from a shoot.

Whenever you're working with hairstylists at a job, talk to them before they start working to let them know what condition your hair is in. If you've just been through three grueling weeks of fashion shows, where your hair has been blown and curled, swept up and combed down, puffed and fluffed five times a day, and it can't take the strain anymore, let the stylist know and ask (politely) if they can be extra gentle.

Most models' hair does experience some damage, especially if they're working a lot. If your hair does start to show the signs of damage, treat yourself to a deep-conditioning hair treatment once a week (you can find deep-conditioning products in the hair-care section of the drugstore). You may also want to make an appointment at a salon that does special hair-conditioning and repair treatments.

The morning before a shoot, you shouldn't bother doing much to your hair, because whatever you do, the hairstylist is probably going to undo. Just make sure it's clean, conditioned, and not tangled.

During your downtime, try to do as little as possible to your hair; it needs a rest from all the styling it gets when you're working. Wash and condition it, but avoid blow-drying it. Let it hang free or tie it back in a loose ponytail. If you go swimming, protect it with a swimming cap; if you're out in the sun, wear a hat or apply a hair product that contains sunscreen.

Before you make any drastic changes to your hair, it is mandatory that you talk to your agent about it. She is selling you in a certain way, and even minor changes in your hair color could totally throw off her sales pitch. A change of hair color could cause a client to cancel a booking, because they thought they were hiring a brunette, and suddenly you're a redhead. Also, if you have an endorsement deal, your contract may state that you can't make any changes in your appearance without the client's permission.

The Skinny on Skin

Skin is so important to the success of a model's career. People pay much attention to skin. Your face says to the world that you're healthy and alive; its coloring is a badge of pride for your ethnic group, whether you have pale, milky skin, warm olive skin, or rich dark skin.

There are more beauty products for the skin than for anything else—wrinkle creams, sunblocks, alpha-hydroxy-acid lotions, scrubs, exfoliators, toners, tighteners, bleaches, and hair removers. No matter what you want to do to your skin, it seems there's a product for you. Most models have naturally good skin. If you suffer from acne flare-ups or other skin conditions, you should consult a dermatologist, who can recommend a number of treatments. Because the truth is, a model without good skin may have a tough time getting bookings.

Even though makeup can cover a lot of flaws, such as acne, when a client is selecting a model, they want someone who's as perfect as possible when they first start out. In the modeling industry, makeup is used as a beauty enhancer, not a camouflage. That's why skin texture, glow, color, the size of your pores, and the way the light reflects off your skin are so important.

As soon as I get home from a shoot, I wash my face, using a mild cleansing cream. I prefer ones that contain no perfumes or dyes (L'Oréal and Maybelline both make good ones). Then I go over my face with a damp wash-cloth, which acts as a mild exfoliator, removing dead, dull-looking skin.

Next, I apply my own skin cream. You may be surprised to hear that I mix it up myself, but I find it works better than any commercial product. It is a combination of vitamin E cream, aloe vera juice, and a capsule of vitamin E. (You can find all these things at your local drugstore.) I apply it at night before I go to bed, in the morning when I wake up, and during the day whenever I feel a little dry. Because I wear makeup everyday, I have to make sure my skin is kept well moisturized.

Roshumba's Rules

Drinking lots of water—at least eight glasses a day—is one of the best things you can do for your skin. It flushes out your body and keeps your skin well hydrated and moisturized.

Once or twice a week, I moisten a cotton pad with witch hazel, and wipe my face with it. This acts as my astringent. Once a month, I steam my face, either by going to the steam room at the gym or by boiling a pot of water to which I add eucalyptus leaves. I put a towel over my head and hold my face above the pot (be careful not to burn yourself!). This cleanses my pores and leaves my skin glowing.

Whenever I'm working outdoors on location or enjoying myself in the sun, I always make sure I'm wearing sunscreen. Any dermatologist will tell you that it's the most important beauty product you can use. It's essential that you protect your skin from the sun, which can lead to skin damage and discoloration, skin cancer, and premature wrinkling.

I also love to take warm, relaxing baths with oils, sea salts, and bubble baths. Not only do I love baths, but, because I do a lot of body work (modeling bathing suits, lingerie, or short dresses—anything where I'm showing a lot of skin), I have to make sure that the skin on my body looks its best. I usually add some kind of oil—baby oil, bath oils from the Body Shop, sesame oil, olive oil—to the bath, anything that softens the water and lubricates the skin. I also exfoliate my skin well, using body scrubbers, Buf-Pufs, scrub beads, and scrungies.

I usually bathe at night. Afterward, I don't apply any lotion, because the oil in the tub provides sufficient moisture. The next day, however, before I leave for work, I apply body lotion all over. In the winter, when my skin is extra dry, I use a heavy moisturizer; in summer, I use a lighter one.

Makeup Moves

Once you decide you want to be a model, it's to your advantage to learn as much about makeup as soon as possible. The first thing you should do is study what you look like in your natural state, without any makeup; how you look with some makeup on; and what you look like fully made up. This will help you learn which makeup looks enhance your face, and which detract from your natural beauty.

The more you know about the makeup that works for you, the more information you can share with the makeup artist on the shoot before she starts to do your face. Can you wear blue eye shadow? Which type of *foundation* (liquid or cream) works best on your face? Does red lipstick make you look sexy or does it wash you out?

It's possible to learn what makeup works for you without spending a fortune on cosmetics. Go to the cosmetic counter at your local store and use their testers. If you go when the stores aren't busy (weekday mornings are a

Catwalk Talk

Foundation is also sometimes called base. It is the first makeup product an artist will apply to your face. It smoothes out any minor discolorations and flaws and creates a perfect canvas for the rest of your makeup.

good time), the salespeople may be more willing to assist you. Or check out the new type of cosmetic counter that is set up to allow customers to browse undisturbed.

You'll want to get accustomed to doing your own makeup, because once you start working, you may occasionally have to do your own makeup or touch up your own face. Especially at the fashion shows, when the makeup artist has so many models to make up in such a short period of time and there may be tiny flaws in your makeup. It's great to be able to pull out your own set of tools to (discreetly) fix something that was applied crookedly, or change a color that doesn't work on you.

Generally, you shouldn't wear a lot of makeup on go and sees, especially if you have good skin. The only exception is if you're going out for a TV commercial, in which case you may need a little makeup—brow pencil, eye shadow, mascara, blush, lipstick—to look your best.

Your makeup bag should contain these essentials:

➤ Foundation

➤ Loose powder

➤ Eyebrow pencil

➤ Eye shadow in neutral colors—brown, beige, and/or gray and black

➤ Eye pencil

➤ Mascara

➤ Blush

➤ Lipsticks in a variety of colors (clear or natural, medium, earth tones, dark, deep tones, bright red)

Roshumba's Rules

I use the same foundation every day; I bring my favorite brand with me whenever I do a job. I wear makeup so much that I like to use just one foundation that I know won't irritate my skin.

You should also invest in a good set of makeup brushes, which will make application easier and more professional looking. Good brushes to own include a big, fluffy powder brush, a blush brush, an eye-shadow brush, an eyeliner brush, a brow brush, and a lip brush. An eyelash curler and makeup sponger are other handy tools you may want to own.

Basic makeup includes foundation, concealer (as needed), powder, blush, eye shadow, lipstick, and mascara, and groomed brows. Medium makeup includes all of the above plus eye liner, eye shadow in the crease, and lip liner. Glamour makeup includes all of the above, plus contouring under the cheekbones, false eyelashes, and more dramatic colors on the eyes and lips. (For a look at all three types of makeup, check out the color photos in the middle of this book.)

Here are some quick and easy tips on applying makeup, in the order you should apply it:

1. **Foundation.** Start by placing small dots of foundation on your forehead, cheeks, nose, and chin. Use a cosmetic sponge to blend.

Applying foundation with a sponge gives a more sheer, even application.

2. **Concealer.** Use only where needed. Dot it on, then pat it with your ring finger to blend.

3. **Loose powder.** Dip a fluffy powder brush into the powder, tap off excess, then dust over your face.

4. **Eye shadow.** Using an eye-shadow brush, sweep powder shadow from outer to inner corner of your eyelid, then blend.

Applying a dark eye shadow in the crease of the eye enhances them and gives them more depth and drama.

5. **Mascara.** First, wipe excess mascara from the wad. Holding the wand horizontally, sweep through lashes. Reapply to top lashes only.

6. **Brows.** Using your brow brush, brush your eyebrows up and slightly out.

7. **Blush.** Dip your blush brush in the blush and tap off the excess. Place the brush on the apple of your cheek and stroke back toward your ear. Most of the color should be on your cheek. If you make a mistake, use your powder brush to "buff" it out.

Apply blush to the apple of the cheeks, sweeping the brush out toward the ear.

8. **Lipstick.** Dip your lip brush in the lipstick. Outline your lips with the brush, starting from the center and working out in either direction. Fill in the bottom lip, then press (don't rub) your lips together. The excess from the bottom will color your top lip and eliminate the need for blotting.

Apply lip liner first, then fill in with lipstick.

9. **The crease of the eye.** Use a small brush to sweep a darker, coordinating tone in the crease.

10. **Eyeliner.** Use a liner brush. Dip the brush in a dark eye shadow (black, navy, gray), and dot a line along the upper and lower lash lines. For an even more dramatic look, use an eye pencil to line around the inner lash line.

359

Lining the eyes helps define their shape and gives them a dramatic look.

11. **Contouring.** For less mistake-prone contouring, sweep translucent powder under your cheekbones to highlight bone structure.

12. **False eyelashes.** False eyelashes usually come in clusters of three lashes. Lashes also come in different sizes—short, medium, and long. Apply the longest ones on the outside corner of your lashes, the mid-length ones in the middle of your eye, and the shortest ones close to your nose. Because some people are allergic to the adhesive, a lot of manufacturers recommend that you do an allergy test before you apply the lashes.

To apply, pick up the individual cluster with a tweezers, then dip the base of the lash in the adhesive that comes in the eyelash kit. Gently set the base of the false lash exactly where you want it, then hold it there for a minute with the tweezers. As soon as it sets, go on to the next one. Be sure to glue the false eyelash to your eyelashes, not your skin. Apply mascara to blend in the false eyelashes with your natural ones.

Reality Check

Don't abuse your hands. Make sure you protect them from the sun, so they don't get dry, discolored, or splotchy. I also protect mine from the cold by wearing gloves. When it comes to washing dishes and doing housework, I always wear rubber gloves to protect them from chemicals, detergents, and hot water, which can dry out hands tremendously.

Picture-Perfect Nails

You see a photo of a beautiful girl with lovely makeup, gorgeous hair, a to-die-for designer outfit, and stunning lighting. So what's wrong with this picture? The model's nibbled, stubby fingernails. You may not have thought about it much, but a model's hands and nails do attract a lot of attention.

When you go to a photo studio, your nails should be clean and buffed, or clean, buffed, and polished with a natural polish. The preferred look is short nails that are well manicured in a square or rounded shape and polished with a clear or natural color. The cuticles should be smooth and in healthy condition. In general, clients don't want to see long red talons on a model's hands, and they don't appreciate when girls come in with chewed-up nails and bleeding cuticles.

I make sure I get a manicure every week. Sometimes I have my natural nails manicured; other times I get nail extensions (acrylic nails). If I do get nail extensions, I don't leave them on for more than a month; I take them off so my nails can breathe. Also, I don't get those long "cat claw" type of extensions. Mine are a short, manageable length that look natural and healthy. At home, I have a nail file, a nail buffer, clear nail polish, some colored nail polishes, and cuticle oil. So if I'm not able to get to the manicurist, I do my own nails.

Apply hand moisturizers as often as possible. Not only will this keep your hands looking their best, but it will smooth your cuticles and moisturize your nails. Also, massage a cuticle oil into your cuticles once a week to keep them healthy.

Keeping your feet in prime condition is also important, because very often, your feet will be showing on camera, for instance, if you're wearing sandals or other shoes that expose your toes or if you're barefoot. Models are notorious for having the worst feet, because they're always having to squeeze them into shoes that are not the right size. Also, working in high heels all day can damage the feet, as does all that running around on go and sees and other appointments.

To make sure my feet look their best, I get a pedicure every two weeks to slough off the calluses and dead skin and keep the cuticles healthy. I generally get a natural or clear polish on my toenails, unless the client has requested a specific color. (Yves Saint Laurent, for instance, always requests that his models have red nails and toes.)

Roshumba's Rules

If I have a shoot coming up and I want my feet to look their best, I'll slather Vaseline on my feet, wrap them in plastic, then put on socks before I go to bed.

Pearls of Wisdom for Your Pearly Whites

I have met so many gorgeous girls who've signed up for the Elite Model Look model search who appear flawless. Then they smile and reveal a mouth full of bad teeth—crooked, decaying, and discolored. Even though an agency may love the girl and want to sign her, her teeth could be the thing that breaks the deal.

Beautiful teeth can't be faked. You can't have a lovely young model smiling on the cover of *Seventeen* with a mouth full of bad teeth. Sometimes, agents may suggest that aspiring models come back to see them after they get their teeth fixed, because a model can't spend her career with her mouth closed.

If your teeth are a problem, see a dentist and ask her about ways you can improve your teeth to get them in the best shape possible. Cleaning, bonding, and braces may work for you. (Before you undergo a lot of expensive dental work, however, it's a good idea to get some sort of confirmation from an agent that you have the potential for a successful career. But don't forget, a beautiful smile can serve you well in life in general.)

Having braces doesn't mean you can't be a model; it only means your career may be delayed a bit. Agents would much rather see girls with braces than girls with crooked teeth and overbites! If you need braces, try to get them as early as possible—at 13 or 14—so they're off by the time you're ready to start a modeling career full-time.

It's also important that you take care of your teeth on a daily basis. Brush your teeth thoroughly morning and night and after you eat sweets. Floss once a day. Chew sugarless gum, and get regular dental cleanings (twice a year is recommended). Take care of any problem teeth or cavities, and make sure your wisdom teeth are removed or growing in properly.

Sometimes I drink red wine, so my teeth get a little stained. To make sure my teeth stay their whitest, once a week, I rinse my mouth out with hydrogen peroxide (don't swallow it—make sure you spit it out!). Then I put a little baking soda on my tooth-brush and scrub my teeth. The two together bubble in my mouth and act as a scrub-bing agent. Finally, I brush my teeth with my regular toothpaste.

It's a lot of work keeping yourself model-pretty, but when you spend your whole day in front of a camera or in front of a crowd on a runway, it's important if you want to have the most successful career possible.

The Least You Need to Know

➤ Models do eat, but they eat reasonable portions of healthy food.

➤ Most models exercise regularly; it's a good habit to develop.

➤ It's vital that models take good care of their hair, skin, nails, and teeth, and learn how to apply their own makeup.

Catwalk Talk Glossary

agency book   A portfolio that contains pictures of all the models the agency represents.

agency head sheet   A poster that features pictures of all its models.

agent   A person in an agency who finds people who have the potential to be successful models, signs a contract to represent them, markets them to clients (including magazines, advertisers, and fashion designers), and guides their careers.

anorexia   An eating disorder whose sufferers eat little or nothing because they think (erroneously) that they are fat.

Better Business Bureau (BBB)   A private, nonprofit organization with offices around the country that provides reports on local businesses.

body shot   A picture of a model in a bathing suit that shows her body from head to toe.

booker   Booker, agent, and model manager are interchangeable terms that all refer to the person in an agency who develops you as a model, books you for jobs, and oversees your career.

booking   Any job a model is hired to do. When a model is hired for a job, whether it be to pose for a magazine or advertisement or to appear in a runway show, she is said to be "booked" for the job.

bulimia   An eating disorder whose sufferers consume huge amounts of food, then purge it by vomiting, abusing laxatives, or exercising excessively.

call time   The time a model is expected to arrive at the job. It's the time the work of the day begins, when the model and other team members go on the clock—that is, start getting paid.

callback   When an agency or client asks you to come back for a second interview because they're considering representing or hiring you, their request is referred to as a callback.

castings   Another word for go and sees. In America, the term castings usually refers to go and sees for TV commercials. In Europe, the term castings is used more often for all types of go and sees.

catwalk   *See* runway.

client   On a magazine shoot, the client is the fashion editor. On a catalog shoot, it's the representative or art director from the catalog company. On an advertising shoot, it's the corporate client.

collections   Refers to the collective showing of designers' new fashions in one particular city. The New York collections take place when all the top New York designers show their latest designs for the season.

commercial agent   Handles models who don't fall into the traditional "fashion model" category. They are called commercial agents because they book models for commercial work (print ads, TV commercials) as opposed to editorial or artistic work.

commercial models   Models who work primarily in local and secondary markets and appear mainly in catalogs and advertisements.

confirmed   If the client definitely wants to book you, you are said to be confirmed.

contact sheet   A large sheet of photographic paper that has mini prints of all the pictures that were captured on one roll of film by the photographer.

contouring   Applying a foundation in a darker shade to shade and contour a model's face, to enhance facial features or create the illusion of high cheekbones or a slender nose.

cover try   A photo shoot that's done to get a picture that's good enough to appear on a magazine cover. The photo itself must be striking, and the model must look her best.

day rate   The amount of money a model earns for a full day of work. A model's experience, popularity, and the caliber of the client all have an effect on her day rate.

eating disorder   An emotional and physical problem that expresses itself through the abuse of food and the body. Eating disorders include anorexia, bulimia, and compulsive overeating.

editorial   Refers to any work that will appear in a magazine's editorial (as opposed to advertising) pages. It includes stories about the latest fashion and beauty trends, as well as lifestyle (sex, relationships, job, money) pieces.

editorial models   Also known as high-fashion models, editorial models work in the fashion capitals where they appear in magazine stories, designer fashion shows, and high-end advertisements.

fashion capitals   Milan, Paris, and New York City are considered the three fashion capitals of the world because so many fashion and cosmetic companies, fashion magazines, advertising agencies, and models are based there.

fashion credits   In return for being allowed to borrow clothes from designers for fashions shoots, a magazine will identify the designer in the magazine's fashion credits, a listing of which designer created which garment in a photo.

fashion spread   A story spotlighting a particular fashion trend. It appears toward the back of the magazine, where there are no advertisements. Because there are no ads, the pictures can "spread" across the page.

fashionista   A person, often someone who works in fashion or retail, who follows every trend. She is always wearing the latest styles, carrying the most fashionable purse, and sporting the hottest sunglasses.

featured model   The first and/or the last model to appear in a runway show. At the end of the show, she walks down the runway on the arm of the designer. She may be the designer's favorite model or a famous supermodel.

Federal Trade Commission (FTC)   A government agency headquartered in Washington that enforces consumer-protection laws.

fittings models   Models who work in a designer's studio trying on the unfinished clothes; the designer then makes any adjustments in the garment so that it fits perfectly.

foundation   Sometimes called base. It is the first makeup product an artist will apply to your face. It smoothes out any minor discolorations and flaws and creates a perfect canvas for the rest of your makeup.

go and see   An interview for a modeling job. It's called a go and see because a model goes to the client's office so they can see what she looks like in person.

haute couture   Ultra-expensive clothes that are custom-made to fit the few women wealthy enough to afford them. They are made of the most expensive, luxurious fabrics, with exquisite details and hand-sewn seams.

head shot   A head shot is a 8×10- or $9^1/2 \times 11$-inch photo of an actor's or model's head and face. They are given to clients at go and sees to help them remember the models they've interviewed. They're used mainly for TV work.

hobby modeling   Also called modeling for experience, it is done primarily for the experience and fun of it. Hobby modeling is usually unpaid.

image   A physical embodiment of an idea or concept. A company will hire a model that best represents its image. For instance, edgy cosmetic company M.A.C. chose RuPaul to represent it because of his outrageous image.

image models   Models who are still relatively new (with typically three to five years experience in the business) but are building toward supermodel status.

in-store modeling   Also called informal modeling. Models are dressed in clothes from the store; they walk around and let the customers see the clothes up close as they shop.

lingerie shoot   A photo shoot for an ad, magazine story, or catalog in which the model wears a bra, panties, slip, teddy, or other underwear without any other garments over it.

local markets   Any city outside of the fashion capitals (New York, Paris, and Milan) where a majority of models live and work.

look books   Photo albums put together by clothing companies so consumers can look at all of that season's styles in one place. Look books can be in-store photo albums or printed brochures that are mailed out to customers.

masthead   Usually appears between the table of contents page and the first article in a magazine. The masthead lists everyone responsible for putting together the magazine, including the editor in chief, the fashion editors, and the model editor.

matte makeup   Makeup with a flat, nonshiny finish. Most normal makeup for day is matte.

measurements   One of the statistics supplied to prospective agents and clients, usually written as a series of three numbers, for example, 34-24-34. The first number is the bust size, the second is the waist measurement, and the third is the hip size.

meet-and-greet   A short interview that the judges and agents conduct with participants at a model convention. You'll be asked basic questions, such as where you live, what grade you're in, and why you want to be a model.

model editor   Books all the models featured in a magazine, including those used in fashion stories, beauty pieces, and all the other features in the magazine (pieces about jobs, relationships, advice, money, for example).

mother agency   The agency that discovered you, marketed you, and developed your career. If you've changed agencies in the course of your career, your mother agency is your base agency, located in the city you call home.

overexposed   A model is said to be overexposed when she has been working too much in one market—she's appeared in every fashion show, magazine, and ad. Clients get bored with looking at her face and stop hiring her.

P&G child   Stands for the Procter & Gamble child and is a common industry term that refers to a child with perfect, all-American features. Mikey from the Life cereal commercial is a classic P&G kid.

panic attack   An extreme reaction to a situation that wouldn't be cause for abnormal distress for most people. It's characterized by an extreme sense of anxiety, fear, and stress.

portfolio   An album of specially selected pictures you take with you to job interviews.

profile shot   A shot of the side of your face or body.

publicist   Also called a public relations specialist. Handles all your contacts with the press, including magazine and newspaper interviews, photo shoots, and appearances on radio and TV shows.

ready-to-wear   Unlike haute couture garments, which are custom-made, ready-to-wear clothes are mass produced. Nearly all the clothes you see at the local mall fall into the ready-to-wear category.

real-people models   Represent a type, such as a mom, a cute kid, a kindly granddad, a balding regular Joe, or a businesswoman. They appear mainly in ads and TV commercials.

residual   A payment an actor or model receives every time the TV commercial she appears in is broadcast. For a national commercial that gets heavy play, this could be a significant amount of money.

runway   Also known as the catwalk, a long narrow stage that juts out into the audience. At a fashion show, the models walk down the runway, which allows the audience to see the clothes up close.

sample reel   A videotape sampling of an actor's or model's on-camera work, including TV commercials and industrial training films.

set   The area in a photo shoot where the pictures are actually taken. The cameras, lighting, and any necessary backdrops or props are set up on the set.

shimmery makeup   As the name suggests, makeup that glimmers and glows; it is best for evening wear and special occasions.

straight-on shot   A photo in which your head and/or body are facing the camera.

supermodel   A model who is so successful she becomes a household name, well known to an audience outside the fashion industry. Supermodels include Cindy Crawford, Christy Turlington, Linda Evangelista, and Roshumba Williams.

talent   The word used to refer to the models, actors, or other performers working at a still photo shoot, on a TV commercial or movie set, or at a live performance.

team   Refers to the behind-the-scenes people who work together to help the model look her best. This includes the photographer, the hairstylist, the makeup artist, the clothing stylist, and all their assistants.

tent   Short for tentative. If the client likes you but isn't quite ready to commit to booking you, she puts a hold or a tent on you.

testing photographers   Photographers who do test shoots with aspiring models. They are often the assistants of major working photographers and are usually aspiring to become working photographers in their own right.

three-quarters angle   In a photo, you're facing slightly off to one side, halfway between the straight-on and profile shots.

waif   A super-skinny, undernourished-looking, not classically pretty model. The waifs were the talk of the fashion world in the early 1990s. Their heyday put an end (at least temporarily) to the reign of the supermodels.

wardrobe   Refers to both the clothes you'll be wearing on a photo shoot and the area where you'll get dressed. It's where the fashion stylist works and where the model changes from her street clothes into the garment being shot.

wrapped   Means finished. "We're wrapped," is the official word from the photographer or client that the shoot is over, that the work of the day has been completed, and that the model and the team can pack up and go home.

Model Knowledge: Essential Books and Web Sites

These books and Web sites are great sources of additional information on fashion, beauty, modeling, and models.

Model Reads

Aucoin, Kevyn. *The Art of Makeup*. HarperCollins, 1996.

Barrick-Hickey, Beth. *1001 Beauty Solutions*. Sourcebooks Trade, 1995.

Berge, Pierre, and Grace Mirabella. *Yves Saint Laurent*. Vendome Press, 1996.

Brown, Bobbi, and Annemarie Iverson. *Bobbi Brown Beauty: The Ultimate Beauty Resource*. HarperCollins, 1997.

Emme, and Daniel Paisner. *True Beauty: Positive Attitudes and Practical Tips from the World's Leading Plus-Size Model*. Perigee, 1998.

Fried, Stephen M. *Thing of Beauty: The Tragedy of Supermodel Gia*. Pocket Books, 1994.

Gaines, Steven, and Sharon Churcher. *Obsession: The Life and Times of Calvin Klein*. Avon, 1997.

Gaines, Steven, and Sharon Churcher. *Simply Halston*. Avon, 1995.

Gross, Michael. *Model: The Ugly Business of Beautiful Women*. Warner Books, 1994.

Martin, Richard. *Haute Couture*. Metropolitan Museum of Art, 1996.

Martin, Richard, and Grace Mirabella. *Versace*. Vendome Press, 1997.

Milbank, Caroline Rennolds. *Couture*. Stewart Tabori and Cheng, 1997.

Milbank, Caroline Rennolds. *New York Fashion: The Evolution of American Style*. Harry N. Abrams, 1996.

Mohrt, Francoise. *The Givenchy Style*. Vendome Press, 1998.

Pochna, Marie-France, and Joanna Savill (translator). *Christian Dior: The Man Who Made the World Look New*. Arcade Publishing, 1997.

Skrebneski, Victor. *The Art of Haute Couture*. Abbeville Press, 1995.

Summers, Barbara. *Skin Deep: Inside the World of Black Fashion Models*. Amistad, 1999.

Vreeland, Diana. *D.V.* Da Capo, 1997.

Walker, Andre, and Teresa Wiltz. *Andre Talks Hair*. Simon & Schuster, 1997.

Wallach, Janet. *Chanel: Her Style and Her Life*. Doubleday, 1998.

Webb, Veronica. *Veronica Webb Sight: Adventures in the Big City*. Hyperion, 1998.

Model Web Sites

www.carolalt.net
Carol Alt's home page

www.cindy.com
Cindy Crawford's official Web site

www.fashionhouse.net
Information on supermodels

www.fordmodels.com
Ford Modeling Agency

www.frederique.com
Victoria's Secret model Frederique's home page

www.imta.com
International Modeling and Talent Association model convention

www.jc-centers.com
John Casablanca's Modeling and Career Centers

www.modelingschools.com
Barbizon Modeling Schools

www.nikitaylor.net
Niki Taylor's Web site

www.supermodel.com
Information on supermodels

www.victoriassecret.com
Victoria's Secret's Web site

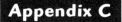

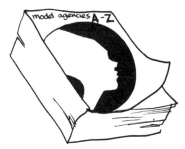

Directory of Modeling Agencies

The following is a list of modeling agencies in the international fashion capitals and in the secondary markets in the United States. To the best of my knowledge, these are all legitimate agencies, but inclusion here does not necessarily mean I endorse any particular one. For agencies in local markets, try the Yellow Pages or the *International Directory of Model and Talent Agencies and Schools* (Peter Glenn Publications, 1999).

New York

Abrams Artists Agency
420 Madison Ave., Suite 1400
New York, NY 10017
212-935-8980

Boss Models
1 Ganesvoort St.
New York, NY 10014
212-242-2444

Click Models
129 W. 27th St.
New York, NY 10001
212-206-1616

Company Management
270 Lafayette St., Suite 1400
New York, NY 10012
212-226-9190

Cunningham, Escott & Dipene
257 Park Ave. South, Suite 900
New York, NY 10010
212-477-3838

Elite Model Management
111 E. 22nd St.
New York, NY 10010
212-529-9700

Ford Models/Children
142 Greene St.
New York, NY 10012
212-219-6150

Ford Models
142 Greene St.
New York, NY 10012
212-219-6150

Gilla Roos, Ltd.
16 W. 22nd St., 7th Floor
New York, NY 10010
212-727-7820

Grace Del Marco-Multi-Cultural Model & Talent Group
350 Fifth Ave., Suite 3110
New York, NY 10118
212-629-6404

ID Men
155 Spring St.
New York, NY 10012
212-334-4333

ID Model Management
155 Spring St.
New York, NY 10012
212-941-5858

IMG Models
304 Park Ave. South, Penthouse North
New York, NY 10010
212-253-8882

Jan Alpert Model Management
333 E. 55th St., Suite 7G
New York, NY 10022
212-223-4238

Karin Models
524 Broadway
New York, NY 10012
212-226-4100

Little Macs/Mac Teens
(children and teens)
156 Fifth Ave., Suite 222
New York, NY 10010
212-627-3100

Major Model Management
381 Park Ave. South, Suite 1501
New York, NY 10016
212-685-1200

Marilyn, Inc.
300 Park Ave. South, 2nd Floor
New York, NY 10010
212-260-6500

Maxx Men
30 E. 20th St., 6th Floor
New York, NY 10003
212-228-0278

McDonald/Richards Model Management
156 Fifth Ave., Suite 222
New York, NY 10010
212-627-3100

New York Model Management
149 Wooster St., 7th Floor
New York, NY 10012
212-539-1700

Next Management
23 Watts St.
New York, NY 10013
212-925-5100

Q Model Management
180 Varick St., 13th Floor
New York, NY 10014
212-807-6777

Spirit Model Management
16 Wooster St., Suite 2
New York, NY 10113
212-226-3004

Thompson Model and Talent Management
50 W. 34th St.
New York, NY 10001
212-947-6711

Wilhelmina
300 Park Ave. South
New York, NY 10010
10/20 (Plus-size): 212-473-4884
Children: 212-473-1253
Men: 212-473-2198

Chicago

Action! Models
1 E. Superior, Suite 410
Chicago, IL 60611
312-664-1609

Aria Model & Talent Management
1017 W. Washington, Suite 2C
Chicago, IL 60607
312-243-9400

Arlene Wilson Model Management
(adults and children)
430 W. Erie, #210
Chicago, IL 60610
312-573-0200

David & Lee Models
641 W. Lake, Suite 402
Chicago, IL 60661
312-707-9000

Elite Model Management
58 W. Huron
Chicago, IL 60610
312-943-3226

Harrise Davidson Talent Agency
65 E. Wacker Pl., Suite 2401
Chicago, IL 60601
312-782-4480

The Palm Group
345 N. Canal, #1006
Chicago, IL 60606
312-382-5368

Premiere Model & Talent Management
27 E. Monroe, Suite 200
Chicago, IL 60603
312-726-8089

Pro-Scout
222 W. Ontario, Suite 520
Chicago, IL 60610
312-642-8880

Stewart Talent
58 W. Huron
Chicago, IL 60610
312-943-3131

Susanne Johnson Talent Agency
108 W. Oak
Chicago, IL 60610
312-943-8315

Miami

Age
1210 Washington Ave., Suite 24S
Miami Beach, FL 33139
305-674-9881

Boss Models
1641 Jefferson Ave.
Miami Beach, FL 33139
305-531-4244

Elite Miami
1200 Collins Ave., Suite 207
Miami Beach, FL 33139
305-674-9500

Ford Models
311 Lincoln, Suite 205
Miami Beach, FL 33139
305-534-7200

Irene Marie Management Group
728 Ocean Dr.
Miami Beach, FL 33139
305-672-2929

Men's Board Management
(305-531-1610)
Women's Board Management
(305-573-3658)
3618 NE 2nd Ave.
Miami Beach, FL 33137

Michele Pommier Models
927 Lincoln Rd., Suite 200
Miami Beach, FL 33139
Women: 305-672-9344
Men: 305-674-7203
Children: 305-531-5475

MMG/Karin Models
539 Euclid Ave., #B
Miami Beach, FL 33139
Women: 305-672-8300
Men: 305-535-8812

Next Management
1688 Meridian Ave., Suite 800
Miami Beach, FL 33139
305-531-5100

Page Parkes Models Rep
763 Collins Ave., 4th Floor Penthouse
Miami Beach, FL 33139
305-672-4869

Los Angeles

Bass International Model Scout
10877 Palms Blvd., Suite 1
Los Angeles, CA 90034
310-839-1097

Bordeaux
616 N. Robertson Blvd., 2nd Floor
West Hollywood, CA 90069
310-289-2550

Brand Model and Talent Agency
1520 Brookhollow Dr., Suite 39
Santa Ana, CA 92705
714-850-1158

Cunningham, Escott & Dipene
10635 Santa Monica Blvd.,
Suite 130
Los Angeles, CA 90025
310-475-7573

DZA&A
8981 Sunset Blvd., Suite 503
Los Angeles, CA 90069
310-274-5088

Elite Model Management
345 N. Maple Dr., Suite 397
Beverly Hills, CA 90210
310-274-9395

Empire Talent Management
6100 Wilshire Blvd., Suite 1640
Los Angeles, CA 90048
323-936-8999

Ford Models
8826 Burton Way
Beverly Hills, CA 90211
310-276-8100

Glamour Kids
(children)
211 S. Beverly Dr., Suite 110
Beverly Hills, CA 90212
310-859-3989

L.A. Models
8335 Sunset Blvd.
Los Angeles, CA 90069
323-656-9572

Next Management
8447 Wilshire Blvd., Suite 301
Beverly Hills, CA 90211
323-782-0010

Nous Model Management
9157 Sunset Blvd., Suite 212
Los Angeles, CA 90069
310-385-6900

Q Model Management
6100 Wilshire Blvd., Suite 710
Los Angeles, CA 90048
323-468-2255

Wilhelmina West
8383 Wilshire Blvd.
Beverly Hills, CA 90211
213-655-0909

Paris

City Models
21 rue Jean Mermoz
Paris
France
75008
1-53-93-33-33

Click Models
27 rue Vernet
Paris
France
75008
1-47-23-44-00

Contrebande
48 rue Sainte-Anne
Paris
France
75002
1-40-20-42-20

Elite
8 bis rue Lecuirot
Paris
France
75014
1-40-44-32-22

Ford Models
9 rue Scribe
Paris
France
75009
1-53-05-25-25

IMG Models
2 rue Defrenoy
Paris
France
75116
1-45-03-85-00

Karin Models
9 avenue Hoche
Paris
France
75008
1-45-63-08-23

Marilyn Agency
4 avenue de la Paix
Paris
France
75002
1-53-29-53-53

Men of Karin
9 avenue Hoche
Paris
France
75008
1-45-63-33-69

Next Management
188 rue de Rivoli
Paris
France
75001
1-53-45-13-00

Paris 30
24 rue Vieille du Temple
Paris
France
75004
1-42-77-22-79

Success
64 rue Rambuteau
Paris
France
75003
1-42-78-89-89

Success Steff
64 rue Rambuteau
Paris
France
75003
1-44-54-94-00

Viva Models
15 rue Duphot
Paris
France
1-44-55-12-60

Milan

Note: Phone numbers in Italy can be either six or eight numbers.

Admiranda Model Agency
Piazza Cincinnato 4
Milano
Italy
20124
02-2952-4813

Christian Jacques Women/CJ Men
Via Tortona 14
Milano
Italy
20144
02-5810-7440

Elite Milano
Via S. Vittore 40
Milano
Italy
20123
02-467-521

Eye for I Model Management
Via Guerrazzi 1
Milano
Italy
20145
02-345-471

The Fashion Model Management
Via Monte Rosa 80
Milano
Italy
20149
02-480-861

Future Model Men
Via Voghera 25
Milano
Italy
20144
02-833-0101

Joy Model Management
Via S. Vittore 40
Milano
Italy
20123
02-4800-2776

Major Model Management
Via Seprio 2
Milano
Italy
20149
02-4801-2828

Want Model Management
Via Borgonuovo 10
Milano
Italy
20121
02-290-6631

Zoom Model Management
Via Franchetti 2
Milano
Italy
20124
02-657-0669

Source: *International Directory of Model & Talent Agencies and Schools* (Peter Glenn Publications, 1999).

Directory of Key Foreign Tourist Offices

I've included these key tourist offices so models can use them as a source of reference when looking for hotels, to get information on transportation, or to provide answers for any number of questions.

British Tourist Authority
551 Fifth Avenue, 7th Floor
New York, NY 10176
Telephone: 800-462-2748 or 212-986-2200
Web site: www.visitbritain.com

French Government Tourist Office
444 Madison Avenue, 16th Floor
New York, NY 10022
Telephone: 410-286-8310
Web site: www.francetourism.com

Italian Government Travel Office
630 Fifth Avenue, Suite 1565
New York, NY 10111
Telephone: 212-245-5095
Web site: www.italiantourism.com

Japan National Tourist Organization
1 Rockefeller Plaza, Suite 1250
New York, NY 10020
Telephone: 212-757-5640
Web site: www.jnto.go.jp

New York Convention and Visitors Bureau
810 Seventh Avenue, 3rd Floor
New York, NY 10019
Telephone: 212-484-1200
Web site: www.nycvisit.com or www.newyork.citysearch.com

Index

387

About the Authors

Roshumba Williams is an established supermodel, spokesperson, and actress. Recognized worldwide as one of fashion's elite faces, Roshumba began her professional career in 1987. She arrived in Paris from her family's home in Chicago with just $150 in her pocket and a dream to make it in the modeling business. Upon arriving in Paris, she teamed up with a small agent and was immediately sent to meet with world-renowned fashion designer Yves Saint Laurent, who hired her on the spot. Roshumba went on to work with the top designers, advertisers, and catalogs worldwide, including Christian Dior, Chanel, Versace, Armani, and Anne Klein. She has graced the covers and pages of *Vogue, Harper's Bazaar, Elle, Top Model, Cosmopolitan,* and *Allure* magazines. Advertisers such as Hanes, Ray-Ban, Samsung, Clairol, Maybelline, The Gap, and Esprit are but a few who have used Roshumba to represent their products. She has been photographed by such important photographers as Oliviero Toscani, Patrick Demarchelier, Peter Lindberg, and Matthew Rolston.

Roshumba is best known as one of the beauties who graced the pages, calendars, and videos of the *Sports Illustrated* Swimsuit Edition. For four years, Roshumba stood out as one of the few African American women to establish herself as an *S.I.* model.

Roshumba has also added television and movies to her resumé. She has hosted shows for the Fox Network's *Fox Style News,* Lifetime Television's *The Wire,* City TV in Toronto's *Ooh La La,* and E! Entertainment Television's *The Making of a Supermodel.* Roshumba also appeared in the Woody Allen film *Celebrity* and has a recurring role as Qali in the *Mortal Kombat* TV series. She can be seen on VH1, where she hosts daily programming and high-profile specials. Roshumba has also been the master of ceremonies, host, and spokesperson for the Elite Model Look model search.

Anne Marie O'Connor is the movie columnist for *Mademoiselle.* In addition, she writes a syndicated beauty and fashion column for the *Chicago Tribune.* She's also written for *Allure, Glamour, Good Housekeeping, George, Epicurious, Publishers Weekly, Ladies Home Journal,* and *American Photo.*